Last King
of the Sports Page

Sports and American Culture Series
Bruce Clayton, Editor

University of Missouri Press
Columbia and London

Ted Geltner

Last King
of the Sports Page

The Life and Career of Jim Murray

Copyright ©2012 by
The Curators of the University of Missouri
University of Missouri Press, Columbia, Missouri 65201
Printed and bound in the United States of America
All rights reserved
5 4 3 2 1   16 15 14 13 12

Cataloging-in-Publication data available from the Library of Congress.
ISBN 978-0-8262-1979-4

∞™ This paper meets the requirements of the
American National Standard for Permanence of Paper
for Printed Library Materials, Z39.48, 1984.

Design and composition: Jennifer Cropp
Printing and Binding: Thomson-Shore, Inc.
Typefaces: Minion, News Gothic, and Krungthep

This book is for Jill Geltner, with love

Contents

Acknowledgments

This project would not have been possible without the help of the friends, relatives, and colleagues of Jim Murray who were willing to answer my questions and offer suggestions as to the best way to pursue this story, and for their assistance I am grateful. Among them were: Kareem Abdul-Jabaar, Dave Anderson, Mario Andretti, Yogi Berra, Walter Bingham, Furman Bisher, Jim Brosnan, Bill Christine, Bob Creamer, Andy Crichton, Rose D'Ambrosia, Al Davis, Frank Deford, Jack Disney, Mike Downey, Melvin Durslag, Bill Dwyer, Marge Everett, Roy Firestone, Doc Giffin, Dan Gurney, John Hall, Carol Hamel, Marie Hewins, Jerry Izenberg, Russell Jaslow, Bruce Jenkins, Gilbert Lilijedahl, Mike Littwin, Michael MacCambridge, Frank McCulloch, Bill Milsaps, Murray Olderman, Scott Ostler, Ferdie Pacheco, Arnold Palmer, Richard Patrissi, Ken Peters, Edwin Pope, Rick Reilly, Eric Sandberg, Jon Sandberg, Joe Santley, John Scheibe, Blackie Sherrod, Dan Smith, Steve Soboroff, Bob Steiner, Jerry Suppicich, Bill Thomas, Al Unser, and Jerry West. I would also like to thank Matt Allen for allowing me to share the valuable research he had previously conducted into the Murray family history.

I would like to thank William McKeen, Ted Spiker, Maria Coady, and Ronald Rodgers, at the University of Florida. Their passion for the project led me to believe it might actually be worth pursuing, and their helpful early reading set me on my path.

At Valdosta State University, Mark Smith, Pat Miller, and Becky Gaskins provided invaluable support, and David Williams offered useful advice about the world of publishing. This project was greatly assisted by the research conducted and guidance provided by Pat Reakes of the University of Florida libraries, Peter Knapp at the Watkins Library at Trinity University, and Brenda Miller at the Hartford History Center. In Connecticut, Ken Buckbee was a godsend who used his investigative skills to dig up documents and news clippings that filled in the early Murray story. In Georgia, the research and editing of Shane

Wilson, Stuart Taylor, and Laurel Kauffman were extremely helpful. Thanks also to Dr. Winkler Weinberg for his medical wisdom.

At the University of Missouri Press, I would like to thank John Brenner for taking an interest in Murray's story and helping a first-time writer through the process. I would also like to thank Sara Davis and Annette Wenda as well as everybody at the press who contributed to the project and helped turn the manuscript into a real, live book.

Together, David Bulla of Iowa State University and I began research into the life of Jim Murray in 2006 and coauthored an article about Murray's role in the creation of *Sports Illustrated.* Dave graciously stepped aside and allowed me to pursue the rest of the story, and for that I am grateful.

My thanks to the *Los Angeles Times* for permission to reprint two columns and a photo from their archives.

Linda McCoy-Murray helped me more than I ever could have hoped for or dreamed. She patiently answered every question I asked, no matter how irrelevant it may have seemed ("What did Jim wear when he wrote his columns?"). She put me in touch with dozens of Jim's closest friends and associates. And she invited me into her home on two separate occasions, allowed me to spend hours sifting through Jim's files and memorabilia in her garage, and even served as my tour guide and recreational director on my research trips to La Quinta, California. For all of the above, I will forever be in her debt.

I wish to thank my parents, Mike and Jane Geltner, for all of the tremendous love and support they have provided me, on this project and in many other pursuits through the years. They have offered unquestioning encouragement in everything I have chosen to pursue, and I will never be able to adequately express my appreciation.

The quartet of Cassie, Bethany, Luke, and Lainey Geltner provided ample assistance by both cheering me on as I struggled to "bang out pages" and giving me a respite whenever needed. They make my life better each and every day with their smiles and laughter.

And above all, I am thankful to my wife, Jill, for everything she does for me and our family. She did her best to act attentive when I felt the need to share what I thought were interesting facts I had discovered in fifty-year-old newspaper columns. All along the way, she has been willing to listen and has picked up the slack for me whenever called upon. Even more, though, I am grateful to her for always being there to help me to remember what is truly important in life.

Last King
of the Sports Page

Introduction

Late in the afternoon on August 26, 1961, Jim Murray looked dejectedly out the window of his motel room, watching the rain wash through the streets of Cincinnati below. The same rainstorm had already washed out that night's Los Angeles Dodgers versus Cincinnati Reds game, which Murray had hoped to use as the subject of his column for the next day's edition of the *Los Angeles Times*. Murray was now starting his second week on the road with the Dodgers, his second week living out of motel rooms, away from his wife and four kids back in Malibu. The first week had taken the team through San Francisco and St. Louis and had included a string of eight consecutive losses that had caused the Dodgers to give back most of the team's second-place position in the National League standings. The mood among the Dodgers coaches, players, and staff had gone steadily downhill. Tension ran high. Younger players were arguing with each other, veterans were snapping at waitresses, coaches and managers were going nights without sleep. Just the day before, Dodger first baseman Norm Larker, coming off a game in which he had struck out twice and dropped an easy foul ball, had nearly come to blows with one of the beat writers along for the trip.

"Would you have given me an error on that foul fly?" Larker demanded of the beat writer.

The beat writer shook his head.

"Why not?" challenged Larker.

"Because I felt sorry for you," the writer answered.

The response sent Larker into a rage. "I don't want you feeling sorry for me," he screamed at the writer. "Get that once and for all."[1]

It was in this atmosphere of losing and disgust that Murray struggled to think of a way to fill the twenty-five column inches the sports desk at the *Times* would be expecting from him in a few hours. He had already turned in six straight columns on the dismal travails of the Dodgers ("This isn't a road trip,

1

it's a death march," he had written two days earlier),[2] covering topics from player nicknames to poker games to their sleeping habits on planes. But now the endless trip was sapping his creativity.

As he struggled, he remembered some sage advice from a city editor many years before: "Son, the best stories are floating right by your front door if you'll only look out there."[3]

It was an epiphany that both gave Murray the impetus to fill those twenty-five inches and sent his column in a direction that would catapult him into the national consciousness for the first time. Murray wrote:

> I mean, people just don't have any appreciation for what us truth-seekers go through on one of these road trips for the honor and glory of baseball.
>
> For instance, you come into a city like Cincinnati at 3 o'clock in the morning. Now, if you have any sense, you don't want to be in Cincinnati at all. Even in daylight, it doesn't look like a city. It looks like it's in the midst of condemnation proceedings. If it was human, they'd bury it.
>
> You have to think that when Dan'l Boone was fighting the Indians for this territory he didn't have Cincinnati in mind for it. I wouldn't arm wrestle Frank Finch for it. To give you an idea, the guys were kidding on the bus coming in here, and they decided that if war came, the Russians would by-pass Cincinnati because they'd think it had already been bombed and taken.[4]

Those three paragraphs, on that rainy afternoon, achieved the short-term goal of chewing up a little chunk of the space Murray needed to fill in the next day's sports section. What he did not know at the time was that he had also gone a long way toward finding his voice as a sports columnist, a voice that, in the next four decades, would become arguably the most recognizable in American sports journalism.

The reaction was immediate. Murray later wrote that Los Angeles is a city of transplants, and most of the twenty thousand transplanted Cincinnatians living in Southern California clipped that column and sent it back to their hometown. By the time Murray and the Dodgers crawled back to Los Angeles, the column was in the hands of the Cincinnati newspapers and the Cincinnati Chamber of Commerce. Murray was now known, and hated, in southern Ohio. By the time the Reds met the New York Yankees in the World Series two months later, women were walking around the streets with homemade buttons that said "Murray for Idiot."[5]

Murray and his editors at the *Times* knew they had struck a nerve. Soon, he was taking on cities from coast to coast, even going on road trips to the remotes of northern Canada with the Los Angeles Blades minor-league hockey club in order to find suitable targets for his barbs. It would lead quickly to national syndication, elite status among his peers, and, eventually, national fame. But though it was his penchant for ribbing cities that gave him the boost he needed, Murray came to the role of *Times* columnist in early 1961 as a skilled writer and an experienced journalist. He already possessed the characteristics that would eventually lead to his success: an extensive knowledge of history and culture gained during childhood, a deep understanding of human nature, a personality that allowed him to relate to even the most adversarial of interview subjects, and, most memorably, a razor-sharp wit with which he wrote laugh lines that would be repeated over and over by peers, readers, and sports figures.

About New York Yankee manager Casey Stengel, Murray wrote: "Casey Stengel is a white American male with a speech pattern that ranges somewhere between the sound a porpoise makes underwater and an Abyssinian rug merchant."[6]

About UCLA basketball coach John Wooden, he wrote: "John Wooden is so square, he's divisible by four."[7]

Writing about oversized Los Angeles Rams offensive lineman Bill Bain, Murray said: "Once, when an official dropped a flag and penalized the Rams for having twelve men on the field, two of them were Bain."[8]

Of everyday golf hackers, of which he was one, he wrote: "Show me a man who's a good loser, and I'll show you a man playing golf with his boss."

He wrote about Ohio State football coach Woody Hayes: "Woody was consistent. Graceless in victory and graceless in defeat."[9]

About basketball referees, Murray wrote: "It's a nice job if you have thick skin, poor hearing, and you like flying through blizzards, room service, old movies and Holiday Inns. A spy has a better social life. The piano player in a bordello gets more respect."[10]

Murray's humor and satire are the most lasting legacy of his years at the typewriter. But the millions of words he typed while churning out the more than ten thousand sports columns are filled with a much wider array of topics, styles, and techniques. He wrote profiles that captured the essence of his subjects with humor and pathos, never glossing over the negative, but somehow almost never appearing overly critical. He traveled extensively, viewing the epic events of the second half of the twentieth century from press boxes across the nation and around the world. He did not shy away from divisive issues. He took moral stands on race, violence in sports, politics. He fielded the reams of letters demanding he "stick to sports," but maintained the principle that his job as a journalist was to report the news, even if the news had little to do with the final score.[11] His column became a must-read in Southern California and beyond, with loyal readers, male and female, who looked to him for humor and sage commentary on issues throughout the world of sports and beyond.

While his contemporaries among sports columnists generally began their journalism careers covering sports in some fashion and worked their way up through the ranks, Murray took a different path, one that gave him a different perspective, and it came across in his writing. In the first two decades of his career, Murray apprenticed under the umbrella of two of the titans of twentieth-century American journalism, William Randolph Hearst and Henry Luce. As a crime reporter and rewrite man for Hearst's *Los Angeles Examiner* in the 1940s, Murray covered the lurid tales of murder and betrayal in Hollywood and beyond. He wrote of death and mayhem, all in a sensational style that fed the cravings of the growing Los Angeles metropolis. As a Hollywood correspondent for *Time,* the beacon of the Luce empire, he covered the elite of the motion-picture industry. Along the way he developed relationships with the movie stars and moneymen of the day, from Bogart to Wayne to Brando. When Luce had the idea to start the first national sports magazine, Murray was one of the team of editors and writers he handpicked to launch the publication. It was Luce, Murray said, who turned him into a sportswriter.[12] Murray was instrumental in the development of *Sports Illustrated* and then spent the next six years covering the West Coast for the magazine (while simultaneously covering Los Angeles for *Time* and *Life*).

From this journalism education, he moved seemingly effortlessly into the role of sports columnist. Because he spent all those years covering news, he did not carry along the baggage of journalism's second-class-citizen status that many sportswriters hang on to. Instead, he used his background and skills to expand the nature of the role he was given. His knowledge of Los Angeles history and culture, both within sports and beyond, allowed him to develop a feel for the city and its inhabitants that made his column fit the city's persona. From February 1961, he could be found on the front of the *Times* sports section without fail, six days a week (though he was rarely seen within the walls of the *Los Angeles Times* headquarters). Although he confronted his share of physical and personal hardship in his life, including two heart surgeries, temporary blindness, and the loss of his wife and youngest son, he rarely missed a column. He complained, as many of the great columnists do, that the column took over his life. It became both his ultimate motivation and triumph and his greatest burden. It was, he said, like riding a tiger: "It's just like any other tiger ride. You may not want to stay on. But you don't dare get off. Either way, it's liable to eat you alive."[13]

By the time Murray was awarded the Pulitzer Prize for Commentary in 1990, he had become one of the elder statesmen of American sportswriters. He lived among celebrities in Bel Air, California. With a vacation home in Palm Springs, he fed his lifelong love of the game of golf at the city's elite country clubs. By this time, most of the athletes he wrote about treated an interview with Murray like a meeting with the president. He acquired journalism awards like the Yankees acquired pennants. He won national sportswriter of the year fourteen times, was inducted into the Baseball Hall of Fame, and received innumerable honorary degrees and honors, accepting each and every one with humor and grace. His friend and protégée Roy Firestone is among many admirers who place Murray's work not just among the greats of sports journalism, but among great writers from any genre. Says Firestone: "I'll say without question, I think Jim Murray was every bit as important of a sportswriter—forget sport writer—every bit as important a writer to newspapers, as Mark Twain was to literature. Could you compare him to Will Rogers? Sure. Twain? Of course. He was that good, and there's no one like him."[14]

The status he had achieved late in life was apparent at the 1992 Summer Olympics in Barcelona, Spain. Murray was seventy-two years old. This was the year of the USA Dream Team, an assemblage of American basketball stars the likes of which had never been seen, including Michael Jordan, Magic Johnson, Larry Bird, and a team full of internationally known names. The hype surrounding the team had reached astronomical levels. Anticipation ran high among the media and throughout the Olympic Village. On arrival, Johnson, head coach Chuck Daly, and some other members of the team were brought in by officials from the Olympic Committee for a press conference with the entire international press corps. The interview room was packed shoulder to shoulder. After a short question period, an Olympic official abruptly cut off the microphones and shut down the proceedings.

"Wait a minute," Magic Johnson said.

The crowd, which had been shuffling papers and heading for the exits, refocused on the dais.

"The great Jim Murray is here, and he didn't get to ask a question," Johnson said.

The Olympic official sneered at Johnson, but grudgingly turned the microphones back on. Quietly, Murray asked his question.[15]

1

The Connecticut Years, 1919–1943

Whatever my fears, I felt that one day I would come upon the meaning of my life, or its lack of meaning, in some flash flood of self-revelation. I think that Aristotle (unless it was "Bugs Baer") called this "the moment of recognition." I called it "the idea."

—Gene Fowler, *Skyline: A Reporter's Reminiscence of the '20s*

A Place Called Sligo

The first line of Jim Murray's autobiography reads, "I was a Depression child."[1] In fact, Murray first came into the world just three days before the dawn of the 1920s, the Jazz Age, the beginning of a run of unprecedented American prosperity. It would be in Murray's formative years that he would suffer along with the rest of America through the Great Depression. The suffering he would live through as a young child, including two near-fatal diseases, the divorce of his parents, and the constant shuffling of the adults in his life, was his and his alone.

Murray was born on December 29, 1919, at St. Francis Hospital in Hartford, Connecticut. By then, the Murrays had been in America for two generations. Before that, the Murrays were a close-knit clan from near the small village of Knockawer, outside Tobbercurry in County Sligo in the farm country of northeastern Ireland. Family records show that Jim's great-grandparents on his father's side, Martin Murray and Margaret Killoran, lived in the hills of Knockawer on land owned jointly by members of the Murray family. The family subsisted on cattle and sheep farming, as did their neighbors and the rest of the rural region around Knockawer. It was an isolated existence. Occasional trips for supplies to the town of Sligo were the extent of contact with the outside world. Jim's paternal grandfather, Michael Murray, was born October 14, 1861. He had five siblings, all of whom would join the second wave of Irish immigration during the final third of the nineteenth century.[2] According to family lore, Michael Murray had the same feeling about Ireland that Jim would have eighty years later about Connecticut: a strong desire to be somewhere else. Michael left Ireland at the age of seventeen and always said he would have left much sooner if he had known how to swim. "He always used to say, if Ireland was a little bit of heaven, he hoped it was from the poorer section of it," Jim wrote.[3]

Michael Murray and his siblings were part of a wave of Irish immigration to the United States that had been going on for most of the century. The Irish potato famine of 1845 to 1849 caused unimaginable hardship in Ireland and left a population ripe for exodus, but the tide of immigration was already going strong by the time the famine began. Including the Great Famine, there were five catastrophic famines between 1818 and 1847. About two million people died of disease and starvation, which constituted nearly a quarter of the Irish population. The Great Famine, though, was a turning point. Many Irish believed they were sacrificed for the survival of the British merchant class. Feeling toward America, however, was just the opposite. Help came from those who had already made the move to the United States. In most major American cities, organizations raised funds for victims of the famine. American relief ships brought cargoes of corn and clothing. The federal government and members of the US Congress became involved in relief efforts. The response to Irish suffering played a large role in convincing the population of Ireland that the United States was their promised land.[4]

In 1860, around the time that young Michael Murray and his siblings came to America, the Irish made up about 40 percent of the foreign-born population of the United States. Irish immigrants were coming to America at the rate of about fifty thousand per year. The majority of them ended up in the Northeast or Illinois. By the end of the century, the Irish population of America exceeded the population of Ireland itself. The first generation of Irish immigrants generally found work as laborers, doing the heavy lifting that was needed in urban America. They were masons, bricklayers, carpenters, and sweatshop workers, longshoremen, street cleaners, tailors, and stevedores.[5] Michael Murray settled in Hartford, Connecticut, in the late 1870s. He had married Bridget Gallagher prior to immigration, and by the early 1880s, he was employed by the Pratt and Whitney Company of Hartford, where he would work for the rest of his life as a machinist. Pratt and Whitney was a successful firm that produced industrial machinery, and later in life Michael Murray spent his working days building airplane engines for commercial and military use.[6] He was a dedicated employee and would arrive at six in the morning and smoke on the steps of the Pratt and Whitney factory until it opened at seven. Once, he was injured on the job and still reported to work, sporting a cotton ball on his head to cover the wound.[7] His occupation was a stable source of income that kept the family fed and clothed and helped the next generation of Murrays live through the Great Depression. The Murrays lived comfortably in Hartford and before 1920 moved to West Hartford, a small, affluent suburb of Hartford.[8] Michael and Bridget Murray, Jim's grandparents, were his primary caretakers for most of his childhood and would play an enormous role in his development. They died within four months of each other in 1934.

James P. Murray, Jim's father, was the third child out of the eight Murray siblings, born on October 31, 1889. Jim wrote very little about his father, so little written description of him exists. James was by all accounts a good student and a sparkling wit. In fact, he was supposed to be the first of the Murrays to attend college. A display of Irish stubbornness, however, kept that from happening. Late in his senior year of high school, James came to Latin class without having completed the day's lesson. He asked the instructor not to call on him, and after agreeing, the instructor called on James anyway. James stood up in class and said, "Look, you son of a bitch, I told you I didn't do the lesson. Why'd you call on me?" He was sent to the principal and thrown out of school. Even after a deal was struck in which an apology would get James back into school and back on the road to graduation, he refused to apologize. He never graduated from high school, and instead of matriculating to Trinity College, where his son, Jim, would go twenty years later, he became a pharmacist.[9]

James married Jim's mother, Mary O'Connell, shortly thereafter. Mary, known as Molly, was born in Ireland. The O'Connells had come to America in 1896 when Molly was five years old[10] and settled in New London, Connecticut. Molly worked as a nurse through most of her adult life. James and Molly had three children. Mary Elizabeth, known as Betty, was born in 1918, Jim in 1919, and Eleanor two years later. During these years, James was a successful druggist, at one time owning three separate pharmacies in the Hartford area. It was in the early years of Jim's life, however, that James's career and marriage would fall apart and send young Jim's life in another direction.

A House Full of Uncles

When he was four years old, Jim Murray had what his family called a nervous breakdown.[11] What he actually had was an obscure disease called Saint Vitus' dance, or Sydenham's chorea, which causes the patient to lose control of his limbs, to lose the ability to walk, to twitch wildly, and to exhibit facial grimacing.[12] Saint Vitus' dance is often associated with streptococcal infection, such as strep throat, and can last for months, which was likely the case with Murray. A disease of this nature can throw a family into chaos even with modern medicine, and at the time there was little in the way of treatment. Murray's parents apparently were not able to care for him sufficiently, and he moved in with his grandparents for what would be most of the rest of his childhood.

Things had already been going badly for the family at the time of Jim's disease. In the first years of his life, the family had been living in Hartford, with Molly's sister Agnes, an insurance clerk, living in the household as well.[13] Prohibition had been in effect since 1919, when the Eighteenth Amendment was ratified. Though the temperance movement had the political strength in the country, the national thirst for alcohol remained, and consumption was pushed underground. Many druggists of the era supplemented their business by selling illegal liquor. Jim's father was no different. He kept a water cooler filled with gin in his shops, as did almost every other pharmacy in Hartford. Liquor laws were indiscriminately enforced, and after James got into a feud with a local cop, the law came down on him.[14] At two o'clock on the morning of January 13, 1922, police officers took him from his bed and brought him to the Hartford Police Station for booking. He was bailed out by his father for one thousand dollars twelve hours later. The arrest made the front page of the next day's edition of the *Hartford Courant.* The newspaper reported that police had arrested a bootlegger named Michael Delaney two days earlier. Liquor valued at thousands of dollars had been stored and sold out of James Murray's shop, and the police had been looking for him for two days. Justice moved quick in Hartford at the time; Delaney was already serving a sixty-day sentence in Hartford County Jail by the time James Murray was hauled down to the precinct.[15]

James Murray pleaded not guilty to the charges, and the case went to court on January 28. In just two weeks' time, all of his drugstores were out of business. The state's case hinged on the testimony of Delaney, who claimed to have sold nine cases of scotch to Murray that were part of a shipment of liquor that had been stolen from Delaney. As reported in the *Courant,* it is difficult to understand why Murray and his lawyer fought the charges in court. Murray admitted to agreeing to buy the scotch from Delaney and admitted to receiving the scotch. His lawyer offered no defense after Delaney's testimony. Upon rendering his decision, the judge said there seemed to be something deeper involved in the case than what was disclosed in court. With or without the truth of the matter, he sentenced Murray to twenty days in jail. James Murray's career as a business owner was effectively over.[16]

Whether it was the strain of their legal and financial problems or the stress of a child with a major illness, the marriage of James and Molly could not withstand the difficulties. They split up when Jim was four, and from then on Jim was raised by committee, with his grandparents taking the lead. Divorce in an Irish Catholic family was a black mark of immense proportions and not to be discussed in public. Jim was now property of the Murrays, and they closed ranks around him. His mother, to them, was as unwelcome a subject as the divorce. Murray's cousin Carol Hamel, who was twelve years younger than Jim and later lived in the same household, said the subject was one that was never broached by family members. "In those days, that was that. That was the end. And the rest of the family hardly mentioned her name. I don't know if you know or not, but the old Irish would, well, they would write her off."[17] Jim's sisters, Betty and Eleanor, remained with Molly, his father moved into an apartment, and Jim moved to West Hartford with the Murray clan.

By the time Jim made the move, his grandparents lived at 21 Crescent Street in West Hartford in a large three-story home built for two families. The house had three bedrooms and a second kitchen on the second floor and three more bedrooms on the third floor—plenty of room to harbor an uncle or two and a few aunts and some cousins and other assorted relatives. During leaner times, more of the extended family would take up residence in the home. The living arrangements throughout the extended family were fluid; at one point during the depths of the Depression, Jim, his father, and sisters all moved into the house at 21 Crescent Street, while Molly was forced to move back to New London to board with her parents. Jim also spent time living with his aunts Margaret, known as Peg, and Katherine, known as Kit. Both took on maternal roles in Jim's upbringing. At times, Jim shared a room with his uncle Frank. He was first exposed to sports by his father and his father's brothers, who would sit around the kitchen table, smoking cigars and arguing about the Red Sox or Jack Dempsey late into the night.[18] The roster would change daily. It included Jim's father, along with Uncle Martin, a fireman who eventually became fire chief of New Canaan, Connecticut; Uncle Jack, a machinist who moved to Fitchburg, Massachusetts; Uncle Frank, who managed and owned apartment buildings in Hartford and later owned a diner frequented by boxers; and Uncle Charles.[19] "They were lively, funny, irreverent. Every boy should have uncles like these," Jim wrote.[20]

But it was Uncle Ed, the black sheep of the family, whom Jim devoted the most ink to when he became a writer. Ed was a gambler, hustler, and con artist who Murray said "hated work so much, he didn't even like to watch it." Ed Murray dropped out of school in the sixth grade and from then on made his living with dice, cards, and assorted other cons. He was a stocky, curly-haired pug with a round face, a squashed nose, and a quick temper. He resembled Jimmy Cagney. In the underworld, he went by "the Gimp," because he had one leg shorter than the other. Murray remembered coming downstairs and watching Uncle Ed boiling eggs and dice in the same pan. "The eggs he ate. The dice he squeezed into a wooden vise until they got in a shape they wouldn't come up a '6' or '8.'" Ed would use the trick dice in illegal craps games. Once, the illegal dice slipped out accidentally, and Ed took a bad beating. Jim woke up to see his uncle's eyes swollen shut. He lanced them with a razor so Ed could get out of bed.[21]

Murray looked up to Uncle Ed and reveled in the tours of Hartford's back rooms and pool halls he received from his uncle. While his father and the other uncles took him to fights and ball games, Ed brought him to places like the Greek-American Club and the Parkville Young Democratic Club, illegal all-night establishments where gambling went on. Throughout his life he repeated the many rules to live by that Ed shared with him: "Never bet on a live horse or a dead woman." "Never take money from an amateur . . . unless he insists." "Never play cards with a man in dark glasses or his own deck."[22]

As an adult, Murray usually played his Uncle Ed stories for laughs, but the Murray family held an honorable reputation in the community, and Ed often brought shame on the family. He was arrested on gambling charges more than a few times and often bullied Murray's grandmother into financing his schemes. As a child, Murray feared him and fantasized about knocking him out. When Murray was a bit older and money was extremely tight, Uncle Ed stole his shoes and slept with them under his pillow. Murray got up the courage and one morning jerked the shoes back from his uncle. When Ed did not attack him, Murray knew he was safe.[23]

Ed also introduced Jim to horse racing. He took Jim to Agawam Race Track in Massachusetts, where Jim won his first bet, on a horse named Kievex. Ed played the angles in the horse game, too, always looking for a way to bend the rules. One scheme he was particularly successful with, for a time, was called past-posting. He worked the scam with his partner, Johnny Pachesnik. Ed would pay a spotter to watch the race and relay to Ed which horse was winning headed into the stretch. Johnny, meanwhile, would run up a minor losing streak, gaining the bookie's confidence. The bookie would get greedy and become willing to accept bets a minute or so after post time. Then Ed would come into the bookie parlor wearing a sweater with twelve buttons. The button that represented the winning horse he would leave unbuttoned. Johnny would place the bet, and the two would split their winnings. Unfortunately for Ed and Johnny, the bookie got suspicious when Ed came into the parlor wearing a sweater in ninety-degree weather. He found their spotter and paid him a little bit more than Ed was paying him. Pretty soon, Ed and Johnny were putting their money on losers, and the house, once again, got its money back.[24]

Ed was generous to a fault when times were good and would be back under his parents' roof when the money ran out. Murray's cousin Marie Hewins, a generation younger than Murray, remembers Uncle Ed coming to Murray family reunions in later years. "He would have the backseat full of pastries, and all us kids just loved it. And another year he wouldn't show up at all. Later on in life, I found out why: he wasn't winning," she said.[25] Uncle Ed's hard living took its toll, and he died in 1954 at the age of fifty-two. As much as anyone in the Murray family, Uncle Ed's outlook and attitudes are reflected in Murray's writing. Characters like Ed and his pals, who knew how to work angles and game the system, but ultimately found themselves on the other end of a con, populate Murray's columns. He would write about crooked fight promoters and shifty horse players with humor and admiration. He would form easy associations with Uncle Ed–type characters he encountered throughout his days in journalism. At Uncle Ed's funeral in 1954, one of the many questionable characters in attendance approached Murray's sister Eleanor and said of Uncle Ed: "They was better crapshooters and better pool hustlers. But for one man for two events by one player, I'd have to take Eddie. He was one of the best."[26]

Though they never assumed the roles of primary caregivers for long stretches after Jim reached the age of four, both Jim's father and his mother remained involved in his life. James Sr. was a natty dresser and the source of Jim's quick wit. He was, according to Gerry Suppicich, a son of Jim's sister Betty, "a very smart guy by common consensus, the smartest of the Murrays, and they were all smart. They were all achievers." Eric Sandburg, son of Jim's sister Eleanor, remembers his grandfather as friendly and bright. In the 1950s, when Sandburg was four years old, he asked James about a belt he was wearing. By the next day, James had bought one for him. "My mother thought it was ridiculous that a four-year-old had a nine-dollar belt," Sandburg said. The Murray family liked to imbibe, and Jim's father was no different. Once, he took Jim to a fight and on the way back stopped into one of his friend's drugstores to play checkers for money. Jim watched as his father kept getting up to fill his glass from the water cooler. Pretty soon, his eyes were red and his speech was slurred. It was an image that stuck with Jim.[27] James and Molly stayed in touch while Jim was a child, and even into adulthood. Among the many letters Jim saved is a get-well card, dated September 24, 1957, signed "Mom & Dad."

Jim had a more contentious relationship with his mother, Molly. Though she was frozen out to a degree by Jim's father's family and often had to go through them to get in touch with Jim, she still managed to be overbearing toward her son, and Jim fought to keep her at arm's length. In later years, she tipped the scales at 250 pounds and was known to berate relatives to the point of tears at family gatherings. Suppicich, who traveled with her years later to visit Jim and his family in Los Angeles, remembers her as a headstrong woman. "She was a tough old Irish war horse, a tough old bitch. . . . I can't describe Jim's relationship with her, other than to say California might not have been far enough away," he said.[28] When Molly died in 1968, Sandburg attended her funeral. After the viewing, he went outside to smoke a cigarette. Jim came over with an anguished look on his face. "If one more old bitty tells me how wonderful she looks," Jim said, "I'm going to tell them to go fuck themselves."[29]

"Don't Call Me Bud"

West Hartford in the 1930s was a melting pot, with Swedish, Italian, and Irish families representing the majority, but with several other ethnicities thrown in. It was a bucolic suburb where preteens played baseball in the street, traded baseball cards, and played checkers on the stoop. Or they sat around outside of Terry's Drug Store, down the block from Jim's grandparents' house on Crescent Street, and drank soda pop (when they could afford it) and argued about the Yankees and the Red Sox.[30] Around the neighborhood, Jim was known as "Bud" Murray, thanks to his little sister, Eleanor, who could not pronounce "brother" and instead called Jim "Budder."[31] Jim developed his sense of humor at a young age, and his lifelong desire to be a playwright surfaced early. He would write and direct neighborhood productions and enlist his sisters, Eleanor and Betty, to star in them. Kids from the neighborhood would watch the results.[32] One of the major radio stars of the 1930s was Kate Smith, known as the "Songbird of the South." Jim would emcee his neighborhood shows, and he would introduce his sister: "You've heard of Kate Smith, the Songbird of the South. Well, let's give a big hand to Eleanor Murray, the Song Horse of the North."[33]

Jim and Eleanor had a close relationship when they were together. On many a snowy winter day, the two of them, along with assorted neighborhood kids, would climb to the top of the Crosby Street hill for a day of sledding. The two Murray kids had a single sled between them, so they would often ride together, making sure to look out for cars on the cross street at the bottom of the hill.[34] Eleanor was a couple years younger, so she didn't tag along on some of Jim's more mischievous escapades. One spring, he and some friends formed the Society of the Red Shadows, a secret organization dedicated to overthrowing South America, or, when that proved too difficult, throwing rocks at West Hartford streetlights. The club's initiation ritual involved stealing elephant rings from Woolworth's five-and-dime. When one member squealed, the rest of the Red Shadows agreed to shovel the dock at Woolworth's in exchange for a promise not to turn them in to their parents.[35]

At the age of ten, Jim was once again felled by disease. This time, it was rheumatic fever, and it was very nearly fatal. As with his earlier bout of Saint Vitus' dance, rheumatic fever is the result of a strep infection, and the fever is usually seen two weeks after a case of strep throat. The virus often attacks and weakens the valves of the heart, as in Jim's case. He developed pneumonia and pleurisy, and last rites were performed for him at Our Lady of Sorrows Church. He hovered between life and death for days.[36] After the development of antibiotics in the 1960s, incidence of rheumatic fever went way down. In the 1920s, however, the only treatment was aspirin, given to reduce inflammation, and the disease was very often fatal.[37] Jim's recovery would take years, during which he spent innumerable hours on bed rest. Even into high school, he was on a reduced schedule that had him attending classes in the morning and back home in the afternoon. Sometimes he would be so overcome with boredom that he would yell and scream, upsetting his aunt Peg, who looked after him through many of these years. Carol Hamel, Peg's daughter, was twelve years younger than Jim. She remembered that as a youngster, she was often told to "keep things on an even keel" so Jim would not get upset. Once, Carol and Aunt Peg heard Jim screaming in anger from his room on the third floor. When they went to investigate, Jim, already a grammar hound, was disgusted with a split infinitive he had found in the *Hartford Times*. He demanded to use the phone so he could call the city desk and complain.[38]

But all the time spent in his room allowed Jim to develop an extraordinary understanding of history and culture. "I read everything. I knew as much about history as Toynbee. I knew about Hitler (from John Gunther's books) before some Germans did and certainly before any Americans," he wrote.[39] He wrote and received letters from the prime minister of Ireland, and he wrote his first award-winning story for a newspaper contest, for which he won five dollars. He devised a baseball game using playing cards (a jack was a single, a queen was a double, and so forth) and refined the rules until the game approximated real baseball statistics.

Despite missing class time, Jim was a good student. He attended Our Lady of Sorrows Catholic School through elementary and middle schools, where writing and language were stressed. Students wrote a theme paper a week, and grading was strict.[40] In 1933, when he was in the eighth grade, Jim made the municipal spelling bee, where he was the most nervous contestant onstage. He misspelled impetus—*I-M-P-E-T-O-S*—and his competitive spelling career was over.[41] By this time, Jim's closest friend was Joey Patrissi, who lived down the block on Crescent Street. The two would go to Terry's Drug Store and read the *Hartford Courant* and whatever sports magazines they could afford. Joey was the best athlete in the neighborhood, and Jim would join him on the fields when he was healthy, or just watch when he was not up to playing. The two went to stay with Jim's uncle Jack's family in Massachusetts during the summer several times. They would go to see the Hartford Laurels, a Class A Minor League Baseball team in the Boston Braves organization. Joey went on to play college baseball at Staunton Military Academy and had an opportunity to play in the Yankees' farm system, but his baseball career was cut short by World War II.[42]

On Labor Day 1933, Jim went to Yankee Stadium to see a doubleheader between the Yankees and the Philadelphia Athletics, a chance to see Babe Ruth, and his other favorite player, Jimmy Foxx of the A's. In a steady rainstorm, Jim got to see a version of the most celebrated sports act of the era: Ruth knocking one over the fence, wobbling around the bases on his spindly legs, and tipping his cap to the crowd. "It was, looking back on it, my first lesson that the event itself had to be dramatized," he wrote. "We were there, in a sense, because we had been lured there by years of purple prose. The home run itself was hardly a cataclysmic event. But Grantland Rice made you think it was."[43]

The First in the Family

Jim graduated from William Hall High School in West Hartford in May 1939, and in the fall, he took the path that his father was supposed to take twenty years before and matriculated at Trinity College in Hartford. He dreamed of attending Dartmouth, but family finances would not allow it.[44] Trinity was a fine alternative, however, and his aunts and uncles were thrilled to have one of their own in higher education. On his application to Trinity, Jim wrote that he expected to become a journalist, "although sometimes I think I'd like to join the diplomatic, or consular service. I consider the latter, perhaps, because I have a lust for travel."

At the end of the 1930s, a college education was still a relative rarity in the United States. During that decade, American universities and colleges would collectively award fewer than one hundred thousand degrees annually. By 1947, 2.3 million students would be enrolled in American colleges and universities.[45] Trinity College was founded in 1823, the second college in the state of Connecticut to open its doors. A small liberal arts college of fewer than 300 students in 1939, Trinity has an Episcopalian heritage, but was a nonreligious entity by the time Murray arrived. The school had undergone an expansion during the '30s, and by the time Murray set foot on campus, it boasted collegiate-style Gothic architecture that gave the campus the feel of medieval academia.[46] The liberal arts doctrine of the school fitted nicely with Jim's interests, and he threw himself into the study of history and English, the two areas where he concentrated the majority of his efforts. He commuted to school, living with the Foleys at 21 Crescent, and worked as a waiter to pay tuition costs.[47] During his spare time, he also wrote for the *Trinity Tripod*, the campus newspaper, and worked as a campus correspondent for the *Hartford Times*.[48]

As an undergraduate, Jim also experimented with fiction and drama, which had been the focus of his literary aspirations since he had begun to envision himself as a writer. He often said that at that age, he wanted to follow in the footsteps of Eugene O'Neill, the famous playwright who had lived in Hartford for a time.[49] Jim began contributing to the *Trinity Review*, a journal published twice yearly by the Trinity Literary Club. In 1941, the *Review* published a play he had written, titled *The Last Tomorrow*. It was the story of a disenchanted engineer,

Tony Karpek, who falls in love with a beautiful ingenue, while fighting off the advances of a smart but desperate female coworker. For the work of a college sophomore, the play is extremely polished. It has the rhythm of 1930s screwball romantic comedy with the tragic undertones of one of O'Neill's stories of despair and disillusionment. The former dominates the first portion of the play, while the latter takes over in the final act, in which the ingenue dies in Tony's arms, and he angrily spurns his coworker, packs his suitcase, and storms out into the rain. In the early section, Jim showed a talent for sharp, witty dialogue, as in the scene where Tony first meets Vivian, the girl he was to fall in love with:

> Viv: You have nice hands.
> Ton: And you have a nice mouth.
> *They stare at each other.*
> Viv: My name is Vivian King. Miss Vivian King. My father's in shipping.
> Ton: Delighted to know you, Miss King. Mine's in his cups.
> Viv (*Good naturedly*): The beast.
> Ton: On the contrary. It makes him docile; and it keeps him from underfoot. You know what a nasty nuisance alert fathers are. (*Vivian starts to leave.*) Are you leaving me? I should like to ask you to dance, but I dance so badly with a girl for the first time.
> Viv: You do have to get used to a person.
> Ton: Besides, the music is terrible.[50]

Jim also contributed short stories to the *Review,* some of which demonstrated the travel lust he had cited in his Trinity application. One story, "Prelude to Defeat," dealt with three Russian generals as they prepare for a battle again a Finnish battalion. The existentialism that was prevalent in much of the literature of the era is very recognizable here: "It was a miserable world for Anastase. Even though a woman loved him, he must die. It puzzled him somewhat, too. He wondered why God so hated the world that he allowed such a situation to exist. It was only those who were not loved that could really afford to die. Anastase shook his head sadly. Surely those Finns were devils for having started this. For a moment he almost became angry at them. But how can one be angry when he's afraid. Anastase wondered if it would help if he wept."[51]

"Melita and the Rose" was yet another story that ends with a death, this one a beautiful Cuban cripple who kills herself when her American lover must return to the United States. While his attempts at fiction established his ability to both craft a sentence and pace a story to its conclusion, he would make these efforts the butt of jokes later in his life when writing about his abortive attempts to conquer fiction.

Jim's first year at Trinity could be called the peak of his competitive athletic career, in terms of actual performance. As a kid, he was fast and athletic, but a nervous outfielder who usually hoped the ball would be hit to somebody, anybody, other than him. He would promote fights in the neighborhood, roping off a ring with clothesline, and grudgingly step into the ring himself when one of the fighters did not show up. His own boxing career ended when a Boy Scout from a rival troop named John McMahon beat him senseless, giving him a bloody nose and a cut lip. "I can still remember wondering why in the hell the bell didn't ring when we had obviously been fighting for a half-hour," he wrote. But baseball was a different story. Jim loved the sport. So when he got to Trinity as a freshman, he earned a spot on the freshman baseball team, his first real shot at organized athletics. He became "the most nervous right fielder the Trinity College frosh team ever had."[52] During his short time on the team, he nearly decapitated the first baseman with a peg from the outfield. He was a college baseball Moonlight Graham, who never even got an official at bat. Once, he was in the on-deck circle as a pinch hitter when the batter in front of him hit into a triple play.

Jim was beginning to get the idea that a baseball career was not to be. His career highlight was a practice home run off the team's top pitcher, Nick Sica.[53] However, it was not Sica, or his coach, or any pitcher who ended Jim Murray's playing days. It was his aunt Peg. Jim was still under his aunt's roof at the time and had joined the team without her knowledge. Education came first, and the family still worried about Jim's health, so he knew they would not be supportive of a baseball career for the family's first college student. Early in the season, Jim inadvertently left his uniform on the bus. Somehow, it found its way back to his aunt, and at her urging, Jim quit the team a short time later.[54]

Despite not achieving success on the diamond, college life suited Murray. He made friends easily, and even with his work responsibilities, he participated in many extracurricular activities. He spent four years as a member of Trinity's Political Science Club, was secretary of the International Relations Club, and was a member of the Trinity Club as well.[55] By that time, Jim's sister Betty was married, and for recreation Jim would bring his friends to Betty's house on the weekends, to deal cards, play croquet, and have a few drinks.[56] While he was pursuing the pleasures and goals of college, however, many of his friends from the neighborhood, kids he had grown up with, were on their way to war zones far away. Hitler's Germany had invaded Poland, and the Second World War had begun in the first month of Murray's freshman year in 1939. The Japanese attacked Pearl Harbor and the United States declared war on Japan during his junior year at Trinity, and Murray, like most young men his age during this era, wanted desperately to be in uniform. The Selective Training and Service Act had become law in August 1940, before the United States entered the war, and in 1941 the age of induction was set at twenty-one to twenty-seven years. Murray and those in his age group were the backbone of the US armed services.[57] Murray tried to enlist but, as he knew he would be, was rejected because of his heart ailment. Nearly 30 percent of enlistees during World War II were given 4-F classification, "not acceptable for military service," and Murray fell into that category. He contacted every political official in the Hartford area in an attempt to get around the classification, but to no avail. He was destined to remain on the sidelines for the duration of the war.[58]

Writing for Money

It is difficult to overestimate the level to which life in America was focused on the war in the spring of 1943. On May 16, the day Jim Murray received his degree, the United States launched the largest air attack yet into German air space, showering the Nazi naval base of Emden with bombs. American and British air forces carried out sweeps in France, while the American air war in the Mediterranean continued unabated. In the Pacific, American troops were making progress against the Japanese on the island of Attu in Alaska, the only battle during World War II to take place on American soil. Japanese planes attacked Allied positions in New Guinea. President Roosevelt and British prime minister Winston Churchill were in meetings to plan war strategy. Adolf Hitler, the day before, had installed himself as the one-man ruler of Germany indefinitely. At home, news was no less concentrated on the war effort. The front page of the *New York Times* on May 16, 1943, included stories headlined "Meat Vanishing: No Relief Seen Here for 2 Months," "144 Seized in City as Draft Dodgers," and "East Must Reduce 'Gas' Use or Face Drastic Steps."

The war seeped into graduation ceremonies at Trinity College as well. Trinity Class Day, a traditional event held at the college the day prior to commencement in which students receive awards and give humorous speeches about their four years on campus, took on a gloomy tone. The Class Day chairman spoke of how the members of the class knew they were living on borrowed time and how some of their classmates were in uniform already, and many more would be by month's end. The featured speaker at the event was a Trinity alumnus from the class of 1918, who related the experience of his own graduating class, full of soon-to-be soldiers headed to Europe to fight in the Great War.[59] So it was a subdued affair on Sunday night at the Trinity College chapel when Murray finally received the first college degree in his family. Remsen Ogilby, president of Trinity, had declared that morning that the class of 1943 would be the last graduation of a normal class at the college for four years. Colonel Robert Butler of the US Army delivered a commencement address in which he heaped invective upon the Germans and Japanese.

But for Murray, it was still a time to celebrate accomplishment. He and fifty-nine of his classmates received their bachelor of arts degrees in the Trinity chapel on a warm Hartford evening. The Murray family brought a large contingent to the occasion, which was celebrated as a milestone for the Murray clan. Murray had little time to celebrate himself, however. Before graduation, he had already lined up a job with the *New Haven Register,* with a weekly salary of $23.50. New Haven is about forty miles south of Hartford, a slightly smaller city, on the Atlantic, best known as the home of Yale University. For the first time, Murray would be living on his own, having secured an apartment in New Haven.[60]

Because of the war, able-bodied men who were still on American soil were scarce. The young men who would normally populate newspaper city rooms were, to a large part, directly involved in the war effort, so cub reporters were few and far between. Murray joined a news staff at the *Register* of mostly older, experienced veterans of the newspaper business and a few 4-Fers like himself. And as the last man in the door, he initially drew the cub-reporter assignments. Soldiers returning home, restaurants short on food due to rationing, New Haven's first woman postmaster, and other similar stories fell to the *Register*'s newest reporter. In his first month on the job, he covered the always divisive issue of the ice cream shortage in New Haven. In a story appropriately headlined "Heat Creates Great Demand for Ice Cream," Murray wrote: "If you're a lover of ice cream (and who isn't?), you'd better call up right now and reserve a stool at your favorite soda fountain for your next treat. Because the way gallons of that priceless dessert have been disappearing from the fountain refrigerators these days with Old Sol doing his best to parboil the poor working people make it likely that you'll no longer be able to drop into the nearest dispensary on the old catch-as-you-can basis and order your favorite double-scoop sundae."[61] Murray went on to supply his readers with the vital information that ice cream had been ranked seventh on the federal government's list of essential industries, and, due to sherbet's lower milk content, hungry New Haveners would be more likely to get their hands on that product in the near future.

As the summer wore on, Murray tried to add flair to his soft-news assignments and society-page features. In the late summer, he earned his way onto the police beat, albeit as a brief writer, mopping up the misdemeanor-level misdeeds of the New Haven criminal element. Murray, from the very beginning, was dutifully clipping his writing, all of it unbylined, and gluing clips into a journal, meticulously writing notes concerning his coverage and delineating the sections of the finished product that he had produced. On a page he marked "Police Beat," he compiled a collection of crime briefs that the city desk had proffered on him. He wrote about a string of four stabbings in New Haven, an illegal Italian lottery, a nineteen-year-old who refused to take his soldier's oath, and, in a story to which Murray could offer a wellspring of personal knowledge thanks to his uncle Ed, a game of chance that turned violent: "A dice game last Saturday night which turned out to have all the markings of a frontier-day barroom melee when two of the participants were discovered to be toting firearms to the scene yesterday resulted in sentences being meted out to seven offenders the aggregate total of which is equal to several months in jail and more than two hundred dollars in fines."[62]

Murray was now working "67-hour weeks," and in that time he was accumulating skills beyond the city desk whenever he could.[63] He wrote movie previews, outlining the new Hollywood offerings premiering at New Haven's theaters, he wrote editorials, he wrote headlines for the copy desk, and he took publicity jobs to earn a little extra cash. (On his first publicity job, he wrote a two-column story for the Yale Hope Mission to earn a cool five dollars.)[64] During the fall, he took on another extra assignment that would lead to his first published sportswriting. The *Register's* sports editor was a man named Dan Mulvey, whom Murray called a "newspaperman's newspaperman," meaning he did not care who did his work for him, as long as it got done. Mulvey let Murray go along on Saturday nights to cover Yale football games and serve as the photographer's assistant, writing cutlines when Mulvey was editing copy. He got a seat in the Yale Bowl press box, the first one he had ever been in. Murray diligently clipped his cutlines and added notations: "Wrote above cutlines on Sat. Midnite of Army game when Dan Mulvey was tied up." He would, he later wrote, "take a few digs at the Yale team and sit back and wait for a reaction that never came." One such dig appeared in October 1943: "Ray Scussel, Yale's standout performer in the 39–7 rout by Army, is shown underway late in the second period on a spectacular dash from Yale 25 marker to Cadet 38. Tackled by Army defensive halfback Minor after the swift 37-yard dash, the 'Scooter' gave Blue fans one of their all-too-infrequent chances to root as he outran the entire Cadet team along the west sideline before being caught by Minor in a last-ditch tackle."[65]

Even at this point, only a few months into his fledgling journalism career, Murray was preparing to move on to bigger things and apparently to get out of Connecticut. He had begun submitting articles on spec to *Time,* with no success.[66] And he began compiling a list of Los Angeles editors and saving them in his clipping book with an eye toward future employment. The effort was beginning to seem justified in the fall of '43, as Murray quickly showed himself to be a determined, energetic reporter who liked to get his hands dirty. By November and December, Murray's stories were appearing on the front page regularly. He took weekend assignments that gave him access to the major crime and disaster stories without the turf battles with other reporters. On Saturday, November 13, he was on cop duty when a shooting made for some weekend excitement.[67] Murray's exhilaration leaks through in handwritten notes he took in his clipping journal from the coverage: "The best part about this story is the wild ride to the scene I had with Ralph Harsh and Eddie Shields. I was sitting in the detective bureau when the call came in and I jumped in the car with Harsh and Shields and rode to the place where the shooting was, past trucks, thru red lights, around corners on two wheels, etc."

Murray's stories became gradually bigger and juicier. In November, he covered the case of a war worker who beat his wife nearly to death after catching her "necking" with an unidentified soldier. "I went up to the jail to see the brute," Murray wrote in his journal. The week before Christmas, he covered a fire that burned an entire city block to the ground, including thirteen businesses.[68] ("What a pip!" he wrote.)

During the winter, fires became a regular part of his beat and often made him a witness to heartbreaking tragedy. As the temperatures dipped, residents of New Haven tenements would stoke the furnace to unsafe levels. The ancient flues on the old flat would reach their ignition point, and the house would soon go up in flames. Murray often arrived at the scene to watch firemen struggling to put out the blaze, the water turning to ice as soon as it came out of the hose. He did his best to take notes with his gloved fingers as his entire body shook from the cold. After being called to one particular fire, he rode in the ambulance with four badly burned young children. At the emergency room, nurses squirted glycerin on their burns, which "sizzled like some grotesque sausages." The children cried "Mommy" and then were silent. Murray asked the doctor about their chances, and the doctor shook his head despondently. "We have no facilities for burned children," he said.[69]

That same month, he covered a story that would illustrate Murray's readiness to move on from New Haven, and at the same time earn him a connection that would help him in the very near future. Acting on a tip from the chief of the Connecticut State Police, Leo Carroll, with whom Murray had developed a relationship, he stumbled on the kind of lurid love triangle that would occupy a good portion of the next decade of his career. An heir to the wealthy Almadon family had been having an affair with a married woman, and the woman's husband had shot him to death. Murray reported the story, his first murder case, and brought it to his editors at the *Register*. The *Register* passed on the story. A disappointed Murray took the story to Walt Cochrane, the Connecticut bureau chief for the Associated Press. The Associated Press was impressed with the story, which was played big in New York and Washington, DC, newspapers. Cochrane would enthusiastically recommend Murray to his colleague Hub Keavy, in the AP's Los Angeles bureau, a month later.[70]

Murray's decision to head West was firm by December. His six-month apprenticeship at the *Register* was short but fruitful, and now he felt ready for the next challenge. A variety of forces had been pushing him in that direction, actually any direction that led him out of Connecticut, for some time. He had clearly outgrown New Haven and the *Register* journalistically. Fires and police briefs had excited him initially, but New Haven was a small city; Murray spent much of his time reporting on incidents that would not merit two lines in a major metropolitan daily. Now he had learned that if he got his hooks into a really big story, his own editors were likely to turn it down. Aside from journalism, Murray was ready for adventure. He had spent his entire life in the Northeast and now was watching his childhood friends and his college classmates leave regularly, headed for places that he had read about and dreamed about. He was also ready to get outside of the grips of his family, particularly the strange and strained relationship he had with his parents. He had developed a kind of claustrophobia related to all of his relatives, and New Haven was the first step toward extricating himself.[71] But by now it was proving to be not far enough. Finally, it was his own 4-F status and the constant reminders that his peers were defending the country in Africa, the Pacific, and across the world and he was still in Connecticut. Worse, his peers were dying. He later said he could not stand to look into the eyes of mothers whose sons had been killed or maimed in the war. He knew they were looking at him, thinking, "Why is my son dead while that Murray boy is still walking around the streets of Hartford?"[72]

Murray stayed in New Haven and worked Christmas Day. He covered two house fires, one fatal; an auto accident; and traffic on Broadway Street. On December 29, 1943, he reported on his first and last real murder that would find its way into the pages of the *Register*. James Streeto, the caretaker of the Boxwood Manor Summer Resort in Old Lyme, Connecticut, fifteen miles up the coast from New Haven, had been stabbed, shot, and bludgeoned with a blunt-force instrument. His sweetheart, Delphine Betrand, said three unidentified youths had done the deed, but she was being held in New London County Jail as a suspect. "A Triumph!" Murray wrote in his journal. "I scooped the AP on this." He had been tipped off by Edward Hickey, the Connecticut State Police commissioner, an "old friend of the family." Murray wrote: "State Police found Streeto already dead, lying in a pool of blood half out of the kitchen door on the floor of the closed-in rear porch. Blood streaks on both the kitchen door and the rear porch door, just short of where he fell, led to the belief he may have been attempting to grope his way out of the building when death struck him. Veteran police investigators described it as a particularly 'vicious' killing and ventured the belief that intense hatred must have driven the assailants."[73] It was, hands down, his bloodiest story yet.[74] And it was good practice for where he would end up next, a newspaper where blood was expected and appreciated, where, in fact, the editors shouted through the newsroom for reporters to pour on the blood in buckets. The year 1943 in New Haven had closed with a deadly flourish, and Murray had only three more days during which he could call the state of Connecticut his home.

2

The *Los Angeles Examiner* Years, 1944–1947

Camelot, we thought it was. Shangri-La. God's city. Just Molly and me. And baby makes three. You hated to leave it for 20 minutes. It was like leaving a great party.

Los Angeles, I love you! we all shouted as we tore off the wing-tips we had worn in Bridgeport or Newark or Port Chester or Winnetka and put on sandals. We bought trunks and swim fins and got a backyard barbecue and a station wagon and on Sundays we drank gin and ate steak. And there weren't any mosquitoes, or sidewalks, and it was cool at night and Man! It would be a bring-down to go to heaven.

—Jim Murray, "Once Upon a Time It Was Dreamsville"

California Dreamin'

So like the gold prospectors, the Joad family, and the Brooklyn Dodgers, Jim Murray succumbed to the great golden dream of California and pointed a course west. Los Angeles held the allure of mystery and opportunity. It was, Murray would find, a place where you could slice away your past and remake yourself, find a new identity, and place a stake in fresh, unmarked territory. It offered endless sun, a topography that, to an easterner, felt as exotic as the moon, and exploding growth that was just waiting to be exploited. Just twenty years before, Los Angeles had been little more than a blip on the United States Census. Between 1920 and 1940, the city's population nearly tripled, reaching more than 1.5 million people in 1940, with nearly 2.8 million in Los Angeles

23

County. The decade of the 1940s would continue the expansion, and by 1950 the city's population would top 1.9 million.[1]

Murray had been planning his exodus for some months and set the end of the year as his launch date. On January 2, 1944, he took the money he had saved from his seven-month tenure at the *New Haven Register* and a few suitcases, went down to the station in Hartford, and boarded a steam train bound for Los Angeles. He also brought along a list of contacts at Los Angeles newspapers and wire services that he had compiled while at the *Register*. Murray was embarking on a trip that would take him beyond the boundaries of the Northeast for the first time in his life. To this point, he had been to New York City and Boston, spent some time at his uncle's home in Fitchburg, Massachusetts, and taken a few rides on the Hoboken Ferry in New Jersey, but that was the extent of his travel. The rails during the war years were overloaded with military personnel, and Murray's train was no different. Around Chicago, he struck up a conversation with a uniformed female traveler, but the stares of male GIs, which Murray interpreted as ominous and slightly threatening, ended the relationship before it began. But the euphoria of discovery was thick, and Murray years later remembered the excitement of the journey. "He told me he went through the town of Rancho Cucamonga as they were approaching Los Angeles, and he loved the name, and the names of the other Southern California towns; they were so lyrical. The windows were down, and he could smell the orange blossoms. He thought he had died and gone to heaven," said Linda McCoy-Murray, Murray's second wife.[2]

When he got to Los Angeles, the euphoria of adventure wore off as he began to realize that he had no job and only $106 to his name. His first stop was the Los Angeles bureau of the Associated Press. Bureau chief Hub Keavy was already aware of him after the recommendation from his colleague, but no position was available at the time.[3] Murray had a list of contacts in the city, including the City News Service, *Los Angeles Herald Express, Los Angeles Times,* and *Los Angeles Examiner,* but no personal connections at those outlets and had no success.[4] Murray rented a room in Ocean Park, a small neighborhood in the southwest corner of Santa Monica that in those days was populated mostly by Jewish immigrants.[5] He went to see Keavy again and received the same response, but this time Keavy put in a call to Bud Lewis at the *Times.* Lewis told Murray to come back a week from Thursday, but Murray knew he would be flat broke by then. With desperation creeping in, he went back to Keavy at AP.

"I hate to do this to you, kid, but go down to see Jim Richardson at the *Examiner,*" Keavy told him.[6]

Murray did as told. On a bright, eighty-degree Los Angeles day, he showed up at the *Examiner* office wearing a rust-colored overcoat, wing-tipped shoes, a button-down collar, and a vest.

Richardson pegged him for a fresh East Coast transplant immediately. "Do you know where city hall is?" he demanded.

"No," said Murray.

"Do you know where the FBI is?" Richardson asked.

"No," said Murray.

"Do you even know where Figueroa Street is, for cryin' out loud?" Richardson barked, his anger rising.

"No," said Murray.

Richardson threw his pencil down. "Well, can you write?"

"Oh, Mr. Richardson," Murray said. "I can write like a son of a bitch."

Richardson hired Murray on the spot and told him he could start the very next morning. Murray enthusiastically accepted and asked Richardson for an advance on his salary.[7]

So, fortuitously, Murray was to start his Los Angeles newspaper career at the *Examiner,* a crime- and scandal-fueled Hearst broadsheet instead of the *Times,* which at that time was a stodgy Republican rag that existed mostly to put forth the antiunionist sentiment of publisher Harry Chandler. Los Angeles in 1944 was a thriving newspaper market with four dailies competing for the ever-expanding readership. There was the *Los Angeles Daily News,* an evening paper that had been founded by Cornelius Vanderbilt Jr. in 1923 as a clean alternative to the scandal sheets of the day but by 1944 had evolved into the city's only Democratic voice. There was the *Los Angeles Evening Herald and Express,* an afternoon tabloid that reveled in sensationalism and was used as a model for Hollywood movies of the day that depicted yellow journalism. There was Chandler's *Times,* which stayed above the fray, and in doing so had made itself a regular presence on the "Worst American Newspapers" list. And, finally, there was the *Examiner,* William Randolph Hearst's favorite paper and the city's leading newspaper since the turn of the century.[8]

By the time Murray joined the chain, the Hearst brand was firmly established in American journalism. Indeed, the term *yellow journalism* came from an early Hearst comic strip, *The Yellow Kid,* and entered the lexicon as a way to describe Hearst's revolutionary approach to newspapering.

William Randolph Hearst had been born into wealth. His father, George Hearst, had set out to pan for gold in 1850 and had made a fortune mining the Pacific Coast for gold, silver, and copper. In 1887, at the age of twenty-three, young William persuaded his father, then a US senator, to let him run the *San Francisco Examiner,* which George Hearst had acquired against a bad debt. W. R. Hearst began to develop his populist style of journalism, which relied on flashy headlines, color comics, gossip, and a healthy dose of jingoism. He quickly doubled the circulation of the *San Francisco Examiner,* and then set his sights on New York. He bought the floundering *New York Morning Journal* and promptly raided the staff of Joseph Pulitzer's *New York World,* then the leading paper in the city.[9] Hearst spent lavishly and led his papers into crusades, most famously fanning the flames of American outrage with headlines and editorials that eventually pointed the country on the course toward the Spanish-American War.[10] During the next three decades, he built a media empire that by 1935 included twenty-eight newspapers, thirteen magazines, eight radio stations, two motion-picture companies, and assorted other real estate and mining entities that together were worth $220 million. At that time, his corporation employed thirty-one thousand people.[11]

In 1904, Hearst had been elected to the US House of Representatives, and he quickly launched a candidacy for president. It was as another outlet to get his message to potential Democratic Party voters that Hearst started the *Los Angeles Examiner* in 1904.[12] The *Examiner* rapidly rode the Hearst formula to the position of number-one morning newspaper in Los Angeles. In the 1940s, the newspaper had the highest circulation in the West, but it was a day-to-day, edition-to-edition battle for supremacy that had editors, reporters, and photographers engaging in anything short of outright crime to gain an edge over the competition. Editors thought nothing of sending staff members into competing newsrooms to surreptitiously steal news pages to get a jump on a story. Reporters regularly blackmailed or bribed police captains and government officials in order to get exclusive information. A favorite practice among photographers and reporters was stealing pictures out of the homes of the families of crime and disaster victims.[13] "In the old days, the competition was fierce," said Melvin Durslag, an *Examiner* sports reporter when Murray joined the staff. "We used to do all we could think of to get a scoop. We used to fight each other like dogs for stories."[14]

And at the forefront of the daily pursuit of the sensational was Jim Richardson, once famously called "the last of the terrible men."[15] Richardson was a bellowing, blustering terror on reporters, editors, and photographers given to thunderous outbursts when he felt his staff was not upholding his standards of cutthroat journalism. Many of these outbursts concluded with a firing. Richardson had started in Los Angeles newspapers in 1913, when, on a family vacation, he witnessed the collapse of the Long Beach auditorium. He left the volunteers helping the dead and maimed and called the story into the *Los Angeles Herald,* fighting off the injured and rescuers so he could keep the phone line open and deliver the entire scoop to the paper.[16] From there, he fought, lied, and backstabbed his way to the top of the Los Angeles reporter pool and became the youngest city editor in the Hearst chain. He lasted only a few months before embarking on a decade of hopping from job to job, bottle to bottle, and wife to wife (there were four of them). He awoke from a bender in a Japanese whorehouse on Christmas morning 1936 and looked around at the dank, depressing room, trying to remember where he was.[17] He never drank again and in 1937 began his second tenure as the *Examiner* city editor. This run would last twenty years.[18] During those years he drove himself and his staff to insanity, throwing tantrums related to the most important of stories and the most inconsequential of briefs. He ran through a string of assistant city editors, who were forced to sit at the desk next to him and take the brunt of his fury. One after another either slipped into alcoholism or left the business entirely.[19] Richardson was despised by a great many of those who worked under him during his tenure, and Murray had his share of dustups with his boss. The two remained friends well after Murray left the *Examiner,* however. "You have to salute Richardson on one big point: it was never dull," Murray wrote ten years after leaving the paper. "In fact, it was fun to work for him."[20]

Life in the Big City

The morning after his impromptu hiring, Murray dutifully reported for work at the *Examiner* office at Broadway and Eleventh Streets in downtown Los Angeles, a five-story cream-colored stucco building with an enormous American flag flying over it. The structure took up an entire city block, and on street level, passersby could view the *Examiner*'s huge black presses whirring away. The building had a small elevator, but reporters normally climbed the thirty-eight-stair marble staircase up to the opaque doors with the words CITY ROOM in large block type.[21] The difference between coming to work in the sleepy newsroom of the *Register* in the one-newspaper town of New Haven and the nerve center of a Hearst newspaper was shocking. The *Examiner* City Room housed more than one hundred staffers, including city side, the sports department, the copy desk, the rewrite desk, the art department, and the society department. Dozens of Remington and Royal typewriters clacked away in the area called "the bullpen," which housed reporters and rewrite men. Editors yelled "Copy!" while copyboys ran paper from desk to desk. The tension level in the City Room would gradually increase throughout the day, and by late afternoon, it would reach a boiling point, said Joe Santley, a writer on the rewrite desk in the 1940s. "About deadline time, for the first edition, the damn place was a mass of smoke. There was pipe smoke, cigar smoke, cigarettes; the second hand smoke was as bad as a 4-alarm fire," Santley said.[22]

Richardson showed no quarter on new reporters. Once, he barked at a cub reporter to get out on an interview. The cub stopped at his desk to leaf through the phone book. Richardson stared through him with his one good eye (he lost the other one in a sling-shot accident when he was seven). "What the hell are you doing?" he demanded.

"Looking up the address," the reporter stuttered.

"Never mind the address," Richardson yelled. "Get the hell out there!"[23]

Richardson had a series of initiation rites that every new reporter was required to go through. He would send each newbie on a bogus meatpacking story at a slaughterhouse, so they would be exposed to blood and organs; they would cover a gory car wreck; they would be required to watch an autopsy be performed; and, in a task that would prove most psychologically damaging to the reporters, they would have to take liquor-drenched dictation from the Hearst movie columnist Louella O. Parsons.[24]

Murray started out like any other greenhorn, writing obituaries and two-graph fire stories (some of which would have made the front page at the *Register*). He was put through Richardson's initiation rituals like any other new hire. On March 4, 1944, he got his chance to interpret Parsons's drunken gibberish, an interpretation that would run coast-to-coast throughout the Hearst chain and beyond. "Some time in late November, Loretta Young and Lieutenant Colonel Tom Lewis will welcome the stork, and if there are any two people happier in the world I haven't met them," he typed.[25]

Murray seemed to survive the phone call, but it was one of his very first *Examiner* stories that left a deeper impression on his psyche. Richardson sent him to report on the story of six-year-old Margaret Wade, whose leg was amputated after she was hit by a car. The fact that the girl's father witnessed the accident raised the drama level enough for Richardson to devote eight inches of column space to it. Murray wrote:

> The child was returning from Huntington Drive School, where she is a second-grader. She saw her father leaving for work and ran across the street to meet him.
> She may never run again.
> Her left leg was amputated at General Hospital while her agonized parents waited in a ward corridor. She had been struck by a car driven by Mrs. Magda Singleton, 73, of 917 Locust Street, Pasadena, and carried under its hurtling wheels for 140 feet before they came to rest against a pole.
> Mr. Wade, whose unhappy task it was to pick up his child's broken body, was bitter:
> "They sent the child home alone at 10 a.m. to get a written excuse for the previous day's absence," he said.[26]

After he finished his shift, Murray took the eight dollars he had remaining from his first paycheck (his starting salary was thirty-eight dollars a week) and spent it on toys for Margaret. He brought the toys to General Hospital, where he was told by the nurses on duty that he would have to take them back. I'm with the *Examiner*, he told them. "Take these to Margaret, or I'll bring the power of the press down on you."[27]

When he was not being put through psychological gymnastics by Richardson, Murray got to savor one of the rewards of Los Angeles journalism, at least for one night. On the night of March 2, 1944, Murray got the plum assignment of covering the Academy Awards. As he did at the Yale Bowl a few months earlier, he tagged along to save somebody else from the menial task of writing captions. Murray's interest in movies reached far back into childhood. Back in Hartford, he spent many hours at the Rivele Theater, taking in Hollywood's latest features. His early infatuation with journalism had much to do with the foreign correspondents portrayed in the Hollywood noir films of the 1930s. He loved the movies of Ronald Colman, David Niven, and any other actor who would put on a trench coat and carry a Luger on-screen.[28] At this time in his career and for years forward, he harbored dreams of writing for the stage and the screen.[29] At the *New Haven Register,* he had been allowed to take a shot at the Hollywood beat, which consisted of writing synopses of the films that were opening that week at the cinemas in the New Haven area. He previewed the films of '40s Hollywood icons Frank Sinatra and Bing Crosby, men who would become the subjects of his profiles a decade later and his close friends a decade after that.[30] New Haven's Paramount Theatre even pulled quotes from Murray's stories and added them to their advertisements. "Deanna was never better— J. Murray, Register," read an ad for the Deanna Durbin–Joseph Cotton film *Hers to Hold.* (Murray's future Hearst colleague Louella Parsons is quoted farther down the ad display.) And Hollywood was still on his mind when he made the decision to come west. Before leaving for Los Angeles, he asked one of his professors at Trinity to write him a letter of recommendation to bring to Hollywood screenwriter Alan Scott. The professor obliged: "The bearer of this note of introduction, James Murray, is a Trinity graduate of the class of 1943. He distinguished himself at Trinity through his writing and as a good and reflective student. His ambition is to be a scenario writer and I thought it worthwhile to introduce him to you, who has made such a good success in your chosen field. If you can be of help to Murray I shall appreciate it as a personal favor."[31]

The Academy Awards ceremony Murray covered in 1944 was the first one in which the festivities moved from a banquet to a theater setting. The event, which originated in 1936, had grown in stature as the movie industry in Los Angeles increased in reach and influence. That year, it was moved to the Grauman's Chinese Theatre on Hollywood Boulevard. Murray joined a crowd of more than two thousand and watched as *Casablanca* scored the Best Movie and Best Director awards.[32] Photos of best actress Jennifer Jones, a twenty-four-year-old first-time actress who starred in *The Song of Bernadette,* and screen veteran Paul Lukas, star of *Watch on the Rhine,* ran in the March 3 *Examiner,* with Murray's captions telling the glamorous story.[33] Less than three months removed from stringing together film capsules for the *Register,* he was roaming the same theater as Ingrid Bergman, Humphrey Bogart, Rosalind Russell, Greer Garson, and the many other top screen superstars of the day.

"Of Passion and Crime and Greed"

Richardson ran off many a cub reporter, but Murray proved immediately to be an asset to the *Examiner,* and the primary reason was the very skill he promised his boss at his interview: deftness with the language. However dedicated Richardson was to getting the ultimate scoop, he was equally dedicated to purple prose that he felt made news stories sing and Hearst newspapers fly off the racks. He was always looking for writers who could turn a run-of-the-mill story into a masterpiece with one glorious lead. Once, Richardson pulled a story of the Associated Press wire about a devastating tornado that had hit a small town in Kansas in the middle of the night. The first sentence read: "The little town off Koming, Kansas, died in its sleep last night." Richardson became apoplectic with excitement and made it his personal mission to find and hire the writer of the lead. He found him a few months later on the copy desk of a Chicago paper and brought him to the *Examiner.*[34]

Richardson demanded the lead of each and every story be given the Hearst treatment. It was a lesson he had learned three decades before, during his first days as a reporter for the *Los Angeles Herald.* He had written a story about a court appearance by a woman who had been arrested for public drunkenness. An older *Herald* reporter who had taken an interest in Richardson looked over his shoulder and offered his advice. "You've got to put a hop on them like a pitcher puts a hop on his fastball," the reporter told him. "Of course we're sensational. So is life. Remember that. The Bible's sensational and so is everything else worth reading."[35]

Murray quickly proved to have the chops to write for Richardson. The straight news leads that appeared on his briefs during his first few weeks quickly morphed into Hearst-style nuggets that earned him praise in the newsroom. When he was given a throwaway assignment about a Pasadena woman who killed herself unexpectedly while out of town, Murray spiced it up enough to earn him fifteen inches of column space: "Born unwanted—and dead by mistake. That was the official version yesterday which Chicago authorities put upon the tragic suicide of Miss Virginia Thompson, beauteous Pasadena girl who poisoned herself in her fiancé's apartment there Tuesday in the apparently mistaken belief that she had lost his love."[36]

The *Examiner's* editors awarded a weekly and monthly prize for the best written story, and Murray quickly began accumulating the twenty-five- and fifty-dollar war bonds that came with winning the awards. In June, he won story of the month when he covered the downward spiral of actress Frances Farmer, who had gone from leading roles in A-list films to debilitating mental illness:

> Frances Farmer lost her way yesterday on the road back to fame and riches in Hollywood. She reached the end of the road—not in the glittering palaces of filmland's greats where she once contributed such a rich and warming heritage, but in a grimy dusty jail cell in Antioch, California, where the listing "vagrant" hung like a tarnished ornament on her famous name.
>
> She was tattered, destitute—clad in blue dungarees and denim shirt, nervous, irritable, "a strange light" in her eyes.[37]

In July, Murray won the best written story award again for his coverage of a blind man who regained sight after experimental surgery. (Murray would have a similar experience himself forty-five years later.) By now, some of his stories were receiving bylines, a sign of privilege among the *Examiner* staff. He wrote:

> Blind for 30 years, and then—
>
> "I looked up and there was a tree—the most beautiful thing in the world."
>
> Simply, in a voice devoid of emotion, William Furber described a miracle of the 20th century—a century in which wise men have said a miracle couldn't occur.
>
> He thinks he's going to be able to see again.
>
> The restoration is as yet only partial, coming and receding with disappointing regularity. It appears, in fact, Furber says, to retrogress with physical fatigue, strong in the early morning and fading into complete customary sightlessness as the day wears on.[38]

Murray continued to monopolize the awards. Within six months of joining the *Examiner,* he was promoted to the rewrite desk and for a time was the youngest rewrite man in the entire Hearst chain. The promotion of a relative newcomer so angered fellow rewrite man Reggie Taverner that he quit the staff, calling Murray "Richardson's bobo."[39] Newspapers in the first half of the twentieth century had a rewrite desk, separate from the copy desk, where the newspaper staff's best writers would take information from reporters, sometimes called legmen, and organize and improve them to prepare the stories for publication. A good rewrite man was difficult to find, and promotion to the rewrite desk would lead to a salary increase of at least five dollars a week.[40] The duties of a staffer on the rewrite battery would vary. About half of the time, they would man the desk and rework the stories of other reporters, often called in from the field. The other half of the time, Richardson or an assistant city editor would send them out on their own assignments.[41]

One downside of taking the promotion and the extra five dollars a week was the fact that as a rewrite man, one would spend a great deal more time within close range of Richardson's wrath. Murray was now in the line of fire. Once, Richardson handed Murray the story of an unknown bum who had hanged himself in a skid-row fleabag motel. Murray did not think it was worth a story, but he wrote it straight: "John Jefferson, 51, was found dead in his room at the Hotel Barclay yesterday. Police dubbed it a suicide." He handed it over to Richardson.

"No, we need something with a little more oomph in it," Richardson said.

Murray thought he was kidding. "Oh, come on," he said with a laugh. He rewrote the lead twice more, and each time Richardson handed it back to him and glared.

Finally, Murray thought, "What the hell? I'll give him what he's asking for." He wrote: "John Jefferson, 68, at the Barkley Street Hotel yesterday knotted a light cord around his neck and stepped off a chair into eternity." He handed it to Richardson.

Richardson looked at it, laughed, and threw it in the wastebasket. He told Murray, "OK, go down to Gallagher's and have a beer."

The incident inspired another *Examiner* rewrite man, Johnny Reese, to write a poem that would later be published and displayed by the Los Angeles Press Club, titled "Jim Richardson's Rewrite Man":

> The rewrite man was writing the death
> Of a miserable Skid Row whore
> From the after effects of a drinking bout
> Some two or three weeks before.
> The facts were simple and dull and brief
> And he had it almost done
> When suddenly came the raucous voice
> Of James H. Richardson.
> "On that murder case," the Great Man said,
> "You can give it lots of play
> "Go into the mystery angle, too,
> "For we're short of news today."
> The rewrite man gave a startled cry
> At the mention of mystery.
> And round-eyed, turned to the desk and said:
> "Were you addressing ME?"
> "Of course," said the Man, and his voice grew thick,
> "Some merciless sadist slew
> "This innocent child of East Fifth Street
> "Tho' he probably loved her, too.
> "Get into your lead that a ghastly smile

"Was pitiful on her face;
"And in saying how she was slain, hark back to
"The Peete and Denton case.
"And somewhere high in your story tell
"Of the marijuana ring
"That made this maid in the seventh grade
"A wretched, besotted thing.
"Oh, yes, in your opening sentence quote
"MacArthur on the Flag,
"Ignoring the coroner calling her
"A syphilitic bag.
"Write wistfully of the cocktail glass
"That broke as her body fell.
"The artist will alter the photograph
"Of the gallon of muscatel.
"Mention a wilted yellow rose
"To tincture it with romance,
"And refer somewhere to an evening gown,
"Forgetting she wore no pants.
"The barroom bum she was living with,
"We'll call her mystery man.
"And try to mention the Japanese
"And the Communists if you can.
"Get excited about the drama here
"Of passion and crime and greed.
"Write a good objective story, and
"Get all of this in your lead.
"Give me a take as soon as you can;
"I want to give it a look.
"But don't start in till you've got the facts.
". . . And hold it to half a book."
The rewrite man, with a ghastly leer
That the Great Man didn't see,
Started again, and finished at last
At twenty five after three.
The climax came the following week.
He was gratified to set
The prize for the finest writing to
Appear in the overset.
MORAL

It served the bastard right, of course,
As philosophers will note,

For being a rewrite man at all
When he could have slit his throat.[42]

Love and Marriage

By the summer of 1944, Murray had settled into his role on the rewrite desk and started to adjust to life in Los Angeles. He lived in a rented upstairs room from a family named Quinn in Ocean Park.[43] When commuting to and from work via streetcars proved untenable, he saved up his rewrite money and bought a used Pierce Arrow automobile, a large, box-shaped four-door used clunker from the turn-of-the-century car manufacturer that had shut down eight years earlier. The car had a statue of an Indian with a bow and arrow as a radiator cap, and Murray said, "It was the last of that run on the assembly line."[44] The car was a gas guzzler, and Murray would have to save his gas-ration stamps to get enough fuel for a trip to the beach.

About three months after Murray joined the *Examiner,* Will Fowler, another young reporter with eastern roots, joined the staff. Fowler was only twenty-one when he started at the *Examiner* in the spring of '44. He and Murray quickly became close friends. They would develop a lifelong friendship; each would be godparents to the other's children. Fowler joined the *Examiner* after a two-year stint in the Coast Guard. He had enlisted on July 4, 1942, and after two successful convoys in which his unit sank Japanese submarines, he had developed a high fever. Doctors discovered that the illness had caused a hole in his lung, and in 1944 he was medically discharged and ready to begin a newspaper career that for Fowler had been a foregone conclusion.[45]

Fowler was destined for the newspaper business, and more specifically the Hearst chain. His father, Gene Fowler, was newspaper royalty, a legend among Hearst men. During the heyday of Jazz Age celebrity journalism, Gene Fowler was a household name who counted among his friends the biggest names of the day, from writers such as Runyon, Lardner, Winchell, and Rice to athletes and sporting celebrities such as Babe Ruth, Jack Dempsey, and John McGraw. He had grown up in Denver during the last years of the Wild West. He drifted into journalism; during a college course he took on the subject, his professor shared the old journalism cliché that a dog biting a man isn't news, but the opposite is. Gene got the point, turning in a sample headline that read, "Hydrant Wets Dog." He went professional and made his reputation at Hearst's *Denver Republic,* where he offered his home to an out-of-work, ragged Jack Dempsey years before the fighter became known to the world as the Manassas Mauler and heavyweight champion of the world.[46] Fowler had made his way east, first in Chicago, then coming to New York. He famously demanded a hundred-dollar weekly salary from Hearst to come aboard the staff at the *New York*

American when the going rate at that time, 1918, was thirty-five dollars weekly. "If the young man from Denver places that value on his services, then he must be worth it," Hearst said.[47] He became the youngest managing editor of a metropolitan newspaper at the *American*. After a decade of New York newspaper exploits, much of it as a sportswriter, Fowler moved his son Will and his family west to Hollywood, where he became a top author and highly paid screenwriter. His circle of friends included W. C. Fields, John Barrymore, and Jimmy Durante, the latter two of whom he penned best-selling biographies.[48]

Gene Fowler was a childhood idol of Murray's, as he was for thousands of young men who idealized the world of 1920s journalism. Will, named William Randolph after the chief, was born in 1922. His father devoted his time to newspapers rather than fatherhood, but as a teenager Will served as a designated driver for his father and used it as an opportunity to develop relationships with his father's famous friends. He was particularly close with Fields, whom he referred to as Uncle Claude. Fowler's first *Examiner* byline would be Fields's obituary, actually written by his father and phoned into the *Examiner* city desk.[49] In the summer of 1944, he and Murray quickly bonded, and along with Joe Santley, Mel Durslag, and a few other staffers, they fell into a routine of chasing stories until deadline and then chasing women and drinks in the bars of Los Angeles after that day's *Examiner* was put to bed. They frequented the famed Ambassador Hotel and some of the clubs that surrounded it, including an *Examiner* favorite, the Balboa Club, on Twelfth and Hill Streets. At the small club near the Ambassador, they met Nat King Cole, who had just formed the Nat King Cole Trio.[50] The City Room at the *Examiner* was populated by heavy drinkers, as was the entire profession in that era, and a long day in the newsroom inevitably ended on a bar stool. "In those days, guys drank, and we went to bars. That's what we did," said Durslag. "I was raised by a bunch of drunks. I started very young on the paper, and I worked with a lot of drunks. They all drank. They kept a fifth in their drawer. The real alcoholic was the guy who kept a half pint in his pocket."

Murray felt comfortable in a bar and adapted easily to the lifestyle. However, his time as a bachelor would be short. In the summer of 1945, Murray stepped into the 575 Club, a small neighborhood bar at 575 South Fairfax, and quickly became infatuated with the girl on the piano. Gerry Brown had come to Los Angeles around the time Murray had. She had grown up in Ann Arbor, Michigan, and played the piano through childhood. In Los Angeles, she had landed a job as a medical receptionist and asked the owner of the 575 Club if she could play for free for customers, to keep her skills fresh. Murray's advances were rejected initially. A short time later, he was on a double date with a friend and two dental hygienists. He excused himself to call the 575 Club, where a friend on the other end told him, "I've got Gerry Brown here expecting you. I've convinced her you were crazy about her but I can't keep her much longer." Murray threw some money on the table, raced out of the restaurant, and piloted his Pierce Arrow through the streets at top speed, arriving as Gerry was leaving. He convinced her to stay that night and less than a year later convinced her to be his wife. The couple was married in October 1945 and honeymooned at the St. Francis Hotel in San Francisco, coming home a day early when they ran out of money.[51]

Murray's rewrite-desk salary had increased to $43.50 a week by the time he got married,[52] enough to move him and his new bride into an apartment in Park La Brea. Park La Brea was an enormous new complex built by the Metropolitan Life Insurance Company that spread across many blocks in the Miracle Mile section of Los Angeles. It consisted mainly of two-story garden apartments amid rows of green lawns, built specifically to mesh with the surrounding neighborhoods. Park La Brea's inhabitants ran the gamut of age, race, and ethnicity, and its quiet streets allowed for a sheltered urban existence.[53] The Murrays' apartment, located at Sixth and Fairfax Avenues, was very close to the hub of Los Angeles professional sports in 1945, a decade and a half before the major professional leagues would make their way west. Three blocks over, at Third Street and Fairfax, sat Gilmore Field, home of the Hollywood Stars Triple-A Baseball franchise. A few blocks to the west was Gilmore Stadium, built in 1934, where the Hollywood Bears Minor League Football club played their games and midget automobiles raced. Also within a few blocks was Pan-Pacific Auditorium, home to the Los Angeles Monarchs ice-hockey team and also the facility where USC and UCLA played home men's basketball games.

Murray's professional life was still devoted to news, but in his new neighborhood he spent much of his free time attending sporting events and familiarizing himself with the Los Angeles sports scene.[54] And the franchise that had the most character at the time was easily the Hollywood Stars. At that time, the Stars were owned by Bob Cobb, owner of the Brown Derby restaurant chain, a local landmark with its flagship restaurant located at the intersection of Hollywood and Vine. It was here that the who's who of show business regularly showed up to eat and be seen eating. Cobb had four Derbies in the Los Angeles area, known for their brown dome roofs and the signature dish that he had invented, the Cobb salad. The walls of the Derby were lined with caricatures of Hollywood's biggest stars—having your caricature on Cobb's wall in the 1940s and '50s meant you had ascended to the top of Hollywood's pecking order. Gilmore Field, named for Los Angeles oil barons, had opened in 1939, a single-deck, all-wood stadium with only a few feet between the baselines and the crowd. For night games, which became more common after World War II, the entrance to the field sported a lit movie marquee announcing that evening's competitors. Spectators flocked to see the games (the Stars were in the first division in the Pacific Coast League in these years), but also with the hopes of spotting Danny Kaye, Jack Benny, Bob Hope, Barbara Stanwyck, Bing Crosby, Gracie Allen, Gary Cooper, or some of the other celebrity regulars, some of whom doubled as minority investors to the Stars.

Cobb was a showman who took his promotional instincts from the restaurant to the ball field. The team for a time fielded female cheerleaders to excite the crowd. Another season, Cobb decided to do away with uniform pants for the Stars and replace them with striped shorts.[55] One opening day, Cobb had papier-mâché stars placed at each position in the field, and as each regular was announced to the crowd, they would leap through the stars.[56]

Murray spent a lot of time at Gilmore Field and at the other venues when he could. Newlywed life, however, did not last very long. The Murray's first child, Theodore (named for Boston Red Sox slugger Ted Williams), was born in July 1946, the same week that millionaire aviator Howard Hughes crashed his experimental plane into a Hollywood mansion. Murray remembered this period in his life as idyllic; he was free to perfect his craft while Gerry devoted herself to the family. In the newsroom, Murray was still consistently winning the *Examiner's* best story awards, and he was developing a higher profile as a writer. Writing under the byline James Murray, his name appeared more regularly in the pages of the *Examiner.*

With the end of World War II, the steady population growth of Los Angeles accelerated. "The city of L.A. . . . was becoming America's Camelot. Every GI who passed through California couldn't wait to get back. As soon as the war was over, he went back to Omaha, Des Moines or Schenectady, picked up his clothes, and made tracks back to California," Murray wrote.[57] The city was beginning to develop the characteristics that would later define it, and Murray was there to cover it for the *Examiner.* He wrote about the financing and building of the Hollywood Freeway, a mammoth undertaking that would put the city on the road to its autocentric personality.[58] He wrote about the air pollution that overtook the city in the 1940s and earned it the reputation as the smog capital of North America. But the *Examiner* paid the bills with crime and passion, and Murray was soon to happen upon a series of stories of that nature that would place his byline on the front page and eventually pave the way for his exit from the world of daily journalism.

The Halls of Justice

Despite the regularity of Richardson's outbursts, Murray normally preferred manning the rewrite desk over accepting assignments that took him out of the office. By 1946, he had some seniority and was occasionally sent on the road for important stories. In February 1946, he went to Phoenix to cover the divorce trial of wealthy socialite Gioia Gould, heiress and great-granddaughter of railroad baron Jay Gould. Gould had married the "short, slightly built Philadelphia socialite" William Grimditch, and the marriage had produced two children. However, while Grimditch was in the army, Gould had come west and fallen in love with wealthy Arizonan Blake Brophy, conveniently recorded it all in a diary, and then let the diary fall into the hands of her jilted husband. Murray wrung all the drama he could out of the trial, and there was plenty. Gould wept daily as Grimditch revealed the contents of the diary and later admitted her love for Brophy on the witness stand.[59] Gould was eventually awarded custody of the children, and the unhappy couple parted ways.

The Gould divorce led to Murray's coverage of another trial later in the year, one that made the front pages on both sides of the Atlantic. In October, Murray went to Las Vegas with a team of *Examiner* staffers to cover the trial of Irish war bride Bridget Waters. Waters had married a US Air Force officer named Frank Waters who had been stationed in Ireland during the war. Shortly after the war had ended, Bridget Waters became pregnant. She informed her husband, who promptly announced he wanted nothing to do with the baby or his war bride, gave her fifty dollars, and left for France. Bridget Waters had the baby, and her husband made his way back to his home state of Nevada, where he met a Las Vegas showgirl named Lucille Griffith. The happy couple decided to marry, and Frank sought a divorce in Las Vegas court. The judge on the case flew Bridget and child across the ocean to contest the divorce. The reunion of the estranged couple was not amicable, and Bridget shot her husband dead with a three-inch pistol while holding the couple's sixteen-month-old baby in her arms.[60]

The Bridget Waters story rang all the bells in the *Examiner* city room. It had sex, infidelity, passion, murder, and for good measure a Vegas showgirl. Sensing a story that could hold the attention of Los Angeles for weeks on end, Richardson sent Murray, Fowler, and photographer Ferde Olmo to Las Vegas, where the team immediately began following Richardson's guidelines for chasing stories, which always placed the emphasis on scoops and was notoriously light on ethics. Las Vegas was still a tiny outpost in the desert that was just beginning to sprout the casinos and hotels that would blossom in the next decade. Waters was being held at the city's four-cell jail, and Fowler quickly sought out and befriended the city official in charge of the jail, supplying him with whiskey, gambling money, and a "whore so high priced he couldn't turn her down." The next morning, he phoned the official and let him know then that he was a reporter for the *Examiner*. With his increased bargaining power, Fowler secured exclusive rights to photograph and interview Waters behind bars. An Associated Press photographer followed Fowler and Olmo to the jail and managed to get a photo of Waters, but Fowler had the antidote for this problem, too.

He broke into the curio shop that the AP was using to transmit photographs, disabled their equipment, and then found a pilot to fly him back to Los Angeles with the film, ahead of the competition.[61]

The trial happened to coincide with the opening of the Flamingo Hotel on the burgeoning Las Vegas Strip. The Flamingo was the brainchild of Los Angeles gangster Bugsy Siegel. Siegel already had a long and confrontational history with the *Examiner,* thanks to the antagonism of Richardson. Siegel fancied himself a Hollywood insider and sought to distance himself from his mobster past. He let it be known that he did not like the name Bugsy, which he had earned thanks to his violent temper decades earlier as part of the New York Mob. Richardson made it a point to refer to Siegel in print as Bugsy, and when that did not get enough of a rise out of the mobster, he began to use the introduction "Benjamin 'Don't Call Me Bugsy' Siegel" throughout the *Examiner* news pages.[62] Murray had not crossed paths with Siegel in Los Angeles, so he was meeting him for the first time when he received a personal tour of the still-incomplete Flamingo along with a delegation of British reporters in town for the trial. He was struck by Siegel's movie-star good looks, as well as the incredible opulence of the new hotel. Siegel was spending freely of the Mob's money and would be dead within eight months, the victim of a Mob-ordered execution in a Hollywood mansion. Murray later surmised that it was the cost overruns at the Flamingo that led to Bugsy's demise.[63]

The Waters trial got under way on October 21, 1946. Murray played up the western-justice angle as the proceedings began: "In this 'last frontier' town where the law of the 'six-gun' is still vividly remembered, Bridget Waters, Irish war bride accused of killing her American husband, indicated today she may rely on that old western defense, 'justifiable homicide.'"[64] The judge seated a jury of "gruff western types,"[65] and the blue-eyed twenty-six-year-old war bride (as she was repeatedly referred to in the *Examiner*) commenced to do her part to gin up the type of story that Richardson had been hoping for. Waters's lawyer made sure the eighteen-month-old child, who had been injured in the shooting, was ever present during the proceedings. Waters regularly shrieked as testimony was read and wept uncontrollably in court, as well as during "exclusive" interviews Murray and Fowler conducted at the Las Vegas jail. Fowler and Olmo pulled off another coup during the trial, securing a photo of Griffith, the showgirl. After Olmo had failed to get a photo of Griffith by roaming the grounds outside her house, Fowler convinced James Young, the Las Vegas assistant coroner, that Griffith needed to be present at the trial. Young brought Griffith to the courtroom, which was packed with locals interested in the proceedings. Olmo snapped a photo of her in the crowd. When the other photographers present asked him which woman was Griffith, he pointed to another woman in the crowd. Another scoop had been secured.[66]

The trial continued, highlighted by the presentation of the murder weapon, a three-inch gun that Murray described as "so small it looked like a watch charm." He wrote: "The fevered flush which has marked her features for the past two days disappeared as her attorney commented when shown the death bullet. 'I can't see it, it's so little.' Waters brow knitted into a frown as the little nickel-plated revolver with which Frank Waters was killed was placed on the table."[67] Bridget Waters's pretrial sworn testimony had portrayed a murder scene in which she had fired the fatal bullet as Frank Waters kneeled near his child, but in court it morphed into a violent struggle and an accidental shooting, according to the defense description. Either way, both judge and jury bought into Bridget Waters's version of events and her woman-scorned portrayal. The defense rested, the judge gave the case to the jury on Saturday, November 2, and by Sunday night Waters had been found guilty of a lesser charge, involuntary manslaughter. Five days later, as the cries of her eighteen-month-old toddler echoed through the Las Vegas courtroom, Judge A. S. Henderson let Waters off with what would turn out to be a seventeen-month prison stint. "My heart goes out to the defendant and her child. But on behalf of the people of the State of Nevada I feel I must sentence this woman to the state prison," he said.[68]

Murray would later write that the Bridget Waters trial and outcome prompted the notion that murder was just a misdemeanor in Nevada.[69] The *Examiner* team had been on the offensive throughout the trial, with their competition following days behind. And Murray's byline had been a fixture on the *Examiner* front page for two weeks. On return to the *Examiner* offices, he found himself in that familiar position for a newspaperman back from a road trip: he had outspent his expense account. To balance his finances, he decided he had spent the discrepancy, ninety-nine dollars, on cab fare. He turned in his expense report to Richardson, including the cab expenses. Richardson, who had been elated with the coverage, immediately focused on the questionable charge. "Good God, Murray, didn't you ever walk anywhere?" he screamed. "Ninety-nine dollars! My God, you could spit across the whole town!"[70]

"We Slept with Our Shoes On"

As the calendar turned to 1947, the *Examiner* was reaching its pinnacle of achievement as a newspaper. It was the circulation leader in burgeoning postwar Los Angeles and, under Richardson, had such a finely honed news operation that Los Angeles police investigators often came to the *Examiner* for leads on fast-moving cases.[71] The staff was experienced and highly motivated, and they fed off the thrills and bloodlust they found when pursuing crime stories. Durslag was on the sports desk in those years and remembers watching the news team in action. "Richardson recognized good work when he saw it. That's why the city side was so good. God, we had some good writers," he said.[72] In the first few months of 1947, they would turn their attention to two of the biggest crime stories in Los Angeles history. One would go down as the city's most sensational slaying ever (until the saga of O. J. Simpson fifty years later). The other would captivate the city for months and eventually lead to Jim Murray's departure from the *Examiner* staff.

On the morning of January 15, 1947, Fowler and photographer Felix Paegel were returning from reporting a story when they heard on the police scanner that a drunken woman was lying in the grass east of Crenshaw Boulevard. When they arrived on the scene, ahead of the police, what they actually saw was the naked body of a young woman. It was in two pieces, having been surgically sliced in half across the middle. Paegel snapped two photos of the body before the police arrived, and the two phoned Richardson and then rushed back to the newsroom with the film. So began the case of the Black Dahlia, and the *Examiner* had been dealt, by luck, a tremendous jump on the story to end all stories.[73] Paegel's photos—one of the body, the other of Fowler kneeling beside it with an *Examiner* peeking out of his jacket pocket—were used on the front of the extra that the paper published just a few hours later. As Paegel emerged from the darkroom with the dripping wet prints, the city staff gathered around Richardson's desk for a gander. "Take a good look," Richardson said. "This is what you'll all be working on today."[74]

The Black Dahlia case took over Los Angeles and the city's newspapers for the next month. Though the *Examiner* was far ahead from the outset, it was Jack Smith, then a rewrite man for the *Daily News,* who wrote the most memorable lead to the story. (Smith's column would later anchor the *Times* news section during many of the years that Murray's column anchored the *Times* sports page.) He wrote, "The nude body of a beautiful young woman, cut neatly in two at the waist, was found early today on a vacant lot near Crenshaw and Exposition Boulevards." An editor had inserted the word *beautiful,* though neither had seen the woman, because, as Smith later said, all dead naked women found in Los Angeles in those years were beautiful.[75]

The *Examiner* was the first to identify the victim, Elizabeth Short, by transmitting her fingerprints to contacts at the FBI in Washington. Short turned out to be the stereotypical Hollywood murder victim, a young girl from somewhere back East, in this case Medford, Massachusetts, who had come to California in search of stardom. *Examiner* reporters were also the first to find Short's mother, Phoebe Short. Under Richardson's direction, a reporter called Phoebe Short and initially told her that her daughter had won a beauty contest. Then, after all the significant information had been acquired, he told the victim's mother the actual truth.[76]

The story crawled forward fast enough to maintain intense reader and editor interest, but not toward any real conclusion. It turned out Short had a series of boyfriends in the months leading up to the murder. One in particular, Red Manley, became the focus of an intense manhunt by police and reporters, but after much newsprint was exhausted, Manley's alibi checked out. An anonymous tip sent *Examiner* reporters on a hunt for a trunk full of love letters and photos of Short with former boyfriends. The trunk was found at the Greyhound station, unleashing another round of *Examiner* exclusives. Scoops were coming so fast, the *Examiner* began pushing all other news off the front page to page 3. In all, the case remained on the *Examiner* front page for thirty-two consecutive days.[77] The *Examiner* also ran sidebars to each major scoop, lauding their own work and fermenting the image of the hard-bitten city reporter to the eager public.[78]

For all the effort and manpower devoted to the case, however, an arrest was never made in the Black Dahlia case. Most of the air went out of the story when the key suspect was exonerated. After the story had faded somewhat, the killer mailed an envelope containing the contents of Short's purse to the *Examiner* building. He had also made taunting phone calls to the city desk. Through the years, more than five hundred people have confessed to the crime.[79]

What pushed the Black Dahlia completely out of the Los Angeles consciousness was the next big crime drama to enrapture the city. For this one, Murray took a starring role in the coverage. The case of the Overell yacht murders made a far lighter historical footprint, perhaps because it eventually came to a satisfying conclusion, but at the time it drove newspaper circulation and interest even beyond those of the Dahlia case. At its height, copies of the *Examiner,* priced at five cents, were selling on the streets for one dollar. "If I am remembered for one thing as a newspaperman," Richardson wrote, "it should be the Overell case."[80]

It was *Romeo and Juliet,* set among the rich and spoiled of Los Angeles. A young, cocky premed student and war hero, George "Bud" Gollum, wanted to marry his girlfriend, Louise Overell, the slightly plump, pampered heir to the Overell furniture fortune. Walter and Beulah Overell did not like the idea. Around midnight on March 15, 1947, a tremendous explosion killed the Overells on their yacht, the *Mary B,* which sank in sixteen feet of water. The young lovers had dynamited the yacht after beating the Overells to death with a ball-peen hammer.

The *Examiner* ran photos on Sunday, but coverage began in earnest on Monday morning. Richardson radioed Fowler and asked him if he had seen the story in the Sunday edition. Fowler said no. Richardson cursed him, slammed down the radio, and turned to Murray on the rewrite desk and asked him the same question. Murray had not read the Sunday edition either, but he did not want to suffer the same reaction. "Sure, I read it," he said. The answer would get Murray a ticket to Santa Ana, where he would spend March 17 to October 6 living in a motel, covering the case along with two dozen other reporters and photographers from Los Angeles newspapers and the news services.[81]

When a second set of dynamite that had failed to ignite was found, wired to a timer, the young lovers were arrested and jailed. Early on in the coverage, Murray was working the courthouse and had heard a rumor that Gollum and Louise had been surreptitiously passing notes to each other at the jailhouse. Richardson had heard the rumor, too, and began to press Murray to find out more. "The letters were reported to be so sensational in nature that they would make the Marquis De Sade blush," Murray remembered. "Richardson knew I didn't have time to steal any letters. One night when I was drinking with Maury Godchaux of the *Times*, and feeling lonely for my family, I phoned Richardson and asked him to let me go home."

Gerry had recently given birth to Tony, the Murrays' second son. It was not the time for an extended road trip. But Richardson, who preferred his reporters to be single and unattached, didn't want to hear it. "OK, if you don't want to cover the biggest story in the country, then you can come home and I'll get you a nice job writing the weather report," he told Murray.

Soon thereafter, Murray crossed paths with "a derby wearing, cigar-smoking Irishman" named George Gallagher who worked for the state attorney's office and was a font of knowledge about the California justice system. Gallagher passed Murray a golden tip: the letters were being passed between Gollum and Louise via a jailer, who was photocopying them before he passed them along. "Bells went off in my mind and a light blazed as I tried to look unconcerned, sidling toward a telephone to call the city desk," Murray remembered.[82]

Richardson made the next move. As city editor for a Hearst paper, he had considerable pull within state politics. Hearst knew how to use his newspapers to influence politics and elections, so politicians understood it was usually in their best interest to remain on good terms with those who made news decisions at the *Examiner* and the other Hearst papers. To anger Hearst or his top editors might mean the end of one's political career. This time, Richardson went to the attorney general, Fred Howser. Howser agreed, and a plan was put in place. An *Examiner* reporter would pick up a motel key at a designated location. The letters would be in the motel room, under the blanket on the bed. Richardson chose Lloyd Emerson, a veteran reporter, to make the pickup. Murray, who was not informed of the plan or the whereabouts of the letters, would unknowingly act as a decoy. When the letters made it back safely to the newsroom, Richardson claimed the story for himself. The *Examiner* editor, Ray Van Ettish, assigned Richardson a single room, with one copy editor and one Linotype operator to set the type. To fool the competition, which regularly sent someone to grab an early edition of the *Examiner* in case of scoops, Richardson had the press run dummy copies without his story.[83]

Readers of the following day's *Examiner* were greeted with a twenty-two-column scoop than ran from page 1 back to page 3, twenty-two columns of news the competition did not even know existed. Gollum's letters, Richardson wrote, were full of "vile salaciousness," much of it unprintable. It is hard to determine what that would constitute by today's standards, however. Judging from the excerpts that Richardson did feel were tame enough for his readers, it would seem the level of vileness that Bud Gollum was capable of was relatively low. Gollum wrote in his letters: "If necessary, I'll kidnap and carry you off somewhere so that no one will be able to find us and I'll make passionate and violent love to you. I adore you. Your lovely hair, your eyes, your lips, your wonderful neck." But the results at the time were undeniable, and Richardson's troops were in awe. "One of my most precious memories is what happened the next morning when I walked into the local room. As I walked to my desk, the reporters simply stared at me in silence. No one said hello or offered congratulations or anything. But I could feel what they were thinking. Why, the old bald-headed son-of-a-bitch really put one over," Richardson wrote.[84]

Murray learned of the transaction when he read it in the *Examiner*. But the rest of the press believed it was he who had pulled off the scoop. Attorney General Howser came down from Sacramento to investigate the "leak" in his office. He declared that a reporter had broken into his safe to steal the letters. Was it Murray? asked Godchaux of the *Times*. Howser indicated it was. The focus of the press now turned on him. Rivals dropped their coverage at the police station and the courthouse to follow Murray around. His notes were stolen. A reporter was found hiding under his bed. He heard strange clicks on his telephone calls.[85] "In fact," Murray remembered, "it wasn't too many days before I began to believe it myself."[86]

The trial lasted for nineteen weeks, and more than 120 witnesses testified. In the end, the jury found the couple innocent, deciding that Walter Overell had mishandled dynamite on his boat, and dismissed evidence of the hammer beating. The letters were declared inadmissible. (Near the end of the trial, Murray had broken a story that the jury was tainted because a juror falsely claimed friends of the defendants had intimidated her.)[87] When the verdicts were read, a tremendous cheer erupted from the crowd of hundreds gathered around the courthouse as reporters raced for the telephone banks in the courthouse hallway and fought their way to Louise to ask her if the marriage was still on. "No!" she snorted.[88]

The Overell case was not only another in the long historical line of miscarriages of Los Angeles justice, but the final major hurrah in Murray's career as a newsman. His coverage of both this case and the Waters case had raised his profile within the industry, if not among the general public. And professionally, he was beginning to feel as though he was outgrowing the *Examiner*. The excitement of chasing Hollywood divorces and sensational crime stories was diminishing, just as the demands of that type of work were infringing on his personal life. He and Gerry now were raising a family and had a life to maintain, one that would work better with more money and a less hectic schedule.

In late 1947, Time/Life approached fellow *Examiner* rewrite man Joe Santley about a position. "I was just back from the war and I didn't feel ready for it, so I suggested they talk to Jim," remembered Santley. Sidney James, *Time's* Los Angeles bureau chief, was aware of Murray from his coverage of the Overell case and some of his other work and was excited to add him to the interview list.[89] *Time* interviewed forty people for the position, but it was Murray who received the offer. It was the money, he said, that sealed the deal. *Time* offered seven thousand dollars a year, a figure that would more than double his salary, as well as much better benefits than he received at the *Examiner*.

As a farewell celebration just before Murray left the staff, Fowler asked his father to bring some of his famous friends along for a night out with Murray. Some of Murray's closest *Examiner* friends were joined by Gene Fowler, former heavyweight champion Jack Dempsey, famed newspaperman Rube Goldberg, and, to Murray's amazement, the dean of sportswriters, Grantland Rice. The group gathered at the famous restaurant Romanoff's in Beverly Hills and celebrated late into the night.[90] It was a fabulous final act for a time in his life that he would always remember fondly. In four years, he had become a skillful writer and an experienced journalist. And now he was going from the Hearst chain to *Time*, a move, he would write many years later, that was like going from a honky-tonk to Park Avenue.[91]

3

The *Time* Years, 1948–1953

Journalism is indeed a form of self-expression. But it is a new form, a very particular form. I will not call journalism art—though with a little courage, I might do so, remembering that there was once some doubt as to whether the novel was properly an art form. But I should liken journalism to art for the sake of expressing the idea that there is a spirit alive today, and especially in America, which may be called journalism-for-the-sake-of-Journalism. In its motivation, this spirit is akin to that compulsion and satisfaction in expressing oneself by giving shape to a stone; there are men today who can only be satisfied if they can give the shape of coherency and accuracy and truth to at least some fragment of human events.

—Henry Luce, January 4, 1939, quoted in
The Ideas of Henry Luce, edited by John Jessup

Joining the American Century

It was 1948, World War II was receding into the past, and Jim Murray had become upwardly mobile, much like his country. The postwar boom in the United States had firmly taken hold. The United States, then nearly three years beyond its military triumph around the globe, had emerged from the war as the dominant economic power in the world. Influence abroad and affluence at home defined the mood of the country. By any historical standards, the economic growth in the country was phenomenal. In the 1940s, the United States made up 7 percent of the world's population, but possessed 42 percent of the world's income and more than half of the manufacturing output around the globe. America produced 57 percent of the world's steel, 62 percent of the world's oil, and more than 80 percent of the automobiles. American per capita income was more than 50 percent greater than the next highest countries, the Western European nations. The economic statistics were indicators that told the story of the new reality that Americans were beginning to feel in the late 1940s. Most Americans ate better, made more money, lived more comfortably, and generally lived a higher quality of life with unlimited opportunity than did their parents.[1]

The influx of money into the pockets of Americans meant tectonic shifts in the country's culture as well. The country was becoming dominated by the middle class. The postwar class system began to resemble a diamond, instead of a pyramid, as it had always in the past, with the middle class accounting for the central bulge, the 60 percent of the population that fitted that description. The country was becoming more educated as well—a college education was now accessible to young people from average families. During the late '40s, millions of Americans abandoned the country's cities and headed for the suburbs to escape the traffic, crime, and congestion. And, in a development that Murray had borne witness to on *Examiner* assignments,[2] the era of television was emerging and beginning to change how Americans received their news and viewed their world.[3]

The cultural changes that had occurred and would continue to occur in the coming years made it an opportune time for Murray to make the move from metro news reporting to national newsmagazine work. And he was landing at a magazine that, thanks to its eminent founder Henry Luce, would come to symbolize, as well as tirelessly promote, the new American dominance around the globe. For a journalist in the late 1940s looking to make his mark, *Time* was the pinnacle of the industry. Time, Inc., was born twenty-five years prior, when Henry Luce and Briton Hadden, recent Yale graduates and editors at the *Yale Daily News,* discovered an unfilled niche in American journalism: the need for a publication that would "organize and departmentalize the news of the week." The idea was to synthesize the important issues of the day—world affairs, science, technology, arts, industry, and so on—and make it accessible to busy Americans. By the end of the 1920s, the idea had taken off, and *Time* had a national circulation of more than two hundred thousand. Hadden died in 1929, and Luce took control of the corporation and directed it to new heights. First, he added *Fortune,* a business publication aimed at those in the top income brackets. The company's research staff and news-gathering organization grew along the way. And in 1936, he launched *Life,* a photo-dominated magazine that soon became immensely popular.[4] By February 1948, when Murray joined the staff, *Life* had far eclipsed *Time* and become a moneymaking juggernaut, with a circulation that had climbed to nearly six million readers. (The circulation of *Time* was then between two and three million.)[5]

Right from the start, Murray had to adjust to a very different working environment. The quiet offices of the Los Angeles bureau of Time/Life, located in posh Beverly Hills and referred to throughout the company as Bev-Edit, were very different from the smoke-filled, cacophonous environs of the *Examiner* City Room. The Los Angeles bureau was the second-largest in the Time/Life Corporation, behind only the Washington, DC, bureau. The headquarters of Time/Life were located at Rockefeller Center in Manhattan. About twenty-five people worked out of the Beverly Hills office. Several were photographers who worked exclusively for *Life;* the majority of the rest were correspondents who reported for all of the company's publications. Murray quickly found that working in the far-reaching Time/Life news service was a completely different type of reporting. Instead of getting his assignments from Richardson or an assistant city editor, just a few desks away, his marching orders now usually came from three thousand miles away, in the New York office. About 60 percent of the work done at the bureaus was at the direction of headquarters. With their remaining time, reporters could pursue stories and pitch them to the bureau chief, who would then try to sell New York on the idea.[6]

The backgrounds of his coworkers had changed as well. *Examiner* writers and editors had often kicked around Los Angeles from paper to paper, or perhaps started out in the newspaper business as copyboys and hung around long enough to find their way onto the writing staff. To find the starting point of the majority of the *Time* staff, however, one needed look only northeast, to the Ivy League. A Time/Lifer was a highly educated, ambitious, and skilled journalist who, Murray would write later, immediately wanted to cover the State Department, the White House, or Winston Churchill.[7]

Hollywood Reporter

Although his beat would eventually include politics, crime, sports, and much of the rest of the happenings in and around Los Angeles, Murray was ostensibly hired to cover Hollywood for *Time*. His duties included writing a regular background report on the ins and outs of the movie business, much of which would find its way into the magazine's "Cinema" section. Bureau reporters would produce lengthy background dispatches, rich in anecdotes, quotes, and human interest, and send them off to New York, where the information would be combined with the work of other reporters and fashioned, by the New York editing staff, into an article that fitted nicely into the *Time* style. "Basically you just sat down and shoveled it out," said Frank McCulloch, who started at the Los Angeles bureau with Murray and later became bureau chief. "Your job was to transport a guy sitting in a New York office some hundreds or thousands of miles to the scene of the story you were doing, and make the sights, sounds and smells real to him. So you always over wrote, unless you were on a very tight deadline, you always over wrote, because that was your function."

Murray found the practice of "writing research," as it was called in the *Time* news service, liberating after his years following the more defined rules of newspaper journalism. "In writing research, you weren't bound by the normal restrictions of journalism," Murray said years later. "You didn't have to put 'alleged' in there, and all that nonsense. . . . The research was sort of a conversation with the editor, but you had to dramatize it, dress it up, find the good quotes, find the punchy lines. You had to sell the story to New York."

Just like he did four years earlier as a cub reporter at the *Examiner,* Murray grabbed the rookie assignments that he was given early on and managed to use them to distinguish himself. He provided research for an early story in *Time*'s "Americana" section and looked at oddities cropping up in American manners and morals. Murray was asked to report on George Hamilton "Ozzie" Osborne, a former circus clown and department store Santa Claus who was attempting to set the world record for time spent sitting atop a flagpole. Flagpole sitting had become a fad during the Depression, practiced by those with no job, no rent money, and a generous amount of idle time. Osborne was an experienced flagpole sitter and ended up spending fifty-two days, thirteen hours, and fifty-eight minutes on a pole atop the Sky Ride at a Long Beach amusement park.[8] *Time* still ran largely without bylines, but the Time/Life news service would include in-house bylines, coveted by writers. On the Osborne story, the brand-new Murray outshone his counterparts and scored points with the home office. "Three guys participated in the research; Murray set the tone of the story by his excellently written piece on Ozzie Osborne[9] but both Jones and Shay . . . had to be rewritten to fit the style that Murray set. If anybody, Murray should have had the byline," wrote a New York editor in a memo to the Los Angeles bureau.[10] The Osborne portion of the article that Murray contributed eventually appeared in *Time* as a single sentence of twenty-six words.[11]

Another early assignment sent Murray back from where he had come, to the *Examiner,* and this time he was much less welcome. The state of William Randolph Hearst's health in 1948 was of great interest, and information was closely guarded by Hearst and his underlings. Hearst had turned eighty-five in May and was living a bizarre, reclusive existence, rarely leaving his Beverly Hills mansion. He had recently moved to Southern California from the Hearst castle in San Simeon, so he could be closer to his doctor. *Time* editors decided that with Murray's connections, he would be able to sniff around the fringes of the Hearst empire and discover how soon the end was coming for its leader.

Murray began working his sources. He frequented the Los Angeles Press Club, but found that Hearst men had been warned against talking shop within earshot of *Time* reporters. He asked a friend from the *Examiner* political desk for information about Hearst. "Christ, Jimmy," the reporter exploded. "I can't talk to you. You guys think we're running a floor show for your benefit." Jack Beardwood, then *Time* bureau chief, spoke with one of Hearst's secretaries on the phone, who, after divulging a few facts about Hearst's condition, suddenly clammed up and referred all questions to Hearst's lawyer, who was conveniently out of town on business.

Despite the information blockade, Murray was able to paint a fairly complete picture for his editors. Hearst, he wrote, was "betraying all the perverse instincts of a beheaded chicken in the matter of dying." For a time, he had barred the word *death* from being spoken in his presence. He had shrunk to 125 pounds. He had a bad heart and palsy, and a friend of Hearst's doctor said he had cancer, a fact Murray was unable to confirm. Still, he was healthy enough to call the city desk at the *Examiner* to demand attention to details as minor as the tone of a friend's obituary. As for Hearst's own obituary, Murray confirmed that Hearst had made sure that no such article existed in the newsroom of the *Examiner*.[12] He ended his report to the editors with a promise to "keep nibbling at this twilight of Citizen Cane story."[13] No mention of Hearst's condition made it into the pages of *Time* for the rest of 1948, and the assignment was soon taken off Murray's desk. Hearst would live, in similar conditions, for three more years. He died August 14, 1951, of heart disease and pneumonia.

As he quickly gained the confidence of his superiors and the New York office, Murray grew into his role as the magazine's chief Hollywood correspondent. The American movie industry at the time was in a state of flux. Several factors were changing the ways movies were made, and the players in Hollywood were struggling to develop a new order. The traditional Hollywood system that had grown out of the early days of the film industry allowed the major studios to control the production, distribution, and exhibition of films. Writers, directors, and actors were usually employed with long-term, fixed contracts with a single studio. In 1948, however, the US Supreme Court ruled that the majors had an illegal monopoly over the industry and ordered distribution and exhibition to be run separately. At the same time, the film industry was looking over its shoulder at the growing influence of television, which many at the time regarded as the death knell for film.[14] The Hollywood box office did decline in the early 1950s as television rapidly became available to the growing American middle class, but the actual threat would pale in comparison to the overreaction among moviemakers. "The movies panicked," Murray wrote later. "No one told them this had merely multiplied the number of theater screens by a few million and that product would be more needful than ever. Hollywood simply got its paws up in the air and rolled over."[15]

Time devoted considerable space to entertainment, and the magazine's top editors liked to break up the weekly parade of politicians and statesmen with the occasional Hollywood starlet. Murray's job, in addition to covering the business angle of the movies, was to identify suitable cover subjects, make contact, and begin the reporting. That part of the job was made more difficult by the fact that the period of the late 1940s and early '50s was a male-dominated era in the Hollywood film industry. Names like Cary Grant, John Wayne, Kirk Douglas, and Humphrey Bogart dominated the screen and filled cinema seats across the country. Many of the female stars of years earlier—Joan Crawford, Bette Davis, Barbara Stanwyck—were no longer causing the box-office stampedes that they did five and ten years prior. Murray's job as a talent scout for *Time,* then, mirrored the work being done by the studios. Hollywood, *Time* reported, was "turning loose an army of assistant producers (and relatives) to scout the nation's soda fountains for blondes . . . a big, fumbling, talent-hunting monster has been set loose in the land."[16] Murray did his part, and during his early years at *Time,* Hollywood's great female hopes such as Betty Hutton, Ava Gardner, Lucille Ball, and Elizabeth Taylor appeared as cover stories. Taylor, Murray said, with her purple eyes, was the most beautiful woman he had ever seen.[17]

Covering the business of the movie industry took up a large part of Murray's time, but one of Luce's philosophies was to focus on personalities, so the Hollywood beat included its share of celebrity journalism. Some of his assignments had the whiff of *Entertainment Tonight,* the 1940s version. He would be dispatched to find out all the intimate personal details of celebrity tiffs, such as a domestic dispute between Humphrey Bogart and his wife or a marital squabble between Frank Sinatra and Ava Gardner.[18] In a report he titled "Guys and a Doll—Marriage by Press-Agentry," he chronicled two days spent in Las Vegas attending the divorce of actor Dick Haymes and subsequent marriage of Haymes to actress and pinup girl Rita Hayworth. Twenty-nine journalists, from newspapers, Hollywood fan magazines, and television stations, were invited to the Sands Hotel. Upon arrival, the Sands "News Bureau" provided each with an hour-by-hour schedule of events that included Haymes's divorce hearing, a trip to the Nevada marriage license bureau, and a marriage ceremony in which television and newsreel cameras were given access to the entire ballroom. The leads, of course, were to be made available for comment several times throughout the proceedings.

Murray's report to his editors was as much a statement about the state of Hollywood journalism as it was coverage of the actual event, and the pages dripped with cynicism. The assembled media were delighted with the cooperation of the principles at first, but, as the festivities dragged on, the proceedings became a "nightmare of popping flashbulbs, snapping plate-holders, smoking hot floodlights and the babble and baying of the press pack in full cry after a helpless vixen." He made sure to point out all the details that showed the ex-tended photo opportunity for what it was, such as a four-layer wedding cake of which the bottom two layers were wood and the icing spelled out "The Sands Wishes Rita and Dick Happiness." "I gotta get the Sands in there somewhere," a hotel spokesman told Murray with a grin.[19]

A Parade of Stars

Murray's eye for female screen talent put him on the trail of Marilyn Mon-roe when she was just a blip on the Hollywood radar. He first met Monroe when she was a mistress of Joe Schenk, chairman of Twentieth Century–Fox and one of the most influential men in the industry. Director Joe Mankiewicz gave Monroe a bit part in the film *All about Eve* in 1950 as a joke meant for Schenk, and she lit up the screen. Soon she was generating enormous buzz and overshadowing bigger names while still playing only minor roles. Murray pitched a story on her to *Time* editors, who agreed, hoping eventually to spin the project into a multipage photo spread of her in *Life*. Murray got to know her during the next few years, detailing her rising career arc in the pages of *Time*. On one occasion, he showed up to take her to dinner at seven o'clock and waited for an hour and a half for Monroe to get ready, during which she went through four to seven dress changes.[20] Murray interviewed her through dinner, but around dessert Monroe began to look distracted. "What's wrong?" he asked.

"Jim," she said, "would you mind if I left with someone else?"

"Not as long as you introduce me," he said.

"OK." Monroe waved her arm, and Joe DiMaggio walked over to the table.[21]

Monroe and Murray had chatted amiably at their dinner together. What he wrote to his editors about her, however, was far from amiable. His network of sources in the industry was extensive by this time, and insiders such as director Henry Hathaway and Monroe's dramatic coach, Natasha Lytess, among others, had supplied him the ammunition to paint a less than flattering portrait of her:

> Marilyn cannot act. Her voice is pathetically inadequate for sound pictures. She is scared to death but is constantly being thrown into pictures with scarred veterans of the screen like Barbara Stanwyck. . . . Stanwyck was so brutally con-temptuous of her that poor Marilyn almost suffered a nervous breakdown and was so afraid to open her mouth in some scenes that her dialogue came out a squeak. . . . Nevertheless, she is a bigger marquee name than many of the estab-lished stars she appears with. . . . In the view of veteran director Henry Hathaway, she has one incomparable talent: She can make any move, any gesture, almost insufferably suggestive.

The report he delivered to New York showed Monroe to be an insecure, overly ambitious narcissist and the owner of a closet that was bursting with skeletons, many of which he went to great pains to identify.[22] His missive to Terry Colman at *Time* headquarters included one chillingly prescient note: "Marilyn claims to live in dread of the fact that her mind will slip, too, and has been known to speak morosely of suicide." On his memo to New York, Murray marked this sentence "not for use."[23]

DiMaggio's courtship of Monroe was in full flight at the time of Murray's dinner with her. DiMaggio was recently retired but still one of the most popular athletes in the country at the time. He had met Monroe after a photo of her in the sports page of a newspaper had caught his eye.[24] The couple would marry in January 1954, in a barely kept secret, at San Francisco City Hall. Murray's description of Monroe as "five feet six inches of whipped cream" never made it into the magazine, but his New York editors could not help but quantify Monroe's sexual powers: "Her figure (5 ft. 5 in., 118 lbs., bust 37 in., hips 37 in., waist 24 in.) inspires whistles across the land."[25] The marriage between the Yankee hero and the sex symbol did not last through the end of 1954, but Murray developed a relationship with DiMaggio that would last years longer.

Another of the many lasting friendships that developed through Murray's film industry coverage was one with singer and actor Bing Crosby. Crosby's reign as a recording and box-office star dated back to the mid-1930s, and Murray would see him from afar at Hollywood Stars baseball games, where Crosby was a part owner. Murray went to Crosby's office on the lot at Paramount Studios to interview him for a story. Crosby's secretary told him to wait in an outer office. Thirty minutes dragged by, and Murray thought the singer had forgotten about him. He approached the secretary and was assured that Crosby knew he was waiting. Another hour passed. Murray told the secretary he had other appointments and was on deadline.

The secretary opened the door to Crosby's office. "Mr. Crosby, the man from *Time* magazine is still here," she called.

"Fuck him!" Crosby called back.[26]

A little mistreatment at the hands of a star with an oversized ego was part of the price to be paid to hold down one of the most coveted beats in the Time/Life empire. Where a few years earlier he attended the Academy Awards as a photographer's assistant, now he was an invited guest with prime aisle seats, as he was at the major movie premieres.[27]

Marlon Brando was another actor who put Murray through his own little initiation rites. Murray went to meet Brando for a cover profile at the actor's home in the fall of 1954, when Brando was just entering the upper echelon of Hollywood stardom. A new breed of star, Brando was a rebellious, independent thinker who delighted in riling the Hollywood power structure and those who ran it. Films such as *The Wild One* and *On the Waterfront* had made him an important commodity. Murray showed up at Brando's five-room bunga-low behind the Beverly Hills Hotel for a scheduled appointment. He knocked, rang the bell, knocked again, to no avail. He sat on the steps and waited, then knocked again. Finally, after an hour, he was pinning a note to the door when Brando threw it open and laughed heartily. He had been reveling in Murray's discomfort from behind the front window.[28]

Later, Murray took Brando to a restaurant for breakfast. Brando ordered eggs, and when the waiter brought them, he was not satisfied. He sent them back and on redelivery sent them back again. Finally, Murray paid the check and told Brando he knew a place where he could get Brando his eggs just how he liked them. The pair drove to the Murray home, and Gerry answered the door with a towel on her head to see Murray and Brando standing before her.[29]

The Brando profile ran as a cover story in October 1954. Brando had already made a habit of sparring with the Hollywood press, and the profile that Murray had worked on exacerbated that antagonism. At the time, Murray's old compa-triot from the Hearst chain, Louella Parsons, was one of two Hollywood gos-sip columnists who wielded tremendous power in the industry—the other was Hedda Hopper of the Esquire Feather Syndicate, whose column ran in the *Los Angeles Times*. The two were rivals, and each was said to have the power to shut down production of any Hollywood film if she so desired. Both had played a large part in the birth of celebrity journalism.[30] The *Time* profile included a lengthy section on Brando's battles with the two, including the revelation that Brando "now calls Hedda 'The One with the Hat,' and Louella Parsons 'The Fat One.'"[31] That little gem, it turned out, was not one that Brando wanted to see in print.

This was one occasion when Murray was helped by *Time*'s no-byline policy. Shortly after publication, Brando wrote a letter of apology to Parsons and for-warded a copy of it to Murray, along with a long, rambling letter to Murray explaining himself. Brando found Murray blameless in the inclusion of the in-sult. He placed the blame for the insult appearing in the article on "the guy who wrote the article." He failed to understand that it was Murray who had given the quote to the New York editors who included it in the published article. At any rate, Brando did not appear overly concerned about the faux pas. Brando wrote to Murray:

> I really think that most of the time [Parsons] is really just a big poop, but out of respect to what I believe to be fair she deserves some consideration. . . . I want you to know that the piece was as fair and truthfully wrought as it could possibly be this side of a lengthy biography. . . . I appreciated, more than any other aspect of the experience, two things: one of which is the new perspective he lent me of myself in relation to the world about me and secondly is your having been as

honest and thorough as you were. Most of all it was your lack of preconception and your insistent openness of mind that made it the most pleasant experience with the press to date. Please give my very best to Frances.[32] I hope that she and the kids are well. Looking forward to having some dinner blabber or something with you.[33]

The ability to turn a somewhat adversarial interview situation into a friendly experience was a gift that Murray would come to rely on and one that would allow him to create profiles that were rich in the human interest his editors demanded. His position at *Time* opened doors, and his character and manner allowed him to take full advantage of the access. "It depended on your personality, knowledge and so forth, as to what you got out of the stars, and Jim was a perfect interviewer," said McCulloch. "Whatever the quality is, he had it in great amounts, empathy, and persuasion. [They] always knew they were going to be treated fairly."[34]

Murray got to know John Wayne while reporting a story on him in 1952. Murray had been promoting the idea of a Wayne cover story for months before, but none of the *Time* editors had ever seen one of Wayne's formulaic westerns or war movies. Theater exhibiters, however, knew all about Wayne, and he was proving to be box-office magic. Murray played poker with Wayne, and the two developed a lasting friendship. As the box-office receipts piled up, the *Time* editors eventually bit on Murray's cover pitch, and Wayne graced the cover in early 1952.[35] During the reporting of the story, Murray went to interview John Ford, the legendary director who was behind the camera for Wayne's latest, *The Quiet Man*. Ford told Murray he did not care for *Time* or its superior attitude and proceeded to browbeat Murray throughout the interview. Finally, Murray had had enough. He told Ford, "Well, I didn't care much for 'She Wore a Yellow Ribbon,' either." He braced for a violent response, but instead Ford hooted with laughter.[36] Wayne was impressed with the cover story when it appeared and with Murray's efforts. "Lots of fellows get paid for doing this kind of work, but lots of fellows don't put in the care and effort that you do to yours," Wayne wrote.[37]

Man of the World

After Murray had a few years of Time/Life paychecks under his belt, the Murrays were ready to graduate from apartment dwellers to home owners. Murray had decided that living in the middle of the city was not the right environment in which to raise children.[38] They moved to a roomy white house in a neighborhood called Pacific Palisades with a walled-in backyard that gave the couple's two young sons a safe place to play. The home was less than a mile from the beach; in the backyard you could smell the Pacific salt in the air.[39]

Pacific Palisades was about seventeen miles outside of downtown Los Angeles. The modernist-style homes became a desirable suburb in the late 1940s and 1950s and attracted artists, architects, writers, and theater people.[40] The Murrays' third child, Pam, their first daughter, was born in 1951, followed in 1953 by Eric, whom the family would call Ricky.

That same year, Frank McCulloch came aboard as a correspondent for *Time*. McCulloch would go on to be one of Murray's closest friends and the man who would play the most direct role in turning him into a sports columnist. McCulloch was the son of cattle ranchers from western Nevada and served in the US Marines in World War II. Afterward, he worked his way from small newspapers in rural eastern California to a position at the *Reno Evening Gazette*, where he wrote for the AP and UPI wire services on the side. His work was recognized by *Time*, and he was hired on, initially as a correspondent in the Los Angeles bureau. He quickly came to be viewed as someone with leadership potential, and after short stints in Dallas and New York, he was back in Los Angeles as the bureau chief.[41] Murray and McCulloch developed an immediate friendship. They felt kinship as two non–Ivy Leaguers in a sea of Princeton, Yale, and Dartmouth graduates. (McCulloch had graduated from the University of Nevada–Reno.) They also shared a similar World War II experience. Whereas Murray's heart had kept him out of the service, McCulloch also had a heart condition that kept him stateside. He spent the war in the Marines' public relations office in San Francisco.[42] McCulloch and his wife, Jakie, became social friends with the Murrays; the two young couples went to plays and sporting events together regularly.

It was during his years in the Los Angeles bureau that McCulloch first made his mark journalistically. Through persistence, he managed to become the one journalist to gain the complete trust of Howard Hughes, then one of the world's richest men and a top film producer and aviation mogul. To secure an interview, he called Hughes's publicist and said, "I know I'll never get to see him, but let me give him 100 written questions. I'll give him a chance to be as careful as he wants." To his surprise, he picked up the phone a week later, and the voice on the other end said, "This is Howard Hughes." McCulloch went on to write more than a dozen pieces on Hughes, and he became Hughes's confidant. McCulloch would go on to have a distinguished journalism career, first as a war correspondent and later as an editor and chief at several California newspapers. He served as *Time*'s Southeast Asia bureau chief from 1963 to 1967 and was considered one of the most distinguished of the early Vietnam War reporters, and one of the first to become disenchanted with the American war effort.[43]

Although the Hollywood beat took up the majority of Murray's time, he got the chance to branch out into other areas of *Time*'s coverage, from politics to crime to religion. He convinced *Time* editors to devote some coverage to the early crusades of Billy Graham in 1949, after the idea had been rejected several times. The article eventually filled an entire page in *Time*'s "Religion" section.[44] Graham later said appearing in *Time* was the most important breakthrough in his rise to fame. In a letter to Murray after the article appeared, Graham wrote, "I have heard comments from various parts of the world on your fair and complimentary presentation of the cause of evangelism. This has gone a long ways to help in putting evangelism to the forefront across our nation in our churches."[45]

In 1952, he got his first shot at presidential politics, when he was assigned to cover the West Coast campaign of Richard Nixon, then a young California congressman running for vice president on the Dwight Eisenhower ticket. Nixon, then thirty-nine, had been chosen because of his influence in California, but was still a relatively unknown politician nationally. Murray viewed the trip, which was to be a whistle-stop train through the Northwest, as a fun little excursion and a chance to get a break from the movie crowd. It turned out to be a stressful lesson in deadline reporting.

Just as Murray joined the campaign, the *Los Angeles Daily News* and the *New York Post* broke a story about a secret slush fund that a group of California Nixon supporters had created. Nixon's men thought it had been overblown and would not catch the attention of the national press corps, but they had miscalculated. The *Washington Post* and *New York Times* picked up the story, and the controversy threatened to force Nixon off the ticket. Eisenhower, who had not been in favor of Nixon as the vice presidential choice, did little to ease the situation. (Nixon famously phoned Eisenhower to ask for public support, telling the general, "There comes a time in matters like this when you either have to shit or get off the pot.")[46] As the firestorm grew, the Eisenhower campaign cut off the train tour early for Nixon to fly down to Los Angeles, so he could appear on television to explain himself. With the press in tow, Nixon and his handlers flew down to LA on a Monday night in preparation for the speech on Tuesday morning. The problem for Murray was that *Time* went to press on Monday night.

Before the flight left from Oregon to LA, Murray received a call from Max Ways, *Time*'s national affairs editor and one of the top men in the company. "We need to know what Nixon will say in that speech tomorrow. Is he taking himself off the ticket, or will he fight on?" asked Ways.

"How am I supposed to find that out?" Murray screamed.

"Just do it," warned the editor.

Murray fretted through the entire flight from Oregon to Los Angeles. Access to Nixon was blocked off by his handlers. Murray decided to wait until Nixon used the restroom. Late in the flight, Nixon made his move, and Murray waited for him to emerge. When he did, Murray grabbed his arm and told him of his predicament, *Time*'s deadline, and how he must know the contents of the speech. Nixon considered the request and then told him to see Jim Bassett, one of the candidate's top men, before the flight was over.

An hour later, Bassett came down the aisle and began reciting pieces of Nixon's campaign speech to Murray. Murray was perplexed at first, but then he understood. Bassett was telling him that Nixon was going to LA to give his stump speech, so he was not going to pull his name off the ticket. When the plane landed, he called New York to deliver the news and then retired to the bar at the Ambassador Hotel, where the press was staying, to celebrate. One drink in, however, his calm was once again disturbed. A reporter for United Press came to the bar and told Murray the wire service was coming out with a "rocket" that said Nixon was getting off the ticket. Murray's stomach shot into the back of his throat. *Time* was about to be 100 percent, irreversibly wrong, and it would be completely his fault. He sprang up, went back to the phone, called Nixon's suite, and got another of Nixon's men, Bill Rogers, on the phone. At Murray's urging, Rogers went to ask Nixon, and when he came back on the line, he said, "The candidate says, quote, Murray's got the story. What's he worried about?"[47]

The next day, Nixon went on television and gave his celebrated "Checkers" speech. It was a maudlin, melodramatic presentation, but it worked to settle the controversy and keep Nixon on the ticket. Nixon looked into the camera and declared that the only gift he had taken was a dog. "It was a little cocker spaniel dog in a crate . . . black and white spotted. And our little girl—Tricia, the 6-year-old—named it Checkers. And you know, the kids, like all kids, love the dog and I just want to say this right now, that regardless of what they say about it, we're gonna keep it," Nixon told the nation.[48] Shortly thereafter, Eisenhower threw his support firmly behind his ticket mate.

Nixon confronted Murray the day after the Checkers speech. Despite helping Murray with his scoop, the soon-to-be vice president did not appear sold on Murray as a confidant. "You're a stinking intellectual," he told Murray.

"Me, Dick?" Murray responded. "Hell, I haven't even read Proust."[49]

During the episode, Eisenhower had made the comment that his campaign should be as "clean as a hound's tooth," so after the controversy died down, Nixon decided to create the "Order of the Hound's Tooth," made up of all those who had played a role in the incident. Murray was invited to join, and in early 1953, after Nixon had assumed the office of vice president, Murray received his official Hound's Tooth membership card and emblem.[50]

Finding a Voice

The life of a *Time* field correspondent had plenty of advantages—money, access, sense of importance—but there were some drawbacks, too, particularly for those with literary ambition, which meant almost everybody in the news service. The correspondent knew that the thousands of words he typed each week would go through layer upon layer of editing and would be virtually unrecognizable when they appeared in the magazine.[51] "If you wanted to encourage yourself, you could find phrases and even paragraphs you had written, and once in a long, long while, especially when you filed a story as the magazine was about to close, once in a long while you'd find your story virtually untouched. But that was rare," McCulloch remembered. The frustration caused some writers to eventually move on to other pursuits, but the majority felt lucky to be on the Time/Life payroll. "Sometimes a reversal of content made you angry, but there were two other considerations," McCulloch said. "One was the prestige of working for *Time*, and the other, more important one was that *Time* put you in position to cover the world's best stories. And so that second one was a huge compensation, and you eventually would adopt an attitude that said 'I know I've done the best I could, and I hit that one out of the ballpark, and what they've done with it in New York, I just can't help that.'"[52]

Murray counted himself among those who were content with the advantages of working in the Time/Life chain, but he, too, would occasionally feel underappreciated, just another cog in the machine. "Frustration is one thing you get used to in seven years of working for TIME 3,000 miles from its nerve center," he wrote in a letter to Sid James a few years later.[53]

One way a correspondent could make an effort to break free of the anonymity was to offer his services to *Life*, which operated out of the same offices. *Time*'s sister publication often ran bylines, gave writers the occasional chance to break out of patented *Time* style, and, of course, had a circulation of nearly six million. *Life* had transformed the magazine industry with its innovative photojournalism, which dominated the publication. It had tremendous power in Hollywood, with the ability to single-handedly destroy a movie or turn it into a blockbuster. Movie producers would send chauffeured limousines to the bureau to escort *Life* photographers to the studios, hoping for an appearance in that week's issue. *Life* photographers were at the top of the totem pole in the Los Angeles bureau.

Murray had gone on assignments with *Life* photographers, but it was not until he serendipitously started up a heated conversation about baseball at a lunch meeting in New York in March 1950 that he received the opportunity to write for the magazine. He told his lunch companions, *Life* staffers, that the Yankees were an economic monopoly, not an athletic success. Two weeks later, he was asked to put that idea into words for the magazine.[54] It was a rare chance to put his name to his words, and he used it to show *Life* editors that he had the ability to generate an emotional response from readers. The article, headlined "I Hate the Yankees," was also Murray's first real published sports opinion piece, though to call it a sports column would be imprecise. Running about thirty column inches in the "*Life*'s Reports" section of the magazine, the first-person piece described in detail why the New York Yankees' domination of baseball for the past three decades was strictly a financial proposition. In 1950, the Yankees had won sixteen of the last twenty-nine American League pennants and twelve of the last twenty-nine World Series. Murray used his space to dispel what he called "the great Yankee myth," that the team had received some mystical quality from the great Babe Ruth that had propelled them to be champions for eternity. Of the myth, Murray wrote:

> Nothing could be more preposterous. For my money the Yankees were and are superchampions for the same reasons General Motors or U.S. Steel or Standard Oil are superbusinesses. They have more fans paying more money than any other club in the history of the game. . . . I would as soon (feel sorry for the Yanks) as I would feel sorry for Standard Oil because it was getting slightly the worst of it in a marketing fight with an independent gas station in East Podunk. . . . So if a lot of people seem to be picking the Red Sox to win, and if DiMaggio is slow rounding into shape again this year, don't shed any tears over it. The "poor old New York Yankees" have always managed to get along somehow.[55]

The New York Yankees had an enormous national following that had grown out of the sports boom of the 1920s, and their stars, from Ruth to Gehrig to DiMaggio, were legendary and beloved from Maine to California. So it was unsurprising that *Life* readers let it be known that they felt the same way about Murray as he did about their team. The magazine devoted two pages to letters, mostly negative, about Murray's declaration of hatred. "'I Hate the Yankees' was the worst article I ever read in *Life*. It upset the whole family, especially my 10-year-old daughter, an ardent Yankee fan," wrote Paul Hahn of New York City. "Mr. Murray must be a crackpot. I do not believe Mr. Murray was qualified to write an article on any major league team, since he is assigned to a minor league town," wrote George Wile of Pottsville, Pennsylvania. "I can't recall ever having read anything so irritating," wrote Charles H. Quinn of Ojai, California. One of the few supporters asked to see "a picture of this brave man who had the courage to write that article," so a one-column photo of Murray, holding a bat over his shoulder and grinning, was included in the letters section.[56]

"I Hate the Yankees" was notable for several reasons. First, as Murray's first bylined article about sports, it was one he cherished and often mentioned in later years when his sports column would touch upon similar issues. Second, the article was his first personal experience with the visceral reaction that an opinionated sports article can engender in his readers. The point-by-point, fact-supported style he used in the piece was one he would repeat in his early sportswriting for Time/Life.[57] The article no doubt led to considerable discussion within the Los Angeles bureau and through the New York offices of *Life*. An article that generated enough of a response to call for publishing a photo of a heretofore anonymous cog in the news-service machine was rare, and after it ran, Murray's name was known to many more of the three-thousand-plus employees of Time, Inc. Third, a line from "I Hate the Yankees" was remembered long after April 1950 and in fact became one of the more enduring lines Murray would write. The comparison of the Yankees to U.S. Steel and General Motors had legs. It soon became a sort of catchphrase that was found often in the baseball writing of the next few decades, or the length of time the Yankees remained dominant.[58] Murray was aware of this and wrote a column in 1966 for the *Los Angeles Times* claiming credit for the line:

> It all began when I heard the guy on television say "Well, it was Bennett Cerf who once said 'Rooting for the Yankees is like rooting for U.S. Steel' because he articulated for so many people what they had already come to feel."
>
> OK, now, you want to know who said it first? You're looking at him. Old Numero Uno. James Patrick Murray.
>
> You don't believe it? All right. Do you happen to have a copy of Life for April 17, 1950 around the house? Gen. Eisenhower is on the cover. He always was in those days. Open to Page 23 and you'll find a story titled "I Hate the Yankees" by a guy identified as "James Murray, Time-Life correspondent in Los Angeles."[59]

Later, the line was most often attributed to Red Smith, who was already established as a leading sports columnist when "I Hate the Yankees" appeared in *Life*. Murray addressed the issue in his autobiography, claiming credit once again, but acknowledging the ephemeral qualities of the public sphere. "Red Smith didn't say it. I did. In the *Life* piece. I lived with it. Because I have since had many things I never said ascribed to me. I call it 'the Dorothy Parker' syndrome," he wrote.[60]

A Hidden Talent Emerges

"I Hate the Yankees" was perhaps the most public in a series of assignments that paved the way for Murray's future evolution into the role of sportswriter. While he was on the Hollywood beat, Murray's knowledge of and interest in sports slowly became known to editors throughout the news service, and eventually many would become dependent on him on those rare occasions that *Time*'s leadership chose to devote column space to sports-related subjects. Murray claimed the responsibility fell to him because "nobody at Time Inc. gave a hoot about sports."[61]

One of his first sports-related assignments came from *Time*'s fact-checking department, and it allowed him the opportunity to meet a personal hero of his, golfer Ben Hogan. Hogan had won the US Open the previous summer, along with nine other tournaments, establishing him as the premier golfer at that time. He would become the first golfer on the cover of *Time*. Time's sports editor, Marshall Smith, spent a week with Hogan in October 1948, but by the time the magazine was ready to publish the piece in January 1949,[62] the researchers assigned to the story decided too much time had passed to rely on Smith's notes and every fact in the piece needed to be run by Hogan. Because Hogan was in Los Angeles for the Los Angeles Open tournament, the researchers sent a five-page, single-spaced list of questions to Murray. He received the list just hours before the magazine was scheduled to go to press.

Murray waited in the locker room for Hogan to finish his practice round and then for the famously meticulous golfer to try putt after putt on the practice green until darkness had fallen. When he finally made himself available to Murray, he showed the same attention to detail with the article that he had with his golf game. He disputed many of the facts on Murray's list, as the Time, Inc., presses in Chicago waited, at a tremendous cost, for Murray to deliver the final version of the story. Hogan refused to okay a statistical chart on his average shot distance, arguing that there could be no "average" shot because of the variables involved: wind, weather, and so on. Finally, Hogan compromised, and the presses were set in motion, several hours behind schedule.[63]

More sports assignments began to come Murray's way, with him taking a more substantive writing and reporting role in the projects. *Time* put sports personalities on the cover of the magazine even less frequently than it did movie stars, but at least a page of each issue was dedicated to sports. When sports topics were chosen that had a Southern California connection, Murray was usually the correspondent who would get the call. He worked on a cover story on Olympic sprinter Mel Patton and did the majority of the research for a cover piece about decathlete Bob Mathias.[64] He said he was assigned the feature on Notre Dame star quarterback Johnny Lattner because "he was A) knowledgeable about sports and B) Catholic."[65] For the Lattner article, Murray traveled to South Bend, Indiana, to cover the football game between Navy and Notre Dame in October 1953. With the majority of the piece written, *Time*'s New York editors sent strict guidelines for his coverage: "During the game watch for at least one well executed defensive play in which Lattner does well. . . . Let us know to whom the game is dedicated. If the first half is dedicated to a Saint let us know. . . . In the event that our heroes lose the story line will change to how the Irish and particularly Lattner act in defeat."[66]

When the Lattner cover story hit newsstands, Murray was already a few months into the next stage of his career with Time/Life. His reputation for sports expertise had gotten him in on the ground floor of the next great proj-ect of Henry Luce's prolific journalism career. The secret project pointed Mur-ray east, to the New York headquarters of Time/Life, where he would assume a new position in the company and begin the transition from news writer to sportswriter.

4

The *Sports Illustrated* Years, 1953–1960

It would not be A sports magazine. It would be THE sports magazine, with a capital T, H and E. It would bring a reader all THE sports news in THE best way, and THE best advice, THE best in adventure, fiction, etc., etc. The writing would be the best we can get. There would be fine color both photographic, painting and commissioned drawings. There would be the finest photographic portraits of sports personalities we can get and the best photographic portraits of animals will be even better if we can make them so. The paper will be of good enough quality to make the most of all of this.

—Sidney James, August 1953, quoted in *The Franchise: A History of "Sports Illustrated" Magazine,* by Michael MacCambridge

"Fair, but Not Objective"

"Henry Luce, indirectly of course, turned me into a sports writer. But first, indirectly of course, he turned me into a journalist."[1] Murray's contact with Luce had been limited prior to 1953, but the famously hands-on CEO made his way to every outpost in the Time/Life chain, so their paths had crossed enough to give Luce an awareness of Murray and his work. Now, however, they would work side by side in the creation of what was at the time known only as Project X.[2] And Luce would prove to be Murray's last true mentor, one who would change the way Murray would view his role as a journalist and a writer.

Having started *Time,* with classmate Briton Hadden, almost immediately after college in 1923, Luce was still only in his late forties when Murray joined the company. Murray, like most of Luce's subordinates, however, considered him larger in life than the president of the United States. Luce, though, was a down-to-earth leader who appreciated and depended on input from his employees. He developed personal relationships with as many Time/Life employees as he could and asked them all to call him Harry. On the day Murray joined the Time/Life staff, Luce was on one of his annual four-week shifts as managing editor of *Time* (a position he had long ago given up as a full-time pursuit). Murray's first piece of advice about Luce came from a veteran of the bureau. "If you don't know, you better say so. Harry's on the deck this month, and he can't abide a lie. He'll forgive you for anything but laziness and lying."[3]

A journalist to the core, Luce had an exceedingly inquisitive nature, and Time/Lifers came to be ready for a slew of questions whenever he was around. When he would make his intermittent trips to bureaus, the staff member who had been assigned to transport him around town would often make a dry run, memorizing facts and names about the geography and history of the region, to be prepared for Luce's inquisition. On one occasion, the Los Angeles bureau reporter who drew the assignment to drive Luce from Los Angeles to San Francisco was unable to go on a dry run. By about halfway through the ride, the writer was becoming overwhelmed by the questioning. After a few more miles, the two passed a large excavation for a new building.

"What's that?" Luce asked.

"Harry," the writer said wearily, "that's a hole in the ground."[4]

Luce's America-first view of the world soaked every page of every publication his company produced, and indeed his idea of journalism held that total objectivity was a myth and it was the job of the journalist to provide analysis and point of view. His formula for team journalism, comprehensive reporting that also offered more than a dash of perspective, raised the level of discourse in America and informed the middle class. "The basic view, in the largest sense, was Luce's idea that this was the American Empire, this was the century of the American Empire, and that was his view of the world," said McCulloch. "And boy that permeated. . . . The editors, all of whom were promoted over time working for him, his editors all reflected that view. They wanted to keep their jobs, so they damn well better reflect that view."[5]

A meeting with Luce could be a tense experience for a young reporter. He had a commanding presence. He was tall and stood straight with ice-blue eyes, thick eyebrows, and a gaze "so piercing it was like staring into the noon sun."[6] He talked rapidly, firing his questions and arguments in staccato bursts, his mind often outracing his speech and confusing those who could not keep up. "Harry Luce," one of his employees once said, "is so damned articulate he can't get a sentence out."[7] But he appreciated and respected those who could match his arguments and often allowed his subordinates to change his positions. On editorial matters, he strived to achieve consensus with his top editors before handing down a decision, a process that would often be exasperating to his editors. One once said to him, "Harry, I wish you wouldn't give us so much argument. Why don't you just give us a few orders?" He was infinitely involved in every aspect of the Time/Life operation. Memoranda "erupted or flowed in an unceasing stream from his desk" on all aspects of the business.[8] But he felt a tremendous kinship toward all members of the Time/Life family and strived to maintain the feel of what he called a "small, big business." It was a tradition within the company that upon the birth of a child, each Time/Life staffer would receive a sterling-silver porringer, engraved to the child "from Henry R. Luce and the rest of her father's friends at Time, Inc."[9]

Luce was always open to ideas from Time/Life employees, and in the early 1950s a development department was created to evaluate ideas from the field and choose the best of them to be considered for implementation. One of the early submissions that came to the department was a memo from a young executive named Robert Cowin. After conducting a readership survey in Columbus, Ohio, Cowin was amazed by the number of women respondents who said their husbands spent too much time devouring various sports publications. Time/Life, Cowin opined, could produce its own sports magazine, one that would far surpass what was currently on the market. Such a magazine would be tapping into the growing market of weekend athletes and sports aficionados who were awash with more free time for recreation.[10] Cowin's memo did not make the cut in the development department, but when it eventually reached Luce's desk, it became, over the objections of many members of the company's brain trust, the next great project for Time/Life, Inc.

The Great Experiment

By June 1953, Luce and his lieutenants had come to the decision that the company should move forward with plans to develop a new sports publication. The idea had been tried before by several different publishers, to varying degrees of success, but no national sports magazine had been able to sustain any real success. Despite market analysis conducted by his own staff that showed there was not enough advertising to support such a magazine, Luce firmly believed sports was the great untapped market in publishing. He had no particular knowledge of or interest in sports himself, but he had noticed that dinner-party conversation always drifted in that direction. "Why does every conversation end up being about sports?" Luce asked an editor. "Because sports, like music, is a universal language," he was told. "Everybody speaks it."[11]

In July, Murray received a phone call from Ernie Haverman, a well-respected reporter and editor at *Life* who had been tapped to lead the new project. Haverman had been chosen because of his experience as a sportswriter at the *St. Louis Post-Dispatch* years earlier. Now he was putting together a small team that would come to Time/Life headquarters in New York and begin the job of developing a prototype. Murray had been recommended by Clay Felker, a *Life* reporter who was picked for the project because, similar to Murray, he was known as the rare Time/Life staffer with a sports background.[12] Haverman asked Murray to come to New York and join the team. Only weeks earlier, Murray had declined a similar offer from another editor who wanted him to participate in the creation of a culture-oriented magazine. With this offer, however, Murray was intrigued. The next week he took the train east.[13]

When Murray arrived in New York, he found the newly formed department already in disarray. At the time there were only seven members of the team, and Haverman kept to himself in a separate office with the door closed. Murray quickly got the sense that throughout the building, the new magazine, derisively referred to as "Muscles," was thought to be a short-term dalliance of Luce's that would soon be abandoned in favor of more important ideas.[14] Editors had already begun taking the opportunity to dump questionable expenses, such as junkets to the Caribbean, on the project's expense account, confident that the expenses would disappear along with the project.[15] Haverman had already become disenchanted with the project, a fact that he would disclose shortly, so the responsibility fell to Murray to determine what the group would cover and who would provide the coverage. He assigned himself to a fight card at Madison Square Garden and sent other writers around the country to events he felt had national significance.[16] And the team's duties went beyond producing editorial content. They even assumed the responsibility of walking dummy pages over to Madison Avenue advertising agencies for early review.

Less than two weeks after Murray's arrival, Haverman dropped a bomb that would almost shut down the project before it got started. His eleven-page memo titled "A Report on Sports" detailed the litany of reasons that led Haverman to the conclusion that a weekly sports magazine was doomed to failure. "I feel that we should abandon the project, that any time or money we spend on it will be wasted and that if we should ever actually publish, it would be a costly failure," he wrote. The reasons he offered were not new, but they were the prevailing wisdom within the halls of the Time/Life building:

- The sports readership did not have a common interest to tie the magazine together. Sure, there were readers for special-interest sports magazines, such as *Field and Stream, Yachting,* and the *Sporting News,* but subscribers to those magazines were satisfied and would not read a magazine that covered their subjects of interest along with others that did not interest them.

- There just were not enough sporting events of national interest to fill the pages each week. It is difficult to imagine in the twenty-first-century climate of twenty-four-hour sports entertainment saturation, but in the early 1950s, sports was heavily regional and seasonal. Baseball, the most national of sports, only went as far west as the Mississippi River on a Major League level, and attendance had been in decline since the late 1940s. Pro football was growing, but was a northeastern and midwestern phenomenon. Pro basketball was relegated to the East and still thought of by many as a bush-league sport, drawing small crowds in minor league towns like Fort Wayne, Indiana, and Rochester, New York. Most believed college sports fans were interested only in their own school and conference. The National Hockey League had only six teams, four in the United States. Haverman foresaw a long winter with nothing to fill the pages of the magazine.

- There were not enough sportswriters who could produce articles that would rise to the level of quality expected from *Time* and *Life* readers. Consequently, the expense of hiring a staff or editing the work of outside writers would be prohibitive.

- The readers who would pick up the magazine were not the type of people that Madison Avenue advertisers were interested in reaching. Sports fans were either actual or overgrown adolescents or working-class types who could not afford the kinds of products that Madison Avenue was selling to magazine consumers.[17]

Two months later, Haverman wrote to Murray to explain himself. "As you probably guessed, I lost faith in the project and asked to be relieved," he wrote. "I still feel that nothing will ever come of it. . . . Of course, Luce can be awfully dogged about one of his ideas, and Sid James is a very persuasive optimist, anyway."[18]

Haverman proved to be prescient, if only on that last point. Luce chose to ignore his well-reasoned arguments, and Sidney James, an editor known for his unyielding enthusiasm and the same man who had hired Murray for *Time* five and a half years earlier, was given the reins. Murray and the staff of the experimental department found out about the change on James's first day on the job when he walked through the doors of the seventeenth-floor offices.

"What are you doing here, Sid?" Murray asked.

James pointed his finger at Murray. "Do you believe in this magazine, Jim?" he demanded.

"Oh, you bet, Sid!" Murray responded with uncharacteristic energy.[19]

James proceeded to pose the same question to the rest of the crew, getting similar responses. It was with that type of overriding passion that James drove the project forward. After his stint in Los Angeles, James had moved up to assistant managing editor of *Life*. Now he took on the project and brought an immediacy to it, refusing to get bogged down by Haverman's arguments and the negativity within the company.

Luce, who had been in Rome, where his wife, Clare Booth Luce, was serving as ambassador, now came back to New York and became intimately involved in Project X. Heretofore an unknown entity to most of the small staff, he now became a regular presence in their lives. "Sometimes it seemed that we saw more of Luce than we did our wives," one staffer said. He had regular lunches with the members, peppering them with his trademark questions.[20] Staffers often got the call to take Luce to a sporting event and provide an explanation of the sport. His total ignorance of the subject was a constant source of humor. At one meeting, Luce recounted a recent outing with an official in Rome who had taken Luce to a basketball game. "He took me to a sports event where he threw the ball in to start the basketball game between the Globemasters and some other team," Luce recounted.

"The *Globetrotters*, Harry," a staffer interjected.

"Globemasters, Globetrotters; it doesn't make a difference," Luce said.[21]

In the fall of 1953, Murray headed back to Los Angeles, but continued to contribute to the project, which now was quickly accumulating staff and beginning to produce copy and pages. He went on trips all over the region to publicize the magazine and to cultivate sources. "I'm glad to be back on the quarter-deck here and report tremendous enthusiasm for our project all up and down the Coast," he wrote to James. "Even those who came to scoff—like a sports makeup editor at the Seattle Times—came away impressed once the reasoning behind the magazine was explained."[22]

In January 1954, the first prototype was produced and sent to *Time* subscribers in Minnesota.[23] It was titled simply the *New Sports Magazine* and was 140 pages long, filled with a mix of spectator and participatory sports articles, from wrestling to fox hunting. On the cover was an overhead shot of spectators, most, as in the fashion of the day, wearing hats, intently observing a sporting event that was taking place outside the frame of the camera. Luce saw promise, in both the final product and Murray's contribution. "I have just read your 'Footloose Sportsman' for the Los Angeles area. It's just fine . . . and I want to congratulate you on this piece and even more, on all the work you have done in the last few months. . . . Fingers must always be crossed about futures, but it does indeed look as if we have a good magazine coming up," Luce wrote to Murray. Murray responded three days later, showing he was both appreciative of the praise and on board with the guiding philosophy of his mentor. "I am indeed sure we have a good magazine coming up," he wrote in his letter, addressed to "Mr. Luce." "It is indeed fun and I know it will be a success in the way I know you want it to be a success, by complementing the other magazines in telling the *total* story of our century."[24]

A second dummy issue went to press in April 1954, but the decision to publish still had not been made. Murray joined the advertising and editorial staffs of the new magazine at a convention in Myrtle Beach, South Carolina, that month, where it was announced that the decision had been made to go ahead. With publication for the first live issue set for August, the magazine still had no name. Murray and some of the others on the experimental staff advocated the title *Fame,* which would nicely tie the company's titles together as *Time, Life, Fame,* and *Fortune.*[25] Luce preferred *Sport,* but the name was owned by MacFadden Publications, which was demanding $250,000 for the rights to the name, a figure Luce was unwilling to pay. In the end, Time/Life was able to obtain the title *Sports Illustrated* from a friend of publisher Harry Phillips for $5,000.

Finally, on August 16, more than a year after Murray had received that fateful phone call, the inaugural issue of *Sports Illustrated* reached newsstands. The cover photo was Milwaukee Braves slugger Eddie Matthews batting in a game at Milwaukee County Stadium. Inside, the magazine was a mix of pieces contributed by Time/Life staff writers, many written in the *Time* style, and others produced by well-known contract sportswriters such as Red Smith and Herbert Warren Wind, writing on their subjects of expertise.[26] Reaction was overwhelmingly positive. Subscription orders poured in. Even President Eisenhower, to whom Luce had sent a copy, complimented it, writing, "I know I shall find much of interest in it, perhaps too much for my own peace of mind." The idea had become a reality, but it would be nearly a decade of tinkering and financial losses before it would finally hit its editorial and financial stride.[27]

Part-Time Sportswriter

As with all start-ups, *Sports Illustrated* struggled to define itself in its first years of existence. Was it a general-interest sports rag geared toward the everyday beer-and-a-hot-dog bleacher bum? Or was it a highbrow literary sports journal for Ivy Leaguers to read over tea in the smoking room at the country club? Or, as longtime *Sports Illustrated* writer Dan Jenkins called it before he joined the staff, "a slick cookbook for your basic two-yacht family"?[28] In the early days, the majority of editors and writers in the Time/Life family thought it should lean toward the latter, while those who were producing the magazine on a weekly basis began to feel like the only route to ultimate success was to move toward the former. Time/Life advertising executives hungrily eyed the wealthy readership of the *New Yorker* and other highbrow publications and believed these were the readers Madison Avenue desired. With James at the helm, the push from above for coverage of upper-crust leisure activities had a willing ear. In the first year of the magazine's existence, one staff writer alone wrote thirty-six articles on yachting.[29] Andy Crichton, an editor who joined the staff of the magazine in 1954, felt at the time there was a growing sentiment that the magazine was being pulled in the wrong direction. "On the first coverage we did of the America's Cup Yacht Race, and we had 8 or 10 or 12 pages laid out," Crichton remembered. "It was dummied up . . . for [James] to go through Sunday evening, and he turned the pages, on this long yacht story, and he closed up the last page, and said 'That's where we live.' And a couple of us said to ourselves, 'I don't think so.'"[30]

Murray, back in his position in the Los Angeles bureau, quickly became *Sports Illustrated*'s de facto West Coast correspondent. His contributions straddled both sides of the leisure sport versus spectator sport debate and, in total, underscored his expertise in an extremely wide swath of sports subjects. One week he would analyze the upcoming college football season; the next issue he would write about Ch. Crown Crest Rubi, an afghan-breed winner at the Westminster Dog Show. Murray's first bylined article appeared in the magazine in January 1955. It was a feature piece about Santa Anita racetrack, Southern California's premier track, which at the time was a runaway financial success and a growing national attraction. As he would through his tenure at the magazine, Murray wove his connections within and knowledge of the Hollywood movie industry into his coverage of sports. Photos of MGM founder Louis B. Mayer and actress Betty Grable ran alongside Murray's text, which lovingly characterized one of the gems of the racing industry:

> Out in Arcadia, Calif., a warm sun dappled down on a million pansy blossoms and a crowd of 30,000 felt a pleasurable shiver of anticipation as a gaudy gentleman in the scarlet greatcoat and furry top hat of a Dickensian outrider strode to the center of the harrowed track and raised his long-stemmed bugle to his lips. It was the call to the colors for the start of the 18th annual Santa Anita Park racing season. A moment later a dozen sleek, shiny thoroughbreds, their jockeys' silks glistening in the sunlight, burst onto the track and minced toward the starting line. To the racegoer, it was the prettiest sight in the world.[31]

It was at that same track, less than two months later, that Murray got involved in his first major sports story, one that would also prove to be an early chance to leave a national footprint for *Sports Illustrated*. In the mid-1950s, horse racing was riding a decadelong wave of popularity and was challenging baseball as the top spectator sport in America. With a little extra money in their pockets, Americans felt free to spend some of their excess at the track. And outside of Las Vegas, there was very little competition for the American gambling dollar. In 1949, 19.7 million patrons visited the country's racetracks; by 1959, that figure rose to 33.5 million. During those same years, the amount of money wagered at tracks rose from $1.4 billion to $2.5 billion.[32]

In late February, Murray covered the Santa Anita Derby, which was the coming-out party for the next great star of the sport, a horse named Swaps. Swaps was owned by an Arizonan named Rex Ellsworth and trained by his friend Mesh Tenney, both devout Mormons. In 1933, Ellsworth, the son of a rancher, had rented a truck and driven to Lexington, Kentucky, with six hundred dollars, money he intended to use to start his racing stable. He had come back to Arizona with six mares and two weanlings and gradually built a thriving thoroughbred business, one that would eventually become the most successful in the western United States.[33] Choosing functionality over appearance, Ellsworth eschewed the Kentucky-style horse farm of white picket fences and majestic barns in favor of the V-mesh wiring of a western cattle pen. With no money for purchasing horses with top bloodlines, Ellsworth and Tenney managed to use their knowledge of conformation and skill of preparation to develop a string of winners.[34] By 1955, the Ellsworth operation was an unquestioned success, and Swaps, a long, tall, and wide chestnut colt with dazzling speed, would be their first opportunity to showcase their stable nationally.

In the Santa Anita Derby, Swaps went off as the second favorite, and after grabbing the lead halfway through the race, "he came into the final turn like a scat halfback—way wide but fast," Murray wrote.[35] Swaps won by half a length, and, as happens following all major stakes races in the winter and early spring, talk turned to the Kentucky Derby. Swaps was both bred and trained in California, and it had been thirty-three years since a California-bred horse had won the Kentucky Derby. California race fans seized upon Swaps as the next great western hope. Arriving at Churchill Downs prior to the race, Tenney became incensed when he noticed a sleeping security guard and decided to bed down in the stall with his prize colt. "Cowboy Sleeps with Horse" was the headline on one of the following morning's newspapers, and soon thereafter Tenney and Ellsworth were dubbed the "Cowboy Race Kings" by *Life*. The public became infatuated with Swaps and his eccentric owners, and an East versus West racing showdown was born.

The other half of the brewing rivalry was Nashua, a quirky, quick-tempered Kentucky-bred colt that had the backing of the eastern racing establishment. Nashua was owned by William Woodward Jr., heir to the Kentucky breeding fortune of William Woodward Sr., a member of American racing royalty. The horse was trained by Hall of Fame trainer Jim Fitzsimmons, who had trained two Triple Crown winners, Gallant Fox in 1930 and Omaha in 1935.[36] On the morning of the Kentucky Derby, western bettors anted up enough to make Swaps the favorite, but by the afternoon eastern money came in and Nashua was the bettors' choice. Swaps was to be ridden by Bill Shoemaker, a young star of the sport in 1955 who would go on to become both a Hall of Fame jockey and a close personal friend of Murray's. On Nashua was Eddie Arcaro, another top-tier jockey, one who was known to have a heavy hand with the whip. When the gates opened, free-running Swaps grabbed the lead, and Arcaro and Nashua waited for "that nice little California sprinter" to come back to them. But

Swaps never did. He turned on the speed down the stretch and pulled away, leaving Nashua in his wake.

"That would have made a fine happy ending for a movie if that were the end of it," Murray wrote later.[37] Instead, the story continued, helped along by Murray himself and his colleagues at his upstart new magazine, less than a year old at the time. To the dismay of the eastern racing chiefs, Ellsworth packed up Swaps and took him home, forsaking the final two legs of the storied Triple Crown, the Preakness and the Belmont. Nashua won both races, and public sentiment for a rematch quickly materialized, helped along by the coverage in *Sports Illustrated*. Whitney Tower, the magazine's lead horse-racing writer, spearheaded the magazine's push for a match race between the two horses. In the June 13, 1955, edition of the magazine, he broke the story that both camps had agreed to such a race, to take place in August at Arlington Park in Chicago, with one hundred thousand dollars going to the winner. Match races were a rare occurrence, a once-in-a-generation spectacle that could ignite the horse-racing world. In 1938, Seabiscuit had beaten War Admiral in a match at Pimlico that captivated the country during the depths of the Depression. *Sports Illustrated* hyped the Swaps-Nashua matchup through the summer, with the help of the trainers, who freely engaged in what would years later be known as trash talk. "Swaps can beat Nashua at any distance from a half-mile to two miles," Tenney said. "Nashua can beat Swaps doing anything," Fitzsimmons retorted.[38] Murray did his part from California. Ellsworth and Swaps took up a good part of his time. He covered the colt's return to the track at Hollywood Park in June, where Swaps trounced the best thoroughbreds California had to offer and set a world record in doing so. In July, Murray contributed a lengthy profile on Ellsworth, complete with a four-page photo spread of the horseman in his trademark jeans and cowboy hat at home with Swaps at "his modest Chino ranch." Murray's piece expressed the pride of the California racing establishment. "Around Hollywood Park they are no longer asking whether Swaps is better than Nashua, it's whether he's as good as Man o' War. . . . A pair of Arizona cowboys has not only crashed the select circle of championship horse breeders, they have temporarily taken it over."[39]

When the race finally went off in August, it was a disappointment. Swaps gouged his foot on a rock weeks before the race, and Ellsworth called for the race to be postponed. But it was scheduled for closing day at Arlington Park, and too much money and hype had been invested. The show would have to go on. When the gates opened, Swaps ran gamely, but was clearly in pain. "Swaps' head veered right and his normally smooth stride was so scrambled, he looked like a drunk coming out of a bar under a push," Murray wrote later.[40] By the stretch, Swaps was far behind and made no real attempt on the lead. Arcaro, who, Murray wrote, had practically started to whip the horse in the paddock, kept flogging Nashua through the finish line, winning by a comfortable six lengths. Nashua would win Horse of the Year in 1955, and Swaps would come back in 1956 with one of the most successful years in the history of racing, winning eight stakes races and breaking three more world records.[41] The two champion colts would never face each other again, but they had helped to significantly raise the profile of a struggling magazine in its first year of existence.

A Deadly Serious Fan

Despite his time and energy being split between the new magazine and his other duties in the Los Angeles bureau, Murray became one of the early writing stalwarts of *Sports Illustrated*. In its early days, the magazine's coverage of major events often was not up to *Time*'s standard of excellence for deadline writing. Time/Life staffers with limited knowledge of sports and writers for hire often slipped into the play-by-play style of newspaper sports coverage, providing little or no perspective. Murray and a few other select writers began to use their space in the magazine to go beyond the plays and the outcome and discuss the scene around the event. The better articles gave a larger context to the events and offered readers analysis not found in daily newspapers.[42] At the same time, Murray made sure the West Coast was not ignored in the pages of *Sports Illustrated*. His Hollywood connections remained evident. He wrote about Humphrey Bogart's love of sailing, Gary Cooper's life as a sportsman, and the penchant some Hollywood titans had developed for playing croquet.[43] He reported and wrote profiles of Southern California sports stars and personalities from a wide variety of sports and recommended many others through his regular backgrounders.

The small editorial staff of *Sports Illustrated* operated on the lower rung of the Time/Life ladder of importance while working at double the pace. (The magazine was producing sixty pages of editorial content each week compared to *Time*'s forty, with far fewer bodies.) But the job was another opportunity to escape the anonymity of *Time*, and the personal recognition that came with seeing their names in print kept the morale of the writers high.[44] For Murray, it was a chance to experiment with another type of journalism. Starting in 1956, he wrote a number of opinionated essays on topics designed to both make his point and raise the passions of his readers. The articles were given prominent play in the magazine, often running alongside artistic representations of the topic and Murray's take on it. He approached the pieces much in the same way he did with his *Life* article titled "I Hate the Yankees" years before: reasoned arguments strongly supported with historical examples, coming down firmly on one side of the debate. The response was similar: pro and con responses would fill the magazine's "Letters" section for weeks afterward.

In June 1956, the editor of a Murray-authored article titled "American League? Phooey!" introduced the piece with a nod to Murray's growing notoriety: "James Murray is no junior circuit upstart but a deadly serious fan who (in the days before his current disenchantment) named his oldest son for Ted Williams. Murray is fully prepared to defend his stand all summer long, if need be, against all serious dissenters." In the piece, Murray charts the long history of American League dominance in professional baseball, which he traces to the early 1920s, when John McGraw's New York Giants were overtaken by the New York Yankees of Babe Ruth. Following "Murray's Law," which states that baseball history is a series of recurrent cycles, he describes how the advent of the black Major Leaguer had brought the National League back to the verge of prominence: "Jackie Robinson, it is my intention to prove, was to the National League what Babe Ruth was to the American. He was a revolution. The sociological aspects of his advent are not germane here. . . . The baseball aspects are." The content of the article, and the flame-fanning headline, led to "a barrage of post-marked garbage aimed directly at me," Murray wrote later.[45]

Later that same summer, Murray used another one of his essay-style articles to perform his journalistic duty and give voice to the voiceless: he made a plea for the poor, persecuted everyday sports spectator. "James Murray speaks with the authority and passion of a fan of many years standing," the editors wrote in a short lead-in to the article. The piece, titled "The Case for the Suffering Fan," recounts the many indignities fans of the mid-1950s suffered, from ancient stadia and hard seats to crooked parking-lot attendants and obstructed views. Alongside the article ran a pencil drawing of cheerless fans and their angry tormentors by famed illustrator Robert Osborn. Attendance was spiraling downward in baseball in the 1950s as television's foothold continued to grow. The great majority of baseball stadia at the time were more than thirty years old, and the amenities had fallen below modern standards. Murray placed the blame squarely upon the shoulders of baseball's cheapskate ownership, from which he saw a casual disregard of the needs and wants of their customers. He predicted that the migration away from the nation's ballparks would continue if circumstances remained the same. To illustrate, he drew upon what must have been a lifetime of slights and humiliations attending sporting events on his own dime:

> People ask: What's happening to the fan? Where is he? Well, I have news. The fan is there, right where he's always been—still tooling around the antiquated ball park in the family sedan looking for a place to park; still emptying out his pockets to pay off that shark who steered him to a fender-denting hold outside the left-field wall, or giving his last eight bits to the usher, the one who's buying income property with the accumulated tax-free tips he gets for dusting off reserved

seats. Could even be, in mid-game, he's still climbing ramps because he didn't tip the usher and so got sent off in the wrong direction. But anyway, he's still around, the fan is, behind his pole or maybe standing in line outside the rest room, the one with only one door and just enough facilities to take care of a Cub Scout den. He's still around, but maybe not for long.

Or maybe he isn't around, at that. Maybe he finally listened when the little woman stamped her foot for the umpteenth time and said: "The ball park? That filthy hole? Not on your life! We're going down to the Loew's High where they have Rossano Brazzi kissing Katharine Hepburn's hand in Technicolor on a Wide Screen with Stereophonic Sound, and where they have those big comfortable loge seats with air-conditioning and hot popcorn and cold Coke if you feel like it." Maybe he thought of the splintery plank seats which he would get for his re-served-seat ticket, and the sweating effort of cheering himself hoarse for a pack of athletes who would make obscene gestures at him or take to the public prints to claim they didn't deserve his services at 50 grand per year. So maybe he did turn to the little woman, thinking: it's just too much trouble to get there, it's too uncomfortable when I am there, they treat me like I'm not wanted anyway; and maybe he said: "Honey, you're right. Loew's it is. And Saturday, instead of going to the ball game, I'm gonna try and break 100."[46]

For the first time, Murray allowed his humor to show in his published writing. The humor of personal experience is present throughout the piece. Murray's fictional fan is placed in satirical situations that run the gamut of the belittling experiences of the everyday fan, or, more accurately, Jim Murray the fan. *Sports Illustrated* correspondents from cities around the Major Leagues contributed anecdotes of fan mistreatment at the various stadia. And Murray incorporated comments from Bob Cobb, Brown Derby proprietor and owner of Murray's favorite hometown Minor League club, the Hollywood Stars, to support his premise. The piece was one of the first in which Murray exhibited an ability to use wit both to entertain his readers and to drive home his point.

The sports essays were an attempt on the part of the editors at *Sports Illustrated* to make better use of Murray's emerging talents. But most of the time, his unique skills as a writer never made it to Time/Life readers. One editor who noticed Murray's flair early on was Robert Creamer, an editor who had been on the staff of the magazine since before the first issue. Creamer said Murray was often handcuffed by the magazine's formulaic design, which did not often allow for writers to employ personal style. Murray's style came through loud and clear in his interoffice background reports for all of his Time/Life assignments. "We all knew Jim could write," Creamer remembered. "It was fun reading his dispatches. . . . And it was great to read. But unfortunately, we weren't smart enough to just run them that way, I guess. . . . I think it hampered Jim, because he worked in this format, he supplied the material for the writers to do their pieces, but I think it kept his light under a bushel."[47]

Ocean of Joy

By 1956, Murray had been in the employ of Time/Life for eight years. The company's great wave of growth had yet to crest, and it paid its employees well. Murray's salary was up to fifteen thousand dollars, a figure that went a long way in California in the 1950s. He was professionally satisfied and well compensated to boot. "I have a great job. I have a New York salary in California," he told Creamer. With Murray's income creeping into a higher bracket, the family made another move, one that would provide both an immediate increase in quality of life and long-term financial dividends. The family left Pacific Palisades and moved about twenty-five miles up the coast to Point Dume, a community at the western edge of the city of Malibu. The new home was on a promontory overlooking the Pacific Ocean, with a sweeping ocean view, something that had long been a dream of Murray's.[48] The city of Malibu had been largely left alone by development until the 1930s, when the Pacific Coast Highway was completed. After that, many movie-industry heavyweights migrated north, and the area became known as the Malibu Movie Colony. Barbara Stanwyck, Jack Warner of Warner Brothers Studio, Clara Bow, and Murray's childhood favorite Ronald Colman were all Malibu residents at one time.[49] Point Dume was still in its infancy when the Murrays arrived. Murray said the move made his commute to the bureau "hideously long," but the view, and the peace that came along with it, was well worth the trade-off.[50] The purchase would also be a profitable one for the Murrays. Once again, they had acquired real estate in a location where land values were soon to go through the roof. When he finally sold the Point Dume property eighteen years later, the buyer was Bob Dylan, and Murray had made a small fortune on the investment.[51]

The Dylans would have never moved in had it not been for the power of *Time,* because the home would have likely burned to the ground. Wildfires are a constant threat in Malibu, where houses are set off on separate hills, surrounded by brush. One day, Murray heard reports of a wildfire in Point Dume while he was at work at the bureau. He rushed home. He soon reached a police blockade and pleaded to the officers that his wife and four children were in the home and he should be let through. Nobody is allowed past this point, he was told. Murray hopped back in his car and drove another route toward the home, only to encounter another police blockade. This time, he pulled out his *Time* press pass and announced he was covering the fire for the magazine. The cops deferred, and Murray was able to get to the house before the fire reached his property. With high winds gusting, he climbed on his roof with a water hose and defended his new home from disaster.[52] Eventually, the family, along with Gerry's parents, who were in town visiting, got into the car and Murray fired up the engine, ready to evacuate to safety. Just before they left, Murray ran back into the house and called the *Life* bureau chief. "God forgive me for this," he said. "We've got to make a run for it quick, and they'd kill me if they knew what I was doing, but Lord, what a beautiful picture!"[53]

Though it was not as dangerous as a fast-moving Malibu blaze, there was another persistent threat to Murray's paradise: the whims of Time/Life editors who wanted to draw him back East. Even before the formation of the sports-magazine task force, the home office had been pushing for him to transfer to another office, with the carrot being career advancement. It was custom-ary within the company for correspondents to move throughout the news ser-vice on their way up the ladder. Murray's close friend Frank McCulloch was transferred from Los Angeles to Dallas to New York and back to Los Angeles between 1953 and 1960.[54] At one point, Murray was offered, in fact strongly ad-vised, to accept the position of bureau chief for the company's Boston bureau. The Boston chief, Jeff Wylie, was slotted for Los Angeles. Fortunately for Mur-ray, Wylie thought even less of the idea than he did and soon left the company to enroll at the Massachusetts Institute of Technology. The switch died in a New York boardroom, and Murray's grip on his beloved Los Angeles was once again safe for the time being.[55] The constant pressure to vacate the West Coast would take its toll, however, and eventually accelerate his departure from Time/Life.

Another minor annoyance to Murray's comfortable existence in Los Angeles was the habit the New York office had of sending reporters west to encroach on what Murray had come to view as his turf. Of course, California was far too large a territory for a single correspondent to cover for a national sports maga-zine. But on occasion, Murray bristled at the idea of a New York writer being sent out to cover what he felt was his story. When the Brooklyn Dodgers moved to Los Angeles in 1958, Murray covered the story for *Time,* doing the bulk of the work on a cover story on Dodgers owner Walter O'Malley. (The New York Giants moved to San Francisco that same year.) However, when the teams be-gan play out West, Creamer was dispatched to cover the inaugural series. The slight was just one example of the type of occurrence that tended to stick in Murray's craw. "I don't know whether it was an injustice to him or not," said his friend Mel Durslag, who was still writing for the *Los Angeles Examiner* at the time, "but he got pissed off at New York and at *Time.* He was mad at them."[56]

A Different Path

At the dawn of the 1960s, Murray's journalism career remained on the slow arc toward the world of sports. He had spent a dozen years in the Los Angeles bureau. He continued to carry out his duties as a correspondent in the *Time* news service, filing his weekly reports, the *Los Angeles Letter* and the *Hollywood Letter*, as well as contributing background dispatches when called upon on California politics, crime, and culture. But his output for *Sports Illustrated* was growing. His byline was appearing as often as many of the magazine's full-time writers. In August 1960, he cowrote a two-part fifteen-page series on a successful mountain-climbing expedition to the summit of Dhaulagiri, a previously unconquered peak in the Himalayas and the seventh-highest peak on earth.[57] In the months following, he covered auto racing, track and field, boxing, professional and college football, and other assorted sporting events and topics, all resulting in bylined articles in the pages of *Sports Illustrated*. In December, he took his first extended road trip for the magazine, spending a week in various eastern cities with the Los Angeles Lakers over the Christmas holidays. The team had moved from Minneapolis to Los Angeles during the summer of 1960. For his piece, titled "A Trip for Ten Tall Men," Murray largely kept the actual basketball game action offstage, instead concentrating on the daily life of professional players in the fledgling National Basketball Association, as they moved through the airports, hotels, and bars of the urban Northeast. Using dialogue and characterization and taking the story beyond the point where traditional sportswriting leaves off, Murray's article was exactly the type of writing that would become the magazine's calling card and foment its eventual success.[58]

Before "Ten Tall Men" ever appeared in *Sports Illustrated*, events had already been set in motion that would send Murray's career in a new direction. After his stints in Dallas and New York, Frank McCulloch had returned to Los Angeles as bureau chief. Like Murray, he felt it was just a matter of time before a transfer order would come in from the Time/Life home office. A few years earlier, in 1957, McCulloch had written a profile piece for *Time* on Norman and Buffy Chandler, publishers of the *Los Angeles Times*. The Chandlers had been impressed with the article and enamored with McCulloch. The three kept in touch. In 1960, the Chandlers' son Otis was promoted to publisher of the *Times* and was putting together a new team of top editors. At the suggestion of Norman and Buffy, McCulloch was considered for the position of managing editor, the second rung on the newspaper's editorial ladder, below editor Nick Williams.[59] "I thought it over, and I said I'd have to have a pretty big salary," McCulloch remembered. "And they said, 'What do you mean by that?' And I said I'd have to have twenty thousand dollars. So they chewed on that for a while and said okay, we'll do it." McCulloch had been earning nineteen thousand at Time/Life.[60]

After he gained his footing, McCulloch began the task of trying to improve the quality of the writing staff at the *Times*. His strategy was essentially to hire his friends away from Time/Life. Eventually, he would hire away enough talent from the Los Angeles bureau to cause Henry Luce to plead for mercy. "I had good personal relationships with them, and I paid them a little more money than they were making at the time," McCulloch said. "And the *Times*, of course, particularly at that time, was enormously dominant in Los Angeles. If you worked for the *Times*, it was just fine in LA. I don't think any of them had a hesitancy about doing it." Murray was the first person on McCulloch's hit list.

Around the same time, the push at Time/Life's New York office to bring Murray back to the East was rising again. This time, however, the offer was much more enticing. He was asked to come to New York to take a position as one of the top editors at *Sports Illustrated*. The magazine was undergoing a shake-up at the top levels in 1960. André Laguerre, the man who would eventually pilot the magazine toward financial and editorial dominance, had been Luce's managing editor in waiting for four years. In April, when Sid James was promoted to publisher, Laguerre was handed the reins of the magazine.[61] Murray's name had been tossed around as a candidate for a top position, and now the offer was beginning to sound like one of the "take-it-or-leave-it" variety.[62]

The Murrays celebrated Thanksgiving in 1960 with his friend Will Fowler and family. Murray and Fowler discussed the apparent turning point in Murray's career. He was sitting on offers from *Sports Illustrated* and the *Los Angeles Times*. A decision needed to be made, and soon. Both offers meant more money. Staying with Time/Life meant security and upward mobility, but, of course, it meant hats, overcoats, and snow shovels as well. The *Times* offer would be a leap into the great unknown. Murray had never written a single sports column for publication. He was well known to Los Angeles–area journalists, but to Los Angeles readers he was almost completely anonymous. But the column, he told Fowler, would be a new challenge. "I never gave it much thought," Murray confided to Fowler, "but what the hell is a sports columnist's routine?"

"You just keep hoping the next guy you talk to will give you an idea for a column," Fowler told him. "If he says 'Come on over to the house for a drink' and nothing else, avoid him."

"Well, I've got four kids now, and I'm really fed up with galoshes," Murray said.[63]

A few days later, he told McCulloch he had chosen the *Times*. After he went downtown to the *Times* offices to make it official, he stopped by the home of Mel Durslag on the way back out to Malibu. Durslag and Murray would now be competing lead sports columnists on the two top newspapers in Los Angeles. Only nine months earlier, the position that Murray had just accepted had been offered to Durslag. *Times* editors had brought him to the Biltmore Hotel for a drink and made him an offer. Durslag turned them down. "Maybe I didn't make the wisest choice, but I passed, because I'd worked for Hearst for all those years," he recalled.

Now Murray was at Durslag's home to tell him he had accepted the *Times* position. Murray was just beginning to comprehend what he had signed up for: six sports columns a week, every week, from now to eternity. "We were talking about writing a column, and he was sort of trying to get himself organized, see. He'd never done that before. . . . And I said the first thing you have to do, Jim, is develop a routine. You need to develop a very rigid routine when you write a daily column," Durslag said.[64]

Luce and the *Time* family were discouraged but resigned to the fact that Murray had chosen California over them. The decision was not unexpected. Murray had burned no bridges and remained held in the highest regard at *Time*. "I salute you especially as one of the pioneers who, along with the rest of the very privileged few, were in at the beginning to stand up before the slings and arrows. There is something very special about a pioneer and something especially special about a magazining pioneer in the mid-Twentieth Century," James wrote to Murray when he heard the news. Murray went home to Malibu and began to prepare himself. "The opportunities for falling off a high wire were certainly present," he wrote later. "I remember going to bed that night thinking, 'I hope I've done the right thing.'"[65]

Murray, right, with his childhood best friend, Joey Patrissi. Patrissi was a stand-out baseball player who spent some time in the New York Yankee farm system.

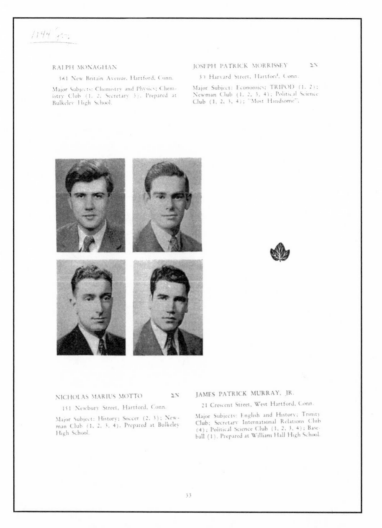

Murray's Trinity College yearbook photo, 1943. While at Trinity, Murray wrote for the school newspaper, published short stories and plays, to the dismay of his aunt, spent a year on the baseball team.

In this 1944 newspaper clipping from the now defunct *Los Angeles Examiner,* Murray removes hail from a car in 1944, shortly after arriving in Los Angeles.

Murray serves as a judge in a drink contest in Las Vegas while he worked for *Time* magazine. No matter what he was covering, Murray seemed to end up spending time in the desert oasis.

A *Life* magazine photographer shot Murray posing with a baseball bat, to run in the magazine with letters that poured in responding to Murray's article "I Hate the Yankees." The article was one of the first to showcase Murray's humor and skill with commentary.

During the 1961 World Series, fans at Cincinnati's Crosley Field show their disdain for Jim Murray. Murray had written columns poking fun at the city of Cincinnati. He would go on to aim his barbs at cities across the country and throughout world.

This is a *Los Angeles Times* Syndication advertisement for Murray's column, circa 1964. Early in his career at the *Times,* Murray became the newspaper's top syndicated columnist, and eventually was published in more than 200 newspapers across the continent.

Murray sits with actors Ty Hardin and Ralph Meeker on the set of the movie 1963 movie *Wall of Noise*. Murray's Hollywood connections landed him a bit part in the film, a now-forgotten horse-racing movie.

Murray poses with (from left) Tommy Bolt, Allard Roen and Phil Harris at LaCosta Resort in Carlsbad, Calif. in this 1965 photo. Bolt was a PGA tour player and close friend (and regular golf buddy) of Murray's. Roen was a Vegas hotelier with underworld connections. Harris was a well-known comedian/actor/musician.

Murray interviews Baltimore Orioles pitcher Moe Drabowsky after the Orioles beat the Los Angeles Dodgers in the 1966 World Series.

(Above) Murray and broadcaster Curt Gowdy pose with awards they received when they were honored by the National Sportscasters and Sportswriters Association in Salisbury, N.C. in 1966. Murray was named sports writer of the year by the organization 14 times.

(Opposite top) Murray and Howard Cosell pose for a publicity shot for an annual football fund-raiser for the Shriners in 1972. The pair had recently returned from the 1972 Munich Olympics, where they were among the first journalists on the scene at the infamous hostage incident.

(Opposite bottom) This cartoon of Murray roasting cities on a grill was published in the now-defunct *National Observer* in 1972. Murray's humorous columns about various locales often drew a huge response from citizens of the offended city.

Murray tees off in a pro-am golf tournament. Golf was Murray's favorite sport and the one he devoted most of his recreational time to.

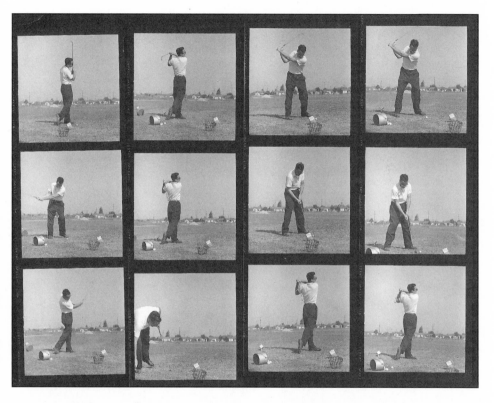

Many a Jim Murray column was devoted to his own trials and tribulations on the golf course. He once said his most common golf shot was either (a) an 18-foot putt which ends up 11 feet short or (b) an 18-foot putt which ends up 15 feet long.

Murray presents a trophy to the unidentified winners of a race at Hollywood park. Murray spent a lot of time at Hollywood Park and eventually a stakes race was created in his honor.

The Jim Murray Handicap race.

Bill Walton addresses the audience as Murray looks on during a celebrity roast held in Murray's honor in September 1979. The roast
was held during the period in which Murray had almost no vision
in either eye.

Murray converses with Gerald Ford at a cocktail party. Murray was acquainted with several presidents, and accompanied Ford to the Major League Baseball All-Star game during Ford's presidency.

Murray is toasted by *Los Angeles Times* editor Shelby Coffey and publisher David Laventhal on the day Murray received word that he had won a Pulitzer prize.

Murray poses with Linda McCoy at Columbia University after the award ceremony at which Murray received his Pulitzer prize. Murray and Linda were married a few years later.

Murray poses with "the Geezers" at a 1989 Super Bowl party. The Geezers was an unofficial group of sports writers who traveled together from sporting event to sporting event. From left are Blackie Sherrod, Bill Milsaps, Bob Verdi, Furman Bisher, Edwin Pope, Murray and Dan Foster.

Murray stands with Linda McCoy, Los Angeles Clippers owner Donald Sterling, and Oakland Raiders owner Al Davis at a celebrity event in 1993. In his later years, Murray disliked public appearances, and often had to be coaxed into social situations by Linda.

5

The *Los Angeles Times* Years, 1961–1962

The sports columnist was the high priest of games then, often less a journalist and more sort of the athletic director of the local chamber of commerce. They were the cheerleaders, often caravanning together to the annual rota of approved events: spring training, the Masters, the Kentucky Derby, the Indianapolis 500, and so on through the athletic liturgical calendar. It was a drummer's life, with deadlines and whiskey and wonderful camaraderie.

—Frank Deford, "*Sportswriter* Is One Word"

Writing a column is a useful but limited talent, like hitting a curve ball or lining up a downhill putt. I ascribe all my success to learning to go to my left on an adverb, changing a compound participle—not letting it play me, in other words—following through on all my prepositions (repeat, prepositions) and learning how to spell Tony Conigliaro.

—Jim Murray, "Finally Won It," *Los Angeles Times,* April 18, 1965

Megalopolis

The Los Angeles of 1961 was an entirely different entity than the overgrown coastal village that Jim Murray had encountered when he stepped off the train seventeen years earlier. The wave of growth that he had been part of had continued unabated. The highway system, the origination of which he had chronicled during his days as a cub reporter, had sent out tentacles in every direction, earning Los Angeles the moniker of the Freeway City. Transplants from every region continued to grow the population, and the residential base was topped with a floating population of tourists, conventioneers, and visitors.[1] The population growth had fueled the rise of spectator sports. In the past three years, the city had gained three professional sports franchises: the Los Angeles Dodgers and the California Angels in baseball and the Los Angeles Lakers in basketball. The Los Angeles Sports Arena had opened in 1959 as a home for the Lakers and other sports and entertainment events. A stadium would be completed at Chavez Ravine as a home for the Dodgers the following year. Los Angeles, which had been drawing more than a million spectators to its minor-league teams for years, was finally in the process of becoming a major-league city.[2]

The playing field in the newspaper industry had changed since Murray had been gone as well. Television, which was just a speck on the media radar in the late 1940s, had by 1961 fundamentally changed the way news was communicated. Though the city's daily newspapers were still recording strong circulation figures and maintained a somewhat loyal readership, a thinning of the herd was in progress, as it was in most major metropolitan areas in the country.[3] And while the *Los Angeles Examiner* was the city's leading newspaper while Murray was on its staff, Hearst's favorite newspaper was on a downward spiral in the late 1950s and early 1960s that would lead to its demise in 1962. The *Los Angeles Times,* Murray's new home, now dominated the market. The previous year, circulation at the *Times* was 532,078 on weekdays and 970,027 on Sundays, while the *Examiner*'s figures were 384,760 on weekdays and 678,280 on Sundays.[4] The two afternoon papers, Hearst's *Herald-Express* and the Chandlers' *Mirror,* still held circulations of between 300,000 and 400,000, but the highway system and the increased reliance on automobiles had drastically reduced the demand for an afternoon news product. Within two years, the Chandlers would shutter the *Mirror* and Hearst would merge the *Herald-Express* and the *Examiner,* and Los Angeles would become a two-newspaper town.

And it was the *Times* that would come to dominate the market. The Chandler family had run the *Los Angeles Times* since the 1880s, when Harry Chandler had married the daughter of General Harrison Gray Otis, who had purchased control of the company a few years earlier from a partner. From the very beginning of the Otis-Chandler partnership, the paper had been a staunchly conservative voice of the city's business elite, always ready and willing to provide a voice for management and be an enemy to labor. For the first half of the century, the paper served as an instrument of the Republican Party in California, a reactionary rag that *Time* called "the most rabid Labor-baiting, Red-hating newspaper in the United States."[5] By the 1940s and 1950s, the *Times* was a national laughingstock. A national poll conducted by *Time* in the late 1950s named it the second-worst paper in the United States. Humorist S. J. Perelman famously wrote that during a train stopover, "I asked the porter to get me a newspaper, and unfortunately, the man, hard of hearing, brought me the *Los Angeles Times*." NBC News anchor Chet Huntley joked that he would "always read the *Los Angeles Times* and know that I could be reasonably accurate by going 100 percent in the other direction."[6]

Circumstances had begun to change in the late 1950s. For one, the *Times,* which had always been the city's dominant paper in terms of advertising due to its close ties to the business community, capitalized on the market growth far more than its competition. In 1960, the *Times* was the top newspaper in the entire country in the amount of news published and in the amount of advertising.[7] The Chandlers felt hurt by their status in the industry as a punch line and longed to join the upper echelon of their industry. With the financial foundation in place, they decided to make an effort to change the paper's reputation. In 1958, the Chandlers handed control of the *Times* over to their son Otis, then thirty-one years old and recently graduated from the family's executive initiation rituals, having worked in various departments throughout the company. Around the same time, Nick Williams was given the post of editor. Upon his hiring, Norman Chandler gave Williams this direction: "I want the *Times* to be fair, and I want it to dig in, to investigate, and to report what it learns." The character of the paper changed completely from that day on, Williams later said.[8] The newspaper began to strive for editorial excellence, and, at the same time, it began to dominate the Los Angeles market. Bill Thomas, who was city editor at the *Times* in the early 1960s and would later become the paper's top editor during the 1970s and 1980s, said the change in attitude and outlook came about quickly under the direction of Otis Chandler. "Two things happened: Otis became publisher, and with that came the infusion of a lot of people with a totally different journalism purposes and methods," Thomas recalled.[9] The editorial staff received a boost when the *Mirror* closed and the top talent from that staff joined the *Times*. And McCulloch did his part with his raiding of the *Time* bureau.

"A Good Man in a Bar"

McCulloch saw the *Times* sports department as yet another way to improve coverage and drive up readership. With the influx of sport franchises and interest, Williams and McCulloch gradually increased the paper's news hole for sports by 20 percent. Unlike the paper's news department, the *Times* sports section had earned an excellent reputation for coverage over the years. When Murray joined the staff, the sports editor was Paul Zimmerman, a veteran of the Los Angeles sports scene who was beloved by his staff. One of the lead columnists was Braven Dyer. Dyer was another old-timer, having been on the *Times* sports staff since the 1920s, when he was one of a group of regional sportswriters who helped Grantland Rice choose the annual college football All-America team for *Collier's* magazine. Dyer was a well-known figure on the Los Angeles social scene, with connections throughout the city's sports scene and within the movie industry.[10] In 1961, Dyer was preparing to cover the California Angels' first season. Frank Finch held the Dodgers beat at the time. Finch had a sharp wit, present both in the newsroom and in his copy, though he had a penchant for using clichéd language from the golden age of sportswriting. The rest of the colorful sports staff included turf writer Bion Abbott; Cal Whorton, who covered boxing and the Los Angeles Rams; Al Wolf; and a team of experienced copy editors and photographers.[11]

Murray was joining a sports staff with a solid core of writers and editors, and he came aboard in an unconventional manner. Generally, sports editors handled the hiring, and a columnist position had to be earned through several years of exemplary coverage on an important beat. Murray was hired by the newspaper's top brass and handed the plum assignment of page 1 sports columnist. (The *Times* also published columnists regularly on the inside of the sports section.) McCulloch and top editor Frank Haven sent a memo to the staff outlining Murray's duties and the chain of command. The guidelines had been set up as part of the negotiations conducted before Murray accepted the position. Murray would report to McCulloch, not the sports editor, and the sports editor was forbidden from assigning stories to Murray, or assigning stories to other writers that would duplicate Murray's theme. In addition, the memo made it clear that Murray was to have complete autonomy. "The sports columnist is on his own, writing on any subject he considers pertinent and writing his daily column at the office, at home, or wherever he may be, as long as the daily deadline is met," the memo read.[12] Murray would operate under these rules for the next thirty-eight years.

Because of the circumstances, Murray knew he would face resentment initially. Dan Smith, who was a copy editor on the sports desk when Murray joined the staff, remembers that there was a detectable undercurrent of resentment throughout the department. "Not everybody on the staff was greeting him with open arms," Smith said. "I remember one of the early columns he did . . . was on one of the pitchers for the Angels named Eli Grba, and he really had a lot of fun with the guy's name. And there were a lot of guys on the sports staff who didn't accept that, they thought it was too 'punny.'"[13]

McCulloch and Murray had discussed the potential for discord before Murray joined the staff. "Jim sold himself as an individual and as a journalist to the other people in the sports department," he recalled. "And his column was so immensely popular so quickly, and it enhanced the sports section so immensely, that everyone, whether they liked him or not, had to recognize that."

Murray's ease at developing friendly relationships with people, which had allowed him to glide freely through the movie industry and create an enormous network of friends and contacts, helped him quickly assimilate at the *Times*. Durslag remembered Murray in those years as having a quiet, friendly, unassuming quality that made people want to be around him. He spent a lot of time socializing and drinking with the other writers, both at the *Times* and at the other newspapers, and was completely comfortable in social situations. He was, Durslag said, "a good man in a bar."[14]

On February 5, 1961, the *Times* announced its new columnist to its readers. In an article stripped across the top of the sports section, headlined "Jim Murray to Write Feature Sports Column in *Times*," Murray's actual biography was recounted, along with a tongue-in-cheek description Murray submitted about his athletic career: "At age 8, he set a new world's record for the 37½-yard dash (the distance from the nearest street corner to the light pole in front of his home)." Murray's "sharp eye and quizzical typewriter" would now appear in the *Times*, the article stated, six days a week, page 1, starting the following Sunday.[15]

The rival *Examiner* took note of their new opposition. The following Sunday, the day Murray's first column was to appear, the *Examiner* ran an article across the top of its sports section championing its own columnist, Durslag. "Durslag's Column Now a National Feature" screamed the headline. The article heaped on the praise of Durslag, with comments from William Randolph Hearst Jr.[16] and sports editor Ben Woolbert, who let readers know that "Mel's column never sends you to the dictionary. He puts simple words together. It's not just the words. It's HOW he puts them together." Get the real sports dope here, the *Examiner* was telling its readers, not from some ex-*Time* man from back East with a multisyllabic vocabulary. The article went on to say that Mel Durslag could now be read regularly at all Hearst newspapers throughout the land, but the focus would still be squarely on Southern California.[17] What Durslag later called a "friendly rivalry" had been formally announced.

"Let's Dot Some *I*'s"

In the winter of 1961, there was no shortage of fodder for a sports columnist. The Los Angeles Lakers, with a rookie named Jerry West and an established star named Elgin Baylor, were in the midst of their first season in the city. The California Angels were preparing to open training camp as a Major League Baseball team for the first time, and the Los Angeles Dodgers were preparing for the fourth season in the city, and their last at the Los Angeles Coliseum. (Dodger Stadium at Chavez Ravine was under construction, not without controversy, and would be ready for opening day of 1962.) Heavyweight boxing champion Floyd Patterson was preparing for his third bout with challenger

Ingemar Johansson of Sweden, with whom he had split the previous two matches. And at the track, the Kentucky Derby prep season was just getting under
way. To announce his newfound presence in the *Times,* Murray chose to touch
on all of these subjects, and many more. Running down the left side of the
sports page, with a pencil drawing picturing an erudite Murray with thick-
rimmed glasses, a bow tie, and the smallest trace of a grin on his face, his intro-
ductory column was a series of one-liners about Murray, his outlook, and the
Los Angeles sports scene. He wrote:

> I have been urged by my friends—all of whom mean well—to begin writing
> in this space without introducing myself, as if I have been standing here all the
> while only you haven't noticed. But I don't think I'll do that. I think I'll start off
> by telling you a little about myself and what I believe in. That way, we can start
> to fight right away.
>
> First off, I'm against the bunt in baseball—unless they start batting against
> the ball John McGraw batted against. The last time the bunt won a game, Frank
> Chance was a rookie.
>
> I think the eight-point touchdown in football has had it. It's added nothing to
> the game unless, of course, you count the extra bookkeeping.
>
> I was gratified by the reaction to the announcement Jim Murray was to write a
> sports column, an immediate and interested "Who??!" Mel Durslag did throw a
> bouquet, though. I'll read the card as soon as I take the brick out.
>
> I came to Los Angeles in 1944 (the smog and I hit town together and neither
> one of us has been run out despite the best efforts of public-spirited citizens)
> and my biggest sports disappointment was the 1955 Swaps-Nashua race, which
> I helped to arrange. I have never believed Bill Shoemaker was properly tied on
> his mount that day when they sprang the barrier. But I will ask Bill—and believe
> what he says because his next lie will be his first.[18]

The tenor of his column was to become apparent to his readers right from
the starting gate. His subject matter for the first month included very little analysis or description of current sporting events or teams. Instead, Murray employed that "quizzical typewriter" that his editors had hyped. His early columns
presented a slightly off-kilter view of secondary sports issues, if they could be
considered issues at all, such as how many vowels a baseball player needs in his
last name to be successful, or how a computer would perform if given the job of
managing a professional baseball team. Instead of the top sports stars, Murray's
early columns more often focused on marginal characters on the fringes of the
sports world: perpetually broke horse players, crooked fight promoters, Minor
League Baseball veterans, or second-rate club golfers. And they were packed
with humorous anecdotes, many going back decades, and a generous helping of

sports (and world) history. His goal was apparent. He was writing to entertain; informing was secondary.

Times readers reacted strongly, some positively, some less so. A reader named Craig Barker wrote the paper to say Murray had just lost one reader because of his "attempt at the Pulitzer Prize for humorous sports writing." Another reader wrote to let Murray know he was not at *Sports Illustrated* anymore, so he could stop writing about "fox hunting, underwater polo and Indian wrestling." Others demanded more baseball writing (Murray responded by saying he would write about baseball when somebody was playing baseball) and fewer history and English lessons. And, of course, he began to hear the familiar request that he go back where he came from. "If you distort the facts and resort to sarcasm, we'd all consider you would be better off back east," wrote reader Robert G. Fitch, who said he spoke for all Dodger fans. Murray received more than one hundred letters of praise in the first month as well, however, including many from his celebrity friends, such as George Kennedy and Frank Capra.[19]

Early on, the pressures of filing six columns a week, and of finding a voice and direction for his new position, weighed on Murray. He had already consulted comedian Jack Benny, someone he felt understood how to create a public persona. Benny told Murray to be himself, and to let his readers see his true personality. The comedian engraved a money clip for Murray with similar sentiments, which Murray carried with him for years afterward.[20]

Only one month in, he reported that the column had already begun to consume his life. It was an observation he would make for the rest of his life. He tried to sweet-talk Gerry, telling her she had not lost a husband but gained a columnist. He said he had already become essentially worthless at any task beyond his all-encompassing chore of filling the column. Like all columnists, he wrote, he was now "a guy who would starve to death on a desert island because he'd spend all his time looking for a Western Union to send the funny line he just thought up for the place."[21]

Boys of Summer

As the Southern California heat index began to rise and Murray grew more comfortable with the life of a columnist, he began to develop his own personal sports beat, which included many of the haunts he was familiar with as a longtime Los Angeles sports fan. Coming up with six subjects a week was a difficult task, even in a sports-obsessed newspaper market like Los Angeles. (Durslag was still required to produce seven columns a week at the *Examiner*.)[22] He found he could get a column or two out of a day at Hollywood Park or Santa Anita racetracks. A major fight card at the Olympic Auditorium would produce one or two preview columns, usually profiles on fighters, trainers, or other assorted boxing riffraff, as well as a recap column the morning after the event. A short trip to Las Vegas for a golf tournament or a boxing card would produce two or three columns, and a trip to Palm Springs, just a ninety-minute drive from Los Angeles, for Angels spring training offered unlimited subject matter. The remaining days could be filled in with think pieces, straight humor columns, and the odds and ends of the sports scene (and his own life) for which he could conceive an angle. In one two-week stretch in the dog days of summer, before the baseball pennant races heated up, he wrote about spending a day with a lifeguard at the beach in Malibu, taking his son Teddy fishing in his new dinghy ("the S.S. Nervous Wreck"), comparing quotations from famous historical and sports figures, and the national chess championships. "Watching a chess match has all the pulsating excitement of watching a pitcher warm up, or a hair fall. . . . It's like watching grass not grow," he wrote.[23]

But baseball was still the national pastime in America in the early 1960s, and both Murray's readers and his editors wanted to see it prominently played in his column. He devoted significant time and space to the Angels, who were struggling through their inaugural season in the American League, and the Dodgers, who seemed to be headed to the World Series, only to give away the pennant on that fateful road trip Murray took with the team in August. The national issue that dominated sports pages across the country in the late summer of 1961, however, was the chase for Babe Ruth's home-run record and the infamous Ford Frick asterisk. By July, New York Yankee sluggers Roger Maris and Mickey Mantle were far ahead of the pace that Babe Ruth followed when he set the record of sixty home runs in a single season, a number that had attained mythical status in baseball. Ruth was a baseball legend, and all that he symbolized about the golden age of the sport was intertwined with the magical number of sixty home runs, set in 1927. For 1961, the baseball season had been expanded from 154 games, which it was when Ruth played, to 162 games. On July 17, Frick, the commissioner of baseball and a close friend and ghostwriter of Ruth's, handed down an official ruling: if it took Maris or Mantle more than 154 games to break the record, it would go into the holy baseball record books with an asterisk. That way, Ruth's renowned number could live on.[24]

Baseball was a house divided. Everybody hated somebody: Frick, Maris, Mantle, or Ruth. Or all of the above. Murray weighed in for the first time on July 25. He took aim at Frick. "Ford Frick isn't the worst commissioner of baseball in history, but he's in the photo. I make him no worse than third place," he wrote. He pointed out the faulty logic in Frick's argument that a new record would be illegitimate because it was set under different conditions. Where do you draw the line? Murray asked rhetorically. Should modern hitters have to face the same number of spitballs that Ruth faced? Hit as many home runs into the wind as Ruth did? Hit as many home runs to left field as

Ruth did? He wrote: "If some batter hits 61 home runs, THAT is going to be the record, as far as baseball is concerned. . . . That ought to satisfy Frick. If it doesn't, he can take his fat pension and retire and become personal custodian of Ruth's record."[25]

The column brought the inevitable letters accusing Murray of being a Yankee hater and much worse.[26] Frick's decision further hyped a home-run chase that had already captured the imagination of the nation. In September, Murray joined the legions of baseball writers covering the story in Chicago to see the carnival for himself. Maris had hit fifty-six home runs at that point, Mantle fifty-three.[27] The games had become a sideshow. Fans, even those of opposing teams, expected a home run every at bat. The stands emptied after each time Mantle and Maris batted, and the home team pitcher was booed for striking them out. There were so many reporters around, Murray wrote, "if we were wearing sheets it would look like a lynching."[28] The 1961 home-run chase was, to that point in time, the high-water mark for sports-media feeding frenzies, with television raising the ante, and the players, the reporters, and baseball management were not prepared for the storm. The Yankees organization offered Mantle and Maris no protection and provided no buffer from the media; reporters, most of whom they did not know, followed them to breakfast, to the hotel, to the stadium, wherever they could find them.[29] On one occasion, Murray surprised some members of the New York press by getting an exclusive interview with Mantle. He woke the moody, hard-drinking Mantle in his hotel room at eight o'clock with a phone call, which the New York writers assumed meant Murray would soon be met with a string of expletives and then a dial tone. Murray, though, used a little psychology to smooth the waters. Mantle, who hated the way the home-run chase had pitted two teammates against each other, was convinced to talk when Murray explained his angle. Murray told Mantle he wanted to write about how Mantle and Maris were about to break the all-time tandem home-run record, which at the time was held by Babe Ruth and Lou Gehrig.[30]

Murray soon grew bored of the chase—both Maris's and Mantle's chase of the record and the media's chase of Maris and Mantle. As would become his pattern, he was loath to follow the crowd of reporters. Pack journalism was not in his nature. He had joined the Yankees press corps in Chicago in mid-September and followed them to Detroit, where the team finally cut off access to Maris (Mantle had fallen behind and was largely out of the race by then).

In the visiting dressing room, the reporters sent a delegation to Yankee manager Ralph Houk to speak to Maris. Houk blew up at them. "It's my clubhouse and I'll run it any damn way I please!" he shouted at them.

Maris was a reticent midwesterner who had neither the skill nor the desire to win over the fans or the media. By late September, the immense pressure had gotten to him. With Mantle out of the picture, he was now the sole focus of the press and the fans. He developed rashes, and his hair began to fall out.[31] Murray was sympathetic to his plight and confessed to be rooting for him to break the record: "The fence, the pitchers, the commissioner of baseball, the ghost of Ruth will be picketed out in right field for Maris—the toughest shift in history. I hope he hits the ball right through all of them and into that glass case in Cooperstown," he wrote.[32]

Maris hit his sixtieth home run on September 26 and went into the last game of the season, on October 1, with one last shot at the record, albeit a record now with an asterisk. By then, Murray had come off the road, and Frank Finch was in New York to record history for the *Times*. In the fourth inning, Maris drilled a fast ball off Boston Red Sox pitcher Tracy Stollard into the right-field stands at Yankee Stadium.[33] He had accomplished a nearly impossible feat, but the record was tarnished, and the press was slow to let up. After the game, a radio reporter asked him if he had thought of Mickey Mantle as he was rounding the bases after the home run.[34] Murray put the feat in perspective the following day, declaring that Maris's accomplishment was far greater than that of Ruth: "Ruth was not battling history as well as the pitchers. And the commissioner of baseball did not level a brush-back pitch at him in the middle of it. He did not have to play with one eye on the calendar. . . . Ruth coasted in. Maris clawed his way in. That's why I'm glad he made it."[35]

Stirring the Pot

The very next month, Murray ventured into an area far more emotionally charged than home runs and asterisks. He traveled to Birmingham, Alabama, to cover a football game between Georgia Tech and the University of Alabama and in the process inserted himself into the growing struggle for civil rights. The University of Alabama was a football powerhouse in the early 1960s, under the leadership of head coach Paul "Bear" Bryant. Bryant, forty-eight years old at the time, was a gruff, hard-drinking Arkansan known to browbeat reporters and do far worse to his players. He had come to Alabama three years before and quickly turned the program into a winner. He had become a hero to whites across the South.[36] The Crimson Tide football team was all white, like the entire student body of the University of Alabama. Segregation was strictly enforced. What drew Murray to Alabama was the brewing controversy over the upcoming Rose Bowl, which was supposed to feature two of the top college football teams in the nation. Both Alabama and UCLA were undefeated, and each was considered a likely candidate for the Rose Bowl. UCLA featured black players, however, and the team was threatening to boycott if Alabama was invited to play in the game.

In 1961, the civil rights movement was gaining steam, and to say the white establishment in the South was on edge is an understatement. The possibility for violence and conflict was present whenever the subject turned to race. The Congress of Racial Equality, a growing civil rights organization, had begun conducting "freedom rides" in the Deep South in the spring of that year. Groups of blacks and whites moving together would deliberately enter segregated restaurants and stores. They were often met by violent mobs and ended up beaten and jailed. Earlier in the year, in Anniston, Alabama, less than forty miles east of Birmingham, a Greyhound bus in which a group of freedom riders had been traveling had been burned. A mob tried to hold the riders on the bus while it burned, and when the riders escaped the vehicle, they were viciously beaten.[37]

It was in this highly charged racial atmosphere that Murray came to Bryant's hotel room in Birmingham's Bankhead Hotel. A soft rain fell outside the window as Bryant leaned back on his bed and began fielding questions from the assembled press.

"Coach Bryant," Murray asked, "what did you think of the announcement out of UCLA that the colored players would not take the field against your team if it got to the Rose Bowl?"

Bryant thought for a moment. "Oh, I would have nothing to say about that. Neither will the university, I'm sure," he responded.

The hotel room went silent as the reporters shuffled papers and looked at the floor.

A local reporter had turned beet red, Murray noticed. The reporter gathered himself and spoke. "Tell them West Coast nigger lovers to go lick your boots, Bear," he growled, his eyes fixed on Murray.

After the meeting broke up, Murray was approached by two southern reporters, Fred Russell of the *Nashville Banner* and Bill Lumpkin of the *Birmingham Post-Herald*. "Forget the remark of that knot-head," Lumpkin told him. "That's not the attitude."

Murray's column the following day was a screed against the racial bigotry of the South. Not a word about the Georgia Tech–Alabama game was mentioned. "It doesn't make any sense," he wrote. "It's worse than un-American. It's un-human. The water fountains in the airport jar you. 'Colored only.' The pretense is that the world is divided into people and non-people. If you don't notice them, eat, drink, or go to school with them, they're not there." Murray went on to write that Russell and Lumpkin had told him that the Alabama football community expected the boycott. "It does seem short sighted. Seem like they're pushing us back in our place and how can this help?" Lumpkin asked Murray, who agreed with the point in print and argued against the boycott. He wrote, "The tragedy I have found in Birmingham is that the bullies of white supremacy have first cowed and terrified their own people. Let's not force them back in those bed-sheets. At least not unless we're sure that's the way they want it."[38]

As Murray now knew would happen, his column in the *Times* was mailed back to Alabama, with the expected results. He was called a "Communist Red Moscow Rat," accused of having a "Negro father," and threatened that he would be tossed from the window. Upon being forwarded the column by a reader, John Bloomer, managing editor of the *Birmingham News,* wrote, "Mr. Murray has a sophomoric intellect that, in this case, is far from amusing."[39] Murray was surprised, however, to see that the outpouring of abuse was smaller than he had expected. He received letters of support from both *Times* readers and some Alabamans. Other *Times* readers, however, wrote to tell him to stick to sports on the sports page. This was something he clearly had no intention of doing:

> I am a journalist, of sorts. I went down to a state in the South which also be-longs to the 20th century. Only, it not only doesn't like it, it doesn't know it. Or won't admit it. A writer—even a sportswriter—is supposed to cover news.
>
> The real news of the game I covered had very little to do with the score. It had to do with the smell of roses and the color of the players. That's what I wrote about. That's what this business is about. That's the way I intend to play it.[40]

Alabama ended up playing in the Sugar Bowl in Louisiana instead of the Rose Bowl. UCLA faced Minnesota in the 1962 Rose Bowl, so the threatened boycott never materialized. Eighteen months later, the federal government forced the integration of the University of Alabama,[41] but Bryant's football squad remained all white. What eventually forced integration of the Crimson Tide team was when bowl committees became uncomfortable inviting segre-gated southern teams to the party. Alabama and the rest of the Southeastern Conference desegregated by the end of the decade (Alabama's first black player joined the team in 1970). Murray traveled back to Alabama in 1970, this time to Tuscaloosa, home of the University of Alabama, when the Tide first agreed to host a team with black players, USC. He was going to the South again not to see who would win the game, he wrote: "The point of the game will be Reason, Democracy, Hope. The real winner will be the South. It'll be their first since the second day at Gettysburg, or maybe, The Wilderness."[42]

City Assassin

While Murray was doing his part for the civil-rights struggle, the wheels were in motion for a chain of events that would eventually bring his column to newspaper readers across the United States. Prior to his trip to Alabama, he had gone to New York and Cincinnati to cover the 1961 World Series. The Reds had overtaken the Dodgers in the National League but were overmatched against the American League champion Yankees, and the series was a glum, one-sided affair, which New York won in five games. In Cincinnati, Murray witnessed the impact of his lighthearted attack on the city just a few months before. His photo ran on the front page of the *Cincinnati Post and Times-Star,* with the tag "most hated man in Cincinnati." He was hung in effigy in downtown Cincinnati, and fans held up signs at Crosley Field that read "Boo Murray!"[43]

The impact was also not lost on the *Post and Times-Star.* The newspaper received more than 250 pieces of mail when it published one of Murray's attacks on the city, more than had ever been received for a single article. *Post and Times-Star* sports editor Pat Harmon contacted the *Los Angeles Times* to inquire about publishing Murray on a syndicated basis. The *Times* turned him down, telling him they did not feel Murray was syndicate material.[44]

McCulloch, however, felt otherwise. He called Rex Barley, then the top executive with *Los Angeles Times* Syndication, and recommended Murray.

"I haven't read him," Barley said.

"Well, you better start," McCulloch urged.

Barley took samples of Murray's column with him on his next sales trip to pitch *Times* editorial content for syndication. He returned with ten newspapers signed on to publish Murray, quite a good haul for a first-time effort.[45]

To that point, Murray had sprinkled in a paragraph here and there poking fun at cities. Now, he made it the centerpiece of his act. In the winter of 1962, he stepped up his travel, and he now began taking road trips in part for their sports value, part for the destination itself. He tagged along on a midwestern swing with the Lakers, which brought him to Detroit; St. Louis; Morgantown, West Virginia; and Dayton, Ohio. Murray took his best shot night after night. Detroit, he wrote, "was like staying up all night on a cake of ice, then taking a cold shower upon arising." In St. Louis, he wrote, the city had a bond issue with the campaign slogan "Progress or Decay," and decay won in a landslide. West Virginia was so poor, he wrote, "it not only didn't know the depression was over, it didn't even notice when it started."[46] Dayton, for some reason, got off scot-free.

Soon, cities began to return fire. The *West Union Record* of West Union, West Virginia, published an editorial in response to Murray's visit: "We have been assailed by the lowest form of the writing profession—the sports hack. The author of this piece of flagrant misrepresentation is a bespectacled Irishman named Jim Murray who looks more like a fugitive from the roof gutter of a post office than he does an Irishman." The article went on to say Murray looked like a gargoyle and was drunk on weak beer when he wrote the column, and it was their fond hope that Murray would eventually starve to death. Murray reprinted the entire editorial in the *Times* and clearly enjoyed the exchange: "Well, Mr. West Virginia *West Union Record,* you're a brave man and a journalist of the old school and I salute you. I wouldn't dare reprint your editorial if it weren't about me. Mr. Chandler and his lawyers wouldn't let me. But tell me: How do you describe Castro?" he wrote.[47]

Durslag, at the *Examiner,* watched the appearance of Murray's city columns and thought it a brilliant way to fill that ever-present empty white space on the sports page. "Jim didn't start out young, so to catch up, he made some noise with the knocking of cities," he recalled. "You see, when you knock a city, you set up two columns for yourself: one, you knock the city, second, you hear from the mayor, and you say 'Boy, is the mayor of Pittsburgh mad at me!'"[48]

Durslag was not the only one aware of Murray's neat trick. Reporters, editors, and even residents in other cities began to be aware of the Murray treatment. Just a few weeks after the Laker road trip, Murray accompanied the Los Angeles Blades, a minor-league ice hockey team, to Edmonton, Alberta, Canada, and Spokane, Washington. A minor-league ice hockey road trip would not ordinarily attract a page 1 sports columnist, but for Murray it was too good to pass up. When he arrived in Edmonton, it was forty below, and it felt like "God had left the door open."[49]

But when he got to Spokane, a delegation of city officials met him at the airport, begging him to rip their city and make them famous. "Listen," a sportswriter from the Spokane newspaper said. "You can say it's the biggest collection of used bricks in the world. They ought to knock it down and ship it to North Hollywood for fireplaces. How's that?"

"Terrible," Murray told him.

The sportswriter tried again. "You can say that on Saturday night, there's nothing to do but watch the trains come in."

"But I've never been here on a Saturday night," Murray protested.

"Who cares?" the sportswriter responded. "I've been here so many Saturday nights it makes me sick."[50]

Murray began to hear it in the press box, too. Bill Christine was a sportswriter for the *St. Louis Globe-Democrat* in the early 1960s when he first met Murray. He would join the *Times* many years later, and the two would become close friends. "If Jim came to a town, and he wouldn't write about the town right off, somebody in the press box would say 'When are you going to knock our town?'" Christine remembered. "It was almost a Don Rickles thing. If Rickles didn't make fun of you, you weren't anybody. Well, if Murray didn't knock your town, then there was something wrong with your town."[51]

Murray enjoyed riling people up and was reaping the benefits. Each month, more newspapers were requesting his column. After one year in syndication, he was appearing in more than fifty newspapers nationwide. He could be read in Boston, Chicago, Las Vegas, St. Louis, and dozens of smaller cities in between. (The *Cincinnati Post and Times-Star,* first to request his column, was now a satisfied customer.)[52] There were always people lacking a sense of humor who were lurking, however, ready to take the fun out of the whole enterprise. In August 1962, another Dodger road trip brought him to Pittsburgh, which he proceeded to eviscerate in print: "They cleaned the smoke out a few years ago and 600,000 people pointed to the sun in dismay and said 'what's that?'" And: "You can tell a native Pittsburgher because he looks as if he's just been rescued from a cave." And: "They have a gastronomical equivalent of silicosis here which is known as a 'Kolbassi' sandwich, samples of which were sent to the FBI and identified as botulism in a casing."[53] Murray was in Cincinnati by the time the column ran in the *Times* and made its way back to Pittsburgh. The mayor of Pittsburgh had spoken out against Murray and had seen no humor in the situation. He demanded an apology, while insulting Los Angeles at the same time. A Pittsburgh television station had offered to pay Murray's way if he would fly back to Pittsburgh and come on the air to explain himself. ("What made me suspicious is he didn't say anything about return transportation," Murray wrote.)[54] The angry letters poured in to the *Times*. "What an ignorant man [Murray] is! He certainly demonstrated his poor sportsmanship in the crude and slanderous article," wrote H. K. Baum of Pittsburgh. Then, in the press box at Crosley Field in Cincinnati, he was told he had a phone call. A caller from Pittsburgh was on the line and said he and several of his friends were going to find Murray when he came to New York (the Dodgers were scheduled to play the New York Mets a few days later) and "have a talk." Murray called the FBI, but was told he was on his own. "He hasn't violated any federal law—yet. If he kills me, of course, that's another matter," Murray wrote.[55]

The Mets games went off with no violence, at least against Murray. It was not the last time a reader would fail to see the humor and threaten some type of retribution. (A few years later, board members at Churchill Downs racetrack considered denying Murray press credentials to the Kentucky Derby after he wrote that Louisville, where the track is located, "smelled like a wet bar rag.")[56] He would continue to take aim at cities from Warsaw, Poland, to DuQuoin, Illinois, for the rest of his career, but never to the extent that he did in his first few years writing the column. He weathered the vicious letters and the humorless city officials through the years and mistakenly gained a reputation, in some areas, as a mean-spirited writer, which he was not. For the most part, his vitriol was aimed at places and institutions, not at individuals. But most took it in good humor. Early in 1962, after a St. Louis sports editor opined that Murray wrote his city material for commercial reasons, he offered a response that summed up his philosophy behind the columns:

> If you care, I'll tell you my thinking behind it. Some years ago, when even President Eisenhower couldn't go there, a sports-writing colleague of mine went

to Moscow to cover a track meet. He was the only guy in a whole magazine empire who could be cleared to go there. I couldn't wait to read the copy.

Know what it was about? A track meet. So help me. For all the clues in the prose, it might as well have been taking place in Compton. I don't know who was at fault—editors, censors or whoever. But I remember I was never so disappointed in my life.

I resolved right then and there never to get so afflicted with press-box myopia that I would not comment on the surroundings if I found them as interesting as the event. I propose to continue to do so.[57]

Murray's profile rose swiftly. The *Times* syndication department aggressively marketed him to newspapers, with tremendous success. Murray received half of the proceeds, which, within a few years, would bring him around fifty thousand dollars a year, on top of his *Times* salary.[58] And the national visibility led to recognition from his peers. In the fall of 1961, his old friends at *Time* published an article acknowledging his "wry humor" and "iconoclastic approach." "Murray has built a reputation and following that, in just six months, qualifies him as one of the best sportswriters in the U.S.," the article declared.[59] He was nominated for the National Sportscasters and Sportswriters Association national sportswriting award, along with Red Smith of the *New York Herald-Tribune* and Furman Bisher of the *Atlanta Journal.* And a resolution was read by the Los Angeles City Council declaring that Murray had "aided in the growth of Los Angeles to acquire the status of sports capital of the world." The recognition, combined with growing comfort in his routine, gave him a more positive outlook about his decision to become a sports columnist than he had exhibited in his early days at the *Times.* On the anniversary of his joining the *Times,* he wrote that being a columnist still felt like riding a tiger: "The only trouble a year later is that the tiger is beginning to look friendly."[60]

6

A National Presence, 1963–1969

Dear Mr. Murray:

I used to hate to get up in the morning. There seemed to be nothing worth looking forward to.

This has all changed since you arrived at the L.A. Times. Now I leap out of my wife's bed and rush for your column.

This is quite a tribute to your literary prowess, for my wife happens to be a very beautiful woman.

Sincerely,
Groucho Marx [March 17, 1961]

Entrenched

Though he was really just a few steps into what would be a thirty-eight-year trek as a sports columnist, the fact was that by the time the calendar turned to 1963, Jim Murray had already climbed to the very pinnacle of his profession. The second half of his lifetime would include numerous challenges, but very few of them would be of a professional nature. In baseball terms, he was a forty-three-year-old phenom who skipped the minor leagues and went straight to starting in the All-Star Game. His superiors at the *Times* had quickly recognized his impact and promoted it. As a result, he already was one of the two most recognizable names to appear regularly in the pages of the *Times,* the other being city columnist Jack Smith.[1] His syndication numbers were escalating. In his second year as a columnist, he had already been nominated for national sportswriter of the year, and he would shortly take over ownership of that award and not relinquish it for more than a decade. And, probably most important to Murray, he had earned the respect of his peers across the country. The denizens of the press box admired him and vied for his time.[2] To the public Jim Murray was now an established brand.

Much of the cause of Murray's rapid rise to newspaper stardom can be traced to a concurrent rise that was being experienced by his employer. Otis Chandler's declaration in 1958 that the *Times* would match its overwhelming financial achievement editorially was beginning to come to fruition. The newspaper had gone from an extremely profitable but underperforming regional news organization to the editorial voice of the western United States. In the 1960s, with its newfound focus on editorial quality, the *Times* began earning its status as one of America's elite newspapers. The newspaper earned a Pulitzer Prize in 1960 for exposing narcotics trafficking in Southern California and won two more Pulitzers for coverage of the 1966 Watts Riots, a series of uprisings in Los Angeles that resulted in thirty-four deaths and more than a thousand injuries. Cartoonist Paul Conrad joined the staff and began winning Pulitzers, and by the end of the decade, the paper would win the prize for local and international coverage as well.[3]

The editorial achievement gave the *Times* the cachet to begin attracting top talent from across the country. The newfound reputation of the newspaper combined with the allure of Southern California brought the *Times* a slew of applications from the Ivy League and an infusion of new talent that further invigorated the push toward excellence.[4] And the *Times* was now experiencing even greater financial success. What had always been a profitable enterprise now reached stratospheric levels. It had become the largest media conglomerate in the West, and it published more advertising than any other daily newspaper in the world for twenty-five straight years.

The *Times* leadership, from Otis Chandler on down, made sure the company's winnings were put back on the table and used in pursuit of editorial glory. *Times* writers and photographers would go to the ends of the earth to pursue a story, always flying first class, dining at five-star restaurants, and hopping from continent to continent to chase down the slimmest of leads.[5] It was a tremendous pulpit from which to preach, and for Murray it allowed him to travel freely in pursuit of any story or subject. And it put his writing in front of millions of readers, in Southern California and across the nation.

What readers could expect was a column that was different from anything else on the sports page. His writing had a comic slant from the outset, and his sense of humor became his calling card. While other sports columnists may include a joke or two in a column, Murray would rile off two dozen one-liners in a row. Many of his humorous profiles read like a full set by a stage come-dian. The laugh lines, however, would feed seamlessly into the overall portrait Murray was painting. He would often take the most arresting characteristic of a subject and set off on a riff that would go on for several inches of his column. A Murray humor column had the feel of a Borscht Belt routine, with the laughs launched rapid-fire, one landing as the next was being launched. Echoes of W. C. Fields, or of comedians of the day, such as Rodney Dangerfield or Murray's friend Don Rickles,[6] could be heard in the margins. Frank Howard, the six-foot-seven, 275-pound outfielder for the Dodgers, was a regular subject in the early '60s:

> Frank Howard is so big, he wasn't born, he was founded. He's only two stories shorter than the Istanbul Hilton. When he falls asleep on an airplane, which he does all the time, he has to bend his knees. Either that, or hang landing lights on his feet. He's the most awesome public monument this side of Mt. Rushmore. It would take a fly a week to walk across his wrists. Mickey Rooney can only com-municate with him by phone. He's Gulliver in a baseball suit. If he shakes hands with you, you have to call a plumber to get loose. And Blue Cross has an auto-matic cancellation clause if he slaps you on the back. You get the feeling he's not actually a man, just an unreasonable facsimile.[7]

Murray's routines in print were not mean-spirited or antagonistic; rather, he would pinpoint the humor in a situation or a subject, hone in on it, and then, in his gentle, sarcastic manner, fire away. As Murray was well known and well read by many in show business, comedians appreciated his writing abilities. He was offered the opportunity to write jokes for performers several times.[8] Steve Allen, comedian and first host of *The Tonight Show,* wrote, "The connection between humor and sports has long intrigued me. One of my favorite Ameri-can humorists is Jim Murray of the *L.A. Times.* God, what a gift he has for the funny line. And yet, simply because his field is sports, the so-called experts in humor never bring up his name when the subject of comic writing is under discussion."[9]

The more affection Murray had for a subject, it seemed, the more humor he would use in his portrayal of it. The Los Angeles sports scene of the 1960s had no shortage of sports personalities, and Murray did his part to create their personae in his column. Another favorite subject was Jerry West of the Los An-geles Lakers. Murray would take what his readers could see on the field of play and explain what it meant in the Murray universe:

> He wears the perpetually startled expression of a guy who just heard a dog talk. He doesn't walk anywhere—he darts. He has the quickest hands and feet

ever seen on a guy without a police record. If they put a cap on him sideways and turned him loose on the streets of London, there wouldn't be a wallet in town by nightfall.

He can hang in the air like Mary Poppins. It would take a week to hang him. He could play Peter Pan without wires. Some night he's going to go up for a jump shot in the first period—and they're going to have to get the fire department to get him down.

His nose has been broken so many times, he sneezes through his ears. Cigarette smoke would come out of his nostrils in corkscrew patterns. His septum is so deviated, he's breathing YESTERDAY'S air. He goes through life with such a s-w-o-o-s-h that there are only a few people certain what color he is.

He's such a bundle of exploding nervous energy that by the end of the season, they don't need a chest X-ray. They just hold him up to the light. If you put a picture on him, you could send him as a post card. Jerry wasn't born, he was pressed. A steamroller would miss most of him.[10]

Murray's humor went beyond one-liners, and he would often use his column to create a set piece with which to satirize that day's subject. Organizing his column as a movie scene with fictional dialogue was a favorite way for Murray to set himself up for laughs. These articles often read like the script to a classic Abbot and Costello vaudeville routine. Readers could be treated to a column-length interview between number-one football draft pick "Stoop" Nagel (a star placekick holder) conducted by broadcaster Triple Tongue Tannenbaum,[11] or maybe read fake dialogue from actual people, like a scene between Dodger manager Walter Alston and star pitcher Sandy Koufax, in which faux Koufax recites Shakespeare while faux Alston implores him to concentrate on the next batter.[12]

Murray would often pick up on an odd quote or circumstance and use it to build an entire humor column. A comment by New York Yankees manager Ralph Houk blaming failure on injuries could lead to a column where Robert E. Lee, Hannibal, and Custer find excuses for losing historic battles.[13] Or he might choose to fill his entire space with baseball puns: "Supposing the Dodgers Jim Lefebvre gets traded to the Reds? If he refuses to go, does that make him Scarlett Lefebvre?"[14] And of course, entire columns would be written at his own expense, whether it be his ineptitude on the golf course, his inability to fix things around the house, or his dreams of athletic prowess in which he battles with the heroes of the day.

The organization of a Murray column also often defied readers' expectations. Murray might spend three hundred words invoking military or sports history, or write half a column about the general wackiness of relief pitchers or referees, before first addressing the actual subject of a profile. Durslag, writing for the competing *Herald-Examiner,* noted the unique structure: "Very often, you see, they'd start him on page 1, and jump him, and you'd get down to the jump and you'd still not know what he was writing about. When you'd jump, he'd finally get into his subject. And he wrote very long, totally undisciplined."[15] The *Times*, however, ran with the most editorial space of any newspaper in the country,[16] and editors in the sports department were loath to touch Murray's copy.

Another Murray trademark was the lack of quotes. Whereas most sports columnists used generous helpings of direct quotations from their sources, Murray strenuously avoided them. The reason, Murray often said, was that "I can write better than they can talk." His readers never had to wade through the cliché'd statements that athletes and coaches regularly spouted in the locker room and sportswriters arduously recorded and played back in their articles. Only the most articulate, or perhaps inarticulate, of sources could find their exact words in a Murray column.

Humor was the linchpin of his writing, but another way his talents as a writer showed themselves was in his ability to elucidate the cultural and historical significance of the places, events, and people he wrote about. He could reveal his own personal affection for a subject, while not slipping into reverence or veneration. Failure, loss, and the seedy underbelly of sports held more interest for Murray and offered more opportunity to create literature. The Kentucky Derby, one of his favorite events, provided annual fodder:

> They all make it for the Derby. The guys looking for a pocket to pick, the "stoopers" checking over the ticket debris for a pasteboard that's still alive—and then up in the boxes are the Whitneys and the Vanderbilts and those kind of people.
>
> They know about horses and whiskey and long jailhouse nights here and they linger for the Derby, they don't throw out the anchor. Tomorrow, they'll be standing in line at a boardinghouse shower again with a towel over their arm and a cake of soap and a toothbrush in their hand, and they'll have to walk a hot mare for the week's room rent. Breakfast will be coffee and a sinker.
>
> The elite will be neither in the boxes nor the track next week, but for one day Louisville gets a tiara in the hair, and it smells of perfume and mink instead of bourbon and sweat.
>
> It's the most uniquely American event of all. It is redolent of Stephen Foster, who died in a waterfront flophouse, and who left America his bittersweet airs of magnolia and losers, and the sounds of banjos in the sick-sweet night downwind of the cotton.[17]

Journalism historians often view American sportswriting through the prism of two rival camps that evolved in the first decades of the twentieth century. Cultural historian Murray Sperber, among others, has called this split the

"Gee-Whiz" and "Aw-Nuts" camps.[18] The former were the shameless promoters of athletics, and the latter were more skeptical about commercialism and sports, functioning as prophets chronicling the excesses in athletics. In effect, the former were advocacy journalists and the latter watchdog journalists. Murray, well aware of his sportswriting predecessors, aligned himself firmly with the "Aw-Nuts" writers. Damon Runyon and Ring Lardner, early-twentieth-century writers associated with the "Aw-Nuts" camp, were heroes of his, often referenced in his columns. To Murray, finding drama in sports was different from manufacturing heroes. "Thank goodness, there are a lot of readers who don't need larger-than-life heroics all the time. They can take their sport with a squirt of humor and a twist of irreverence," Murray wrote.[19]

With the rapid rise of his reputation and the reach of his column, Murray began pitching the idea of a compilation of his greatest hits after only a year on the job. Red Smith and Joe Palmer, newspaper sports columnists whose bylines ran in many more markets across the country, had convinced publishers to release books in recent years, the majority of which sat on the shelves. Publishers were wary. In 1962, Doubleday turned Murray down. "A few easy dollars for the columnist and a loss for the publisher," Doubleday managing editor Tim Seldes surmised at the time. "A very regretful 'no' because this lad really does write amusingly well."[20]

Three years later, Doubleday had changed its mind about the amusing lad, who was now much more established. The company released *The Best of Jim Murray* in January 1965 and had enough sales success that a sequel, *The Sporting World of Jim Murray,* was released four years later.[21] The book was praised by reviewers, many of whom were friends or admirers. "Murray makes his work look easy, which is what Joe DiMaggio used to do," wrote Martin Kane in *Sports Illustrated.* Murray was typically humble yet proud upon the release of the first book. "It ain't Dickens. It's shorter than 'Gone With the Wind.' It hasn't got any sex, any four-letter words. . . . It's written by a very nice fellow who needs the money."[22]

Bedouins in the Night

It was a balmy eighty degrees on Christmas Day 1960 in Los Angeles when Murray climbed aboard an eastbound plane for the first extended road trip of his sportswriting career. The itinerary included six chilly northern cities in nine days where the Lakers, new that year to California, would be spending the holiday season. It was probably not the most enticing yuletide schedule for the snow-and-cold-averse Murray, but it would signal the beginning of a relationship with the team that would be more intimate and personal than his association with any of the other teams he covered. The 1960 holiday trip produced the final article Murray wrote for *Sports Illustrated*. By the time it was in print, under the title "A Trip for Ten Tall Men," in the January 30, 1961, issue, he had left the magazine and was preparing to join the *Times*. But the friends he made on that trip and the style of coverage he employed would influence his basketball writing for years to come.

The National Basketball Association was not even a decade old when the Lakers arrived in Los Angeles in 1960. The team had started off as the Detroit Gems, purchased during a surge in interest in professional basketball immediately after World War II. The team lasted one year in Detroit, before it was sold, moved to Minneapolis, and renamed the Lakers. The franchise quickly became one of the strongest in the National Basketball League (a precursor to the NBA), with early superstar George Mikan as its center and drawing card. The team changed hands again in 1957, taken over by a group of investors led by Minneapolis politician and businessman Bob Short. After three years of hemorrhaging money, the franchise came west. Short, like Walter O'Malley just a few years earlier, saw Los Angeles as the promised land, a sure ticket to major-league status.[23]

The NBA at the time, however, was still decidedly minor league. The league had graduated from cities like Sheboygan, Wisconsin, and Rochester, New York, to major metropolitan areas, but crowds were often sparse. In that first year, the Lakers could play home games at the Los Angeles Sports Arena only on Mondays. Home games scheduled on other days ended up in whatever facility was available, including high school gyms. The Harlem Globetrotters, well known for their comedy skit–fueled exhibition games, were still the biggest draw in the game. Promoters booked them at every opportunity to increase attendance, giving the public the impression that the NBA was more show than competition. On Murray's 1960 trip, the Lakers played the New York Knicks in the first game of a doubleheader—the Globetrotters were the main attraction in Madison Square Garden that night. Other bush-league promotions to draw fans, like ice shows and bowling demonstrations, were commonplace. And small-town promoters from Wheeling, West Virginia, or Dayton, Ohio, could persuade the league to play a regular-season game in their town if they could guarantee the gate.[24]

These circumstances added up to make the life of an NBA player less than luxurious. It also made them more accessible to those journalists who chose to write about them. There weren't many. Murray later wrote that when the Lakers came to town, he had little competition for their attention, and a bond between him and the players formed quickly. It was, he wrote, an opportunity for a different kind of sportswriting. "The players were highly accessible. They were eager for ink. They had not yet been made millionaires. Journalistically, I had them all to myself."[25]

A Laker road trip in the 1960s was an intimate affair. The traveling party consisted of the twelve players, the head coach, and one trainer, who would also act as a traveling secretary. The press would usually be represented by two or three writers and the radio announcer, Chick Hearn.[26] (Hearn, a close friend of Murray's, broadcast Lakers games from 1961 until 2001, at one point calling 3,338 in a row.) The group would fly as cheaply as possible, usually economy class. A cross-country flight in those days was a ten-hour affair, with a stop to refuel in St. Louis. For financial reasons, a trip east would include as many as ten games, with very few days off.

Jack Disney was the Lakers beat reporter for the *Los Angeles Herald-Examiner* in the early 1960s and got to know Murray on the road. The *Herald-Examiner* and the *Times* may have been in direct competition, but the competition was put to bed on the road, and an atmosphere of solidarity ruled the day. "Because of the primitive nature of the travel, and the small size of the traveling group, the atmosphere was one that really created some bonds between the people," Disney recalled. "I think because of the nature of things in those days, there was much more camaraderie, not only among newspaper people, but with athletes as well."[27] Players and writers would fly together, take a cab to the arena together, and go out for dinner and drinks after the game. Their salaries were similar. It was understood that players' personal lives were off-limits. Disney's closest friend and drinking buddy on the road was not a fellow writer, but Laker starting guard Frank Selvy.

Laker star guard Jerry West, who would become a lifelong friend of Murray's, said writers were allowed to become part of the team's inner circle. "At that point in time, it was like the stone ages for Christ sake—you lived together, you laughed together, and the sportswriters were there to see it all," West recalled. "It made for a different kind of environment, when writers traveled with the team, went to dinner with them, had drinks with them."[28]

Road trips were almost all downtime, with long hours spent in airports, musty hotel lobbies, and empty coffee shops. Players and writers were always looking for ways to amuse each other and fill the time. One favorite game among the players in airports was for three or four of the taller players to find an unsuspecting traveler, surround him, and begin conducting a conversation above his head, literally. When the traveler cried foul, the players would continue chatting as if he was not there. Writers were in on the laugh for some of the pranks, but Disney quickly learned not to share a cab with the players—writers always got the bill.

After a game, players and writers would go out for drinks. The *Herald-Examiner* was an evening newspaper, so Disney did not have to file a game story until six in the morning. After a game in Boston one night, Disney, Murray, and a few Lakers went out drinking, and Disney had a few more drinks than usual. The party moved back to the hotel, and Disney's deadline was approaching. Murray, who had written his column earlier in the day, deemed his friend unfit for typing and proceeded to write and file a game story for the *Herald-Examiner* under Disney's byline. "The next day I chided him for using a bad angle," Disney joked.[29]

On another late night, Disney, Murray, Hearn, and one of the Lakers were out drinking in St. Louis after a game when the bars closed down. Bars were still serving in East St. Louis, however, so the group grabbed a cab and headed over the bridge. Before they reached their destination, they were pulled over, and before the officer approached the car, the cab driver informed them that he did not have a driver's license. As their driver was outside of the cab being questioned, Hearn grabbed the microphone and began doing play-by-play on the incident for a rapt audience back at the cab company.[30] The group never made it to East St. Louis that night.

Murray, who was always less fascinated by games than he was by the people who played them, saw the details of road life as a way to bring his readers behind the curtain, into the world of the professional athlete. To do that, he wrote about the Lakers differently than he did any other team. "A Trip for Ten Tall Men," the *Sports Illustrated* article, was structured like a travel diary, with 95 percent of the action taking place away from the court. The games, stats, and outcomes were beside the point. Instead of newspaper-style quotes, he used dialogue between players, which offered insights into their off-court personalities. And he created scenes, on airplanes and in bars and hotels, in which to show the players' interactions with each other and with an often rude and dismissive public. It was the type of writing that, a decade in the future, Tom Wolfe would christen "New Journalism" and would be heralded as an innovation in the field.

After joining the *Times*, February with the Lakers became an annual affair for Murray. He made a trip east with the team every year from 1962 to 1965. He often wrote in a style similar to the *Sports Illustrated* article. He also used his close proximity to the players to write profiles of Laker stars like West, Elgin Baylor, and Wilt Chamberlin and personalities such as Ray Felix, Hot Rod Hundley, and Jimmy Krebs. Some columns gave the impression that Murray was a silent observer, hiding in the overhead compartment on a team flight or in somebody's locker before a game:

North Central Airlines flight No. 579 kicked and bucked and groaned its way out to the flight line, and in seat No. 17A, Elgin Baylor surveyed a map with distaste as if it were a missed layup.

"Thirty minutes from Chicago to Milwaukee and it ain't but 68 air miles," he complained loudly to the gods.

"Ninety miles, it's 90 miles," Wilt Chamberlin corrected him. Wilt Chamberlin is always correcting him.

Elgin turned his imperious gaze on Chamberlin. "It's 68 air miles. It's 90 miles by dogsled. But we're going to fly there. At least, I think we are, if they ever get the rubber bands around the props on this thing. Where'd they get this airplane—in the Smithsonian? How many wings it got? The squatters made it in 30 minutes 100 years ago.[31]

Though West was a budding superstar, Baylor was the leader and backbone of the team in the early 1960s. He was extremely proud and could come off as aloof and surly and was considered a tough interview for many writers on the pro-basketball circuit. In Murray's behind-the-curtain portrayals, the Lakers, including West, deferred to Baylor on the court and off. He was always in the middle of the quips and insults that circulated among the players. Murray developed a friendship with him and, in his columns, painted a very different portrait of Baylor than came across in mainstream NBA coverage. "It was easy to get on a first-name basis with Elgin. All you have to do is let him know three years in advance and always speak first," Murray wrote.[32]

Five years can be a lifetime in professional sports, and by 1965, Murray's fifth year of February road trips with the Lakers, he was already beginning to feel like his class had graduated and it was time to move on. Baylor and West continued to anchor the squad, but many of the bit players with whom Murray had shared so many flights and late nights had moved on and been replaced by "impostors." Embarking on a ten-thousand-mile trip through Pittsburgh, St. Louis, Cincinnati, and Detroit with this new group left him feeling melancholy, old, and slightly out of place. Baylor had similar feelings, and the two reminisced about playing cards by flashlight and about old times, "100 hotel lobbies ago, when points—and people—were more familiar." Murray wrote that he looked around the cabin and saw unknown faces inhabiting the seats of ghosts: "'Call yourself the Lakers?' I want to yell at them. What's that young man in the funny hat doing in Jim Kreb's seat? Why isn't 'Hot Rod Hundley here? And Ray Felix, what have you done with him? What's going on around here, anyway?"[33] Murray could sense that the annual ritual had run its course. He would go on one more regular season trip with the team in 1969. By that time, Wilt Chamberlin was on the team, and the Lakers were thriving. The NBA was now a major league, but, to Murray, not nearly as much fun.

In This Corner, Death

On the night of March 21, 1963, Murray and a dozen or so other sportswriters were milling around outside Dodger manager Walter Alston's Dodger Stadium office, which that night was serving as boxer Davey Moore's dressing room. Moore had just lost his featherweight title after being knocked out in the tenth round by a Cuban-born Mexican fighter named Sugar Ramos.

Moore was hustled into the dressing room by his handlers, who shut the door on the press. The sportswriters cried foul and, on Moore's order, were allowed into the room.

Moore sat on the dressing table, an enormous welt under his eye, and tried to focus on his interrogators. "It wasn't my night," Moore said weakly. "Just like you writers, if you'd only admit it. Can't write a lick some days. Well, that was me tonight. I just wasn't up to my best."

The writers dutifully recorded their quotes and shuffled out toward ringside for the night's next fight. Minutes later, Moore grabbed his head and shouted to his trainer, Willie Ketchum, "My head, Willie! My head! It hurts something awful!"[34]

The match had been a close one. Through nine rounds, a clear victor had yet to emerge. In the tenth, Moore sent Ramos into the ropes with a left hook, but Ramos rallied and unleashed a two-handed attack that would eventually kill the champion. The round ended with a Ramos punch that knocked Moore backward, where he toppled over and hit his head on the bottom ring rope. The collision caused swelling in Moore's brain, swelling that was slowly killing him as he entertained the sporting press minutes later.[35]

Murray came back to Moore's dressing room an hour after the impromptu press conference, saw the door closed, and pushed his way through. There he saw Ketchum stripping the trunks off an unconscious Moore, who was lying prostrate on the dressing table. An ambulance had been called. Moore would never again regain consciousness.[36] He remained in a coma for the three days, during which his condition was front-page, above-the-fold copy in the *Times*, culminating in a seventy-two-point screaming front-page headline when he finally succumbed on the morning of March 25.[37]

Moore's death was the third in a string of high-profile boxing tragedies. A year earlier, Benny "Kid" Paret had been killed in the ring by Emile Griffith, who pounded Paret with twenty-one straight blows as he hung over the ropes. And heavyweight Alejandro Lavorante, who had fought for the heavyweight title within the year, was in a coma from damage he sustained in a fight six months earlier. Now, with Moore's death, antiboxing sentiment reached a fever pitch. It was not that boxing had just recently become violent and potentially fatal—boxers had been dying since the sport was invented. In fact, there had been 216 ring deaths since 1945, when *Ring* magazine began compiling such figures, and 16 deaths in the year before Moore's unfortunate demise.[38] But the issue was now a hot one. California governor Pat Brown called for the sport's abolition,[39] and even Pope John XXIII weighed in on the debate, calling boxing barbaric and "contrary to natural principles."[40]

The barbarism of boxing was an evil Murray had been fighting in print since he joined the *Times*. But it was also an issue that left him vulnerable to criticism and charges of hypocrisy. He was caught in a web of contradiction: On one hand, he loved the sport's rich history, the spectacle of it, and the fascinating characters associated with the fight game. On the other hand, he was disgusted by the brutality of boxing and railed against it in print so strongly and so often that he alienated readers and fellow sportswriters.

The roots of Murray's love of boxing had formed early in childhood. As a preteen, he organized boxing matches in the neighborhood, complete with regulation rings and referees. He even participated himself, until he found the taste of gloves and canvas not to his liking. Among the first professional athletes he met in person were "Battling" Bat Battalino and Kid Kaplan, boxers who frequented his uncle Frank's diner in Hartford.[41] Jack Dempsey was Murray's childhood hero, and he would view Dempsey as the ultimate symbol of the America of his youth for the rest of his life. He covered fights at every opportunity from his earliest days as a journalist and found ways to be around the sport even when it had no relevance to his beat. As a columnist, he made fight night at the Olympic Auditorium in Los Angeles a staple of his coverage. Television had helped raise the popularity of boxing, and Murray joined the growing herd of sports media at most heavyweight championship bouts.

And he did not limit his coverage to heavyweights and big-name fighters. He would dedicate his column to second-tier fighters like Billy Daniels,[42] who was a barber by day, or Amos "the Train" Lincoln,[43] who worked in his grandmother's drugstore in Watts. Colorful characters—the con men and hype artists, ring jockeys and palookas—found their way into Murray's column as well. It was a community for which he had deep affection, which made it that much harder for him to stand on the mountaintop calling for its demise.

But that is what he did from the earliest opportunity. Boxing fatalities proved to be an issue that brought out the moralist in him. With Paret hovering near death, Murray launched an attack on the sport. "Boxing should have to go back to the barges, I'm afraid," he wrote. "Its calloused indifference to its own, its disdain for the simple dignity of a human being has earned it no other consideration. No civilized society can put its stamp of approval on it in its present form." Paret died days later, and Murray continued to write in the same vein. His earlier column had drawn out a forceful response, both from readers and from fellow writers, who failed to understand how a sportswriter could attack a sport he covered. Murray's rebuttal: "That sort of cynicism depresses me, but I suppose a lot of the hyenas we have let into the newspaper business over the years have earned us this reputation. But the goal of journalism is, or should be, truth. To say a sports writer is supposed to be an apologist for an evil thing is to say a doctor is supposed to defend cancer."[44]

The sad circumstance of Alejandro Lavorante hit Murray on a more personal level. Lavorante was a shy, handsome Argentine who became a top contender in the heavyweight division during an era in which there was no dominant champion. His star rose quickly in the early '60s as his manager, Pinkie George, padded Lavorante's record against weak competition. Eventually, he had to fight actual competition, and he was quickly exposed. He was badly beaten by ex-champion Archie Moore, who George thought was further over the hill than he actually was. Murray covered that fight at the Los Angeles Sports Arena and said watching Lavorante that night was like "watching a drunk cross the freeway, just a question of time."[45]

Just a few months later, he was matched against Cassius Clay, then twenty years old, already loud, fast, and lethal, and on a rapid climb toward the top of the division. Murray brought Gerry to a banquet held to promote that fight, and both became enamored with Lavorante. Murray described him as a "quiet, polite giant in a black tie and white coat, a modest boy who hung on the fringes of the crowd and did what he was told." Clay predicted he would dispatch Lavorante in round 5 and proceeded to pummel him unrelentingly for five rounds, knocking him out on cue with a right hand as the fifth drew to a close.[46]

Lavorante's quick spiral downward culminated in his next bout, just eight weeks later, against unranked, unheralded Johnny Riggins, a San Francisco club fighter. Now a thoroughly exposed fighter and a beaten man, both physically and psychologically, at just twenty-four years old, Lavorante's fight career, and indeed his life, ground to a halt in the sixth round, when he walked into a right hand and was carried out of the ring on a stretcher. He was in a coma by the time he reached California Lutheran Hospital.[47]

Ironically, Murray was in Chicago to cover the Sonny Liston–Floyd Patterson heavyweight championship match when he read the news about Lavorante's condition. Again, he was faced with the inherent contradiction of his position. He was actively participating in the ultimate hype and publicity hurricane in boxing: a good-versus-evil heavyweight championship fight. He agonized over the fate of Lavorante and wept for the fallen fighter: "What did this boy do to deserve anything like this?" At the same time, he attempted to explain his actions: "As long as society countenances it and man consents to it, I will cover it, because I am a reporter, not the general manager of the world. . . . But as a reporter, I must label it for what it is."[48]

Two months later, Murray went to visit Lavorante in Room 254 at California Lutheran Hospital. He sat by the stricken boxer's bedside and watched as he was fed. A clown visited the room and placed a tape recording under Lavorante's pillow in an attempt to wake the boxer. Murray interviewed Lavorante's doctor and confirmed his own worst fears: "It will reach the bottom of the barrel and Alejandro's family will reclaim this human vegetation which they sent out as a loved son."[49] Lavorante's parents eventually brought him back to Argentina, and, after two more brain operations, he died in Buenos Aires on April 1, 1964.

So with Paret recently killed in the ring and Lavorante hovering near death, the fate of Davey Moore in March 1963 brought the issue of ring violence front and center. The Moore story held page 1 of the *Times* for a week. A resolution was introduced to outlaw boxing in California, and similar resolutions calling for regulation were brought to the floor of both houses of Congress in Washington.[50] But despite the outcry of Murray and others, the furor was not sustained. There were no other high-profile ring deaths in the succeeding months and years to keep the controversy alive, and it gradually drifted to the back pages and out of the nation's consciousness. The commission that Governor Brown formed in the aftermath of the Moore death delivered its formal report two and a half years later. The issue was no longer front-page news. In an article on page 2 of the sports section in the *Times,* the commission chairman stated that "Governor Brown was most receptive to the report."[51]

With the nation's ire diminished, Murray gradually cooled his rhetoric as well. The controversy had done nothing to decrease interest in the sport. Television ratings remained constant both nationally and in California.[52] The saga of Sonny Liston and the emergence of Muhammad Ali filled hundreds of column inches for Murray, who remained a fixture at high-profile boxing events and more mediocre matches. He maintained his admiration for most of those involved in the fight game, while often saving his derision for boxing fans, whom he viewed as callous and bloodthirsty. A boxing crowd, he wrote, is "a collection of 16,000 sick jokes" who would "cackle at watching a sledgehammer on the Venus de Milo."[53]

Whether he liked or not, however, Murray was one of those sixteen thousand. When his son Ted was young, Murray took him to see a fight card, just as his uncles used to do when Murray himself was a boy. On this night, one of the matches was a particularly vicious bloodbath between two welterweights.

Ted turned to his father as the violence became too much for him. "How can you sit here and watch this?" he asked.

"Teddy," Murray said, "there is no greater theatre."[54]

For his readers, however, he added an addendum: "It is great theater," he wrote. "But so is a hanging."[55]

Winds of Change

If the 1960s was the decade in which Murray finally found his calling in life, it was also a decade in which the culture shifted out from under his feet, as it did for many of his generation. Those, like Murray, who had survived the Great Depression appreciated the material abundance and position of international power felt in the United States. Between 1961 and 1969, the US economy grew every single month, the longest period of economic growth in the country's history. The next generation, however, was beginning to question the country's rampant materialism and blatant inequality.[56] A confluence of events and changes—the Kennedy and King assassinations, the civil rights movement, the Vietnam War, the sexual revolution—combined to strike at the core of all the beliefs and values held by Americans in the post–World War II era.[57] Though Murray would find himself politically in support of some of the calls for change, his value system was firmly rooted in an earlier era. For him, the '60s vibe did not register.

The Murray household was built on traditional family roles: Gerry was in charge of the home and the kids; Jim dedicated himself to his work. Using his Time, Inc., retirement money, he had built himself an office separate from the main house, where he would do most of his writing. The building housed an office, a desk, shelves of books, and Jim's typewriter. He was a ferociously hard worker who would log hour after hour in the office. The children knew they had better have a good reason to knock on the office door. On many nights he would rejoin the family for dinner and then head back to the office, working late into the night. Covering a sporting event was a six- or eight-hour affair; he arrived before many of the players and coaches got to the venue and often stayed late, doing more interviews or having drinks with fellow writers.[58]

The road had also become a regular part of his life. After a few years as a columnist, he developed an annual routine. In February, it was a trip east with the Lakers, often followed by a swing through Canada and the northwestern United States with the Blades. March was spring training. Murray would make the trip to Vero Beach, Florida, to spend a week at Dodgers camp, as well as spend time in Phoenix with the Angels. In April he would head south, usually taking a trip to Salisbury, North Carolina, for the National Sportscasters and Sportswriters Association awards, and possibly the Masters in Augusta, Georgia. May would begin with the Kentucky Derby and end with the Indianapolis 500. The summer often would kick off with a trip to the US Open golf tournament and end with a Dodger-Angels road trip. He would cover the World Series each October and, starting in 1967, the Super Bowl each winter. Throw in heavyweight championship fights, the occasional golf tournament, the Olympics every four years, and a few other miscellaneous trips, and it all added up to more than one hundred days away from home each year.

The column took up most of Murray's time and attention, and for that he often felt guilty. His children were growing up too quickly, he complained. "One minute, they were all in the back of the car, shiny-faced, on their way to Disneyland. In no time, they were growing mustaches, letting their hair grow, insisting on torn jeans to wear to school," he wrote later.[59] In his column he would highlight the Norman Rockwell aspects of fatherhood—fishing trips with Teddy, watching Pam march with the Sergeanettes at halftime of Santa Monica High

School football games, nights at the Little League ballpark. After each family vacation, Murray would pen a column, ostensibly in the voice of his youngest son, Rick, recapping the trip, with Murray as the butt of the joke:

> Well, we stopped at Morrow Bay and Dad sez, "I and Tony will play golf as I wish to show the kid a thing or two I picked up from Palmer" but when they come back that nite Dad don say much and Mom axes why and Tony who is my second big brother sez "Oh, Dad had a little troble with his woods," and Mom sez "His driver?" and Tony sez "no the trees" and like to bus laffin an Dad hollers and sez "Wut can you expeck as this whole dam golf course is tilted toward the ocean and is better suited to Tony's type of game which has not got any finny ess like mine has" and mom sez "Cheer up, maybe the British Open will be more suited to your type of game" and Tony sez "I beat him by 13 shots" and Dad sez "If they's anything I can't stand it's a 17-year-old wise guy."[60]

Real life, of course, was far more complicated. His children would eventually inflict much emotional pain on both him and Gerry. In the '60s, however, they were growing up and going in different directions. By the midsixties, Ted was in the army in Germany. Tony, the athlete of the family, was a high school baseball star who eventually pitched for the University of California at Berkeley. Pam was a strong student, and Ricky, just eight when Jim started writing his column, grew into a guitar player and surfer.

Bruce Jenkins was Tony Murray's closest friend through junior high and high school. Jenkins, who went on to become a sports columnist and colleague of Murray's, grew up in Malibu, three miles from the Murrays' house in Point Dume. Jenkins's father, Gordon Jenkins, was a prominent musician who had arranged songs for Frank Sinatra, and the Jenkinses and the Murrays were social friends. A regular joke between the two families was that Bruce was interested in Murray's sports memorabilia, while the Murray children had no interest; at the Jenkins house, the opposite was true, as the Murray kids reveled in Gordon Jenkins's musical notoriety. Bruce Jenkins was an only child who relished his time with the Murray clan and was taken in as part of the family. Jim, he said, was basically a separate entity from the rest of the group. Most of the time, he was locked in his office writing, or away working. When the entire family got together, however, the Murray humor was on display from all members.

"The best times of all were when Murray would come in for dinner," Jenkins recalled. "Sitting around the dinner table with that family, I swear, there were times when you'd be laughing so hard that you could barely even stand up. They'd go around the table just shredding each other, just unbelievable sarcasm, firing away rapid-fire, one after another, everybody holding their own. Nothing was sacred—not me or anything else. They would just be killing each other, in what for them passed for good-natured fun. I think a prude would have been horrified and recoiled from it all."[61]

Because of Murray's absence, Gerry inherited the role of disciplinarian. When the children were young, she exhibited tight control over every aspect of their lives, down to minute details. On trips to Connecticut to visit their family on Murray's side, the kids were amazed when their cousins were allowed to get a snack without asking permission first. Murray often felt guilty about forcing Gerry to be the heavy hand and manage the children and believed it contributed to health problems that she developed later on.[62] Gerry went along with Jim on many of the social outings associated with his job and was the perfect companion, able to converse comfortably with sports and Hollywood personalities. What free time Murray had was devoted to his wife. At parties, Gerry would often dust off her piano skills and lead Jim and friends in an Irish sing-along.

Tony Murray was the sports fan among the children, and he often invited Jenkins along to Dodgers and Lakers games, where they would reap the benefits of attending with the famous Jim Murray. Murray would drive them to the game hours before it began, give them floor seats for the Lakers or box seats for the Dodgers, leave the two of them on their own, and head up to the press box. "The main reason I became interested in sportswriting through Jim wasn't so much that I was learning at his feet, because you couldn't even find him," Jenkins said. "I don't think he ever told me one thing about how to do the job. I just sort of learned by being around him, getting this incredibly close up look at sports." Though Tony attended dozens of professional games at his father's side, Jim rarely returned the favor. Jenkins went to all of Tony's games from junior high through college and can recall Jim coming to only one or two during his son's entire playing career. "He was really distant from his kids," Jenkins said. "They were Jim Murray's kids, but they didn't feel like they were getting much out of the deal."[63]

Murray acknowledged his disconnect in his autobiography. When it came to parenting, he wrote, Gerry knew it by instinct, but he did not have a clue. "I began to lose contact with my boys. I was bewildered, they were defiant," he wrote. "Part of the problem was the famous father syndrome. But it was part paternal neglect. I had gone chasing my career, and, in so doing, had lateraled off the main work of raising the kids to my wife while I went after 'success.'" The countercultural influence, of which California was the epicenter, also played a role, Murray believed. For him, everything was being turned upside down. He had an Irishman's understanding of the bottle, but the concept of illicit drugs was foreign to him. He looked up to athletes, statesmen, war heroes as a kid; now young people worshiped long-haired, bare-chested guitar players.[64] To Murray, it was a world slipping out of control. Once, he attempted to put his skills as a writer to use against the problems of society. He wrote a pamphlet laying out the evils of drugs and the peril of the youth and distributed it to parents throughout Malibu.[65] It was a wasted effort.

The sports page of the *Times* remained largely free of Murray's cultural and parental despair. The column, he said, was an escape. The assassination of Robert Kennedy, however, pushed Murray to reveal, in print, his feelings about what he saw as a dangerous road down which the nation was headed. Kennedy was shot on June 5, 1968, in Los Angeles after winning the California primary. Murray viewed the incident as a bellwether and lashed out at the younger generation: "Freedom is being gunned down. The 'right' to murder is the ultimate right in this country. Sloth is a virtue. Patriotism is a sin. Conservation is an anachronism. God is over 30 years old. To be young is the only religion—as if it were a hard won virtue. 'Decency' is dirty feet, a scorn for work. 'Love' is something you need penicillin for. 'Love' is handing a flower to a naked young man with vermin in his hair while your mother sits home with a broken heart. You 'love' strangers, not parents."[66]

The column drew intense reaction, and, predictably, readers lined up for and against him. Each side of the cultural divide could be seen in the letters written in response to the column. "Murray's understandably emotionally bitter but nonetheless irrational outburst expresses a feeling with which the martyred Robert Kennedy would be the first to disagree," wrote George Pascoe of San Marino. "There are teeming numbers of people in America who are not red-necked Southern sheriffs, wizened old reactionaries, or money grubbing sell-outs who feel exactly the way Murray does, and I'm one of them," wrote Elliot West of Hollywood.[67]

The Kennedy column was a departure for Murray. In most cases, his writing remained free of politics. His apprenticeship at the feet of Henry Luce, a fierce cold warrior, probably was behind some virulent anti-Soviet rhetoric that would occasionally slip into print. One such column nearly caused a Soviet boycott of an international track meet. On another occasion, editors moved one of Murray's anti-Soviet rants onto the editorial page.[68] Generally, however, it was hard to get him to engage in political dialogue in public.

Magazine journalist Gussie Moran tried to do so for a profile of Murray, to no avail. "Do you have any political convictions?" Moran asked.

"Yeah. I'm against daylight-savings time," Murray said.

"What do you think of Cuba?"

"It's a nice place, but I wouldn't want to live there."

Moran tried one more time. "Don't you think everyone should vote?"

"Only if they're alive," Murray answered. "Back where I come from the cemeteries sometimes swung more elections than free beer. Sometimes you weren't too sure about the people you put in office, either."[69]

"America's Earache"

Of all the millions of words Jim Murray tapped out during his sixty years perched in front of a typewriter, none left more of an impression than these four: "Gentlemen, Start Your Coffins." It was an example of his true gift—the zinger, the laugh line, the one-liner, the ability to take the entire issue, whatever it may be, and crystallize it into one quick snippet of wordplay. And with that particular line, he had stripped down his personal take on auto racing to a single easy-to-repeat catchphrase.

That line did not appear until 1966, three years after Murray's first appearance at Indy for the *Times*. The Indianapolis 500, or "the 500" to the thousands of race junkies who made the pilgrimage each year, was the largest event on the American sports landscape by the early 1960s. The Indianapolis Speedway opened in 1909, just a few years after automobiles began appearing on American roadways alongside horses and carriages. And, as Murray would note regularly, people began dying shortly thereafter.

The Indy 500 of the 1960s was a weeklong carnival of beer, sausage, traffic, vandalism, heat, and, above all, noise—deafening, 750-horsepower, rattle-your-vital-organs noise. The Speedway offered seats for more than 150,000 spectators, and the infield of the two-and-a-half-mile track held more than 40,000 cars, which would bring with them another 200,000 warm bodies. The population of Speedway, Indiana, where, most of the year, the carburetors outnumbered the people, topped 400,000 on race day, more than the total attendance of a seven-game World Series.[70] A 1,000-strong brigade of state, county, and city police was mobilized to control the roving bands of fans who killed time before the race by wrecking homes and property. Buses served as portable jails. Cars lined the roads for twenty-four hours before the Speedway opened, with fans consuming drink after drink to lubricate themselves for the coming spectacle. Once the gates opened, great enclaves of spectators formed, the largest of which came with their own security. A great many race goers were either unconscious by race time or willfully ignored the actual race, going about the business of drinking, lounging, and carousing all the while immersed in the 125-decibel roar of the Fords and Offenhausers.[71]

The *Indianapolis Times,* a Scripps-Howard newspaper, had recently begun syndicating Murray's column, so when Murray showed up for race week in 1963, the paper's sports editor, Irv Liebowitz, asked Murray to write a "Welcome to Indianapolis" column to improve his visibility with readers. Murray happily agreed. He gave Liebowitz a column that was equally divided: one half insults aimed at Indianapolis and its residents, the other half attacks on the dangers and annoyances of auto racing. The *Indianapolis Times* editors, intent on raising Murray's name recognition, ran the column on the front page the day before the race, complete with Murray's pencil-drawn head shot to seal the deal. The response was immediate, and, as the editors hoped, passions had been aroused. When Murray arrived at the track the next day, he was a marked man.[72]

As long as there has been auto racing, death and injury have been along for the ride. By 1963 fifty-six people had been killed at Indy alone, including drivers, mechanics, track personnel, and spectators. The subject of death and danger, however, was not a popular one at the Speedway. To most drivers, it was part of the contract they signed when they chose to get behind the wheel. Their bravery and the inherent danger were what gave the sport its electrifying edge. Auto racing was a distinct subculture, and one of the unwritten rules that had developed throughout the racing community was: Don't say things that portray the sport in a negative light. The great fear was that the wrong people would get interested, and the whole party would be shut down or cheapened by people who "didn't understand racing."[73]

Dan Gurney was a driver from Riverside, California, who raced at Indianapolis through the 1960s, part of a Hall of Fame career in several branches of auto racing. He met Murray in the early 1960s and became a close friend and regular source over the years. Gurney explained the attitude that Murray was up against. "When we were on the airliner flying to Indy back in those days, we used to say, 'Okay, we're about to land at Indianapolis. Everybody set your watches back to 1940.' And there was a certain aspect of things that you just didn't talk about," Gurney said. "So, here comes Jim, and he's not necessarily under the influence of that traditional way of not talking about it. He just came out, and he really stood on the gas about those issues. So, it, I'm sure, it made a lot of wives and sweethearts and family members say, 'What in the dickens is going on here?'"[74]

Murray's method of standing on the gas included lighthearted columns that made fun of the obliviousness of the sport and its participants, as well as more pointed attacks on the disregard for the safety of the drivers and everybody else. His reputation grew. Many drivers, such as Gurney and Mario Andretti, read deeply enough into Murray's rhetoric to understand that he had tremendous respect for the drivers and their bravery and incorporated that respect in the majority of his columns. But others saw him as an outsider just playing the sport for cheap laughs. One race day, Murray approached Denny Hulme, Peter Revson, and a number of other drivers in the garage area. Hulme eyed Murray combatively. "Oh, you're the bloke who's got everybody bloody scared to death about this place," Hulme said derisively. The other drivers laughed loudly in support.[75]

Andretti, a racing superstar from the mid-1960s, said it did not take long for the drivers to understand that Murray was writing from a different perspective from the rest of the racing press. Andretti himself was so nervous that his knees were shaking the first time he was interviewed by Murray. "Most of the PR people, they would say to stay clear of him, or be very careful what you say, you know what I mean? He wasn't one you felt comfortable with."[76]

Murray weathered the cold reception among the drivers in 1963 and managed to enjoy himself. One of the drivers who welcomed him despite his reputation was Eddie Sachs. Sachs, thirty-six at the time, was an accomplished driver who had been racing at Indy since 1953 and, after finishing second in 1961 and third in 1962, was one of the favorites. Murray was already acquainted with Sachs, a witty, gregarious fellow who wore a perpetual grin and was a favorite of the writers because of his penchant for regaling them with stories of his misadventures. Murray waded through many silent stares in the garage area at the Speedway until he came across Sachs. "Jim!" he shouted. "Come on in. Step over that rope there!" Sachs, Murray wrote, was not offended by Murray's position on safety, because he was aware that he was "performing in the court of death."

Murray profiled Sachs a few days before the race. The column included an ominous passage. Sachs loved everything about the Indianapolis 500 and told Murray that when "Back Home Again in Indiana" was played over the speakers before the race, he could not help but sob during the entire parade lap. "One of these years, I expect I'll cry, too," Murray wrote.[77]

It did not take long. The following year, Murray stayed back in Los Angeles for the race. In 1964, for the first time, the race was broadcast on closed-circuit television across the country, including at the LA Sports Arena, and Murray took up a seat. Just two laps in, twenty-six-year-old driver Dave MacDonald's car spun and hit the wall and exploded into flames. In those years, cars carried up to seventy-five gallons of fuel at the start of the race, and many of the cars, including MacDonald's, ran on gasoline instead of the less combustible alcohol. Sachs, blinded by the smoke, crashed into MacDonald, as did five other drivers, and an enormous plume of jet-black smoke, three stories high and a hundred yards wide, consumed the track.[78] It was a spectacularly frightening sight. Sachs's car burst into flames. On the closed-circuit broadcast, the crash was shown three times, then, at 12:50 p.m., audiences were told that Sachs was dead. Shortly thereafter, a pretaped interview with Sachs was shown. Sachs was asked if he was ever frightened behind the wheel. "No, I've never been scared at the race track," he answered chillingly.[79] MacDonald, like Sachs, died of burns.

There was no trace of humor in Murray's remembrance of Sachs in the *Times* a few days later. He wrote of beating his fists against the theater walls as they announced the death. He recalled spending the evening before the previous year's race with Sachs and his wife, listening to music and making predictions about the race. Now the one prediction he did not make that night had come true. "Drive straight, old buddy," he wrote. "Find a nice little track where everybody gets the checkered flag, and where you don't have to cry the first time around. And don't worry about the parade lap next year. I'll cry for you."[80]

The death of his friend may have crystallized Murray's feelings about racing's dangers, but he was back at Indy the following year just the same. And his writing on the sport and the safety question continued to take a satirical approach the majority of the time. One of his favorite auto-racing truisms to mock was the argument that races such as the Indy 500 served as research and development for the auto industry and, in the long run, saved thousands of lives on America's public highways and roads. That was the focus of the prerace column in 1966 that included his immortal line. The setup to the column was the Indy track announcer introducing some changes to the race, which Murray had renamed the "Memorial Day Safety Contest." The race, Murray's fake announcer told the crowd, was being altered to approximate road conditions on US highways:

> Announcer: "The driver in Car No. 4—the Schenley Special—will be drunk. The driver in Car No. 5 will just have had a fight with his wife. The driver in Car No. 7 will be color blind, the driver in Car No. 11 will have an IQ of 12 or exactly 490 points below his horsepower. The driver in Car No. Zero will have his arm around a girl and 19 traffic citations for reckless driving. He will be called upon to light her cigarette at 195-miles-per-hour.
>
> "Car No. Blank will have no brakes. We are keeping the number secret because we want it to come as a complete surprise to the driver. Car No. 13 will have 14 teen-agers and 9 surfboards in it and will have bald tires and a burned-out clutch. It will, however, have a souped-up engine, too, and the teen-agers will be instructed to throw pop bottles into the path of oncoming cars at stated intervals. The will also have the radio on too loud to hear sirens. Car No. 70 will have two little old ladies from Pasadena.
>
> "Now, ordinarily, for tests like these, automotive research uses articulated dummies to study crash effects, but today instead of articulated dummies we're using race drivers. Gentlemen, start your coffins!"[81]

Copy editors in the *Times* sports department recognized a memorable phrase when they saw it and played it as the headline above Murray's column, which may account for some of its resonance. His association with the race grew subsequently, and between 1967 and 1973, he missed the event only once. These years were some of the more deadly at the Speedway. After the Sachs crash, gasoline was banned, but cars still carried up to seventy-five gallons of fuel. The start of the race, when thirty-three full gas tanks accelerated into the first straightaway, was a virtual powder keg. That keg finally ignited in 1973.

For the 1973 race, Murray was invited to watch the event with the family of racer David "Salt" Walther in the Dayton-Walther Corporation suite, above turn 2 at the Speedway. Driver Art Pollard had already been killed during a practice run prior to the race. The field averaged 192 miles per hour in practice that year, more than 8 miles per hour faster than the previous year. At those speeds, cars covered the length of a football field in one second, leaving little or no reaction time for drivers. Many were braced for tragedy.

It was a rainy Memorial Day, and the race was delayed for four hours as tow trucks drove lap after lap in an effort to dry the asphalt. The weather, which increased the odds of a shortened event, turned the race into a sprint. The green flag finally started the race late in the afternoon, and only two hundred yards later, disaster struck. Walther's car veered to the right, climbed another car, smashed into the wall, and exploded into a fireball, spraying flames, metal, and fuel into the grandstand, where spectators watched just a few feet beyond the wall. Walther's car spun down the track, spraying fuel all the way. The front of the vehicle had been clipped off on impact with the wall. Walther was upside down as the car spun, his feet visible through the missing front end of the car. Flames burned his legs, body, and face.[82]

In the Walther suite, family members were in denial. "It's not Salt," a family member said hopefully. "I just saw Salt go by." Murray knew better. He considered tiptoeing out of the room. Journalistic practice, he said, compelled him to stay and ask questions. He approached Walther's uncle Fritz and began interviewing him about his nephew. Murray was sure the driver was dead and had to try hard to refrain from saying "was" when referring to him.[83]

The race was a debacle. Walther spent six minutes inside the melting car and suffered third-degree burns over 40 percent of his body, but survived. Thirteen fans were injured by the flying debris and fuel. The rains came again, and the race was postponed. It finally went off two days later, and the results were not any better. Driver Swede Savage suffered hideous injuries in a crash in the fifty-ninth lap and would die weeks later. A crewman in the pit was killed by a fire truck responding to the accident. Then the rains came again, and the race ended under a red flag after just 333 miles.[84]

The 1973 Indy 500 was a publicity disaster for the sport. The resulting outcry led to major changes almost immediately. By the following month, the fuel limit was lowered from seventy-five to forty gallons.[85] Other changes followed. And by next year's Indy 500, the Speedway had been revamped to protect both drivers and fans. As Murray pointed out regularly, it took more than the immolation of a few drivers to goad the racing executives into reform. It required a financial threat. Andretti, who was involved with driver-led boycotts in Europe in the late '60s that forced reform in Formula One racing, believes Murray's stance helped along the way: "As the sport became more commercial, we were looking like a very irresponsible bunch. That's not going to sell. I've always said if companies want to spend millions of dollars to be part of a team, it's not because they want to go to funerals, it's because they want to celebrate and they want to get the positive side of the sport. You could almost say Jim was a pioneer, pointing those things out, no question about it."[86]

A few months after the 1973 Indy race, Murray called out his fellow scribes. A driver had been killed in a Formula One race in Europe. Murray noted a typical auto-racing article about the incident, which, in his eyes, buried the lead: "Scotsman Jackie Stewart reached a milestone in Formula I racing today with his 26th career victory in the Dutch Grand Prix, in an event marred by the death of British driver Roger Williamson." This was akin, in Murray's view, to saying "the maiden voyage of the S.S. Titanic was 'marred' today when the luxury liner hit an iceberg and sank with all hands."[87] After a decade writing about racing, he was still amazed that fellow journalists failed to see beyond the lap counts and standings to the actual human tragedy.

If he saw death as the lead, Murray knew the nut graph of auto racing was bravery. That was the thing that drew him back to Indianapolis year after year. His writing always clearly distinguished between the villains, racing executives in fourth-story corner offices, and the heroes who climbed behind the wheel to risk their lives. "They're the same people who drove wagon trains, fought Indians, risked sailing off the end of the earth—or went to the moon," he wrote. "They're what makes this race fascinating, with their pitiful defenses against it, of flameproof suits, dust masks, goggles and fire extinguishers. They're crazy. They'd rather be dead than bored. They think they're having the time of their lives. Alas! Maybe they are."[88]

A Moving Target

Thanks to his penchant for skewering cities and his willingness to satirize all aspects of sports in print, Murray had developed a reputation in some circles as a negative writer. But in actuality, he very rarely unleashed personal attacks on specific individuals. Most of his jibes came with a dose of humor, and most were aimed at groups or institutions. There were a few select people, however, who could engage Murray's wrath. Sometimes, he could be provoked. While covering a Dodgers-Phillies game in Philadelphia in the summer of 1965, he approached Phillies outfielder John Callison for an interview. Callison's teammate Dick Stuart intervened. "Hey, don't talk to him," Stuart said. "I'm not kidding. If he can think of something bad about you, he'll say it. And he'll hunt until he finds it." Callison shrugged Stuart off. "The way I'm going, who can hurt me?" he said.

Murray had been offended, however, and he responded in kind in the following day's newspaper. In an effort to remove the label of "ripper," Murray wrote that he concentrated on Stuart all game in an effort to write something nice about him. Finally, in the ninth inning, Stuart struck out on a wild pitch and was able to make it to first base. "This had to be the farthest distance a swinging bat came from a thrown ball in the history of the game. At that, it wasn't a great deal worse than the first two pitches Stu swung at but this pitch was so far away from everybody with a glove or a bat the first impression in the press-box was that Stuart had swung at a pickoff attempt." In the field, Murray wrote, Stuart played first base "like he was trying to hatch it." He continued in this vein for ten column inches, before settling into a flattering profile of Callison, probably his intention in the first place.[89]

Ted Williams was an occasional target of Murray's. Though Murray had been a fan during Williams's playing career, and even named his first son after him, at some point he had decided that Williams was interested only in personal success and cared little about his team. He had written such in the pages of *Sports Illustrated*,[90] and continued the same line of reasoning in the *Times*. When Williams became eligible for the Baseball Hall of Fame in 1966, his election was a foregone conclusion; his statistics placed him among the top hitters of all time. Murray, however, once again stated his case against Williams: "Ted Williams was on the Red Sox but not of them, a subtle but nonetheless real distinction. HE gave recitals. The business of winning and losing appeared to belong at a different level. HE played the Yankees four times a game. The rest of the team played them 9 innings." Williams was elected to the Hall of Fame easily, with 93.4 percent voting in his favor. And, as with most of Murray's in-print quarrels, it eventually dissipated; years later Williams sought Murray's help in his unsuccessful efforts to get Dom DiMaggio elected to the Hall of Fame.[91]

It seemed that in order to draw out the true "ripper" in Murray, one needed to be wearing the heavyweight championship belt. The boxing press in the early 1960s was reluctantly chronicling what they saw as the inexorable, inevitable climb to the top of the mountain by, to many, the most detestable of contenders, Charles "Sonny" Liston. Liston had served time for robbery,[92] was known to have Mob connections, and eventually came to fully inhabit the role of the villain that he had been stuck with by the press. Floyd Patterson had held the belt since 1954, save for a short stretch when he had relinquished it to Swedish fighter Ingemar Johansson, only to reclaim it a year later. Patterson was a reserved, introspective champion who was well liked, though not well respected, by most writers, Murray included. Liston was nearly unanimously despised. Much of the rhetoric was reminiscent of sports journalism from earlier in the first half of the twentieth century, when black fighters were routinely discussed almost entirely in racial terms. With Liston, the overwhelmingly white press corps used terms like *jungle cat* and *gorilla* with regularity.[93] Before the long-anticipated Patterson-Liston match in September 1962, Murray wrote: "The first look you get at Sonny Liston, you only hope it don't bite." And "You half expect it to roar. Two people saw him doing roadwork one morning and called the circus to see if any of their cages had been vacated."[94] Patterson was no match for Liston, as most of the writers had predicted. He knocked the champion out in the first round and then repeated the feat in a rematch the following year. Murray and many others in the press predicted the demise of boxing. Instead of doom, however, boxing received an enormous boost, in the form of Cassius Clay.

During the 1960s, Murray directed more negative ink in the direction of Clay, soon Muhammad Ali, than he did toward everybody else combined. He was not alone among the scribes. "Murray was just like all the sportswriters," said Ferdie Pacheco, Ali's doctor and adviser through much of Ali's career. "Everybody hated Ali. He was loud, he was brash, and he wouldn't shut up."[95] Ali had won a gold medal as a light heavyweight at the Olympics in Rome in 1960 and began fighting as a professional heavyweight shortly thereafter. He first appeared in a Murray column after Murray covered a fight card at the Los Angeles Sports Arena headlined by the Eddie Machen–Bert Whitehurst heavyweight match. Clay fought George Logan, the pride of Boise, Idaho, and bloodied him for four rounds until Logan's corner threw in the towel. "You could hardly recognize Cash," Murray wrote. "He had his mouth closed."[96]

Throughout Clay's climb toward title-contender status, the majority of writers continued to portray him as a loudmouth and a clown, not to be taken too seriously. Murray's columns were generally dismissive, and his barbs were delivered with a dose of humor as Clay moved through the ranks. He signed to fight Liston toward the end of 1963, with the fight scheduled to take place in Miami the following February. "It will be the most popular fight since Hitler and Stalin—180 million Americans rooting for a double knockout," Murray wrote.[97]

With Liston now in his path, the press gave Clay a lateral promotion from carnival barker to sacrificial lamb. Much of the prefight newspaper copy expressed genuine fear for Clay's safety. According to one prefight poll, 93 percent of the accredited writers in Miami were predicting a Liston victory.[98] And the great majority of the writers, Murray included, were calling not just for a Clay loss but for a savage beating with a good chance of ending with Clay's death or debilitating injury.

Of course, things did not turn out that way. Clay famously gained the upper hand before he ever set foot in the ring. He chanted threats through a bullhorn outside Liston's home. He raged and screamed and threatened the champ at the prefight press conference in a display that went beyond confident and seemed to edge past the fringes of sanity. Murray and most in the press interpreted the act as the ultimate display of fear, but it apparently convinced Liston that Clay was indeed crazy. When the fighters finally stepped into the ring on February 25, 1964, Liston was the one paralyzed with fear. Clay danced circles around Liston, battering and taunting him as he went. Liston sat on his stool as the bell rang to start the eighth round. A new era in boxing had begun. Clay, a practicing Muslim since a few years before, publicly announced his desire to be called Muhammad Ali shortly thereafter.

Despite Ali's cries for them to "eat their words," most of the writers still did not give him his due. Instead, many made vague references to the fight being fixed, and few proclaimed him a worthy champion. The result was such a surprise, in fact, that the athletic commission in Florida held up Liston's purse to investigate whether he had taken a dive.[99]

Murray seemed to be in step with much of the press corps in the immediate aftermath of the fight. Two nights later, however, he had an encounter with the new champion that would forever alter his perception. Murray accompanied two black journalists, Brad Pye of the *Los Angeles Sentinel* and A. S. "Doc" Young of the *Chicago Defender,* to Ali's home in a working-class Miami neighborhood. The raving madman that had been Ali's public face before and immediately after the fight was gone; in his place was a quiet, contemplative Ali, still coming to terms with what he had accomplished. He reclined on a couch in a pair of white shorts and gray socks. Howard Bingham, Ali's lawyer and photographer, was the only other person in the house.

As Murray, Pye, and Young listened, Ali delivered a half-hour soliloquy. He told the reporters that he had prayed for his life in the dressing room before the fight. His eyes welled up with tears as he told of his prayers: "I say 'Lord, I'm a clean liver. I don't smoke, I don't drink, I don't chase women. I'm going to live right if I win the championship. I'm not going to turn against you. I treat little children right. I'm not around rich people. I'm the champ now and god wants me to be the champ."

As he continued to talk and began to describe the fight, Ali became more animated. He jumped up and started throwing punches in the air. "Now what are they going to say? See how Almighty god turns the tide? I'm going to make boxing alive." He pointed at Murray. "You a wise reporter. YOU need me. You think you can talk to Sonny Liston like this?" he demanded.

At three thirty in the morning, Archie Robertson, whom Murray understood to be a liaison between Ali and the Muslim group with which he was aligned, entered and demanded to know why the reporters were there. "I'm the boss here," Ali retorted. But the impromptu press conference had come to an abrupt conclusion.[100]

The journalists took the intrusion as an ominous sign. Murray's writing about the champ would take a much more serious turn after that night in Miami. Where he had viewed Ali as a one-dimensional cartoon character prior to the Liston fight, he now realized he was dealing with a complicated figure with many intellectual layers.

Ali signed to fight a rematch with Liston, slated to take place the following May in Boston. Just weeks before the fight was to go off, Massachusetts boxing authorities banned the fight due to the questionable credentials of the promoters and the whiff of organized crime. It was moved to a high-school hockey arena in the textile town of Lewiston, Maine, population forty-one thousand. The fighters, entourages, and press descended on the little town, bringing with them rumors of violence and mayhem. Ali's training camp was surrounded by a large Black Muslim presence, which was not appreciated by the press or local authorities. Rumors swirled that the Muslims threatened to kill Liston if he did not take a dive, or that Malcolm X had sent assassins to kill Ali. The Muslim connection had begun to dominate the coverage and the portrayal of Ali.[101]

Murray arrived in Lewiston a week before the fight, after having spent some time in Massachusetts prior to the change of venue. He was already predisposed to abhor New England and everything about it and promptly let loose on its northernmost state. "Maine, America's rockpile. The only thing that grows here is moss—and moose. Its state emblem should be a snow shovel. Or an earmuff.[102] Jerry Izenberg, who was covering the fight for the *Newark Star-Ledger*, spent a lot of time with Murray during the run-up to the fight. "I remember some guy . . . was passing out handbills about this bar in the only hotel downtown, and he had brought in a stripper," Izenberg recalled. "So that night Jim said, 'What are you going to do?' And I said, 'Oh, I guess I'll just have some dinner.' And he was going to have dinner with me, and he said, 'You mean we're not going down to the Leopard Room to see Miss So-and-So?' He said we just had to go to the Holly Hotel, the pride of Lewiston. But of course it was the only one in town."[103]

As one would expect, the fight would turn out to be an entirely amateur promotion. Even the national anthem was botched. The night before the fight, Murray, *Times* columnist John Hall, and Dan Jenkins of *Sports Illustrated* attended a cocktail party at the Poland Springs Lodge, just outside of Lewiston, where Liston was staying and training. "We gathered on the great veranda of the lodge for cocktails and stuff," said Hall. "And our table had Dan, Jim, me, and the singer Robert Goulet, who was going to sing the national anthem. And we all drank quite a bit, particularly Goulet. The next night at the fight, he got the words mixed up in the anthem. He had to stop, and start over. We all kidded him that he couldn't keep up with us. We took him out of his game."[104]

Murray's column, where it concerned Ali and not the quaint village of Lewiston, expressed his opposition to Ali's Black Muslim principles. "Cassius belongs to a menacing cadre of the community which calls itself 'the Fruits of Islam.' History has shown this fruit is bitter and poisonous. It is the Gestapo in blackface. Its stock-and-trade is terror, its payoff is death." While he still mocked Ali for his mouth, now he incorporated jabs about his new name and association with Islam. "If Clay wins, he may retire to his tent in the desert with his camel and a mirror."[105]

The actual fight was quick and confusing. Ali came out dancing again, and Liston lumbered after him to no avail. Just a minute into the first round, Ali threw a short right hand that clipped Liston on the side of the head and sent him to the canvas. Most in the crowd thought Liston had slipped, but he was counted out as Ali stood over him,[106] and the fight was over. As the press corps and the sparse crowd began the eternal debate about whether Liston had taken a dive, Ali began celebrating, leaping around the ring with, as Hall wrote at the time, "all the dignity of a wounded giraffe."[107]

Once again, cries of "fix" rang out. Most in the press decried the "mystery punch" and hinted again that Liston had not fought a true fight. This time, however, Murray went against the conventional wisdom. "I sat right next to him, and my story was about the phantom punch, like everybody else," Hall said. "And Jim wrote that he saw the punch, it was a corkscrew deal, but it was a real punch. We kidded each other about that for years." Editors at *Sports Illustrated* noted Murray's contrarian interpretation and republished most of his postfight column in the following week's issue.[108] Murray spent the next few weeks fending off letters from incensed boxing fans. "Maybe you're writing your columns too far in advance—or maybe you should at least see a fight if you're going to write about it," sniffed Robert Cody of Pasadena. "Maybe you should too. I was at ringside. Where were you?" Murray retorted.[109]

Almost the entire sportswriting establishment refused to acknowledge Ali's chosen name and continued to refer to him as Clay.[110] Pacheco saw the stubbornness as yet another racial slight from the press. "They all just refused to do it. Like Ed Pope [of the *Miami Herald*]. He refused to call him Muhammad Ali for ten years. Ten fucking years! He still called him Clay. Pope's one of my best friends. And I'd tell him, 'Eddie, you're just showing your ass.' You look like a Georgia cracker, or the Ku Klux Klan," Pacheco said.[111]

Murray was no exception. He was happy to create new monikers like "the Emir of Babble-onia" or "the Arabian Nightmare," but his name was still Cassius Clay. Murray seemed to relish the dispute. Prior to Ali's title defense against Cleveland Williams in the fall of 1966, Murray used part of a column to replay a phone conversation he had with Ali on the subject:

Murray: "Hello, Cassius, how's the old . . . ?"

Cassius: "Ali, Muhammad Ali."

Murray: Ah, yes. We seem to have a bad connection, Cassius, I can't hear you too clearly . . ."

Cassius: "I say, ALI! MUHAMMAD ALI!How's come you always call me by my slave name?"

Murray: "Well, you can call me by my slave name, Cassius, JIM."

Cassius: "That's your slave-master name. You were slave masters."

Murray: "Well! That would have been news to my grandfather, Cash. The part of Ireland where he came from, they would have thought Uncle Tom's Cabin was the high-rent district. The only slave they had around the house was called 'Ma.'"

Cassius: Johnny Carson, HE call me Muhammad. Huntley-Brinkley, HE call me Muhammad."

Murray: "Maybe they don't know your real name, Cassius. Remember, I knew you BEFORE these guys—BEFORE you were going to fight poor Alejandro Lavorante, to use his slave name."

Cassius: "Well, I got to go now."[112]

Through the remainder of the 1960s, Murray's portrayals of Ali continued to tilt toward the negative. If race had been at the heart of Ali's problems with the press, then the Vietnam War inflamed things even more. Ali was drafted into the US Army and promptly refused to serve on religious grounds. "I ain't got no quarrel with them Viet Cong. . . . They never called me nigger," he famously said. He was stripped of his title as his case moved through the courts. Murray, like most of the establishment press, saw his refusal as an affront and derided his lack of patriotism. He wrote: "You see, Cassius Marcellus Clay, one of the greatest heroes in the history of his people, has decided to secede from the Union. He will not disgrace himself by wearing the uniform of the Army of the United States. . . . From the safety of 103 years, he waves his fist at dead slave owners. Down to his last four Cadillacs, the thud of Communist jackboots holds no dread for him. He is in this country but not of it."[113]

Ali was a divisive figure in a divisive time, and he was a character type that had no clear forebearer in sports history. And Jim Murray was nothing if not a traditionalist. To him, a champion was Jack Dempsey, humble in victory, gracious in defeat. Or Joe Louis, quietly dispatching contenders while inhabiting his role as deferential champion, palatable to white fans, a shining example for blacks. Both were symbols of true greatness, and Murray returned to them again and again in his work. Ali was different and new, and it would take a decade before Murray and his brethren would give him his due. In the end, the new champ would have to taste defeat to achieve acceptance in their eyes.

7

The 1970s

Top of the Heap

I woke up Monday morning and looked in the mirror—and an imposter winked back at me.

That fellow in the mirror was 50 years old that day. Not me. I'm somewhere between 26 and 39.

—Jim Murray, "Ravages of Time," *Los Angeles Times,* December 30, 1969

Outside the Ropes

As the sun rose on a new decade, Jim Murray was beginning to feel a bit like a relic. He was experiencing the effects of middle age, and spending his days covering the world's greatest physical specimens made his personal decline that much more pronounced. By his own admission, he had put on some weight, his golf swing sounded "like twigs snapping under an elephant," and he often felt the urge to wrap himself in a blanket and do a crossword puzzle.

He was sensing his age at the typewriter as well. He worried that he had become infected by the dreaded disease of nostalgia. He rattled off references to Dempsey, Ruth, Grange, and his other childhood heroes, all the while worrying that the readers and younger writers viewed him as stuck in the past.[1] And though he held the title of national sportswriter of the year five years running, and would hang on to it for the entire decade save 1978,[2] he was already envisioning the end of his run, his obsolescence. "By the time I'm 60, I will pretty well have written myself out," he told an interviewer in 1972. "Even now I feel

145

I may have gone to the well of words once too often. I write two bad columns a week."[3]

In November 1972, Murray took Gerry back to Hartford to attend a class reunion at Trinity, receive an award, and watch his alma mater's football team lose to Amherst. As he showed Gerry the local sights, Murray commented on how everything had shrunk. Sisson Avenue, which he remembered as a half-mile wide, was now only two shallow lanes. And the Connecticut River, once as wide as a Great Lake, now looked like a creek. The couple visited Murray's old dorm room, where he had lived with his roommate, Jack Cohane. One of the room's current residents let him in to look around. On the walls, Cohane's posters of Roosevelt had been replaced by George McGovern, and, even more disconcertingly, there were girls on the hall. As they walked away from the room, Murray heard the student's girlfriend ask who he was. "Oh, just some old grad, I guess," the student responded, unknowingly driving a dagger deep into Murray's psyche.

"Old grad!? Me!? No! I'm not," he wrote in response. "I'm young and slim in my white buck shoes and it's the summer of '43 and the chapel bell is ringing and I've got an 8:30 in Philosophy 4A and none of us is ever going to be old, ever. And just who are these grey-headed old imposters who say they went to school with me? My classmates were young and shining and carefree and gay, not these somber insurance men. Besides, we always beat Amherst."[4]

Despite his insecurities, Murray's writing was as vibrant as ever. And he was influential and confident enough to challenge some of the sacred cows of the sports landscape. Racial equality was a subject that could ignite his sense of outrage. And though golf was his passion, discrimination was built into the fiber of the sport. The Masters, one of the most venerated events in golf, was the target Murray chose to bring the sport's racism into the public discussion.

Murray had come to the subject early in his *Times* career. He had been writing his column for only three months when the Professional Golfers' Association of America struck down a clause in the organization's bylaws that said only Caucasians could be members and participate in PGA events. The organization had planned to hold the PGA Championship in Los Angeles in 1962. California attorney general Stanley Mosk demanded the bylaws be changed if the PGA wanted to continue holding tournaments in the state. The PGA pulled the tournament, but also rescinded the offending clause.[5] Murray, writing with less confidence at that early stage, called the PGA "an exemplary group in the main but one which has found an occasional fellow who would kick the ball out of the rough in its midst." The column applauded the move to eliminate the Caucasians-only clause and mentioned Charlie Sifford, the best black golfer of the era and one whose cause Murray would champion just a few years later.[6]

Sifford was to golf what Jackie Robinson was to baseball. Robinson's racial trailblazing was immediate and far-reaching, however, while change in racial

attitudes took much longer to develop in Sifford's sport. He was born in Char-
lotte, North Carolina, not an area of the country noted for its forward-thinking
racial ideals. His family lived down the street from the Carolina Country Club,
and Sifford began caddying as a youth. He would earn fifty cents a round plus
tips. He gave most of the money to his mother, saving a few dimes to support
his cigar habit, which he developed at age twelve, and which became his trademark on the golf course throughout his playing career. By the age of thirteen,
he was a scratch golfer, and in the 1940s he began playing competitively and
winning with regularity. He won the National Negro Open five times in the
1950s and was able to enter a few PGA Tour events, at northern locales, where
the PGA racial code was not strictly enforced.

In 1960 he managed to get his PGA tour card, but had to fight to get accepted into tour events. The following year he entered the Greater Greensboro
Open in his home state and was atop the leader board after the first round. He
received threatening phone calls that night, and the next day, a dozen young
white men harassed him with racial epithets and taunts for nearly the entire
round before being removed by police. Word spread about his treatment, and
Sifford received sympathy from a few players, but no apology from the club or
the tournament. Somehow, he managed to hang on and finish the tournament
in fourth place. Sifford fought on, becoming the first black player to win a PGA
tournament, when he took first place in the 1967 Hartford Open. He would go
on to win the Los Angeles Open twice.[7]

By the 1960s, the Masters invitation had taken on the status of the mecca of
American golf. The event and all that surrounded it were steeped in golf lore,
and its home, Augusta National Golf Club in Augusta, Georgia, had long been
considered hallowed ground. The club was founded by Bobby Jones, the most
revered golfer in the history of the sport. The Masters tournament had debuted
in 1934 and quickly became the sport's seminal event. On the suggestion of
Grantland Rice, it was played in late March, so sportswriters on the way back
north from baseball spring training could attend and publicize the event. The
plan worked, and the Masters became an annual celebration of Jones, Augusta
National, and the grand old game of golf.[8]

The problem for Sifford, or any other black golfer, was that they were not
invited to the celebration. The Masters was an invitational and was organized
not by the PGA Tour, but by the small cabal that ran Augusta National, which
included Jones and his cofounder, Clifford Roberts, a businessman and friend
of Jones. Despite his tour success in the '60s, Sifford felt he was being excluded
from the Masters. The tournament's guidelines for choosing the field seemed
to change based on Sifford's actions. When he won the Hartford Open, a rule
that had granted invitations to all tour winners was abolished and a complicated point system installed. Sifford did not have the required points. When he
led the Canadian Open after two rounds, a notice was placed on the bulletin

board prior to the third round stating that the Canadian Open winner would no longer receive an invitation to the Masters. Sifford thought it was personal and spoke out about it. He claimed that Roberts had said, "As long as I live, there will be nothing at the Masters besides black caddies and white players."[9]

In 1969 Murray took up Sifford's case, and this time he pulled no punches. Golf, he wrote, had started as "the recreational arm of the Ku Klux Klan." He pilloried the Masters for developing a formula for selecting its field that made it easy to get in if one was from Taiwan, but impossible if one came from a cotton patch in North Carolina. And he quoted Sifford, who said he had received a threatening letter from Bobby Jones, urging him to keep quiet.[10]

Shortly after the column ran, Murray received a letter from Jones. The golf legend had never publicly stated his position on racial equality, but, to Sifford, his silence had spoken volumes. In his letter to Murray, Jones defended the Masters' selection process. "It seems completely obvious to me that we cannot invite any golfer simply because he is black," Jones wrote. He also told Murray that he had never threatened Sifford. Jones enclosed his letter to Sifford, which supported his claim. The letter to Sifford, however, strongly urged Sifford to cease and desist from questioning the Masters' field-selection process and seemed to have been written in an attempt to keep the entire issue out of the press.[11]

Murray wrote back to Jones, questioning the Masters' practices and offering his opinion that the tournament should consider inviting Sifford to make up for all the years he and other black golfers were barred. It was Murray's position that eventually a black player would get to tee it up at Augusta, and that honor should be bestowed on Sifford or some other player who had suffered racial indignities in the sport for decades, not a younger player who managed to qualify. Jones responded once again in defense of the Masters' policies and denying any racial bias in the system.[12] His letter was filled with appeals for peace: "Honorable disagreement is by no means a bar to friendship," he wrote.

Sifford won the Los Angeles Open the following weekend, and Murray came back at the Masters in print soon after. He meticulously went through the current Masters' selection formula, point by point, showing how the nature of the formula made it nearly impossible for Sifford to get on the list. "The barriers thrown up remind me of the guy who shoots a kid's parents and then the kid is deprived of his inheritance on the grounds he's an orphan," he wrote.[13] One of the eligibility criteria allowed for a vote among all past Masters champions, with the winner of the vote receiving a bid. Murray had lobbied his friend Art Wall Jr., a former champion, on the merits of choosing Sifford, and, indeed, Wall turned out to be the lone vote in Sifford's behalf.

Sifford's last chance to qualify that year was by winning the Greater Greensboro Open, the same tournament where he had been called "nigger" and "darkie" for fourteen holes just eight years earlier. He missed the cut, and as he signed his scorecard, he bitterly told reporters, "Now they can keep their tournament down there lily-white."

Jones's entreaties for friendship apparently had little effect. Murray's anger was palpable in the *Times* the following day. "OK, rest easy, Jefferson Davis! Put down that gun, John Wilkes Booth. . . . Tobacco Road is still safe from the 20th century," he wrote. "The Masters golf tournament is as white as the Ku Klux Klan. Everybody in it can ride in the front of the bus."[14]

The Masters remained all white for another six years. The tournament changed its fluid selection criteria soon thereafter, reinstating the rule that allowed for tournament winners to receive a spot in the field. Since the rule was not retroactive, Sifford remained on the outside looking in.

Murray made his feelings toward the Masters known with another gesture: he simply stopped going. What had been a regular stop on his annual southern swing was removed from the itinerary for seven years. He returned in 1974, and in 1975 he was there when a black golfer finally was allowed to join the field. Lee Elder won the 1974 Monsanto Open, earning him a position in the field for the 1975 Masters. The Masters resisted the urge to change the formula in the interim.[15] (Jones had died in 1971. Roberts would die in 1977, shooting himself at the par-three course at Augusta National and leaving instructions to be buried in an unmarked grave.) Murray walked the course with Elder, with whom he was friendly, but chose to write his column about Elder's caddy for the day, Henry J. Brown. He wrote: "At 11:17 a.m., Eastern Daylight Time Thursday, 110 years after the death of Lincoln or a millennium as the Jim Crow flies, a historic first took place on the No. 1 tee at the Augusta National Golf Club here. For the first time in memory of man, Henry J. Brown took out a wood and handed it to a man who was neither (1) blond, (2) rich, (3) Caucasian, (4) Anglo-Saxon nor (5) a member."[16]

If the Masters' racial barrier seemed to be overcome only after years of pressure, the Baseball Hall of Fame rolled over in 1971 with one good shove. The subject was the admittance of Satchel Paige, perhaps the greatest star in baseball's Negro Leagues. Paige joined the Cleveland Indians of the Major Leagues in 1948, a year after Jackie Robinson had broken baseball's color line. Paige was in his forties by then, but still managed to play for five years and compile a respectable record.

In 1964 Murray began lobbying the Hall of Fame to induct Paige based on his Negro League career. The hall had not accepted any Negro League players to that point. "If Satchel Paige doesn't make the Hall of Fame, they should call it the Hall of Shame. No one did more for baseball. Because no one did it for both Negro and white leagues."[17]

Murray and other columnists and commentators continued to press the case for Paige through the '60s, and in February 1971, the Hall of Fame announced a sort of compromise: a special wing would be added to honor Negro League greats. The irony of the hall bestowing an honor upon black players that sounded eerily like "separate but equal" was not lost on Murray and many other writers. "This notion of Jim Crow in Baseball's Heaven is appalling in its own right," Murray decried. "I can't think of a more terrible idea. . . . What is this—1840? Either let him in the front of the Hall—or move the damn thing to Mississippi."[18]

The hall went with the first option, just a few months later. In July baseball commissioner Bowie Kuhn and Paul Kirk, president of the Baseball Hall of Fame, announced that Paige and all future inductees from the Negro Leagues would be given full membership into the main Hall of Fame.[19] Murray saw it as a victory for all Negro Leaguers. When Paige was admitted later that summer, Murray celebrated by addressing his column to Cool Papa Bell, Josh Gibson, Buck Leonard, and all the Negro League stars he hoped would follow Paige into the hall. He wrote, "You're all invited to Cooperstown! Old Satchel Paige made the Hall of Fame, and not by the tradesmen's entrance, and you all know he's surrogate for you. . . . As long as Satch is there [your] names will never die."[20]

Racial politics seemed to become more complicated as the years went by. Undisputed examples of prejudice offered a writer like Murray a chance to take a strong stand against a clear villain. Sometimes, however, the waters were a little murkier. Murray waded into some of that murky water when he wrote about the case of James Harris, Los Angeles Rams quarterback, in 1977. Harris was black and had been the Rams' starting quarterback on and off for four seasons. Amazingly, that made him the black quarterback with the most games started in the history of professional football to that point. A sensitive, quiet veteran player and a graduate of Grambling University, Harris seemed to be the favorite among Rams players. But he had been injured midway through the 1976 season and replaced by rookie Pat Haden. Haden had led the Rams to a 7–2 record, a playoff victory, and an eventual loss in the NFC Championship game, one step short of the Super Bowl.

As the 1977 season developed, race inevitably became part of the equation. Rumors swirled that Rams owner Carroll Rosenbloom had pressured head coach Chuck Knox to play Haden over Harris, which Rosenbloom denied. Haden was a blonde, handsome University of Southern California graduate, a hometown hero, and many felt him to be more marketable than a black quarterback. (The Rams had a third talented quarterback, Ron Jaworski, who had also seen significant playing time.) As the dissension mounted, Knox further exacerbated the situation by threatening to leave the Rams to become head coach for the Detroit Lions.[21]

The *Times* did its part to publicize the feud. Skip Bayless, a talented, high-energy sports reporter in his early twenties, wrote a lengthy three-part series parsing every aspect of the quarterback controversy. Letters began flowing into the *Times* on both sides of the issue. The Los Angeles City Council even joined the fray, passing a resolution that praised Harris and attacked Rams management and some members of the media.[22]

Though Murray seemed to regard the racial element of the story as a contagious disease to be avoided, he wrote a few lines deep in one of his columns that pulled him into the controversy. On the issue of whether Knox had been racially motivated in his choice of starting quarterback, Murray took the position that cries of racism are often indefensible: "If a man calls you a crook, he has to prove it. If he calls you a cheat, you can shoot him. But if he calls you a bigot, you might as well become one. There's no known defense for it. You might as well pack up and move."[23]

The comments enraged Murray's old friend Doc Young. Young saw the Harris circumstance as symbolic and elevated it beyond the football field. He wrote to Murray, condemning Murray's stance as dismissive of what Young saw as rampant racism. "I cannot condone the flippancy with which you attempt to treat one of the world's most serious problems. You *should* know better; you should be a better person. Bigotry is evil, barbaric, murderous, and you know it." Young attacked Murray in print as well: "I hate to mention Jim Murray's name in a critical context because he is a truly great writer, but the fact also is that Jim Murray—out of carelessness, overzealousness in straining for the 'cute' or 'erudite' saying, one or the other; or simply because, deep down, he doesn't give a damn—has committed a terrible boo-boo, casting a serious problem in the format of frivolity."[24]

Murray steered clear of the controversy completely for the remainder of the year. A few weeks later he wrote a tongue-in-cheek faux-interview column between a congressman and his chief "sports meddler."[25] The column poked fun at the involvement of the LA City Council, which Murray thought preposterous. And the Rams put the entire situation to rest later in the spring by trading Harris to the San Diego Chargers, letting Jaworski go to the Philadelphia Eagles, and acquiring Joe Namath, the former superstar quarterback who would ride out his career on the Rams' bench.

Racial equality was the social issue that Murray came back to most often during his lifetime. He viewed sports as a reflection of society in areas of race, as opposed to a tool for change, but he felt the athletes who persevered and triumphed despite obstacles of prejudice were true heroes. As he did for society, Jackie Robinson personified these qualities for Murray.

Robinson had retired from baseball by the time the Dodgers came west to Los Angeles in 1958. When Robinson was enshrined in the Hall of Fame in 1962, Murray applauded the honor in print, and Robinson responded with a letter of gratitude. The two corresponded intermittently after that. Where he let his actions speak for him during his playing days, Robinson was extremely outspoken on racial issues after his retirement and often took issue with Murray's columns.

In 1967 a University of California at Berkeley sociology professor named Harry Edwards led a movement urging all black athletes to boycott the 1968 Summer Olympics in Mexico City. (Edwards's actions were associated with the infamous Black Power salute that occurred during those games.) Murray blasted Edwards's idea in his column, arguing that the exploits of Robinson, Jesse Owens, Joe Louis, and other black athletes had done much more for the plight of blacks than any boycott could accomplish. "I can't help but feel it's the most self-defeating form of social protest short of holding your breath in the corner," Murray wrote.[26] He also equated the boycott to Adolf Hitler's insults toward American black athletes during the 1936 Berlin Summer Games.

Robinson's response illustrated the feeling of disillusionment felt by many in the civil rights movement during the late 1960s. Robinson vehemently sided with Edwards in a letter to Murray shortly after the column appeared in the *Times*. Robinson wrote, "You point to examples. The black man is tired of examples. . . . I'm sorry you can't understand. We want the same rights in everyday life as we get in athletics. . . . Olympics occur periodically. Justice must be practiced every day, and none of this has the faintest relationship to Hitler."[27]

The two continued their correspondence on the issue, which took on a more conciliatory tone. Soon thereafter, the two men dined together in Phoenix and stated their cases. Robinson heard Murray's argument and allowed that Murray was not a bigot, just a bit misguided. After the dinner, Murray concluded that the two had become friends. Robinson objected to several of Murray's columns in the succeeding years and responded with angry letters, but each time the two were able to work out their differences amicably.

Two weeks before Robinson's death in the fall of 1971, Murray bumped into Robinson outside of Riverfront Stadium in Cincinnati, where both had come to attend the World Series. Robinson's health had declined appreciably, and diabetes had robbed him of his eyesight.

"Oh Jim, I'm sorry I can't see you anymore," Robinson said apologetically.

"No Jackie," Murray said. "I'm sorry we can't see YOU anymore."[28]

"They're All Gone"

Of the more than ten thousand columns Murray wrote over the course of his tenure with the *Times*, only two made it onto the front page. One was a touching tribute Murray wrote to his favorite athlete, Ben Hogan, when the golfer died in 1997. The column is structured around a round of apocryphal golf between Hogan and God on Hogan's first day in heaven. The other was also about death, but of a far more tragic nature.

Covering the Olympics was and is one of the great perks in the life of a sportswriter. Journalists who spend most of their professional lives in and out of press boxes, locker rooms, and airport terminals in places like Cleveland and Detroit get a chance every four years to see the most beautiful parts of the world and meet athletes and journalists from dozens of nations, all on their employer's dime. Starting with the 1964 Summer Games in Tokyo, Murray made a habit of covering the Olympics for the *Times* and then tacking on a week or two of sightseeing afterward.

In 1972, the Olympics returned to Germany for the first time since 1936, when Adolf Hitler used the games to advertise his message of Aryan superiority. Now, twenty-seven years after World War II, German officials hoped to portray to the world the image of a country that had been completely rehabilitated. The stain of the Nazis would be wiped clean through athletic competition. German officials went so far as to title the event "The Games of Peace and Joy." At the opening ceremonies, five thousand doves were released into the skies over the Olympic Stadium. The German security forces were outfitted to appear as the anti-Nazis: powder-blue uniforms holding nothing more dangerous than a walkie-talkie.[29]

Murray was not in the mood to let the memory of World War II die just yet. His first column from the Continent laid out ways for Americans to remind the Germans, lest they themselves forget about their past. "If there's a lull in dinner-table conversation," he wrote, "lean over to your host and inquire 'Didn't Hitler get his start around here?'" Or one could ask, "Did they award you the Olympics, or did you capture them?" Murray had come through Paris and had missed a connecting flight to Munich days before the games were scheduled to start. Writing about the incident, he penned a line that would ominously foreshadow the looming tragedy. His traveling party was forced to spend the night in an airport hotel, "which seemed to be patronized exclusively by Arab hitchhikers."[30]

The games were a spectacular success for the first week. American swimmer Mark Spitz shattered world records on his way to earning seven gold medals. Crowd-pleasing seventeen-year-old Russian gymnast Olga Korbut became a media darling on her way to capturing three golds and a silver. Murray stuck to track and field, writing about Russian sprinter Valeriy Borzov, the disputed pole-vault competition, and Eddie Hart and Reynaud Robinson, American sprinters who missed their heats when their coach got the starting time wrong. The games as a whole appeared to be fulfilling the stated goal as a symbol of international harmony and athletic sportsmanship.

On September 5, Murray was awakened by a phone call from Joe Alex Morris, a *Times* reporter stationed in Bonn, Germany. The Olympic Village has been stormed by Arab terrorists, Morris told him. They had taken over the Israeli building and taken hostages.[31] Murray dressed quickly and made his way down to the lobby of his hotel, where he ran into Howard Cosell, covering the games for ABC Television; Shirley Povich, a columnist for the *Washington Post*; Tony Triolo, a *Sports Illustrated* photographer; and Rick Giacalone, director of photography for ABC. The group climbed into Giacalone's car and drove to the ABC bungalow, just outside the entrance to the Olympic Village.[32]

The group correctly assumed the village would be locked down by German security. Cosell assumed it would be simple to gain entrance, thanks to the affability of the powder-blue German peace officers. "Don't kid yourself, Howard," Murray told him. "These are the sons of the Gestapo."[33]

After being turned away at one entrance, the group removed all items identifying them as media members. They found another entrance, and Triolo convinced the security officers that he and Cosell, each wearing Puma sneakers, were actually Puma shoe salesmen. Murray and the others used the Puma debate as a diversion and made it into the village.

The Arab commandos had stormed Building 31 of the Olympic Village at five o'clock, killed two Israeli athletes, and taken nine more hostage. The body of one of the murdered Israelis had been rolled into the street outside the apartment building. The terrorists, members of a violent faction of Yasser Arafat's Palestinian Liberation Organization, took their hostages to the second floor and released their demands via a few sheets of paper tossed over the balcony to the waiting German police. If Israel did not release hundreds of Palestinian prisoners, they would shoot a hostage every hour starting at nine o'clock.[34]

The journalists had entered the village around eight thirty and, once inside, were free to roam the streets. Povich got within eyeshot of the terrorists patrolling the balconies, brandishing their Kalashnikov assault rifles. Cosell filed reports for ABC News, watching as more and more German police and security forces poured into the area.

What Murray found in the village was a bizarre scene in which oblivious athletes went about their everyday Olympic business while a military operation was undertaken. Armored cars, tanks, and fire vehicles were now parked on the main street of the village, while athletes pedaled by on bicycles or jogged by on foot. He encountered the Munich chief of police, issuing orders from his command post in a government van, surrounded by hundreds of officers with walkie-talkies. Nearby, American sprinters listened to music and played cards. Dozens of athletes crowded around a television, watching not the reports on the terrorism but the boxing match between Cuban Teofilo Stevenson and American Duane Bobick.

Murray interviewed American decathlete Bruce Jenner. (He would finish tenth in the decathlon in Munich and go on to win the gold medal in the same event in 1976 in Montreal.) Jenner was getting a rubdown in preparation for his event. Through the window he could see the terrorist lookout positioned on the balcony of Building 31. "It's all a bunch of shit," Jenner said. "Why do we have to cancel a day? We can walk around that building on the way to the track, can't we? We don't have to go through it."

The atmosphere in the village surrounding Building 31 made up the crux of the column Murray filed that evening. It ran in the bottom-right corner of the *Times*'s front page, under the headline "Olympics' New and Tragic Event—Murder." He wrote: "Eight guys with hate in their hearts and guns in their hands have turned this whole billion-mark festival into a Middle East incident. They've hijacked the Olympics."[35]

Morris's lead article in the *Times* told the rest of the tragic tale. The terrorists had gone with the hostages to an airport after being promised transportation out of Germany. That evening at the airport, German snipers had opened fire on the terrorists, who were preparing to leave in helicopters. The terrorists immediately shot their bound victims and then engaged in a gun battle with German forces. Six hostages were killed, two captured.

The following day, Murray returned to the village. Building 31 was now heavily guarded by German security. There was nothing left to guard but bloodstains and bullet holes, Murray noted. He interviewed members of the Hong Kong delegation, who were also staying in Building 31. The group had been ignored by the terrorists, who were intent on killing only Israelis. One Hong Kong athlete who had a plane to catch had calmly marched down the stairs and, once he informed the terrorists he was with the Hong Kong team, was peacefully shown the door.[36]

The conclusion of the games of the XX Olympiad took on the attitude Jenner had displayed on September 5. A ceremony for those killed in the incident was held on the morning of September 6 at the Olympic Stadium. Eighty thousand people attended and watched the Olympic flags lowered to half staff as the Munich Philharmonic played Beethoven's Funeral March. At the conclusion of the ceremony, International Olympic Committee president Avery Brundage delivered an embarrassingly inappropriate speech in which he announced "the games must go on," and the following morning the competition resumed.[37]

In print, Murray had argued that the games should not be continued under the circumstances. He admitted, however, that with the cost and preparation involved in an Olympics, it was understandable that the show must go on. And how could a nation (the United States) that played an entire slate of professional football games two days after the assassination of its president really argue for suspension in this case? But the games would be remembered, not for the athletic feats, but for "the somber silhouettes of Building 31 or the members of the German rifle team that had them in their crosshairs during the long, tense, afternoon hours, or the gun-carriers and tanks being moved into position at dusk, or the hovering helicopters, or the smell of death in the air."[38]

Stage and Screen

After eighteen years in Malibu, the Murrays decided it was time to move closer to the city. Los Angeles had exploded into a sprawling metropolis, and traffic had multiplied since the family made the move. Murray found himself commuting for hours at a time to attend games and conduct interviews. Malibu was undiscovered country when the Murrays arrived in the '50s, but now it was some of the most desirable real estate in Southern California. Jim Murray had unwittingly become a savvy real estate investor.

Around that time, Murray called his sister Betty, and the subject of the sale of the Malibu house came up. Murray's relatives back in Connecticut were always interested in the details of his Hollywood lifestyle.

"So you sold the house," Betty said. "Did you sell it to anybody famous?"

"Yeah, as a matter of fact I did," Murray said.

"Who?"

"I can't tell you that."

"Who do you think you're talking to?" Betty asked incredulously. "I'm your sister, and I live in Connecticut. I'm not ABC News."

"No, you don't understand," Murray explained. "It's in the purchase of sale contract that I wouldn't tell anybody, and I wouldn't write about it in my column."

Murray did indeed withhold the details, but a year later was back in Connecticut to visit family, and Betty brought it up again. "Jim, who did you sell your house to?"

"This guitar player, his name is Bob Dylan."[39]

Dylan in fact bought three other houses in adjacent lots and created a compound for his family. The Murrays took their windfall and began shopping for a home closer to downtown Los Angeles. Jim had always dreamed of living on a golf course and being able to step out of his back door and tee up a golf ball. He put an offer down on a house overlooking the eighteenth hole at Riviera Country Club in Pacific Palisades, his favorite golf course. Ben Hogan had won the Los Angeles Open three times at Riviera and had won the US Open there in 1948, so the course was often referred to as Hogan's Alley. Alas, the Murrays were outbid, and the dream of golf course living would have to be postponed.

Instead, the Murrays settled in Bel Air, a few miles to the east. Their new home, on Bellagio Terrace, was a spacious, split-level house on a cul-de-sac. In the back, it boasted a large bay window with a sweeping view of Los Angeles. And though it did not have Hogan, Bel Air had its share of celebrities. Mike Downey, a sportswriter and columnist who joined the *Times* in 1985, remembered driving Murray to the Bellagio Terrace home after a Dodgers game. As they were pulling into the driveway, Murray mentioned that the singer Peggy Lee lived nearby.

"Really?" Downey said. "How far does she live from you?"

"Oh, about $900,000," Murray said.[40]

The move to Bel Air signaled the end of an era in Murray's personal life, and he marked the change with his Christmas Day 1973 column. Running under the headline "Missing: Ocean of Joy," he composed a tender ode to the great Pacific:

> I have abandoned my great shining sea for the ease and access of the city. I have left the ramparts for the soft center. I have left my love for my comforts. I have left the sunset land and wild acres for the sedate, the secure.
>
> I have traded white caps for white houses. I shall never be exactly the same person again. Did you ever watch a sun sink into a molten sea? Have you ever had a chance to watch the changeling moods of a mighty ocean—THE mightiest of oceans?
>
> An ocean is like a person—now stormy, raging, passionate, dangerous, now spent and placid and resting from its labors of anger.
>
> A view of the ocean is a great healer in bad times. Its very immutability is a reminder that what has gone wrong in your little life is not a flyspeck on the grand and mysterious design of things. It can be an ocean of tears. But in the best of times, it can be an ocean of joy.[41]

The move to Bel Air, just a few miles from Beverly Hills, brought Murray back into close contact with many of his Hollywood connections, formed years before, during his days on the Hollywood desk at *Time*. His wish to always stay in the orbit of the movie business may have been one way for Murray to hang on to a fantasy he had harbored since his youth. Even after he had become a sports celebrity in his own right, he still spent much energy dreaming and scheming about achieving success on another stage. He had come to California in 1943 carrying that letter from his professor recommending him as a screenwriter, and he never kicked the urge to conquer Hollywood and Broadway, to have his name spoken alongside Hemingway and Tolstoy. "There's only one regret I have," Murray told D. L. Stewart of the *Dayton Herald Journal* in 1974. "It's too late to become a serious writer."[42]

He did not give up easily, however, and there are more than a few examples of Murray's attempts at fiction, drama, and screenwriting to be found in his personal archives. In 1961, shortly after he joined the *Times* sports department, he sent two movie treatments to an acquaintance at Paramount Pictures, story editor Curtis Kenyon.[43] Both dealt with sports. Murray, long an aficionado of sports films, seemed to be hoping his new public persona might warrant some consideration from the studios.

"A Number on His Back" reads like a 1950s Hollywood B-movie college-football picture, populated with a cast full of the usual campus suspects: Buddy Hart, all-American, who plays at "Tech" for Coach Butch Donaldson, dates Shirley, the girlfriend, and struggles in class with Dr. Googheim, the professor of economics. The story opens with Buddy's recruitment:

> The bell rings and Poppa hurries to living room door, throws it open. He spreads his arms wide: "Butch! And Docky! Come in. We were just watching the movies of last Saturday's game. Coach, that's a mighty fine-looking bunch of ball players you got there, yes sir." There is loud laughter from a burly overcoated man he ushers into the room, and echoing laughter from his cigar-smoking friend.
>
> "If you think this team is something, wait till next year, Mr. Hart. Yessir just wait till next year." He stops short as he sees the son standing there grinning awkwardly. "And is this the boy?" he asks quickly, sizing the youngster up like a piece of prize stock at the state fair. He is obviously impressed with what he sees. Buddy Hart is a well-muscled, alert-looking hunk of athlete. The coach quickly approaches, seizes the youngster's hand.
>
> "Buddy, I'm sure glad to meetcha, I sure am."[44]

The second screenplay is a boxing story that launches into backroom skull-duggery from the very first sentence. An out-of-town fighter is offered "five bills to lose close" while newspapermen wait outside the dressing room, "dipping into the anchovies and free booze provided by the gambling casinos for the occasion."[45] A film-noir story of ring subterfuge and backstabbing launches from there.

Kenyon lauded Murray's sportswriting, but let him down gently in regards to his screenwriting. "A Number on His Back," Kenyon wrote, was too conventional for the studio. The boxing script, however, could be a good vehicle for Sidney Poitier, one of Paramount's rising stars. Poitier was already filming another Paramount feature, Kenyon wrote. (Two years later, Poitier would become the first African American actor to win an Academy Award.) "In the interim, let's just put it on the back burner; and please continue to keep me entertained with your fine column." On the back burner was where it apparently died.

In early 1962, Murray turned his attention to television. He was offered the opportunity to join the writing staff of a fledgling program, *The Andy Williams Show*. Williams was one of the most popular singers of the day, and NBC decided to capitalize on that popularity by creating a variety show with his name on it. Murray was feeling a bit isolated after a year of the column and jumped at the chance to work collaboratively with other writers and to try a new genre. "The whole idea sounded glamorous and thrilling. I pictured myself as a kind of latter-day Florenz Ziegfeld. I saw each show as opening night. I saw myself in a muffled great coat, opera hat and carrying a gold-headed cane—lavish budget, champagne parties, milk baths and diamond tiaras," he wrote.

What he found was a much different experience. The show was in preproduction when Murray joined the writing team. The other members of the team were head writer Mort Green along with Bill Persky and Sam Denoff, all three veterans of another popular television variety program, *The Steve Allen Show*. The Williams program was to debut in September, so the four began meeting in June to hammer out the early scripts. The goal was to come up with some themes for comedy sketches that would complement the musical portion of the show. Murray would be paid $350 a week, half what the other members were making, but a significant supplement to his *Times* salary.

Murray's excitement drained very quickly once the actual work began. He found the job of television writer to be an endless parade of boring conferences. And, worse, he found himself unable to contribute to "the community sing" of the comedy writers, in which members would call out jokes and themes, and others would try to build off those ideas. "I would think of a gag in my head and automatically reject it before I could articulate it," he said. "Even if it was funny (which it seldom was), I couldn't make it sound funny. . . . My communicating had always been between my typewriter and myself. Suddenly, I was called upon to be a coffee-house raconteur and wit. All I got was stage fright."

His career as a television joke writer lasted six weeks. Though he began to feel more comfortable near the end of his run, he came to the conclusion that being a scriptwriter was a full-time career, not something that one could do while simultaneously covering sports for a newspaper. His fellow writers continued on, and eventually *The Andy Williams Show* became a hit, lasting until 1971. Its success, however, was largely based on the musical talents of Williams, and, after the show was established, the comedy content was decreased in favor of musical acts.[46]

A few years later, Murray decided to pitch his own television ideas. He developed an idea for a television series called "Washington Correspondent." The hourlong drama was to follow the adventures of a newspaperman writing for a large New York daily or wire service who would investigate government agencies, looking for stories. In Murray's description, plots would range from international spying to the kidnapping of the president's daughter to returning POWs who had been indoctrinated by communists. "This show could be as exciting and melodramatic as 'Gangbusters' for the blood-and-thunder audiences while having high appeal for the adult segment who prefer a dramatization of problems which cannot be solved with one squeeze of the trigger."[47] Again, Murray apparently found no takers for "Washington Correspondent."

The closest Murray ever came to seeing his work on the big screen came at the behest of his old friend and hero Ben Hogan. Hogan's life story had already been filmed once, under the title *Follow the Sun,* in 1951. The film starred Glenn Ford, included appearances by golfers Sam Snead and Jimmy Demaret (Hogan served as an adviser but did not appear on-screen), and featured a cameo appearance by Grantland Rice. But the director, Sydney Lanfield, had little understanding of golf, and the result was what Murray later called "a triple bogey."

Hogan wanted a mulligan. After Murray had become a columnist, movie producer Tom Laughlin approached Murray about taking another shot at the Hogan story. Murray turned him down, but Laughlin returned later with the same request, this time with Hogan's name on it. Murray relented and agreed to give it a shot.

It was another lesson in the all-consuming nature of "the Column." To produce a good screenplay, Murray wrote later, you have to devote all of your time and mental energy to the story until it is done. But Murray had to turn out a column almost every day before he could even start to think about the Hogan script. And interruptions such as the World Series or the US Open kept popping up, shutting down progress for weeks. Eventually, he gave up. He wrote a letter of apology to Hogan, blaming his failure on his newspaper responsibilities. The column, once again, had granted a curse to balance out its blessings.

If he never fulfilled his screenwriting dream, Murray did at least get to perform somebody else's dialogue on-screen. In 1962, an acquaintance at Warner Brothers called him for some advice. The studio was in production on a horse-racing film called *Wall of Noise,* starring Suzanne Pleshette, Ralph Meeker, and Ty Hardin. The director was filming a race scene and was having trouble getting the correct horse to win the race. In other words, nobody on the set knew how to fix a horse race.

Murray, of course, saw column potential in their situation. He advised the filmmakers to hire actual jockeys and trainers, who, they could be assured, would have no trouble fixing their fictional race. And he offered several more suggestions to help in the production. The advice earned him an offer of a bit part in the film.

When Murray's day on the set arrived, he joked with the producers that he had perfected a made-for-the-screen move where he would light a cigarette and then crush it out in a particularly debonair manner. Unfortunately, he was told, he would not be on the screen long enough to light a cigarette. Murray played a sportswriter (he felt he was miscast) and was given a single line: "So then this race was just a tune-up?" He executed it flawlessly, after writing it on the notebook he carried in the scene as a prop.[48]

The performance of *Wall of Noise* at the box office could be described, in horse-racing terms, as "struggled out of the gate, did not challenge." Reviewing the film for the *Times,* Margaret Harford wrote that the horses offered the film's best performances. The actors, on the other hand, "were losers all the way." Hardin was expressionless and appeared to be thirty pounds overweight, and Pleshette offered limp love scenes. Murray, Harford observed, was typecast as a widely read syndicated sports columnist.[49]

On the strength of his performance in *Wall of Noise*, Murray's acting career apparently stalled. Hollywood remained a closed door. He contented himself by creating fake movie treatments and dialogue and using them as columns, one of his favorite techniques for satire. Though his skill at one-liners and humor writing would seem to be a good match for movies or television, his particular writing talents somehow shined brightly only in that comfortable eight-hundred-word format that served him so well. "Jim was a natural," said Frank Deford. "He was just made for columns—just like Red Smith, who never wrote anything much good outside his column. But he and Red were perfect for what they did."[50]

The Pursuit of Infinity

Golf is the cruelest of sports. Like life, it's unfair. It's a harlot. A trollop. It leads you on. It never lives up to its promises. It's a boulevard of broken dreams. It plays with men. And runs off with the butcher.

—Jim Murray, quoted in *The Gigantic Book of Golf Quotations: Thousands of Notable Quotables from Tommy Armour to Fuzzy Zoeller*, edited by Jim Apfelbaum

In the summer of 1974, Murray received a call from his friend John Marin. "How'd you like to be the first person ever to play the new course up on Mulholland Drive?" he asked.

"Wait a minute," Murray said. "You mean NOBODY's played it—EVER?"

"That's right," Marin said. "Never had a cleat mark on it. Won't open for a couple of months. Mountain Gate, 6,900 yards of sylvan beauty. Might have to chase the deer off if they're in our line. I'll get a foursome."

"No, no, don't do that!" Murray exclaimed. "There'll just be the two of us. PLEASE! Uh, how're you playing?"

"I haven't had a club in my hand in six months."

"Get your clubs! I'll meet you at the first tee!"

After a lifetime as the ultimate duffer, Murray was about to achieve a lifelong dream. "Do you have any idea what a thrill it is to stand on a tee and KNOW you're going to set a competitive course record? To know that EVERY shot is history?"

Of course, what followed was the kind of golf records that are recorded not on the PGA Tour, but on thousands of public courses by thousands of twenty-five handicappers every weekend of the year. Murray recorded the first eight at Mountain Gate, the first lost ball at Mountain Gate, the first "ball-to-bounce-off-a-tree" and the first "man-ever-hit-in-the-face-by-his-own-golf-ball." A short while later, he reported becoming the first golfer ever at Mountain Gate to take seven shots to the edge of the green and say out loud, "Let's see, I lie 3 to here."[51]

The incident at Mountain Gate was just one of dozens of golfing exploits, with himself as the foil, that Murray recounted for his loyal readers. Golf was the one sport of which he was more than an observer. His boxing career ended in preadolescence; his baseball playing days were over in college. But he golfed all the way through. He was a hard-core addict. Golf was part of every vacation and every road trip and a part of every possible workday. Through a life in which his eyesight deteriorated to the point that he had no hope of seeing the flag until he tripped over it, he always found a way onto the course.

Either because of or in spite of the fact that he tried and failed at the sport three times a week, Murray, when pressed, would say golf was his favorite of the sports and Hogan his favorite athlete. And since the best of the golfers have extended careers, greats like Hogan, Arnold Palmer, and Jack Nicklaus were among those to whom he devoted the most ink over his writing life. Golf is the sport that allows for the greatest amount of interaction between writers and players, and Murray's relationship with some of the stars of the sport, from Palmer and Nicklaus to Gary Player and Tommy Bolt, often crossed the line from journalistic subject into personal friendship.

Most of the pros knew of Murray's adoration of Hogan. At one particular tournament Murray was covering, Palmer hit his ball into a deep ditch, leaving him with an impossible shot out of a thicket. Palmer noticed Murray watching from the gallery. "Well," Palmer said. "You're always writing about Hogan. What would Hogan do in a situation like this?"

"Hogan wouldn't be in a situation like that," Murray said.[52]

Murray, though, always found himself in situations like that. Bill Thomas, managing editor of the *Times* in the '70s and '80s, played in a regular foursome with Murray and got to view his travails firsthand for years. "We played golf, more or less. I say more or less, because Jim wasn't very good," Thomas joked. "He loved the game, and wrote about it beautifully, but he just couldn't play very well."

One major problem, Thomas said, was that Murray was unable to hit the ball very far. Once, he was entered in a pro-am event prior to a tournament in Los Angeles. He was on the tee, taking some practice swings before teeing off for the first hole. Fans lined both sides of the fairway. Nicklaus saw Murray and came over to give him some pointers. "You've got to turn your hip," Nicklaus instructed.

"Jack, I'm afraid I'm going to hit somebody," Murray said, looking out over the gallery.

"Don't worry," Nicklaus responded. "If you hit somebody, you won't hurt them."[53]

His blunders and misdeeds on the course and those of his playing partners were an endless source of humor and column material. And his golf buddies often contributed to his writing, with both words and deeds. One such occasion was a friendly round at Bel Air. The foursome that day consisted of Murray, Dodger announcer Vin Scully, Dodger Stadium concessionaire Tom Arthur (inventor of the Dodger Dog), and advertising executive Vic Hunter,[54] one of Murray's closest friends. Murray found himself looking at a shot over a deadly sand trap onto the green.

"That's a Felzer," Arthur announced, after PGA Tour player Forrest Felzer, who had lost several tournaments thanks to pivotal trips to the beach.

With that, the word creation commenced. A "Scully," it was decided, was any shot that was headed to the green, but was stopped short on the way by a tree. A "Roddy," named after bartender and friend John Roddy, was committed whenever a golfer used his foot to advance the ball out of the rough.

Another of Murray's closest friends and golf mates was Bob Williams, Riviera regular and owner of a successful pasta company. A "Williams," the group concluded, was an unsought lesson, delivered in the middle of a hole, that resulted in utter confusion for the recipient of the lesson. And Murray's friend Jimmy Henghan, a Hollywood trade reporter, was honored with a "Henghan," defined as a mysteriously found ball that arrives at the perfect time, often with a clear shot to the green.

Murray himself was recognized for his exploits on the green: A "Murray," it was decided, was either an eighteen-foot putt that ends up eleven feet short or an eighteen-foot putt that ends up fifteen feet long.[55] But if he overshot or underhit thousands of putts on thousands of greens, there were always those perfect strokes that brought Murray, like every other golf junkie who carries a bag, back to the game again and again.

In April 1981, Bill Dwyre joined the *Times* sports staff as assistant sports editor and was promoted to sports editor just two months later. Murray wanted to get to know his new boss and decided to do so at Riviera. Dwyre was just thirty-six years old and in awe of Murray. "I wasn't playing much golf then, but I said, 'Sure. I'll do that,'" Dwyre said.

> He brought us to Riviera Country Club. We went out and played Riviera. The first hole is a very famous hole. You tee off right next to the clubhouse. It's a par 5, not too hard of a par 5, and he hits it onto the back of the green in about five shots or something, but I think he somehow got there in 3. And he has about a fifty-five-foot killer putt. I'm watching him, and he hits it, and it turns left and turns right and breaks in and breaks out, and, finally, it goes right in the hole. So

I think he got a birdie on the first hole. And this guy's in his sixties already, you know, and I'm thinking, "My Lord, he must be a hell of a golfer." And he doesn't say a thing. He just walks over and picks up the ball out of the cup.

So I finish up, I get my eight or something, and we go and we sit in the golf cart. We sit there for a minute, and then Jim looks over at me and says, "You know, sometimes I miss those left."[56]

Burning Words from a Flaming Heart

Somewhere during the cultural and political upheaval of the late 1960s, the ocean liner that was American public opinion on the subject of Muhammad Ali began to bank and slowly reverse directions. When his title was stripped for his refusal to join the army, he was still, to most, the obnoxious buffoon and the religious zealot from a frightening Muslim group who had taken most of the shine off the heavyweight championship belt. But in exile, he became something else entirely. Unable to fight, he undertook a series of questionable ventures to earn a living, from performing on Broadway to participating in a computer-simulated faux fight on film against another ex-champ, Rocky Marciano.[57] He also signed on for a series of lectures on college campuses and found that he was adored by the get-out-of-Vietnam, antiestablishment youth movement. And though he was largely forgotten to the majority of the boxing public, his banishment engendered sympathy and led to a renewal of his status as an underdog.[58]

Sportswriters, for the most part, were slow to catch on. When he finally made it back to the ring, he was still Cassius Clay to most of them, though six years had passed since his conversion. In the *New York Times,* he was often referred to as "Clay, also sometimes known as Muhammad Ali," a stylistic decision that annoyed some of the younger writers. Murray continued to call him Clay in his columns through his match against Oscar Bonavena in December 1970. On the eve of that fight, Ali's last tune-up before the highly anticipated match with the new champion, Joe Frazier, Murray was still playing the name game, calling Ali "Marcellus Muhammad Ali Herrod Hussein Clay" in his fight preview.[59] After the fight, Murray retired the game and the name, and Ali was Ali from then on. Murray's attitude toward Ali remained the same prior to the Frazier fight, however.

The hype for Ali-Frazier I in Madison Square Garden on March 8, 1971, was overwhelming. Thanks to the media publicity machine, and the penchant of boxing writers for creating drama beyond that of two men exchanging blows, the lines were clearly drawn: Ali was the countercultural hero; Frazier was the working-class, lunch-pail representative of the establishment. And, due to closed-circuit television contracts and timing, it was the last "fight of the century" in which the results reached a news-hungry public via newsprint. The fight ended well after the 11:00 news and was shown live to only 1.6 million closed-circuit viewers, so most people woke up on March 10 without a clue. In Manhattan, readers grabbed up newspapers as they fell off the delivery trucks.[60]

What they saw was Ali crumpling to the floor from a Frazier left hook in the fifteenth round of a thrillingly violent display of pugilism. Whether it was due to age, the long layoff, inadequate preparation, or an underestimation of his opponent, Ali was no longer the unhittable dancer who faced Liston years earlier. Instead, he showed another side of himself in the ring: the ability to absorb punishment. And Frazier meted it out in large doses. Murray had long believed that when Ali met resistance, he would turn and flee or succumb quickly. As far back as the first Liston fight, Murray had felt he saw weakness and quit in Ali, and ever since he had been expecting it to return. Even against Bonavena three months earlier, Murray had written that Ali was in retreat when he knocked down his overmatched opponent.

Now, in defeat, Ali had finally earned Murray's respect. "He came out and fought—like every broken-nosed but great-hearted club fighter who ever lived, he was going to go out throwing his best shots. Boasters usually give way to rout quicker than strong, silent types," he wrote. "Ali hoisted all flags and gave battle. It's a way only champions have. And he was a champion. . . . When he could not, he attacked. It may have been his finest moment in a ring. Or anywhere else."[61]

To be sure, Murray continued to have fun with Ali's showmanship and to compare him unfavorably to the champions of his own youth. But an undertone of humor and affection now crept into his writing. Ali, for his part, usually enjoyed the company of the reporters who hung around his training camps and fights, though he reveled in proving them wrong. Murray maintained a civil, if not friendly, relationship with Ali and now shared a lengthy history.

But Ali had his fun with Murray, too. In 1973, Ali came to Los Angeles to promote an upcoming bout against Ken Norton. From the podium, he denounced a certain Los Angeles sportswriter, whom he did not name, for writing the phrase "muzzle the Muslim." The diatribe was clearly aimed at Murray. Incensed and absolutely sure he had never written those words, Murray called the *Times* research library and had a staffer read him his last dozen columns about Ali. "Muzzle the Muslim" was nowhere to be found. Confident, Murray went to Ali's hotel room ready for a confrontation. Ali was lounging on the bed waiting for him. Murray angrily bet Ali one hundred dollars that he was not the source of those words. Ali accepted the bet and then produced a yellowed clipping with the offending phrase, written many years earlier.[62] Murray was dumbfounded. He swallowed his pride and apologized in the hotel room, and then later in a letter to Ali in which he included a check for one hundred dollars. Soon thereafter, Murray received a response, which contained the check, uncashed, and a gentle, hand-printed lecture. "Jim, I have nothing bad to say about what you write, because burning words arise from a flaming heart," Ali wrote. "Jim, forget it my friend. It's impossible to be human and not make mistakes."[63]

The following year, Murray joined the press caravan on a trip halfway around the world, to Zaire, where Ali would finally reclaim his title belt from the current champion, George Foreman.[64] For the press, the entire undertaking was a debacle from the beginning. First, Murray and a troupe of national sportswriters and columnists began the trek to the Dark Continent only to learn that Foreman had suffered an injury and the match had been postponed six weeks. Murray had flown over the North Pole from California to Paris when news of the postponement reached the writers. They booked their tickets back to the United States and planned to try it again the following month. Murray was convinced the fight would never happen.

But a month later, he stepped on African soil for the first time, armed with a quiver full of African clichés. But instead of pith helmet, drum-beating natives, and Katharine Hepburn, he and the rest of the writers were confronted with Zairean officials with a decidedly un-American interpretation of freedom of the press. "Every day was a crisis," said Jerry Izenberg, in Zaire representing the *Newark Star-Ledger*. "There were government censors, everything went wrong, the machines didn't work, and we were kept under strict guard. We all had guys assigned to us to be interpreters, but if you put lemon juice on their foreheads, it would have said C-O-P. They were there to spy. The government was everything, they ran the fight."[65]

Zaire had been liberated from Belgium just thirteen years prior (when it was called Belgian Congo) and, after a series of tribal confrontations, was now run by the dictator Mobuto Sese Seko, who sported a leopard hat and saw a heavyweight championship fight as a way of introducing his country to the world. He sought to control the content of that introduction, and soon writers began noticing that the stories they submitted were very different from what their editors were receiving back in the United States. Twelve-hundred-word articles were mysteriously shrinking to 650 words in transit. But the government censors were so inept, the versions they sent on to the United States were completely nonsensical.[66]

Eventually, the censors were called off, but Mobuto's men found new ways to torment the writers. Murray and the others spent much of the week waiting in long lines for documentation or on bus rides over the forty potholed miles between N'Sele and Kinshasa. African officials changed rules and schedules on a whim, so the writers were constantly in the dark and getting progressively angrier.

On the day of the fight, they were told press credentials would be distributed at 3:00 p.m. in Kinshasa, so Murray and the rest planned to get their tickets and go back to the compound to rest up for the fight, which was scheduled for 4:00 a.m. to accommodate television back in the States. In Kinshasa, they were informed that no, the credentials would actually be distributed back in N'Sele. Back at the compound after yet another bus ride, a smiling interpreter ordered them back on the bus to get their credentials at the stadium in Kinshasa. On and on it went, until the group was led into a swelteringly hot room in the bowels of the stadium after midnight. A mob of 150 writers, now sweating and seething, fought each other and their guides for their fight tickets. It was well after two when, finally, the "sleepless, bearded, blood-shot, saddle-sore" group made it to ringside.[67]

For their troubles, the press was treated to a classic bout. The Ali mystique was cemented. The intimidating and heavily favored Foreman was duped into punching himself out by the now legendary "rope-a-dope," and Ali knocked him out in the eighth round. Murray wrote, "Foreman hit the floor like a load of cantaloupes falling off a truck. It was the first thing he hit squarely all night long."[68] The drama for Murray, however, was still to come.

About fifty phones had been installed for the press at ringside, and before the fight Murray made a test call to the *Times* sports desk. To his amazement, the call went through, and Avrum Dansky, 17,500 miles away in Los Angeles, sounded like he was in the next room. The postfight call, however, was a different story entirely. On first dial, Murray connected with a Southern California dentist's office. He begged the receptionist to stay on the line, to no avail. On the next try, he got accounting at the *Times*. He finally connected with Dansky and dictated two pages of copy, but then the line went dead. And as workers leisurely tried to breathe life into Murray's phone, the skies opened up and loosed a downpour of biblical proportions. The boxing ring and the press tables were located under a corrugated sheet-metal roof, and now the rain pelted the roof and made hearing impossible. The water came in at an angle, dousing the writers and disabling their phones. Murray stood in two inches of water, trying, unsuccessfully, to block the rain with an umbrella as he screamed over and over into the dead receiver.

After an hour of pouring rain, *Times* reporter Dial Torgerson was able to find an open line on an inside phone in the basement of the stadium, and Murray's column finally made it to America, only one hour late. In the end, his battle with the elements to get his column into the paper proved exhilarating. "The Africans kept saying everything would be all right, and in the end, it was. Africa taught me one thing. Efficiency is no fun," he wrote.[69]

The "Rumble in the Jungle" was the apex of the Ali story. The next year he faced Frazier for the third time in a bout Murray later called "the most terrible fight ever seen in a ring," one he believed ended the careers of both men.[70] Ali's victory on a fourteenth-round technical knockout (Frazier did not answer the bell for the fifteenth round) cemented his reputation as a true champion. Ali stayed atop the heavyweight division for another four years, save a stretch in which he lost the title to upstart Leon Spinks and regained it within a seven-month period in 1978.

By the time Ali came to Los Angeles in July 1979, Murray's opinion of him had reversed. He had taken to saying about Ali that "he didn't have fights, he held recitals." Ali called a press conference at the Los Angeles Forum to announce his retirement and discuss his plans to start a charitable organization. Before the conference, which was attended by more than a hundred media members, Murray was escorted to a private room to talk with Ali, and the two chatted for a half hour before Ali spoke from a podium with the rest of the media. Ali, for his part, now incorporated Murray into his act. "Jim Murray! Jim Murray! The Greatest Sportswriter of all-time!" he shouted outside a Los Angeles Lakers game a few months earlier.[71]

Like almost all boxers, Ali could not stay away from the limelight. A year later he was back in the ring with the new champion, Larry Holmes, who battered Ali until his trainer, Angelo Dundee, stopped the fight after ten rounds. Murray was finally ready to include Ali on his Mount Rushmore of boxing. "He belongs with the Joe Louises, James J. Jeffries, the Jack Johnsons and the Jack Dempseys now. He's yesterday's roses, he belongs to the scrapbooks."[72]

Even before the fight against Holmes, Ali was exhibiting signs of physical deterioration, and the progression continued through his retirement. By the 1990s, Ali suffered from full-blown Parkinson's disease, moved slowly, and had trouble communicating. Murray's early laments about the brutality of the sport of boxing now came full circle and enveloped perhaps the largest figure to come across the sports landscape in his lifetime. "The most stunning physical specimen any sport ever produced" had become "a shambling, stumbling, stuttering, mumbling replica of himself," Murray wrote. It was, he said, just another in the long line of boxing tragedies. "Even though he may have been the best of all time, he was miscast as a fighter," he wrote in his autobiography. "He paid the price. He was right. He was too pretty to fight."[73]

A Year in the Dark

The old adage says bad luck comes in threes. Starting at the National League Championship Series in 1978, Murray hit on a trifecta of physical trauma that got progressively worse and culminated in an entire year, 1979, of near-total blindness.

Philadelphia hosted game 1 of the playoffs. The Dodgers beat the Phillies, and Murray filed his column from Veterans Stadium and headed back to the press hotel with a gaggle of sportswriters. The group reached the lobby after two and, with everybody in a hurry to get to sleep, crammed into the elevator eleven strong, well over a ton of sportswriter. It proved to be more than the elevator could handle. The machine made a valiant effort and then shuddered to a halt between floors. Murray suffered from claustrophobia and seemed to have a physical makeup that would regularly bring elevators to a halt; this was the third time he had been stuck in a stalled one. So after a half hour of manic button pushing and alarm pulling, he pleaded for the escape hatch to be opened. His fellow scribes boosted him through the hatch, whereupon he tripped over the steel bar on top of the elevator. His shin swelled to the size of a grapefruit, his bicep developed a ripe bruise, and intense pain shot through his elbow. The wounds required treatment, administered by Dodger doctor Bob Woods, but Murray was able to play through the injuries and finish out the 1978 baseball season for the *Times*.[74]

Injury no. 2 happened two months later, at the World Cup golf tournament in Hawaii. Gerry came along, and the two made a vacation of it, staying at the luxury Princeville Resort. One morning at seven, Murray awoke from a deep sleep to the sound of a ringing phone. Startled, he ran for the phone and tripped on a throw rug and came down hard on his foot. He crawled to the phone, expecting an urgent message, and was greeted on the other end of the line by a cigarette executive casually inviting him to a cocktail party. He never made it to the party. Instead, he went to the hospital, learned his foot was broken, and was outfitted with a cast and a pair of crutches.

Navigating on crutches proved to be a difficult task, but the fall in Hawaii caused a much more sinister injury, one that revealed itself gradually. Murray began to notice blurriness in his left eye. It got a little worse each day. His right eye was already barely functioning due to a cataract, so he relied almost entirely on the left eye. In late January, he flew to Miami to cover Super Bowl XIII between the Pittsburgh Steelers and the Dallas Cowboys. He never made it to the game.

In Miami, the left eye deteriorated rapidly. By midweek, he had to feel his way through the lobby with his hands, going from wall to wall. The day before the game, Murray and a group of sportswriters went to Gulfstream Park Race Track to kill time before the big event. Murray ordered an egg salad sandwich for lunch. When it arrived, it looked to him as though it were growing red worms. In fact, his eye was filling with blood, thanks to four tears on his retina that had been expanding ever since that early-morning phone call at the Princeville Resort.

So while the Steelers and the Cowboys were engaged in the most thrilling Super Bowl to date, Murray was across town at Mercy Hospital, participating in what he called his own personal Super Bowl. "I won't say I was in deep trouble, but Jimmy Greek said that if you took me that afternoon, you got 40 points," he wrote.[75] Doctors determined the surgery could be performed with only local anesthetic, so Murray, lying on the operating table, got the pleasure of staring directly into the needle that was being stuck into his eye. His blood pressure shot up to 260. The surgery was performed by Dr. David Sime, who, coincidentally, had been an Olympic sprinter and subject of a Murray column years before. Sime operated on Murray for five hours, the tears were repaired, and when the bandages came off a few days later, the left eye was back in business.

It did not last long. Murray flew back to Los Angeles and began to get back into his daily rhythm. Doctors told him he could start driving—both cars and golf balls—and his column returned to the sports page. But in April the eye deteriorated again, and this time it was much worse. The day after Easter, he was watching TV when he told Gerry that the television suddenly "appeared to be flowing down to the floor." The next day, doctors delivered the latest in his ever-expanding string of bad news: his retina was now completely detached from his eye. He was blind.

Surgery no. 2 was performed a few weeks later at the Jules Stein Eye Clinic at UCLA, and the retina was reattached. Before he could even leave the hospital, however, it came off again. A third surgery was scheduled and then canceled after doctors determined the chances of success were minimal. Murray was sent home to contemplate life without sight. Doctors reconvened, and the decision was made to perform a victrectomy, which would have a one-in-twelve chance of success. On May 19, the surgery was performed at Huntington Memorial Hospital in Pasadena. Once he was off the table, another waiting game began.

This time, the physical and mental pain was far worse. Murray was required to lie facedown for three weeks, even while eating. Back in Miami while he was confined to the hospital, at least he could attempt to watch television; now he was completely in the dark. His eye filled with blood. He could barely eat or sleep, and his weight dropped precipitously. He suffered from constant debilitating headaches. Then, after nearly a month of suffering and hoping, it was all over. The retina had come off for good.

Nearly half a year in and out of hospitals, fighting for his sight, had worn him down. He could read the tea leaves; in his heart, this was the outcome he had been expecting. "That was a shock to open the eye and see nothing but a black hole," he said. "But I didn't have high hopes; I went into that operation without an eye. It gets to a point where if something happens that you kind of wish hadn't happened, you can cry and feel kind of bad. But when something catastrophic happens, crying doesn't help."[76]

The left eye was done. The right eye provided very little sight due to the cataract. But, Murray thought, at least it was something. He decided to forego cataract surgery for the time being. After his six months of hell, he was putting off a decision. He would wait. And in the meantime, he would try to resume his life. He told *Times* sports editor Bill Shirley of his plan. He couldn't type, he couldn't see the field of play, he couldn't transport himself, but, by God, he could still produce a column. Shirley and the *Times* editors signed off, and it was announced that his column would resume on July 1.

What he produced for his return from surgery proved to be the most celebrated column of his career. It was a eulogy for his eye, and a wistful remembrance of all he had seen with it. The loss of Murray's sight became an occasion to memorialize his own past, but also for his readers to mourn, and celebrate, their collective histories. It ran at the top of page 1 of the sports section with a headline "If You're Expecting One-Liners, Wait a Column . . ."

OK, bang the drum slowly, professor. Muffle the cymbals and the laugh track. You might say that Old Blue Eye is back. But that's as funny as this is going to get.

I feel I owe my friends an explanation as to where I've been all these weeks. Believe me, I would rather have been in a press box.

I lost an old friend the other day. He was blue-eyed, impish, he cried a lot with me, laughed a lot with me, saw a great many things with me. I don't know why he left me. Boredom, perhaps.

We read a lot of books together, we did a lot of crossword puzzles together. He had a pretty exciting life. He saw Babe Ruth hit a home run when we were both 12 years old. He saw Willie Mays steal second base. He saw Rocky Marciano get up. I thought he had a pretty good life.

One night a long time ago he saw this pretty girl who laughed a lot, played the piano and he couldn't look away from her. Later he looked on as I married this pretty lady.

He saw her through 34 years. He loved to see her laugh, he loved to see her happy.

You see, the friend I lost was my eye. My good eye. The other eye, the right one, we've been carrying for years. We just let him tag along like Don Quixote's nag. It's been a long time since he could read the number on a halfback or tell whether a ball was fair or foul or even which fighter was down.

So, one blue eye missing and the other misses a lot.

So my best friend left me, at least temporarily, in a twilight world where it's always 8 o'clock on a summer night.

He stole away like a thief in the night and he took a lot with him. But not everything. He left a lot of memories. He couldn't take those with him. He just took the future with him and the present. He couldn't take the past.

I don't know why he had to go. I thought we were pals. I thought the things we did together we enjoyed doing together. Sure, we cried together. There were things to cry about.

But it was a long, good relationship, a happy one. It went all the way back to the days when we arranged all the marbles in a circle in the dirt in the lots in

Connecticut. We played one-old-cat baseball. We saw curveballs together, trying to hit them or catch them. We looked through a catcher's mask together. We were partners in every sense of the word.

He recorded the happy moments, the miracle of children, the beauty of a Pacific sunset, snowcapped mountains, faces on Christmas morning. He allowed me to hit fly balls to young sons in uniforms two sizes too large, to see a pretty daughter march in halftime parades. He allowed me to see most of the major sports events of our time. I suppose I should be grateful that he didn't drift away when I was 12 or 15 or 29 but stuck around over 50 years until we had a vault of memories. Still, I'm only human. I'd like to see again, if possible, Rocky Marciano with his nose bleeding, behind on points and the other guy coming.

I guess I would like to see Reggie Jackson with the count 3-and-2 and the series on the line, guessing fastball. I guess I'd like to see Rod Carew with men on first and second and no place to put him, and the pitcher wishing he were standing in the rain someplace, reluctant to let go of the ball.

I'd like to see Stan Musial crouched around a curveball one more time. I'd like to see Don Drysdale trying to not laugh as a young hitter came up there with both feet in the bucket.

I'd like to see Sandy Koufax just once more facing Willie Mays with a no-hitter on the line. I'd like to see Maury Wills with a big lead against a pitcher with a good move. I'd like to see Roberto Clemente with the ball and a guy trying to go from first to third. I'd like to see Pete Rose sliding into home headfirst.

I'd like once more to see Henry Aaron standing there with that quiet bat, a study in deadliness. I'd like to see Bob Gibson scowling at a hitter as if he had some nerve just to pick up a bat. I'd like to see Elroy Hirsch going out for a long one from Bob Waterfield, Johnny Unitas in high-cuts picking apart a zone defense. I'd like to see Casey Stengel walking to the mound on his gnarled old legs to take a pitcher out, beckoning his gnarled old finger behind his back.

I'd like to see Sugar Ray Robinson or Muhammad Ali giving a recital, a ballet, not a fight. Also, to be sure, I'd like to see a sky full of stars, moonlight on the water, and yes, the tips of a royal flush peeking out as I fan out a poker hand, and yes, a straight two-foot putt.

Come to think of it, I'm lucky. I saw all of those things. I see them yet.[77]

The column brought tears to thousands of healthy eyes across Southern California and the country. After wiping away the tears, however, many readers probably read the tagline, which announced that Murray's column was resuming, and thought to themselves, how is that possible? What is the point of a blind sports columnist? How can one tell the story of a game they can't see? Pete Rose, for one, asked him point-blank: "How can you write a column if you can't see the fucking game?"[78]

Murray knew that those were not the pertinent questions. His skill never lay in descriptions of games or plays. "My bread and butter is to talk to Steve Garvey, not to watch him," he said at the time. No, the one question that kept repeating in his head was: how can I produce words and sentences that I cannot see? He would now have to dictate his column into a cassette recorder. As one who had spent forty years writing, he understood that writing and talking were two separate skills. "What plays on the written page often does not play on stage," he wrote later. "One romances the eyes, the other falls on the ears."[79]

For his return column, Murray had dictated directly to *Times* secretary Marilyn White. It had been an emotional experience that had left White in tears, and she told Shirley she was unwilling to go through it again. Shirley and the top editors at the *Times* were worried that if Murray remained absent from the sports page much longer, it would begin to be reflected in lost circulation. Murray would need his own personal assistant, someone to drive him around, walk him from point A to point B, and help him look up facts and phone numbers. Shirley chose John Scheibe, a night-desk assistant who had been with the sports department for eight years. At the time, Scheibe felt he had been languishing in his current position and was upset at being passed over by Shirley for writing positions. He had been circulating his résumé when Shirley told him about his new assignment.

The following week, Scheibe drove to Bellagio Terrace to meet Murray. From the outset, Murray explained what he wanted. His two biggest problems, he said, were that he could not drive and he could not look up facts and statistics. Also, he would need Scheibe to observe the scene while Murray conducted interviews. "I can call up Jim Palmer on the phone anytime but it's not the same as interviewing someone in person," he said. Scheibe found that part of the assignment most challenging. Soon thereafter, Scheibe took Murray to Dodger Stadium. Murray asked Scheibe to follow Dodger second baseman Davey Lopes around before the game and record everything he saw.[80]

For the next six months, Scheibe shuttled Murray from Bellagio Terrace to Rams training camp, to Dodgers and Angels games, to press conferences, and to personal interviews. In October, he would fly with Murray to Baltimore and Pittsburgh for the World Series. At first, Scheibe said, Murray did not open up much, and their conversations centered on that day's sports topic. But over time, Murray would drop tidbits of history from his career, observations about the newspaper profession, and words of journalistic and life wisdom. One day, the two had planned to cover a Dodgers game, but Scheibe had forgotten his press pass, so they had to go back to Scheibe's apartment to retrieve it. Scheibe still had responsibilities in the sports department as well as his duties for Murray and had neglected to clean his apartment for more than a week. Murray looked at the sink overflowing with dishes. "You know, your house is where you live," Murray said gently. On another occasion, Murray asked Scheibe to read the newspaper to him, a task that Scheibe would perform regularly during his time as Murray's assistant. The newspaper, Murray told him, is like a three-course meal. The news section is the meat and potatoes, the local news is the vegetables, and the sports section, of course, is the dessert.[81]

The outpouring of support for Murray came not just from his colleagues and readers, but from his celebrity friends, from the worlds of both sports and entertainment. In late September, many of them came together for Jim Murray Night at the Friars Club. The Friars Club was, and still is, famous for staging not-ready-for-prime-time roasts of celebrities. Comedian and roastmaster Hal Kanter opened the festivities: "You will hear things here tonight that can't be repeated when you get home to your wife," he said. "Unless, of course, you're married to a hooker." The head table included Jerry West, Bill Walton, broadcaster Brent Musberger, former Rams head coach George Allen, comedians Bill Cosby, Norm Crosby, and Jackie Vernon as well as Bill Thomas, Mark Murphy, and Chuck Garrity from the *Times*. Most of what was said was unpublishable when John Hall sat down to write about the event for the following day's newspaper. He did his best to quote one of Crosby's lines: "All this talk about a guy who can't see! I'm sitting next to George Jessel and his (unprintable) pacemaker blew out both my (unprintable) hearing aids and I can't hear an (unprintable) thing!" Murray laughed along with the proceedings, and when it was his turn to speak, he told the crowd that he wished Howard Cosell had been there, so all the derision could be have been heaped on Cosell instead of him.[82]

The recognition and good wishes helped, but Murray often had difficulty staying in good spirits. He traveled to Boston to consult with Dr. Richard Kratz, a cataract surgeon, and Dr. Charles Scheppens, a well-known retinal surgeon whose clients included Ella Fitzgerald, Lauren Bacall, and California Angels owner Gene Autry. Murray was told that an operation to fix the cataract on his right eye could cause the retina in that eye to detach. He returned from that trip extremely dejected. When Scheibe arrived to pick him up, Gerry intercepted him. "Yesterday, he was walking around the house, wearing an old man sweater, all bent over like an old man," she said. "I yelled at him, 'You straighten up and stop feeling sorry for yourself. I never want to see you like that again.'" Her voice was cracking, and she had tears in her eyes as she told Scheibe to keep an eye on Murray for signs of depression.[83]

In Boston, Murray had been fitted for a small optical device that he could place over his good eye to increase vision. Later, it would allow him to write his columns in long hand. He would scribble large letters that took up a page per paragraph and hand the sheets to Scheibe to dictate back to the sports desk at the *Times*. When walking, Murray did not like to be guided by the arm and would ask Scheibe to walk a foot or two in front of him. He could make out the outline of Scheibe's body and follow along. Once, the two of them were at Rams training camp, and the path they were traversing crossed into the shade. Murray lost sight of Scheibe, stepped off the path, and fell into a rusty sprinkler pipe, leaving a long, bloody gash on his leg. Rams doctors taped up the wound, but it became infected and sidelined Murray for more than a week.[84]

Through the autumn he continued to prove, four times a week, that he could produce a column virtually blind. (Indeed, he would be named national sportswriter of the year again for his work in 1979, even with his limited output.) But his right eye was gradually getting worse. In early December, Scheibe took Murray to the Los Angeles Coliseum to cover the Minnesota Vikings–Los Angeles Rams football game. After the game, Scheibe led Murray outside of the stadium, toward the players' dressing rooms, for postgame interviews. Murray was moving even slower than usual. Police had set up wooden barriers to keep traffic off the street that led to the Coliseum. Scheibe stepped between two of the barriers slowly and then turned back to make sure Murray made it through safely. But Murray walked straight into the sawhorse, pitched forward, and bent over at the waist before Scheibe was able to grab him and return him to his feet. Murray slowly adjusted his glasses and followed Scheibe into the locker room.

On the drive back to Bellagio Terrace, Scheibe sensed that Murray's situation had deteriorated. When they arrived, Murray got out of the car and walked tentatively toward the door. "Is everything okay?" Scheibe called. Murray did not answer, and the door shut behind him.

Two days later, Shirley announced to the *Times* sports staff that cataract surgery would be performed on Murray on December 17. The risk of complete blindness was just as great as it had been six months before. But the advantages of staying pat had clearly diminished. There was, Murray now felt, really nothing to lose. Kratz would perform a procedure using the Kellman phacoemulsification technique, in which a supersonic drill liquefies the cataract, allowing doctors to remove it without any residual retinal trauma.

The surgery was performed, and that night the bandages were removed. Murray blinked and then focused on the television in his hospital room, which was tuned to *Monday Night Football*. Before the surgery, the television looked to him like a white spotlight. Now, he focused on the screen, and could make out Denver Broncos quarterback Craig Morton running on the field. The green of the grass, the orange of the Broncos' uniforms, even the number 7 on Morton's jersey were clearly visible.[85] "I will never forget that sight," Murray wrote. "For some men, the most beautiful sight they will ever see in this world is a Canadian sunset or the changing of the leaves of autumn. Not me. For me, it was Craig Morton on Channel 7."[86]

The veil had been lifted, and, almost immediately, the possibilities of daily life expanded as the claustrophobia of eternal darkness receded into his memory. Within weeks, he was able to type and see the words as the ink struck the paper. He opened his desk drawer and put away the telescopic device, the tape recorder, and the special distance glasses that had been his crutches through the darkness and pulled out his pad and pen. He could even drive himself to the Bel Air market or the Duck Blind, his favorite liquor store, both short distances from his home. He would still require drivers for long rides and was unable to drive at night. And he was less than exact when he did get behind the wheel. Friends would notice that the washer and dryer that sat at the back of the garage at Bellagio Terrace had multiple dents and dings received during Murray's attempts to bring his car to a rest.[87]

The Murrays had purchased a home in Palm Desert earlier in the year, and now they spent the last Christmas of the '70s there. His dream of stepping out of his living room onto the golf course had been realized and was made all the more delightful now that he could drink in the greens of the fairways and palm fronds against the desert tans of the San Jacinto Mountains.

A few weeks later, Murray called Scheibe for a ride to a media event in Newport Beach. Super Bowl XIV would be played in the Rose Bowl in Pasadena, with the hometown Rams facing the Pittsburgh Steelers. Murray had not seen Scheibe since the operation. Scheibe pulled his car into the Bellagio Terrace driveway as Murray was coming out of the house. Murray paused and gazed into the vehicle. "Scheibe, you're a white man," he observed.[88]

Murray had another scare two years later, one that would again require major surgery. Preparing to fly to Detroit for Super Bowl XVI, the world went dark once more. Gerry drove him to the hospital immediately, and he was soon back on the operating table. This time around, Dr. Otto Jungschaffer, who had been involved in the earlier procedures, used a new technique to freeze the retina back onto the eye. The surgery was a success, and the retina held.[89]

The decision to go through with the surgery had clearly been the correct one. The retina would never again tear loose and plunge Murray into darkness. Still, his vision would steadily weaken through the remainder of his life, and he would require a driver and, in later years, assistance with routine daily activities. To friends and acquaintances, physical frailty and weak eyesight would become part of Murray's persona for the rest of his years and his drive to fight through them a sign of courage. It was a badge Murray rejected. He still viewed himself as the slightly clumsy athletic wannabe of his younger years. But these daily battles to confront the personal obstacles he faced to cover the games and produce the columns would become etched in the memories of his friends and colleagues. For Blackie Sherrod, Murray's close friend and a revered sports editor and columnist, it was Murray's defining trait. "In view of all the adverse circumstances," Sherrod said, "Jim was the toughest rascal I ever knew."[90]

8

The 1980s

Brave New World

It's not often the American public opens the paper anymore to find out who won and how. The famous five "W's" of our business have pretty much been reduced to the one "W" for "Why?" TV takes care of the Who, What, When and Where. On the big stories, anyway.

—Jim Murray, "Amateur Night," *Los Angeles Times,* March 12, 1971

Changing the Channel

One of the constants in the career of Jim Murray was the ever-looming specter of television. When he was a beat reporter in the '40s, television cameras first began appearing at crime scenes, forcing print reporters to step over wires and then watch as their stories aired on television hours before they could get them into print. When he moved over to cover Hollywood in the '50s, he encountered a movie industry gripped by the fear that television was about to kill their golden goose. It did not, but it did end the studio system. Once he made the move to sports journalism, he watched from the press box as television transformed that industry, too. Boxing matches, baseball and football games, golf tournaments—events that were originally created for live spectators—were remade to suit television viewers, and television advertisers. Sports now lived and died with how they suited the four-cornered screen.

Before television, a trip to the ballpark had been a special occasion. The anticipation of attending a game added to the excitement. Television was now a way of life. A professional sporting event, once a distant occurrence and romanticized by a newspaper, was now as commonplace as a trip to the dentist. In 1978, a national poll conducted by *TV Guide* showed that, with the exception of baseball, the majority of Americans preferred to witness sporting events on television rather than in person.[1] Between 1960 and 1980, television broadcasts of sporting events doubled.[2]

By the 1980s, the small screen had imperial status in sports. And the money it had brought with it was staggering. In 1984, the three major networks were operating under a two-billion-dollar contract to cover the National Football League. From 1970 to 1980, the average Major League Baseball salary increased 417 percent, the average pro-basketball salary went up 375 percent, and the average National Football League salary doubled.[3] Top stars like tennis player Bjorn Borg earned more than two million dollars annually in endorsements. (Just twenty years prior, Sandy Koufax, then Major League Baseball's best pitcher, boycotted Los Angeles Dodgers spring training because the Dodgers organization refused to give him a raise to seventy thousand dollars.) And though television was putting obscene amounts of cash (by the standards of the time) into the hands of athletes and franchise owners, they were saving the biggest piece of the pie for themselves: the sports divisions of the three networks earned more in profits than was earned by all of the American professional sports franchises combined.[4]

The enormous interest in sports generated by television was a rising flood that brought everybody along for the ride. In sports, it was a boom time. Players, owners, and coaches were reaping huge monetary benefits, and those who wrote about them were enjoying the trickle-down effect. And though they may have been among the last to feel the trickle, it was not a bad time to be a sports columnist, either.

From 1983 to 1985, salaries for sports columnists at big-city newspapers increased from an average of thirty-two thousand to nearly forty-seven thousand dollars—pocket change to athletes and television announcers, but a windfall for those who made their living with a notebook and pen. The confluence of booms in newspapers and in sports made the top names in the sports-columnist field desirable to newspaper executives, and some newspapers came calling with large salary offers to lure away top talent. Murray's friend Blackie Sherrod jumped from the *Dallas Times-Herald* to the rival *Dallas Morning News* when the *News* dangled an unheard-of six-figure salary in front of him. The *Times-Herald* countered by paying Murray's former *Times* colleague Skip Bayless a similar figure.

Now, for the first time, a sportswriter might be able to brag about perks other than a seat in the press box and a complimentary hot dog. Some were negotiating company cars, first-class travel, bonus packages, country-club memberships. In the gossipy, underpaid newspaper industry, journalists from other departments took note. At an Associated Press convention in November 1984, Bayless, Dave Kindred of the *Atlanta Journal-Constitution,* and John Schulian of the *Philadelphia Daily News* were the speakers in a panel discussion in which they were asked to defend their high salaries to the assembled journalists. The three, Schulian said, were like lambs in a lion's den.[5]

Since the *Times* was the most profitable American newspaper in an era of gargantuan newspaper profits, its sports department waded into the fray, battling the biggest papers in the country to attract the nation's top sportswriting talent. Mike Littwin was among a number of writers lured away from smaller newspapers to join the *Times* sports staff in that era. Littwin came to the *Times* in 1978 from the *Norfolk Virginian-Pilot.* "The *Times* was at its height probably around that time," Littwin said. "It was considered to have one of the two or three best sports sections in the country. And the newspaper itself had tremendous ambition and was making a huge amount of money. We used to fly first-class on any flight that was over two hours. You could go wherever you wanted to and pursue any story you wanted to do at that time. Basically, the only limitations on you were your own ability to make it great."[6]

The *Times* sports department had been run by Bill Shirley since 1964, when he took over from Paul Zimmerman. Shirley was a visionary who was cognizant of television's effect on sports and sought to adapt his product to suit the brave new world that was now ruled by TV. He looked past what he saw as small-time competition, like the *Herald-Examiner* down the street, and instead focused on *Sports Illustrated*[7] and, even more ambitiously, ABC Sports. "Shirley didn't care too much if we got beat on a story by the *Herald-Examiner,*" said Scheibe, who returned to desk duty after his stint as Murray's driver. "He saw TV as the competition, so he started hiring young writers like Skip Bayless, Ted Green, Alan Greenberg, Scott Ostler, and Richard Hoffer. . . . Under Shirley, it also was just a transformation from this kind of little hometown newspaper into this, you know, this bigger idea."[8]

In 1972, Shirley had sent sports staffer Dwight Chapin to cover the Summer Olympics in Munich and had given him instructions to emulate the coverage of ABC Sports and its esteemed chief, Roone Arledge. Chapin was the *Times's* best reporter at the time, called "the dean" by his colleagues in the department. But Shirley had high expectations, and Chapin was not meeting them in Munich. He called Chapin in his hotel room. "Dwight, ABC is beating us," Shirley demanded. "Then hire ABC, Bill," Chapin replied.[9]

But it was Shirley's vision of the future that shaped the department. The young writers were given the latitude to pursue stories and think big. "We were similar of style," said Littwin. "A lot of us were basically home-run hitters who also struck out a lot. But we were always swinging for the fences."[10]

Another characteristic the new hires shared was that they were in awe of Murray. Most had grown up reading his column and emulating his style. Meeting him was something akin to an audience with the pope.

Ostler joined the *Times* in 1976 after a childhood of reading Murray every morning. "The first time I ever met him, I guess, was when I first went to the *Times* as the prep editor," Ostler recalled.

> He only came in [to the office] maybe once or twice every two months. He came in one day to pick up his mail, and he walked by my desk. I don't think we had met; maybe he briefly introduced himself. And somebody had given him a promotional item, a basketball. And he kind of walked around up behind my desk, and he said, "Hey, do you want this basketball?" And I said, "Yeah, great." So he gave me this free promotional basketball. I thought, *Wow, this is the greatest gift I ever got. Jim Murray just gave me a basketball.*[11]

Littwin remembered on his first story for the *Times*, fresh from Norfolk, covering the Bob Hope Classic in Palm Springs. Murray was being followed around by a television crew who was working on a story about him. "I remember thinking, *Man, you get to the 'LA Times,' and TV stations follow you around.* I ended up learning that that was only if you were Jim Murray," he said.[12]

Murray also received his share of the sincerest form of flattery. The imitations took place at newspapers across the country, with varying degrees of success, but it crept into the work of the *Times*'s young writers, too.

"We all had a little bit of the Jim Murray disease," said Littwin.

> I think I was struck as hard as anybody by him. There's a story that Chuck Garrity, who was then the assistant sports editor, one day he took me aside and put his arm around my shoulder and said, "There's only one Jim Murray. Try to be somebody else." So, yeah, for a young writer, you've got the guy who just wrote the funniest, most brilliant, smartest lines of anybody in the country. It's like having *The Show of Shows'* writing team all in one guy, right there. So it was very difficult not to try to emulate what he was doing.[13]

Shirley's eye for talent raised the level of journalism in the department immensely. Employee relations, however, went in the other direction. John Hall wrote a column for the *Times* for the entirety of Shirley's reign as sports editor, mostly appearing on page 3 of the sports section. "Let's see, how should I put it? He was a narrow-minded, selfish, crooked jerk," Hall said. "He was so nasty . . . to all the guys on the staff. Nobody liked him. He would leave nasty notes for people, that they had to improve their prose, and he was very jealous of people. . . . Several people left because they didn't want to be around him."[14]

Shirley sought the approval of his superiors in management and viewed the staff as cogs in the machine. (Murray was an exception to this rule, and the two maintained a strong professional relationship by all accounts.) His level of empathy was nonexistent. He would remove writers from beats or demote them via a note in their mailbox. He barred writers from bringing their wives on road trips. Once, he called a writer in the hospital room and accused him of freelancing while on sick leave.

The corporate mentality had infiltrated the *Times* over the years, and the company expanded and became more than a family-owned newspaper. Littwin remembers a disconnect between the top editors, including Shirley, and the frontline writers, editors, and photographers: "All the top editors ate lunch in this editors' cafeteria upstairs on the tenth floor. They ate at noon, and Bill Shirley, no matter what was going on, no matter what you were doing, would leave to be there at noon. He would be in the middle of a conversation, and bang, noon, he was gone to lunch."

Shirley's illustrious career as sports editor, to the glee of his employees, came to an ignominious end, after an incident that took place around Super Bowl XV in January 1981. While he had the vision to bring the *Times* into the new era of sports journalism, he had come of age in the business during an earlier time, and the standards and mores of the industry had shifted beneath his feet. For as long as there had been a sports section, sportswriters had been receiving complimentary tickets, meals, drinks, and gifts and had happily accepted whatever was offered. In the post-Watergate era, all journalists, sportswriters included, began to take their roles more seriously. Conflicts of interest, large and small, were ferreted out. Many newspaper vets went down in the process.

Shirley either was blind to the sea change or didn't much care. Either way, he had the misfortune of getting swept up in a ticket-scalping scandal, one brought about by his own newspaper. The Oakland Raiders were matched in the Super Bowl against the Philadelphia Eagles in January 1981. Littwin was in Fresno to report a story about Raiders coach Tom Flores the week before the game. "I picked up the *Fresno Bee,* and the lead story in the sports section of the *Fresno Bee* was this article on Super Bowl tickets. About the sixth paragraph in, there's this: 'Among those getting Super Bowl tickets and trading them was Bill Shirley, sports editor of the *Los Angeles Times.*' And this is pre–cell phone days, so I run to a pay phone and call the office and say, 'What the hell's going on here?' So yeah . . . he was caught by his own newspaper."[15]

The article, written by two *Times* news reporters, ran on the front page, above the fold. It was an investigation into Super Bowl ticket scalping, and the story that was uncovered swept up players, coaches, team and league officials, and sportswriters and editors. Everybody, Shirley included, was getting complimentary or face-value tickets, turning around and selling them to ticket brokers, and pocketing the profits.[16] Shirley's offense was made worse, to his superiors and his employees both, by the revelation that he had been confiscating complimentary tickets meant for the staff, selling them, and keeping the money. Shortly thereafter, he was demoted from sports editor and replaced by Bill Dwyre, who had joined the newspaper only a few months earlier. To the horror of his staff, however, Shirley was kept on as a staff writer, allowed to keep his salary, and given a private office and his choice of which stories to cover, an arrangement he kept until his retirement in 1986.[17]

Murray was of the same generation as Shirley and was also slow to adapt to the changing ethical standards. Littwin recalled a special staff meeting Dwyre called in the wake of the scandal to address the issue of complimentary tickets. There was a new sheriff in town, and the rules would be changing. "Dwyre came in, and at that point, teams gave comp tickets to people who were covering the team. It was routine, in the '70s, among sportswriters," Littwin said. "So Dwyre came in and said, 'All this stuff has to stop. All this shit has to stop.' So we had this big staff meeting. Everybody was there. Murray was in the office, sort of a rare, really rare, sighting. And Murray raises his hand and says, 'What if your wife wants to go to a game?' We all covered our eyes. 'Well, Jim, you know, you buy a ticket.'"[18]

"Hey, Aren't You Jim Murray?"

On one of the many occasions that the Yankees were playing in the World Series, Murray arrived in New York City in the company of columnists Blackie Sherrod and Ed Pope. The three made their way to the reception desk at the Waldorf-Astoria in Manhattan, where they were informed that, despite their reservations, no rooms were available. Sherrod and Pope were dismayed, but Murray asked the clerk for the phone and began dialing. Within a few minutes, he began chatting amiably with somebody on the other end of the line. Then he calmly handed the receiver to the clerk. "Son," the clerk heard a man say. "This is Conrad Hilton. Could you please find Mr. Murray and his friends a room in my hotel?"

Though he rarely acknowledged it as a fact himself, Murray had become a genuine celebrity. He lived among the glitterati. Tourists carrying phony maps of the stars, hoping to catch a glimpse of Liz Taylor or Tony Curtis, were a staple in his neighborhood. Peggy Lee and John Forsythe lived just a few houses away, and a couple of blocks over, on Bellagio Drive, the more adept star-seeking tourists could find the homes of Cary Grant, Jimmy Stewart, Greer Garson, Warren Beatty, Diane Keaton, Ricardo Montalban, and many others.[19] He counted among his friends scores of '60s and '70s A-listers, people whom every American could identify by just one name: Sinatra. Hope. Crosby. Newman. Heston. Matthau.

Murray's sister Betty made a rare visit to Los Angeles in the early '80s, and Murray brought her to the Bel Air Country Club, where he was now a member. As he was showing her the grounds, he noticed something and directed her toward the practice tees. "Come on, there's somebody I want you to meet," he said. Betty saw what was about to happen and tried to pull away. Murray forged on, and soon they were upon one of the golfers. "Betty, there's somebody I'd like you to meet," he said. "This is my friend Dean Martin. Dean, meet my sister Betty."[20]

On another occasion, Murray needed a ride to a red carpet–style fundraising event and had arranged to be driven by Angie Dickinson and Dinah Shore, both Bel Air neighbors. The two glamorous actresses arrived at the Murray home on Bellagio Terrace. Murray saw them through the window but remained in the house. Soon, the honking started, and neighbors peered across their yards, just as Murray had hoped. ""I wanted my neighbors to see that not only were these gorgeous women, Angie and Dinah, picking me up, but they were so impatient to see me that they were honking their horn," he told a friend.[21]

His connections to the luminaries of Hollywood had developed into a network of friends and sources throughout Southern California. But the wide distribution of and respect for his column raised his profile across the country, even in the halls of the White House. From Nixon forward, Murray was acknowledged by every president through the remainder of his life. His relationship with Nixon, of course, went back to Murray's years at *Time* and continued forward. Once, during Nixon's truncated reign in the Oval Office, Murray covered a Texas-Arkansas football game in Fayetteville, Arkansas, which Nixon attended as well. After the game, Murray got caught up in Nixon's Secret Service brigade. One of the agents thought Murray looked suspicious and slammed him up against a fence. As Murray struggled, Nixon strolled by. "How ya doin', Jim?" Nixon asked. "I'd be better," Murray said, "if you could get this monkey to put me down."[22]

Nixon was famously a sports junkie, but his successor, Gerald Ford, was a former star athlete, a veteran of the offensive line from the University of Michigan football squad in the 1930s. Ford was a sports fan, a golfer, and a devotee of Murray's column. It earned Murray his first trip to the White House and a ride on *Air Force One*.

Ford put together a baseball roundtable to accompany him to the 1976 baseball All-Star Game in Cincinnati. Along with Murray were former player and then television announcer Joe Garagiola, Chicago Cub Hall of Famer Ernie Banks, John Underwood of *Sports Illustrated,* and David Israel of the *Washington Star.* The group met up at the White House, took a Secret Service limousine to Andrews Air Force Base, and flew with Ford on *Air Force One* to Cincinnati in time for the game. During the flight, Ford summoned Murray and the base-ball crew to his quarters on the plane as he dined on lobster and crabmeat. Murray asked for a beer and then posed a question to Ford. "Mr. President, did you ever tackle Pug Rentner?" Rentner, Murray said, was one of his favorite all-time football names.

"Many times, Jim," Ford said. "But I got this eye kicked open by Jay Berwanger."[23] The president fingered one eye. "Or maybe it was this one."

Once at the game, the group followed Ford's entourage through the locker rooms and up to the owner's box, from where they were to view the action. Murray had difficulty getting into the conversation. Finally, in the seventh inning, Ford addressed him again. "Jim, who's that at shortstop? He's in a Dodger uniform."

Murray attempted to show off his extensive baseball knowledge to the president. "That, Mr. President, is Billy Russell. He's one of the fastest runners in the league. It's very hard to double him up," he advised. Russell soon hit into a double play. He was out at first by forty-five feet, Murray wrote later.[24]

After his presidency, Ford became a staple on the pro-am golf circuit, where Murray and he developed a closer relationship. Ford regularly turned up in the column, with Murray often poking fun at the former president's golf game. Ford enjoyed the repartee and corresponded on occasion: "Over the years, I have read a number of columns in which I've been mentioned. You can be sure that some pleased me and other provided a less desirable reaction," he wrote to Murray in 1977.[25]

A year later, Murray invited Ford to deliver the presenting speech when he was inducted into the National Sportscasters and Sportswriters Association Hall of Fame. Ford declined, so John Wayne was called in as a replacement. Wayne became ill immediately prior to the ceremony, so Murray went down his list, and in the end, the speech was delivered by Tennessee Ernie Ford and Andy Griffith.[26]

So Gerald Ford never presented Murray with an award, but years later another former president did. In 1992, Murray attended a charity gala in his honor at the Beverly Hills Hotel. It was a high-dollar, star-studded affair, emceed by broadcaster Roy Firestone, organized by Merv Griffin, with tables filled by sports and movie celebrities. After a string of presentations in Murray's honor, Firestone announced that one last friend wanted to say a few words. Ronald and Nancy Reagan walked out from behind the curtain. Reagan spoke about his relationship with Murray, which dated back to the days when Reagan starred in films and Murray wrote about film stars. Eventually, Reagan concluded his speech, and applause rang through the ballroom. Murray slowly and delicately made his way onto the dais. The applause reached a crescendo, and he waited patiently for the audience to quiet. The room finally grew silent. "Did I die?" he asked.[27]

His celebrity status, such as it was, could often be a hindrance in his work and his personal life. He would be recognized at golf tournaments and prize-fights and field autograph requests from sports fans and readers. He found himself constantly in demand for personal engagements, which he detested. He was not comfortable as a public speaker and felt he had no skill for it. "I don't do it if I can get out of it gracefully," Murray told his friend Murray Olderman. "And I certainly don't do it as much as people would like me to do it, because I don't do it well. You know, I'm a writer. I'm not a talker."

In the late 1970s, he was offered the chance to go on a public speaking tour, where he would be paid three thousand dollars per appearance. "I rejected it out of hand," Murray said. I told them, 'You're gonna expect Bob Hope, for that kind of money.' Well, make a long story short, these guys are now getting $20,000 an appearance, and what I should have done was developed a talk, and then polished it up and revised it as I went along, and got comfortable with it. And if I had done this, we wouldn't be sitting here now, we'd be doing this on my yacht," he told Olderman.[28]

Worse, in his mind, than the inconvenience of public speaking and auto-graph hounds was the effect his celebrity status had on his journalism. The type of work he had done in his precolumn days—cultivating inside sources, break-ing stories, investigative reporting—were long gone. He accepted it, but not without some regret. "When I first started out, I was an experienced reporter and probably a better one then than now," he told Walt Cieplik of *Writer's Digest*. "But also, I was anonymous. I could go to a cocktail party and not be JIM MURRAY. People would misbehave, or, rather, open up more to me then. Now, it's easier to get a hold of a guy, because he's probably heard of me. But, by the same token, he's on his guard."[29]

That was the trade-off—anonymity for access. And the level of access Mur-ray achieved was legendary among colleagues in the sportswriting business. Promoters and PR men fought to get their events or athletes into the column, and the athletes, for the most part, viewed an appearance in the column as the highest of honors. Athletes who would not give most reporters the time of day would rearrange their schedules to talk to Murray. Often, he would gladly share his access with his lesser-known colleagues. Murray's friend Bill Milsaps, then a columnist for the *Richmond Times-Dispatch*, was with Mur-ray during the 1975 World Series in Boston. After several days of rain, writ-ers were starving for column material. "Jim found me in the hotel and said, 'Pete Rose is coming up to my room to talk this afternoon. Would you like to join me?' And I said, 'Yeah, sure,'" Milsaps remembered. "So, Pete Rose sits down in Jim Murray's room and talks for an hour and a half, just the three of us. And Pete treated Jim as he would treat someone he respected a great deal. I wish like hell that I had a tape recording of the whole thing. I could have sold it."[30]

Sometimes, sports legends would turn the tables on Murray. At a World Series in St. Louis in the '80s, Murray was with Sherrod and a few other columnists, taking the hotel elevator down to the lobby. As the group made their way from the elevator to the door, they heard a voice shouting, "Hey, Jim! Jim!" The man turned to his companions. "That's Jim Murray," he said proudly. "Jim! Come over here, there's some people I want you to say hello to." The rest of the columnists wearily moved out of the way as Stan Musial escorted Murray over to his entourage.[31]

With his stature and name recognition came influence. Promoters, league officials, public relations people, and others with a stake in sports-related issues courted him and coveted his approval. In 1981, Oakland Raiders owner Al Davis decided to move his franchise to Los Angeles, over the stringent objections of NFL commissioner Pete Rozelle and the league's other franchise owners. A court battle of epic proportions ensued, with the Los Angeles Rams, the LA Coliseum, the San Diego Chargers, and others pulled into the fray. Davis was already viewed as an unpredictable outsider, and much of the national coverage at the time painted him as aggressive and vindictive. Murray's writing, however, was detached. He had relationships with both Rozelle and Davis that went back two decades. In his column, he pointed out that franchise movement was historically common and often successful, for teams and leagues. According to Davis, Rozelle and the league sought to sway Murray's opinion on the subject of the move. "People were dispatched from Palm Springs, where we were all having the league meeting, to Los Angeles, to get a hold of Jim, to try to turn him around," Davis said. "They sent the owners, officials, PR people, everything they could think of." He contended that Murray's tacit support was instrumental in the move's eventually going through. "I would say if you were to pick five guys in America at that time who carried weight . . . nationally, it would include Jim Murray and Melvin Durslag [of the *Herald-Examiner*] and maybe a few guys from the *New York Times*."[32]

Murray placed the highest importance on his relationships with sportswriters and was often embarrassed by his celebrity status. His fellow scribes appreciated Murray's lack of ego. "You'd sit with him and some third-string beat guy from Bakersfield would come up to meet him and pretty soon, you were convinced the beat guy was the star and Murray was the nobody," said Rick Reilly, who worked at the *Times* with Murray from 1983 to 1985. "He was that humble and self-effacing."[33]

Despite the inconveniences, Murray clearly enjoyed the trappings of celebrity life. His childhood of deprivation never left his mind. So he would bristle when confronted with athletes who mistreated reporters and acted ungrateful toward the media and fans. Fame, as he saw it, was the price for success in the sports business. "Anyone who is famous aches to be anonymous. Anyone anonymous aches to be famous," he wrote. "It's kind of like the deal between Faust and the devil. You have sold your soul, you pay the price. There's an implicit contract. With money comes fame. With fame, out goes privacy."[34]

Just Another Day at the Lathe

Though he mingled with the beautiful people, Murray was still a sportswriter, and with that label came some of the same insults and indignities that beset the greenest scribes covering the lowest levels of the minor leagues. Many athletes do not read newspapers (or anything else) and therefore did not know Jim Murray from Anne Murray. Or maybe they knew who he was and did not care. Either way, the job of covering sports includes a deep downside, of which Murray was not exempt.

During his period of blindness, Murray was in San Francisco covering a series between the Dodgers and the San Francisco Giants. The players on the two rival California teams were not fond of each other, to put it mildly, and the Giants players saved some of their animus for the writers who traveled with the Dodgers. Oblivious, Murray went into the Giants locker room and started a conversation with Giants pitcher Vida Blue, who apparently was not in on the team code. His teammates quickly set Blue, and Murray, straight. "Hey, get out of our clubhouse," yelled John Montefusco, another Giants pitcher. Murray and Blue went on chatting, and the chorus got louder. Players began to close in on the two as they continued their conversation. The mood quickly became more threatening. "Get the fuck out of here," another player shouted at Murray. Finally, John Scheibe, who was assisting Murray on the road trip, escorted him to safety. As they left, the Giants surrounded Montefusco and started chanting expletives about Murray and the Dodgers.[35]

In the interest of safety, backing down was usually the right move when a confrontation developed. But Murray often made his feelings known when he thought he was being mistreated. One year when he had made the trip to Indianapolis for the Indy 500, he entered the garage area looking for A. J. Foyt, a premier driver at the time. Foyt was known to be very cantankerous, and the press treated him delicately. Murray approached him and asked for an interview while Foyt was working on his car. Foyt ignored him, and Murray waited for him to look up from the engine. Several minutes went by. Finally, Murray approached again. "A. J., can I ask you a question?"

Foyt looked up and stared at Murray with disgust. "Can't you see I'm working here?" he said.

"What do you think I'm doing?" Murray retorted.[36]

Owners and executives invariably knew Murray, but sometimes lower-level club officials could make his life miserable. He traveled with five other *Times* writers to Boston in 1986 to cover the World Series between the New York Mets and the Boston Red Sox. Seating in the press box at Fenway Park was limited, and the *Times* was allotted only two seats. Two other writers were given the press-box seats, so Murray found himself, on a freezing Boston night, viewing the game from an outdoor auxiliary box with a severely obstructed view.

One of the writers came around to coordinate the *Times*'s coverage. "Jim, I'm just checking," he said. "The office just called in to see what you were writing."

"The fucking game," Murray spat back.[37]

It was a rare display of disgust from a man who seldom displayed any trace of ego. In describing Murray, other sportswriters make a point to mention that he appeared unaware of his exalted status in his field. "It was one of the best things about him. He was the biggest of big-timers, yet he never acted like a big-timer," said Milsaps.

If he rarely reacted to personal mistreatment, he had an opposite reaction to attempts to change his writing, especially if he was not consulted first. If what appeared in the morning paper was different from what he had submitted to the copy desk, he would become livid. He would refer to the desk censors as "the thought police." On one particular column, he included the phrase "life's a bitch." Somewhere in the editing process, it was softened (without Murray's consent). The change, he felt, weakened his wording demonstrably. Enraged, he complained to *Times* managing editor Bill Thomas. He told Thomas that he read smut in the entertainment section on a daily basis, but for some reason he was being held to a different standard. He even threatened to resign, but Thomas managed to talk him down from the ledge.[38]

With television at the top of the media food chain, television reporters and cameramen were another source of misery for sportswriters, Murray included. At the conclusion of the Los Angeles Open golf tournament in 1988, winner Chip Beck was preparing to address the media, and Murray walked in front of the platform of TV cameras. An overzealous cameraman from KTLA Channel 5 tried to push Murray past the row of cameras. Murray was incensed and fired off an angry letter to the station's general manager. Shortly thereafter, he received a letter of apology from both the station's vice president and the offending cameraman, but his opinion of TV people remained the same.[39] Many would receive the title of "prick," Murray's favorite slur for those he disliked.[40]

Like television, the computer had become part of a sportswriter's life by the 1980s. Murray, a devotee of his 1946 Remington portable typewriter, resisted electric typewriters for as long as he could and said he preferred writing in longhand if possible. But the computer's ability to shorten transmission time made it a journalistic necessity. For Murray, it was a constant source of frustration. At the 1984 Olympics, writers were given "porta-bubbles," which were essentially word processors that could transmit copy electronically. A writer would finish his story and then attach the phone receiver to the machine, and in two minutes the story would be transmitted to the desk. At the closing ceremony, Murray, Ostler, Littwin, and reporter Randy Harvey of the *Times* were watching from the press box and writing on deadline. Toward the end of the presentation, the Olympic flame was doused and the stadium went dark. Writers had been given flashlights so they could see their computers, and many were holding them in their mouths to see as they typed. Under these conditions, Murray began attempting to transmit his column via porta-bubble. Littwin watched as Murray's fuse burned. "He calls in, dials up, and sticks the [receiver] in the word processor. And it won't go, it won't go, it won't go, it won't go, and Jim starts to panic. And I'm sitting here writing on deadline. I love Jim, but he's not really up on the electronic computer era," Littwin recalled.

> He couldn't get it to send, and he was really starting to panic. So I tried to do it for him, and I couldn't get it to go either. The place is pitch-dark, and they're announcing the years of the Olympics, and after each year of the Olympics, starting with 1896, they set off fireworks, so there are fireworks going off everywhere. It's like being in Beirut, like we were being bombed. Lights are all out, bombs are going off everywhere, we're trying to write, and he's trying to send his column. So I say to the desk, "Jim can't send his column." And the guy at the desk says, "Tell him to dictate." And I move away and say, "The fucking guy is blind."

After an extended battle with the porta-bubble, a runner was sent over to the stadium to pick up Murray's uncooperative machine and bring it back to the office.[41]

Though he hated it, Murray thrived under deadline pressure. At major events, other writers were amazed at the speed with which he would write a column. He was often the first one finished typing, though he might have been one of the last to start. He would stare off into the distance, deep in thought, and then, in a flurry of typing, pound out his eight hundred words with barely a break in keystroke. Ed Pope remembered one World Series he covered along with Murray. Pope was about two paragraphs into his column when he looked over to see Murray zipping up his typewriter. "Another writer leaned over and said to me, 'Doesn't that just break your heart to see somebody write that easy?'" Pope recalled. "And I said, 'No, he works hard. He thinks about it a lot.' And the other writer said, 'No, he doesn't. He doesn't work hard at all. It's a gift. It comes naturally to him.' And that was true."[42]

To Murray, however, they did not all come easy. He would often say that he never found that elusive column that "wrote itself." When he was not writing on deadline at an event, most of his columns were composed in his office at his home in Bel Air. Sometimes, he would find himself in what he called a "knife fight" and would struggle for four or five hours to find the right words. Those words might not come, and, dissatisfied, he would send the column in and declare it a "Tuesday column"—a subpar performance, in the Murray lexicon.[43] And the sole judge and jury allowed to render a decision on the quality of a column was Murray himself. "If 8,000,000 people tell me it was a great column and I know it wasn't, it doesn't matter. And if I write a great column and nobody says anything, that doesn't matter, either," he said.[44]

As an interviewer, Murray placed more importance on what he learned through observation than from answers to questions. Always deferential to other journalists, he would often remain in the back of the pack and allow the other writers to ask the questions. Bob Steiner first met Murray when he was the sports information director for the University of California at Berkeley. Murray asked Steiner to introduce him to the school's star running back at the time, Chuck Muncie. "I brought him over and introduced him to Muncie," Steiner recalled. "And Jim never asked him a question; he just listened and listened. Muncie played with glasses. And Jim's column the next day began something like, 'Finally the guy with glasses gets to bully somebody.'" Murray believed that most of the time, the questions and answers that came out of locker-room interviews were banal: "When I go into a locker room, I may sit and watch Maury Wills across the room, and I'll tell you more about Maury Wills watching him when he doesn't know he's being watched, than I will if I sit down and talk to him for six hours and ask all these questions," he said.[45]

None of the frustrations—the failing computers, the spoiled and greedy athletes, the pissed-off letter writers, the bitching publicists, and all other manner of "pricks"—was enough to sour Murray on his profession. If it did momentarily, he could always conjure up a vision of Hartford. He would imagine the workers in the Connecticut Valley "putting the lathe away for the night," and he would count his blessings. "Writing is hard work, but there is a certain satisfaction to it," he said. "And it beats the hell out of digging coal, or driving a truck, or tending bar."[46]

Rules of the Game

Journalism students were yet another group who placed demands on Murray's time. Occasionally, he used his column to both answer their queries and question their work ethic. "The full-throated, patch-elbowed, blue-jean college work shirker is abroad in the land, the guy who has been dozing through lectures all winter and now must find someone to do his final paper," he wrote. Then he would, with tongue firmly in cheek, answer their questions:

Q: What are your working hours?
A: Depends. I try to get to the World Series by the fourth inning or two hours

after the game starts, whichever comes first. Basketball, the last 10 seconds is enough. Football, you only have to get in the game about as often as the Cypriot place kicker. In college, you just spend 10 minutes a year licking stamps on questionnaires.

Q: When you cover an event, what materials do you take?

A: Paper, pencil, eyes, ears—and a good book to read in case it gets dull.

Q: What are your days off?

A: Every.

Q: What tips would you give a person who wants to make a career of sports writing?

A: Disregard all of the above and start doing your homework. You can't cover the Super Bowl by questionnaire. If you could, I would.[47]

The truth was, however, that through the years Murray had developed firm beliefs about how to operate in his business. When asked, he had a few truths he would share about what constituted effective writing and what made good journalism. He offered a set of stock stories that would illustrate his points. Usually, he followed his own advice. Occasionally, his counsel was more of the "do as I say, not as I do" variety. If the anonymous journalism student from what Murray had christened "Shiftless U" wanted a serious answer to his questions, the Murray rule book would look something like this:

Focus on People: This was a guiding philosophy for Murray, dating back to *Time.* To illustrate his point, he often retold a story from the Beverly Hills bureau. He was filling in as bureau chief, and another correspondent, John Coffin, brought him an article about a remarkable development in the production of airplane fuselages that would reshape the aircraft industry. Murray was fast asleep by the third sentence. He told Coffin that the story belonged in a graduate school thesis, not *Time.* Go find some old German scientist who invented the new fuselage, Murray told his subordinate, and write about him. The "people-first" strategy came with him when he became a sportswriter, and he would articulate it regularly. "People are interested in people," he said. "People are not interested in things. People *think* they're interested in baseball, per se, but they're not. They're interested in Mickey Mantle. They're interested in what he had for breakfast."[48]

Don't Make Friends: This rule was one that ran counter to Murray's own behavior, but he championed it regularly nonetheless. His nephew Jon Sandburg went into journalism after college in the '80s and soon landed a job in the newsroom at the *Hartford Courant.* Around that time, he was in Los Angeles and visited Murray. "What do you tell young journalists just getting started?" Sandberg asked him.

"Trust me, you don't really want to know," Murray said.

"Tell me."

"Okay, here it is. Don't ever make a friend in this business," he told his nephew. "You're only going to have to fuck somebody in the end."[49]

No Cheering in the Press Box: It is the oldest and perhaps most ignored of sportswriting tenets. Sportswriters, Murray said, must root for leads. He would admit to dreaming up his ideal outcome at events that he covered and then hoping the dream would come true. He might pull for his favorite athletes, he said, but only because it made it easier for him to write his column. "You sit there on a Sunday night writing about a nobody who just won the United States Open, and you think to yourself 'If Palmer had won, I'd be all through by now,'" he said.[50]

That's Entertainment: Every time he sat down to write, Murray often said, his goal was to give readers a laugh or brighten their day a little. If they were to learn something, it would only happen if they were amused enough to keep reading. In the '80s, Murray bristled at the penchant young writers had for turning every story into investigative or confrontational journalism. "There's a tendency now to take a sour attitude in all of journalism," he said in 1985. "It's Watergate. Everybody wants to become famous."[51]

Don't Forget the Fairer Sex: Murray understood that half of newspaper readers were women, and he did not want to write them out of his audience, as most other sportswriters did. He went to great pains to make sure his writing was not too technical and was accessible to as many readers as possible. "If I write something like 'blitz' or 'bogey,' I'll explain it. Guys in my business, they don't realize the public, particularly female readers—of whom I have a lot—don't know what the hell you're talking about. It doesn't interrupt the flow too much to define 'blitz.'"[52] *LA Times* Syndicate brochures peddling Murray's column to other newspapers routinely championed his ability to woo women readers.

His success with drawing women to his column continued even after feminism became more prevalent in the culture. It was a movement that clashed with Murray's traditional values. His humor had always included an element of playful sexism—poking fun at the ineptitude of women drivers, or complaining about women on the golf course. With the rise of feminism, editors occasionally asked him to pull back. Once, a column he turned in about tennis star Gabriella Sabatini, which suggested that she was too beautiful to devote her life to tennis, earned Murray a call from the desk. "The paper called me and said, 'Some people around here think this is going to bring the feminists out of the woodwork. Do you really want to say this?' And I said 'Shit, yeah, I'm sick of them,'" he said. "Those [feminists] are so tiresome. People with no sense of humor bore me. It was a joke. I said 'Who was the criminal that gave her a tennis racket?' Did they really think I meant it?"[53]

Don't Overwrite: The great New York columnist Red Smith, an influence and later a close a friend of Murray's, was known to bleed over every sentence he wrote and would rework a column over and over in an attempt to achieve perfection. Murray was the opposite. He was a first-draft writer. "I think you strip all the joyousness out of your writing when you do that," he said. "I feel that my first elated feeling is probably the right one, and . . . I just feel that if you tinker with it, you destroy the spontaneity."[54]

Finally, Forget the Score: Murray often illustrated this point with a story about a colleague who covered a decathlon competition in Moscow between American Rafer Johnson and Soviet Vasily Kuznetsov. The meet took place in the late '50s, and US-USSR relations were at a low point. Americans were not permitted to travel in the Soviet Union. The *Time* correspondent turned in a story devoted exclusively to the results of the competition, devoid of any color from inside the USSR. "I didn't want to read about the bloody decathlon," Murray pointed out. "I didn't want to read who had the highest marks in the shot put, or who threw the javelin the farthest. I wanted to know what it was like, what these Russians were like watching this American athlete, and this Russian athlete, what the city was like. We got none of that," he recalled. "And in the back of my mind, I thought don't ever get so wrapped up in who won and lost, so that you overlook the setting."[55]

Seasons of Pain

While his professional life had been sailing along, Murray's personal life had been on the brink of disaster for some time. It went over the brink on a warm afternoon in the summer of 1982. He and Gerry returned from a trip to Las Vegas to find a card in the door. The card read: "Please contact the L.A. County Coroner at 226-8001 re: case #82-7193." Murray rushed in and, shaking, dialed the number. "We've got your son down here in the morgue," the voice said. "Which one?" Murray asked.

The Murrays' youngest son, Rick, had been found dead in his apartment hours before, the victim of a deadly mixture of alcohol and drugs. It was the conclusion of a tragic arc that had consumed the Murrays for years. Like his older brothers, Rick's interest was in music, and he had spent his youth and his young adulthood in and out of bands, and in and out of trouble with drugs and the law. His relationship with his parents followed the same sad ritual that besets families into which drug addiction invades—screaming, crying, eviction, rehabilitation—all followed in a circular progression in which the problem advances and retreats, always ready to reassert its control over the lives of all involved. Rick was no different.

Murray offered a loose account of the last years of Rick's life in his autobiography. When Rick's behavior proved unmanageable, Jim and Gerry threw him out of the house, invited him back, and inevitably threw him out again.

They took him to a psychiatrist, who undervalued the depths of Rick's addiction. Murray admittedly had little interest or faith in Rick's musical abilities, but nevertheless used his connections to set up interviews with a few friends in the entertainment business. Nothing panned out. Jim and Gerry paid for Rick to move to England, where he spent a year playing guitar in train stations and living in abandoned buildings. After a year, Rick was ready to come to America, and, again, Jim and Gerry paid his way. This time, Rick tried New York, with similar results. Soon, he was back in Los Angeles. Jim got him a job in the *Times* mailroom, but a short time later he received an apologetic call from Rick's supervisor, who had fired him for sleeping on the job. From there, Rick drifted around Southern California and served time in jail for a variety of drug-related offenses.

The last time Murray saw his youngest son was following a court appearance. Rick had had been in a fight, and his parents accompanied him to court. Rick wore one of his father's suits. The judge let him off with a warning, and Jim and Gerry dropped him off at his apartment, still wearing the suit. Two weeks later, they would bury him in the same suit.[56]

The Murrays' middle son, Tony, had addiction problems as well. Tony had been a baseball star in high school, the one son who took an interest in sports. Murray brought him along to sporting events and, when he showed promise, introduced him to some of his sports contacts. Bruce Jenkins, one of Tony's closest friends through high school and college, remembers going out to dinner with Jim, Tony, and Dodgers manager Tommy Lasorda when Tony was choosing where to play baseball after high school in the late '60s. He eventually chose the University of California at Berkeley, where he pitched for four years. After his eligibility ran out, however, his life took a course similar to Rick's. He got involved in hard drugs, and soon his parents were dragging him to counselors and fretting over his whereabouts.[57]

Tony's addiction got worse and worse, and by the early '80s he had little or no contact with his parents. Jenkins said he was one of the few people who stayed in contact with Tony. In later years, Tony was hopelessly bitter, his weight ballooned to more than three hundred pounds, and he sank further into the grips of alcohol and hard drugs. His relationship with his father was nonexistent. Jenkins remembered an exchange that took place after he had become a sport columnist for the *San Francisco Chronicle*. He ran into Murray in the press box at the Los Angeles Coliseum before a 49ers-Rams game. "I saw Big Ton' the other day," Jenkins told Murray. Murray looked at him quizzically. "What? Did you lose a bet?"[58]

Murray's guilt over his parenting increased as the troubles continued. He worried that being a famous father had crippled his children's emotional development, and he cursed what he saw as the corrupting influence of the Southern

California music and drug culture. But the deepest source of his guilt was the belief that the failures of his children had damaged his beloved Gerry beyond repair. He blamed himself, and he blamed his kids. And the guilt and pain were about to get much, much worse.

In early 1983, with the Murrays still deeply mourning the death of Rick, doctors examined Gerry and found cancer in her brain, colon, and liver. She was told she had a year to live. An operation was conducted to remove the cancer from the colon, but the brain cancer was inoperable. Radiation treatments followed. Chemotherapy slowed the advance of the cancer, and the Murrays tried their best to be brave in the face of the inevitable. Gerry accompanied Jim to golf tournaments, they spent time in Palm Desert, and they got together with old friends and relatives, where Gerry would go to the piano and play her favorite old songs. Their daughter, Pam, was married and brought them a granddaughter, and Gerry spent as much time with her as she could.

Jim and Gerry were in Palm Desert for the Bob Hope Classic golf tournament in January 1984 when the beginning of the end arrived. Gerry fell in the bathroom and hit her head, and a day later slipped into a coma, from which she would not emerge for three months. After a medical procedure in March, she regained consciousness for a few days, but slipped back into a coma and died on April 1.[59]

The day after Gerry died, Jim and his children were at the house on Bellagio Terrace, mourning and making funeral plans. To the surprise of the family members, Murray excused himself and told them he had to go to his office. "I have to go write," he said.[60] "He was only gone an hour, maybe less," Ted Murray said later. "It was the fastest column I ever saw him write. He asked me to go read it. I did, and I was blown away. I told him that, and he said 'There are a lot of tears on those typewriter keys.'"[61]

In any conversation about Jim Murray with those familiar with his work, the column he penned on the occasion of Gerry's death will invariably be mentioned. It is a tear-drenched lament to a lifelong love lost, and the depths of Murray's pain bleed through with every sentence:

> This is the column I never wanted to write, the story I never wanted to tell.
>
> I lost my lovely Gerry the other day. I lost the sunshine and roses, all right, the laughter in the other room. I lost the smile that lit up my life.
>
> God loved Gerry. Everybody loved Gerry. She never went 40 seconds without smiling in her life. She smiled when she was dying. She smiled at life and all the people in it. When you thought of Gerry, you smiled.
>
> She had these big gorgeous brown eyes and they were merry all the time and they looked at you with such trust and happiness. She never looked down or away. She never did anything to be ashamed of. Nothing. Never. She never did

anything she didn't think God wanted her to do. She was in charge of smiling for Him.

She never grew old and now, she never will. She wouldn't have anyway. She had four children, this rogue husband, a loving family and this great wisdom and great heart, but I always saw her as this little girl running across a field with a swimming suit on her arm, on a summer day on the way to the gravel pit for an afternoon of swimming and laughing. Life just bubbled out of Gerry. We cry for ourselves. Wherever she is today, they can't believe their good luck.

I don't mean to inflict my grief on you, but she deserves to be known by anyone who knows me. She has a right to this space more than any athlete who ever lived. I would not be here if it weren't for her. I feel like half a person without Gerry. For once, I don't exaggerate. No hyperbole. If there was a Hall of Fame for people, she would be No. 1. She was a champion at living.

She never told a lie in her life. And she didn't think anyone else did. Deceit puzzled her. Dishonesty dismayed her. She thought people were good. Around her, surprisingly, they were. Her kindness was legendary.

She loved God. I mean, He made the trees, the flowers. He made children, didn't He? And color and song, and above all, babies. She knew He'd take care of her.

She loved babies. Anybody's. She played the piano like a dream. Ask any of the football coaches, the basketball players, baseball pitchers or just newspapermen who leaned across their drinks and implored her for one more chorus of "Melancholy Baby." She played "Galway Bay" every St. Patrick's Day for a maudlin husband who wept over a moonrise he'd never seen or a sunset that existed only in a glass and an ice cube. She was fun.

She wasn't afraid to die. She didn't want to. But she knew she'd see the mother she lost, the son she lost. In a place where she could never lose them again.

You have funny ways of remembering things. The thing I remember clearest today, for some reason, is the habit she had of leaving notes for the kids when she was only going to be gone for the shortest times, the briefest moments. She would leave these notes on a table in this huge lettering, for her handwriting was like her heart, large and overflowing and joyous. "Gone to store," it would say. "Be right back, Love, Mom." She didn't want the kids to think they were without her love for even a few minutes.

She has left no notes this time. But she has, as usual, left her love.

There is a line at the end of "Alice in Wonderland" that always hurt me to read because it reminded me of my Gerry. Alice's sister is dreaming of Alice: "Lastly, she pictures to herself how this same little sister of hers would, in the aftertime, be herself a grown woman; and how she would keep, through all her riper years, the simple and loving heart of her childhood; and how she would gather about her other little children, and make their eyes bright and eager with many a strange tale, perhaps even a dream of Wonderland of long ago; and how she would feel with all their simple joys, remembering her own child life, and the happy summer days."

Gerry took the magic and the summer with her. It wasn't supposed to be this way. I was supposed to die first. We would have been married for 39 years this year and we thought that was just the natural order of things. I had my speech all ready. I was going to look into her brown eyes and tell her something I should have long ago. I was going to tell her, "It was a privilege just to have known you." I never got to say it. But it was too true.[62]

In the *Times* sports department, tears filled the eyes of many of the writers and editors as they discovered it, one by one. Bill Dwyre said later that "for a few magical minutes, the entire department was purged of the cynicism that was its operation lifeblood." "The Column," which was an ever-growing vine wrapped around every aspect of Murray's very existence, had now become the outlet for him to express and release his indescribable grief and pain. He shared that pain and love with his readers, who responded in kind. Letters poured into the *Times*. "Surely there must have been enough tears shed today to flow the Los Angeles River to its crest," wrote one, expressing the abiding sentiment.[63]

The day after the column was published, Geraldine Murray was buried in Holy Cross Cemetery, where her youngest son had been laid to rest less than two years before. Murray's old friend Will Fowler was a pallbearer at the funeral, as he had been at Rick's funeral. Murray, Fowler later said, had never looked "so crushed and seemingly helpless." At the end of the requiem mass, Fowler approached Murray and placed his hand on Murray's shoulder. Murray turned his gaze toward him. "What am I going to do?" he asked.[64]

The Column Must Go On

Rick Reilly was another of the many talented sportswriters to come through the *Times* sports department in part with the hope of coming into the orbit of Jim Murray. He and Murray became close in his two years in Los Angeles, and shortly after he was hired at *Sports Illustrated,* he pitched the idea of a profile on Murray to his editors. "I saw a way to write about him that would allow me to dig into his life deeply but also tell a story that might move people who'd never even heard of him," Reilly remembered. In early 1986, Reilly spent time with Murray while reporting the story. He discovered that his friend and mentor was nowhere near recovered from Gerry's death. Reilly's article was a portrait of a desperately lonely man still deeply in mourning. "The thing about Jim Murray," Reilly wrote in his lead, "is that he lived 'happily,' but somebody ran off with the 'ever after.'"[65]

Reilly followed Murray as he went through the motions and joylessly per-formed his professional duties. The two attended a promotional dinner for Miller Beer, where sports celebrities approached Murray and expressed their concern. At the home on Bellagio Terrace, Murray went about his life in a house of sorrow—around every corner was something to trigger a memory of Gerry. He vowed not to forget, but spent much of the time in a small corner of the big house, wallowing in his grief. Reilly ended his story with a scene in which Murray is holding a picture of Gerry, near tears. "The final curtain is pretty bad, isn't it? That last scene, the last act, is pretty bad," Murray told Reilly. "Put it this way, it'll never play in Dubuque."[66]

The article gave a much wider audience to Murray's personal struggles. "I remember after the piece came out, he sent me a note which said something like, 'That was very well written. Too well. I felt like a naked man being paraded down Main Street in a cage,'" Reilly said. "I was never sure if that was a compli-ment or an accusation."[67]

Though it must have felt like it to Reilly, the curtain was not ready to fall on Murray just yet. His grief did not seem to slip over into his professional life. In-stead, he poured himself into his writing and produced at as high a level as he ever had. Prior to Gerry's death, Murray had been toying with the idea of re-tirement. He had been saying for years that it was nearing the time for him to vacate his position and let someone from the next generation assume the man-tle. He wanted off the treadmill of daily journalism. Friends told him he would miss being somebody, but he always disputed that perception. No, he would say, he would be fine hanging around playing checkers at the corner store, or spending his days reading mystery books. But with Gerry gone, he clung to the column. A colleague told Ostler that Murray had planned to retire follow-ing the 1984 Olympics in Los Angeles, but when Gerry died shortly before the games, he changed his plans. "He decided that 'This is all I've got. I'm just going to keep writing,'" Ostler said.

During his bleakest hour, Murray received a ray of light from a most unex-pected source. All the way across the country, in Upstate New York, a long-lost acquaintance was about to reenter his life. Murray had first met Linda McCoy, then known as Linda Carothers, at the 1969 Indianapolis 500. Murray was in town to cover the event and, due to his eyesight issues, was looking for some-body to drive him around for the week. A friend at the *Indianapolis Star* recom-mended Linda, an attractive, bubbly twenty-four-year-old Indiana native with connections throughout the Indiana sports scene. Linda and her four siblings were from nearby Columbus, and she knew the region inside and out. At the time, she was working as an assistant to John DeVoe, president of the Indiana Pacers. Bob Collins, sports editor at the *Star* and a close friend of Murray's, ap-proached Linda with the proposition. "At first, I told him no. I said, 'If he's a colleague of yours, he must be old,'" she remembered. But Collins was persistent. "He said, 'You know the city. You can talk sports. And I need you!'" Linda was still hesitant, but Collins had an ace up his sleeve. He held up the keys to a '69 Camero convertible, fully loaded, and shook them in front of her. "I thought, 'Oh, this is great. I get my own pace car,'" she said.

So she took the bait from Collins and proceeded to drive Murray around Indianapolis for the next four days. Murray would spend time at the Speedway during the day, and in the evening Linda would take him to the many social events staged for racing sponsors and members of the media. "We went to a lot of parties," she recalled. "I knew a lot of people in the racing industry, and, you know, I was a Hoosier. I was born with a basketball in one hand and an oil can in the other." After the sponsor and track events were over, Linda brought Murray along to gatherings with her friends. "He loved that," she said. "He loved getting the chance to see how the young people partied."

After the race was over, the two parted ways, and each forgot about the other. A few years later, Linda got married and moved to Southern California with her husband. She ran into Murray at a golf tournament and the two exchanged pleasantries, but that was the extent of their contact until 1985. In the interim, Linda had a son, Bill, moved to Upstate New York with her husband, and eventually divorced. When her friend was in town visiting from Southern California, Linda inquired about Murray and learned of his troubles—the blindness, the deaths of Rick and Gerry. Soon after that, Linda found an address in an old directory and sent Murray a Christmas card, offering her condolences. He wrote back a few months later, and soon they were talking on the phone and considering the possibility of getting together in person. "He said, 'Well, you know, I don't come east.' I said, 'Well, I don't come west. It's been nice talking with you,'" Linda said.

But it turned out Murray was coming east. The 1986 US Open golf tournament was scheduled for June in Shinnecock Hills, New York, on Long Island, just a few months after Reilly had witnessed Murray at his lowest point. Linda arranged to attend the tournament, and the reunion was a success. "I drove down, met him, and we were together from that moment on," she said.

"Together," however, for the new couple, had a different meaning for a bi-coastal couple with entirely separate lives. Bill was still in middle school, and Linda did not want to uproot him. So, for the next five years, the two conducted a relationship based largely on the American sports calendar. When Linda could arrange time off from work, she would meet Murray at an event. If Murray was coming east to cover something, Linda would drive to meet him, sometimes bringing Bill along.

After a few years of this arrangement, Linda moved back to Indiana so she and Bill could be closer to her immediate family. At the time, she assured

Murray that she wanted to be with him, but she felt her son needed to be near his relatives. Linda recalled the discussion: "He said, 'Look, you know, when Bill goes off to college, maybe you'll think about coming to LA, if we're still speaking at that time.' And I said, 'Okay. We'll look at it.'"[68]

Murray's friends noticed the transformation in his life. Gradually, he began to emerge from the depths of his depression. Those close to him attributed it largely to his relationship with Linda. Roy Firestone, who had become a friend of Murray's and was deeply worried about him in the mid-1980s, believed Murray would have continued on the path toward ruin if the relationship had not blossomed. "Linda McCoy saved his life," Firestone said. "If not, he would have died. . . . He had lost everything, he had lost his bearings as to who he was." *Times* editor Bill Thomas noticed a change as well. Thomas had become a close friend and golfing partner and began inviting Murray to senior writing meetings, where *Times* veterans could share their wisdom about various areas of the *Times* operation. Thomas noticed Murray emerging from his years-long funk, taking an interest in all aspects of the newspaper. Thomas and his wife socialized with Jim and Linda as well. "He was just so much happier with her," Thomas said. "They were clearly happier together."[69]

As he prepared to head up the coast to cover the 1989 World Series, Murray was in a much better place emotionally than he had been in years. The fall classic matched the Oakland A's and the San Francisco Giants, so he made plans to spend a week in the Bay Area. Oakland had won the first two games, and Murray was preparing for game 3 in the press box at Candlestick Park in San Francisco. At 5:04 p.m., Pacific standard time, the stadium began to move. For a few seconds, there was a low rumble, and then the entire stadium began to shake violently.[70] In the press box, Murray leaned over to his *Times* colleague Ross Newhan. "They never last more than a minute," he said hopefully.[71]

This one did not either. But Murray wrote that it was the worst one he had ever been in, and he had been experiencing earthquakes since 1943. The Loma Prieta earthquake, as it came to be known, registered 6.9 on the Richter scale. It had struck about forty miles south of Candlestick Park. Before it was over, parts of the Nimitz Freeway and the San Francisco Bay Bridge had collapsed, and fifty-seven people had been killed.

Luckily for the sixty-three thousand people on hand, Candlestick Park held up. Players scurried out of the dugout onto the field. In the main press box, writers lunged to get under the door frames. Because of the large number of writers on hand, an auxiliary press box had been set up in the upper deck, behind home plate. Reporters grabbed hold of the makeshift tables set up for them and nervously rode out the quake. "A World Series that had been as deadly dull as a chess game in a firehouse suddenly became more wildly exciting that you would ever want," Murray wrote. When it was all over, most of the spectators stood up, looked around, and waited for the game to start.

There would be no game that night. At 5:35 p.m., Major League Baseball commissioner Fay Vincent canceled the game, and a short time later an announcement was made on the public address system. Fans left the park in an orderly fashion, only to spend the next several hours in gridlocked traffic caused by the surrounding road damage. Murray made his way down to the field with the help of his friend Ken Peters of the Associated Press. The two found Oakland A's players Jose Canseco and Mark McGuire on the field, noticeably shaken.[72] They did some interviews, and then Murray and every other reporter and columnist in attendance began to think the same thought: how am I going to get my story into the paper?

Murray found his way to the parking lot and caught a ride with Ed Pope, Blackie Sherrod, and Dan Foster, another close friend and a columnist for the *Greenville News* in South Carolina. The group went in search of a working pay phone. It would be a long search. The only available way out of the traffic gridlock took them south, around the San Francisco Bay. The four veteran columnists drove cautiously through several darkened towns before they finally came across a gas station with a light on, and, more important, a working pay phone. Pope dictated his column back to the desk at the *Miami Herald* and then handed the phone over to Murray. As Pope emerged, he noticed what appeared to be a motorcycle gang approaching through the darkness. The members were dressed in black leather, sported greasy hair and long beards, and seemed extremely impatient. "Hey, you," one yelled at Pope, gesturing for him to approach. Pope warily made his way over to the bikers, all the while planning his escape. The lead biker pointed toward the phone booth. "Is that Jim Murray in there?" he asked. Pope, his anxiety gradually easing, nodded yes. The biker nudged one of his cohorts. "That's Jim Murray!" he exclaimed.

The confrontation quickly became a love-in, and everybody's earthquake story made it successfully into the hands of the appropriate editors. Murray, in his column, had tried to put what had happened into proper perspective. "They do not know when and if the World Series will resume," he wrote. "The important thing is to get San Francisco to resume. It is a city living with an unpredictable sociopath. It may go years, even decades, living as normal as a postal clerk. Then it goes into maniacal rages. The ballparks, the bridges, even the highways and electrical circuits are at its mercy. A World Series is the least of its victims."[73]

Hours later, the group finally arrived back at the hotel by the bay. Murray, Pope, and a few others were discussing plans for the next few days before going to sleep. "Jim, it looks like there's going to be some aftershocks," Pope advised.

"No, no," Murray said. "There's not going to be any aftershocks."

"Well, that's what a seismologist just said on television," Pope said.

Murray looked back at him. "Who are you going to believe, me, or a seismologist?"[74]

9

The 1990s

Literary Lion of Sports

Burnout is a lousy modern invention, a sign of the times, like rap music and call-waiting. It's a disease that inflicts only the affluent. A product of prosperity. It's a good thing for us Thomas Edison needed the money. Or Rembrandt. Or Michelangelo.

—Jim Murray, "Susceptibility to Burnout Increases with Income," *Los Angeles Times*, March 14, 1993

Trophy Case

If you hang around long enough in the newspaper business, you inevitably become what Furman Bisher refers to as a "walking statue." Murray knew the feeling. He had long ago graduated to "lifetime achievement" status, and every sports, academic, and civic organization competed to bestow upon him its highest honor, provided Murray would agree to attend a dinner and make himself available for pictures and questions. "What did you think of Ben Hogan, Jim? How about Sandy Koufax?" Murray deflected the invitations when he could and labored through them when he could not. He hated giving speeches and never felt comfortable speaking in front of an audience, and his eyesight issues made public appearances even more difficult. "He'd write this fabulous speech, and he'd get to the place, and the podium wasn't lit very well, and he couldn't read it, so he'd kind of stumble around," said Dwyre.

The invitations kept coming, and Murray hated to say no, so Dwyre devised a plan. He, Dwyre, became Murray's screener, chauffeur, and master of ceremonies, all in one. He would wade through the requests, decide which ones were worth Murray's time, and accompany Murray on the night of the event. On the dais, Dwyre would moderate. He would start Murray off with a few prearranged questions and then let the audience loose to mine Murray's fifty years of anecdotes.

Walking-statue status extended to the press box as well. The Rose Bowl was one of Murray's favorite events, and he made sure to cover it every year. A few minutes after he made his way to the *Times* section of the press facility, a line of out-of-town sportswriters would slowly begin to form around him. The scribes of Minnesota, or Iowa, or whatever Big Ten school had the honor of facing the Pac-10 champion that year, each wanted the chance to shake Murray's hand and hear a quip or two about their home state. Murray was happy to provide a lifetime memory, but, again, his eyesight made things difficult. His admirers would approach from the left side, his blind side, and Murray would be forced to execute a 270-degree head twist for each introduction. He always worried he would be surprised, snap his neck around, and detach his last remaining retina. To solve this particular problem, Dwyre would arrive with Murray and take up residence on his left side, blocking access and forcing the line toward Murray's good eye. And there Dwyre would stand, for an hour or two, watching as the throng moved past him, each writer leaving the encounter with a smile on his or her face as they made their way back to their assigned seat, and eventually back to Peoria.[1]

Murray's likeness was hung in halls of fame of dozens of sports and journalism organizations over the years, and eventually the honors became, for him, about as much of a thrill as taking off his shoes. Winning the J. G. Taylor Spink Award from the Baseball Writers Association of America, however, certainly held special significance. The award is presented at the annual Baseball Hall of Fame induction ceremony, so the winner gets to share the stage with that year's crop of baseball greats entering the sports pantheon. Murray traveled to Cooperstown, New York, in August 1988 to accept the award on the same day that Pittsburgh Pirates legend Willie Stargell was inducted into the hall.

Baseball Hall of Fame representatives are quick to point out that winning the Spink Award does not mean one has been "inducted" into the hall. Instead, their plaques hang in the "Scribes & Mikemen" exhibit in the hall's library. Still, to the many Pirate fans and assembled visitors on August 1, 1988, it certainly appeared as if Murray was now a Baseball Hall of Famer. And that is how Murray took it as well. He climbed to the podium after his introduction and announced, "I don't know what the hell I'm doing here, either. I have to be honest with you: Putting me in the Hall of Fame is ridiculous." He then shared with the crowd a litany of one-liners dedicated to his athletic deficiency: "You've heard of guys who couldn't hit a fast ball? I couldn't hit a slow ball. You've heard of guys who couldn't hit a curve ball? I couldn't hit a straight ball. I couldn't hit, throw, or catch anything going more than five miles an hour."

The crowd sufficiently warmed, Murray shared the story of his earliest memories of baseball and how those experiences transformed into a lifelong love affair with the sport. Watching his teams lose had hooked him at an early age, he said. From the day his beloved New London Nine had lost to their hated rivals from Watertown, he found a perverse pleasure in being on the losing side. "Losing solidifies you," he told the crowd. "Losing is such sweet heartache and there are no tears like the tears of a fan whose favorite pitcher has just walked in the winning run." From there, he ended on the note he hit throughout his life when describing his love of the sport that has no time clock. He answered the hundred-year-old critique that baseball is just too slow. "I never went to a ball game in my life in a hurry. Who wants it to end? You want to go home and do the dishes or wash the windows? What for? I always wanted baseball to go into extra innings and I always felt the way Ernie Banks felt—let's play two or three."[2]

Though his Hall of Fame moment placed him among the legends of his profession, from Damon Runyon to Ring Lardner to Red Smith, there was one award out there that was the Holy Grail to sportswriters, mainly because it was largely withheld from them. When the year 1990 began, they had been awarding the Pulitzer Prize to the country's best newspapers and journalists for seventy-three years, and precisely three sportswriters had won the honor. Over the twentieth century, the Pulitzer name had become the ultimate expression of excellence in the profession, but, for some reason, sportswriting had been deemed by the powers that be to fall below the threshold for recognition. Arthur Daley, Red Smith, Dave Anderson—after seventy-three years and hundreds of awards, that was the roll call in Pulitzer's sportswriter wing.

Joseph Pulitzer is an odd choice to represent journalistic purity. He was the late-nineteenth- and early-twentieth-century newspaper baron who came up with the idea for the Pulitzer Prizes in journalism after a lifetime of accumulating wealth by producing some of the worst journalism on record. His newspapers brought sensationalism to the newspaper page. Pulitzer put the *yellow* in yellow journalism. Exaggeration, scare headlines ("Startling Confession of a Wholesale Murderer Who Begs to Be Hanged!"), fabrication, and warmongering were all fair game as his papers, with the *New York World* as his flagship, made him one of the country's richest men.

His newspapers did have an investigative, social-justice element to them (there was profit in crusades in the age of yellow journalism), and Pulitzer wished that to be his legacy. Toward the end of his life he was overcome with guilt, repented, and began spouting the language of journalistic principle. Upon his death, he left a large chunk of his fortune to create Columbia University's Graduate School of Journalism and to endow the first national prizes for books, drama, music, and journalism. (He had the idea for the prizes, not coincidentally, right after the first Nobel Prizes were awarded.) The success of the school, at the time of creation only the second such school in the United States, and the prizes helped to transform his place in history.[3]

The Pulitzer Prize, despite its namesake, quickly ascended to a position of the highest esteem in the profession, and over the years the triumphs of journalism and most of its greatest names received the honor. Pulitzer's will laid out a complicated judging operation in which editors and writers from top newspapers, along with a few educators and freelancers, are tasked with rendering a decision on the work of their peers. Those jurors, divided into committees by prize category, recommend winners to the Pulitzer Board, which chooses the eventual winners. It is often an incestuous process. Though it is easy to enter (in 1990 the entry fee was twenty dollars), the country's largest newspapers enter every category (in 1990 there were fourteen journalism categories) and dominate the awards. And at the top of the list is the *New York Times*. By 1990, the *New York Times* had won sixty-three Pulitzers, or three times as many as any other newspaper. Through the twentieth century, the newspaper came to represent the beacon of American journalism, and its stranglehold on the Pulitzer no doubt helped. During that time, the Columbia Graduate School became a feeder school to the *New York Times* newsroom. The Sulzberger family, owners of the *New York Times,* donated considerably to the school while receiving its highest honors. And the newspaper had more jurors and board members on the Pulitzer Board than any other newspaper. In short, the *New York Times* appeared to control the awards from the inside and out.[4] Daley, Smith, and Anderson, the three men in the Pulitzer sports club, all won while writing for the *New York Times.*[5]

The three men form an unlikely trio if one was choosing the Mount Rushmore of the sportswriting profession. Daley joined the *New York Times* in the 1926 at the age of twenty-two and took over the newspaper's "Sports of the Times" column in 1942. For the next thirty-four years, until his death in 1976, he wrote workmanlike prose filled with pleasant anecdotes and remembrances, with his point of view usually in lockstep with the sporting establishment. And he did it prolifically, writing seven columns a week, forty-eight weeks a year, always looking over his shoulder for his replacement. (He had originally been awarded the column temporarily.) He received his Pulitzer in 1956 and was as surprised as anybody. Daley, like almost everybody else in the business, had believed Red Smith would be the first sportswriter to win the Pulitzer.[6]

If there was a dean of sportswriters in the mid-twentieth century, for the generation that followed the Golden Age of Sports, it certainly was Red Smith. He worked his way from St. Louis to Philadelphia to New York through the

1930s and '40s, settling at the *New York Herald-Tribune*, and finally joining the *New York Times* in 1971 in the twilight of his career. His writing, even relegated to the sports page, was viewed as literature beyond the realm of sports and journalism. Ernest Hemingway declared Smith his favorite sportswriter and alluded to Smith in his fiction. The college textbook *A Quarto of Modern Literature* placed a Red Smith column between an essay by Winston Churchill and a short story by Dylan Thomas.[7] His work was studied in the hallowed halls of Harvard and Yale. A master of irony with an ability to craft the perfect line, Smith's literary abilities afforded him recognition beyond his peers, so it was little surprise when the Pulitzer Board called his name.

Smith had deep reservations about the award when he was finally chosen for it in 1976. He had been hurt when Daley, who he felt was a pedestrian writer, won it. For years, he would pick up the *New York Times,* look at Daley's column, and sarcastically say, "Aha, another Pulitzer Prize winner." Once he was on the receiving end of the award, he still felt conflicted, but chose to accept it with grace publicly. Privately, he was dismissive. "Oh, it's just part of being with the *New York Times,"* he said. "I always swore I'd refuse it, but I've decided that 70-year-old crocks who are bitter are boring."[8]

Anderson received Pulitzer's blessing in 1981, after fifteen years on board at the *New York Times*. Like Smith, Anderson was a friend of Murray from many years on the columnist circuit, and the two played golf together on occasion. Unlike Smith and Daley, Anderson and Murray shared a mutual respect for one another. When Anderson won the award, however, the drumbeat for Murray to win had already been growing louder and louder. "I was surprised I won it before he did. Let's put it that way," Anderson said.[9]

Dwyre began nominating Murray for the award in the mid-1980s, and each year was astonished when Murray's entry was not chosen, even as a finalist for the prize.[10] For the 1989 nomination, he added a "last chance" element to his pitch. By next year, he told jurors, Murray would be fading, Pulitzer-less, into the sunset. It was now or never. "On January 28, Jim Murray will go to New Orleans to cover his last Super Bowl," Dwyre wrote. "Probably in late 1990—all too soon for readers of The Times and followers of sports journalism and its history in this country—Murray will stop writing columns all together." Dwyre believed it at the time; Murray had told him one more year was all he had left in him. Though he had said it before, this time it seemed more definitive.

For the prize for general commentary, entrants have to submit ten articles. Dwyre chose Murray's piece from the San Francisco earthquake; deadline columns from the Rose Bowl, Super Bowl, Kentucky Derby, and Indy 500; along with profiles on California Angels pitcher Jim Abbott, San Diego Chargers kicker Rolf Benirschke, former University of Southern California Heisman winner Mike Garrett (who had become a community activist in inner-city Los Angeles), and Dallas Cowboys head coach Tom Landry, who had been fired after a legendary career. He wrapped up the entry with a column featuring Murray's analysis of racial politics in sports. Absent in the collection was the trademark Murray rim-shot column of his younger days, with laugh lines from start to finish. However, the collection offered its share of zingers: In the Rose Bowl, the USC Trojans tackled so poorly they "appeared to think they were playing tag." In the Super Bowl, San Francisco 49ers wide receiver Jerry Rice caught passes that were so far over his head, they "seemed to be reachable only by phone." And Sunday Silence, the horse that won the Kentucky Derby, was "so ugly he was almost 2 years old before they were sure he wasn't going to be a camel." The entry was heavy on melodrama as well. Abbott, born without a hand, writes a letter to a young girl who lost her hand in a violent crime. Garrett mourns the loss of his brother and niece to street crime. Benirschke is misdiagnosed with Crohn's disease. It was a solid sample, but, in a way, the contents of the entry were less important than the idea behind it. What Dwyre was actually selling to the jurors were the memories of three decades of sustained brilliance. "Many people win Pulitzers for many reasons, all of them valid. Some even win them for seniority, which is valid," he wrote.[11]

Word had spread throughout the *Los Angeles Times* newsroom that Murray was a finalist and that he had a good chance to finally be anointed by the gods of journalism. The results were scheduled to move on the Associated Press wire at noon, and the sports department on the third floor of the *Times* building was buzzing by 11:30. At 12:11 p.m., associate sports editor John Cherwa looked up from his computer, smiled, and gave a thumbs-up sign to the assembled group. As had become an annual newspaper tradition in big-city newsrooms across the country, champagne corks popped and applause filled the room. Murray accepted the award with a shrug. "This is going to make it a little easier on the guy who writes my obit," he quipped.[12] But he enjoyed the goodwill of his co-workers and spent the day accepting phone calls from colleagues, friends, and admirers and fielding media interviews from news outlets across the country. Notes of congratulations came in from President George Bush, as well as Reagan and Ford. The next morning, he was up at three for an appearance on ABC's *Good Morning, America*.[13]

Many in the community of sportswriters, especially those close to Murray, treated Murray's Pulitzer as an acknowledgment of their little corner of the profession. Finally, a working stiff from the press box was up on the wall. "I don't care what happens now," Blackie Sherrod told Murray when he called to congratulate him. "One of our gang has finally won the Pulitzer Prize."[14]

In May, Murray invited Linda, Dwyre, and *Times* publisher Dave Laventhal to accompany him to the Pulitzer award luncheon in New York a few weeks later. It is a reverential affair, held in the Low Library in the heart of the

Columbia University campus. Prizewinners, jurors, and board members mingle and exchange congratulations. Winners accept their medals and checks without making a speech. The 1990 ceremony included a few well-known literary names—playwright August Wilson won the drama prize for *The Piano Lesson*, and writer Stanley Karnow won the history prize—among the mostly anonymous group of journalists. When the ceremony drew to a close, a line slowly developed, snaking around the room and ending at the *Times*'s table. Award winners, jurors, and other attendees were waiting patiently for the requisite Murray handshake and autograph.

A few days later, Murray was at Churchill Downs for the Kentucky Derby. He sat in the press box, hunched over a word processor, when he began to feel a presence looming over him. Many of the sportswriters and columnists on hand had quietly inched toward him and now surrounded him. Billy Reed of *Sports Illustrated* sat a bottle of Dom Perignon on the table in front of him, and, without a word spoken, the entire press box stood and applauded.[15]

Rather than send him off into the sunset, the award reinvigorated Murray. All of those well-thought-out retirement plans quietly faded away. "The Pulitzer could take him either way," Dwyre said. "He could say, 'That's it, that's the crowning achievement. I'm done, see ya. I've got this on my way out the door, and I'm happy.' Or he could say, 'Hey, this has validated me. I can go on some more.' And the combination of that feeling, the attention he got, and people telling him, 'Hey, you're the best,' was a plus. . . . I think that kind of inspired him to go on."[16]

A Not-So-Secret Society

The Pulitzer Prize is often the trampoline that launches the winning journalists into a higher tax bracket, but Murray's financial windfall opportunity had actually come months before he won the award. In 1989, Peter Price, the former publisher of the *New York Post,* noticed the success of national sports newspapers in Europe and South America and decided to bring the idea to the United States. With the financial backing of Mexican media magnate Emilio Azcárraga, Price began putting a staff together in April of that year for a new publication, christened the *National Sports Daily.*[17] Frank Deford, Murray's old colleague from *Sports Illustrated* and one of the most recognizable sportswriters in the country at the time, was hired away from *SI* to be editor and publisher. Deford immediately began raiding sports departments in the top newspapers. Deford was given a blank checkbook, and the numbers he offered were leaps and bounds beyond the average newspaper sportswriter pay scale. Murray was the first name on Deford's hit list.

Deford called Murray and offered him a contract to join the *National.* His starting bid was $200,000 a year, but he planned to negotiate up to $250,000 if necessary. The negotiation never got that far. Murray was shocked by the initial figure. He had never played the salary-negotiation game with the *Times,* and as a result the company had paid him well below what he was likely to be worth on the open market. "I was surprised to find out how little Jim was making," Deford remembered. "I believe he said $125,000."[18]

Shortly thereafter, Murray called Dwyre and asked him to come out to his house on Bellagio Terrace. Dwyre drove out to Bel Air, not knowing what Murray wanted to discuss. Murray invited him in and told him about the offer. "I thought, 'Oh, Jesus, he's gone,'" Dwyre said. He had heard about the figures Deford was offering. "As much as we wanted him, we weren't going to get up that high."[19]

He did not have to. Murray had already turned Deford down. Loyal to the core, he told Dwyre, as he had told Dwyre's superiors, that he still remembered how the *Times* had stuck with him during his period of blindness and that he felt he owed it to them to stay with the company. In the end, he made a few moderate demands—a salary increase well below the *National's* offer, the option to fly first-class on all travel—and remained safely in his position at the *Times.* Deford hired Ostler, the *Times's* other columnist, and then moved on to other targets. Once again, Murray's financial acumen had proved sound. The *National* lasted only sixteen months, done in by a flagging economy and a weak distribution network.

So with a Pulitzer and a new salary, Murray was ready to make another big change to his lifestyle. Bill McCoy, Linda's son, had graduated from high school and enrolled at Ball State University in Muncie, Indiana, in the fall of 1990. Once Linda was comfortable that her son was thriving in the collegiate environment, she felt ready to leave his side. She called Murray and told him she was ready, if he was still willing. With Murray's approval, Linda bought a one-way ticket to Tampa, Florida, site of Super Bowl XXV, and after the game the two flew back to Los Angeles to begin their new life together.

From the previous five years of her relationship with Murray, Linda had already become acquainted with what had, over the years, grown into another type of family for Murray—a family of sportswriters who had, somewhere along the line, taken on the sobriquet "the Geezers." Because he worked from home and spent a prodigious amount of time on the road, Murray actually spent much more time with columnists from other newspapers than he did with his colleagues at the *Times.* As a result, deeper friendships developed with his friends from the road. Though he was friendly with dozens of writers from across the country, a close-knit group of his travel companions had formed. Murray, Sherrod, Milsaps, Pope, and Dan Foster of the *Greenville News* formed the core of Murray's inner circle. "At first, we called ourselves the Senior Tour," recalled Milsaps. "But as things moved along, we became the Geezers."

Foster was both the traveling secretary of the Geezers and Murray's chauffeur on the road. "Foster would always get the car and give Jim a ride," Milsaps said. "Because [Jim] couldn't see, sometimes he thought you were going to have a wreck, when you weren't really going to have a wreck at all. And he'd say, 'Jesus Christ, Foster! Slow down!' Or 'Shit, Milsaps, slow down!' We'd say, 'Jim, it's okay. We're not going to wreck.' Because his sight was so bad, he always had the feeling that something terrible was going to happen."[20]

Foster was a native South Carolinian and a graduate of Furman University who spent his entire career at the *Greenville News*. As a young sportswriter, he had befriended Jesse Jackson and helped the future civil rights leader gain a football scholarship to the University of Illinois after playing at segregated Sterling High School in Greenville. Foster eventually became sports editor and assigned himself to be the eyes and ears of the *News* at major national events like the Kentucky Derby and the Masters.[21]

Foster and Murray first met at the Masters. Both loved golf, and enjoyed playing together, so the two ended up spending the most time together of the Geezers. "Whenever I'd see one of them in the lobby, I'd say, 'Where are you going?' and they'd say, 'I'm waiting for Jim, or I'm waiting for Foster,'" Izenberg said. The two often became a sort of two-man comedy team for the rest of the group, Murray peppering Foster with faux insults, Foster as the comic foil. "[Foster] was Murray's favorite whipping boy," Pope said. "Murray would sort of be abusing Foster, in a funny sort of way, but he'd never let him up; he'd always have something else to say."

Milsaps said that getting together with the Geezers eventually became more of a draw for him than the events themselves:

> We would write our columns, and then we would want to go sit around and talk with friends. So we would finish, and then we would go sit around and go up to one of our rooms, and sit on the bed and drink whiskey and talk. And sometimes we'd talk very late, to one thirty, two o'clock in the morning. And then we'd get up the next day and do it all over again. . . . As I got near the end of my sportswriting career, I was not as excited about the events I was going to cover as I was the prospect of seeing my friends. And I guess that's, I think, when I knew I had to get out of sports. If you're not excited about covering a World Series or Super Bowl, and it got to the place where I wasn't, then you've got to do something else.

So in 1991, Milsaps decided to leave the sports desk and take the position of managing editor of the *Richmond Times-Dispatch*. It was at that point that the group decided to formalize their arrangement. "I said this is terrible," remembered Pope. "We're not going to be able to get together like this anymore, we'll splinter, and eventually more guys would quit, go off and do other things. So that's when we said we're going to start having a little reunion every year." In the 1990s, the Geezers began meeting once a year, getting together when, for a change, they had no deadlines to meet. Foster would make the arrangements, and everybody would gather in some warm-weather locale, like Dallas or Phoenix, for a weekend of golf, cigars, and old stories. As the years went on, a few more writers, including Furman Bisher and Dan Jenkins, joined the group, and it has survived to the present day. "The most common word spoken is 'What'd he say?'" said Milsaps.

The reunion became something Murray looked forward to each year. He still covered his share of the big events, but his schedule was becoming lighter. His writing output was lower as well; he had not dropped to two columns a week as threatened in the Pulitzer nomination, but most weeks saw Murray appearing in three or four editions of the *Times*. Though the Olympics had always been one of his favorite events to cover, he was less than thrilled with the prospect of making the trip to the Summer Olympics in Barcelona, Spain, in 1992. On the request of Dwyre, and with Linda's prodding, he agreed to the assignment, which would turn out to be the last Olympics of his career.

Once he was in Spain, the event energized him, and he attacked the assignment with a vengeance. He wrote a column every day of the sixteen-day event, focusing on a different sport for each one. Dwyre hired a friend of his wife to serve as a translator, to make things easier for Murray. One day, after Murray had finished writing, he attended a concert of the Three Tenors with Linda, the translator, and a few others. The musical trio of Spanish singers Plácido Domingo and José Carreras and Italian singer Luciano Pavarotti was an international sensation at the time. Murray and his group were seated close to the stage. As the singers came out on the stage, Domingo scanned the front rows. "Oh, my God, look," the singer said. "Jim Murray is in the audience." With that, he strolled down and chatted with Murray, making the auditorium of stunned opera fans wait a few more minutes for the show to begin.[22]

The Seventh at Hollywood Park

Way back in December 1967, Murray was in the winner's circle at Los Alamitos Race Course to present a check for twenty-one hundred dollars to Earl Brown, owner of Bright Rockette, the winner of the first-ever Jim Murray Classic. The race was a 350-yard sprint for quarter horses, and Bright Rockette clocked a winning time of eighteen seconds. It was about as far as one could possibly get from the Kentucky Derby, a fact Murray reveled in the following day. Quarter horses, he wrote, "can be as much as seven-eighths thoroughbred, which means that they can be within one-eighth of being complete loafers, but, by and large, they come from the lunch-pail set. This is fine, because so does the guy they named the race after."[23]

That was many years before Murray became "the legendary Jim Murray," and a two-thousand-dollar quarter-horse race on a Wednesday night in Los Alamitos was a nice little honor. Murray loved the denizens of any racetrack, be it Los Alamitos or Churchill Downs, and needed little excuse to spend time in and around the sport. Dan Smith worked with Murray at the *Times* in the '60s and later became a public relations man for Del Mar Racetrack, north of San Diego. He worked with Murray occasionally through the years on horse-industry stories. "Jim loved the characters in horse racing. He loved that whole scene," Smith said. "He loved the fact that you had the richest people and the poorest people in horse racing, the highs and lows economically."

If Los Alamitos was the first track to name a race after him, Hollywood Park was likely the track at which he spent the most time. Hollywood Park had been founded in 1938, with its original shareholders dominated by movie moguls like Sam Goldwyn and Darryl Zanuck and stars like Bing Crosby and Ronald Reagan. It was a luxurious environment, known as the track of lakes and flowers, and it attracted celebrities and those who wanted to see them. It was the most popular track in the United States through the 1950s. Marge Everett, the daughter of an Illinois racetrack owner from Illinois, became CEO of the track in 1972, and Murray became a staple at the Marge Everett Sunday-night parties. They were star-studded affairs where you were as likely to run into Cary Grant or Burt Bacharach as you were a jockey or a trainer from that night's races. The media were represented by Murray, John Hall, and radio host Jim Healy. Gerry often came along with Jim and played the piano for the assembled crowd into the early morning.[24]

Everett was still running Hollywood Park in 1990 when the modern version of the Jim Murray Handicap first went off. This time, the Murray was a true thoroughbred race, with a prize of seventy-five thousand dollars.[25] Bill Christine was on hand for the race, which set the track's attendance high for the summer. "Marge can snap her fingers, and fifty celebrities turn out," Christine said. For Murray's race, Cary Grant, Milton Berle, Pete Rozelle, and Fred Astaire were among the attendees. "It was like a Hall of Fame of entertainment, and they all came because Marge asked. But they also came because they knew Jim, and they were familiar with Jim's work, and they wanted to honor him in that way. It was just a tremendous gathering," he said.

As he had with his Los Alamitos race, Murray used his column to jokingly announce that his event would someday, somehow, become a race of immense importance: "I have no doubt that, in a year or two, it will be right up there with the Kentucky Derby. Maybe it'll be another jewel added to the Triple Crown. Or, maybe, it'll replace the Belmont. I'm a little worried it might upstage the Breeders' Cup. I'll bet Bill Shoemaker is sorry he retired too early to add the

Murray to his illustrious list of stakes wins." From there, he turned the article into a tribute to his uncle Ed, who had introduced him to the ponies six decades prior. He recounted some of Ed's illegal schemes and finally gave credit to his uncle for turning him away from the gambling life and toward a life of writing: "He taught me to read a *Racing Form*, but one day, when I showed up with a pool cue, Ed just took one look and shook his head. 'Put that down,' he said, 'and pick up a book. You'll make more money out of a book than you ever will out of a pool cue.'"[26]

In later years, Murray enjoyed going to the racetrack more than most other recreational pursuits. As much as he liked Hollywood Park, he was partial to Del Mar. Another track with a Hollywood background, Del Mar was founded by Bing Crosby in 1937 and frequented by his entertainment-industry friends through the years. Murray was a regular at Del Mar's Pacific Classic, a million-dollar race of national interest held in August. Christine remembered one particular Pacific Classic he covered along with Murray for the *Times*. Murray approached him a few minutes before the race. He told Christine that he had been researching the entries and had enough background to write his column should any of the seven horses in the field win, with the exception of one horse, Missionary Ridge. That horse was a long shot, and Murray knew absolutely nothing about it. Despite Uncle Ed's sage advice, Murray liked to put some money down at the track, though never more than a few dollars. Now, he decided he would put his money on Missionary Ridge. "That's an old racehorse charm," Christine said. "Down-and-out bettors say, 'I know what I'll do, I'll put some money on him; that'll stop him.' A guy who hasn't cashed a ticket in a month says that."

Of course, Missionary Ridge won going away. The twenty-four-to-one shot paid fifty-one dollars on a two-dollar bet, and Murray had placed all of five dollars in his failed attempt to jinx him. "So the race is over, we finish our postrace interviews, and we're back in the press box, and we go to our respective computers to start writing," recalled Christine. "And I look over at Jim, and I say, 'Well, Jim, what can I tell you?' And he says, 'I made a lot of money, but now I'm also going to write a lousy column.' But of course, he didn't." To solve his dilemma, Murray followed the old sportswriter's mantra: the best story is in the loser's locker room. He focused his column on the favorite, a filly named Paseana, who was badly beaten. Missionary Ridge, who had just added about $125 to Murray's wallet, did not appear in the column until the nineteenth paragraph.[27]

Only Fools Rush In

It was hard to argue that, having reached his midseventies, Murray had become a bit curmudgeonly. His personal rules for public and private attire had been set in stone years before, and he followed them religiously. Around the house, he preferred to wear old golf shirts, tattered sweaters, and old polyester slacks with holes in them that Linda referred to as "God-awful." He hated wearing tennis shoes, a hatred that was surpassed only by his hatred of jeans. Once, when he and Linda were invited to a western-themed party, he at first refused to even consider wearing the despised denim monstrosities. At Linda's insistence, he went with her to Macy's and bought his first pair in years and proceeded to curse their very existence from then on.

When he was working or out in public, he insisted on always wearing a jacket and tie. (For covering sporting events, he would relax this rule; sportswriters, as a rule, will fight to the death to protect their most coveted perk: the right to dress casually on the job.) "He wouldn't dream of going to a restaurant at night without a jacket and tie," Linda said. On one vacation, the two were flying to Hawaii. The plane was full of boisterous vacationers dressed in T-shirts and Bermuda shorts. Murray had on a jacket and tie, a pair of gray slacks, and loafers. The flight attendant, a young man, approached Murray. "Sir, do you work for the airline?" he asked.

"No," Murray responded. "Why do you ask?"

"Because we rarely see anyone on this flight in a coat and tie," the flight attendant said. "I thought you might be my boss."

Late nights at the bar were a thing of the past for Murray as well. He had given up alcohol cold turkey after Ricky died in 1982 and now often avoided alcohol-fueled events whenever possible. He would tell Linda that he wanted to arrive after cocktail hour, so he would not have to walk around with a Diet Coke for an hour, trying to avoid the drunks. And his daily schedule was still ruled by "the Column." He preferred to be in bed in time to watch Jay Leno or David Letterman and to wake up by eight to start writing. He would not sleep well if he did not know what he would be writing about the following day. In the morning, he would arise and head down to his office, which was a converted bedroom. He would shower and dress, plant himself behind the keyboard, and get to work. If the words came easily, he would be done by lunch. On more difficult days, he would tell Linda, "This one's a real toe sucker," and fight with it until two or three in the afternoon, still in plenty of time for his 7:00 p.m. deadline.

The Column had long been a Los Angeles institution, and a large percentage of his readers read it, rain or shine, by force of habit. Though Murray's mind remained sharp, the substance of the Column had changed subtly over time. No longer did he produce twenty-five column inches of laugh lines and sparkling witticisms, as he had two decades earlier. Though he would toss off a few one-liners now and again, he concentrated mainly on straight profiles of sports personalities, tackling the occasional hot-button issue that bubbled to the surface of the sports culture. And he went to the well of his accumulated sports and history knowledge often. His tendency to refer to people and events from as far back as the 1920s did not go unnoticed. Mike Downey liked to kid him about the regularity with which Jack Dempsey and Gene Tunney appeared in Murray's columns. Readers noticed as well. Manny Weisbord of Marina del Rey offered a humorous take on a common observation:

> When I saw that Jim Murray's column today dealt with the Lakers and Jazz, I feared momentarily that I would lose my regular bet with an old UCLA golfing pal.
>
> The bet is that Murray will mention Babe Ruth, Jack Dempsey, Ben Hogan or a racehorse from the 1920s in any column. When he does, I win $10. When he doesn't, my friend wins.
>
> Fortunately, Murray somehow saw a parallel between a 1998 basketball series and Ruth and Gehrig.
>
> My daughter may be able to go to college on the Ruth-Gehrig-Dempsey-Hogan scholarship.[28]

Three decades earlier, the majority of his readers had probably seen Dempsey fight, or at least had a sense of Dempsey's public persona; by the 1990s, Dempsey, like the rest of the sports icons of the '20s, was just a faded black-and-white memory. The younger generations in the *Times* sports department still revered Murray, but some wondered just how much he connected with modern readers in the age of twenty-four-hour cable television and the burgeoning Internet. He was, after all, at an age where most of his contemporaries were long retired and now swapped their stories of lore on the golf course or around the shuffleboard court. Murray was still performing his act for millions of readers of all ages. "There was somewhat of a feeling that Murray was becoming a little bit irrelevant," said Scott Ostler. "He wasn't dealing with the day-to-day issues, he wasn't at the ball yard, knowing who's playing, who's the backup third baseman, stuff like that. Not that anybody said, 'Geez, let's get this guy out of here.' But there was a little bit of undercurrent, I guess."[29]

While he struggled to stay current, he worried about his mental health as well. He did the *New York Times* crossword puzzle religiously and was able to plow through it in fifteen minutes, but he still somehow believed he was developing Alzheimer's disease. Linda would find brochures around the house; Murray had highlighted passages detailing how to spot the early warning signs of the condition. And he liked to spend his time at home. He was still an avid reader, but not necessarily of sports-related topics. He liked to plant mystery novels around the house and would usually be involved in three or four of them at any given time.

With fewer responsibilities, Murray and Linda spent a lot of time at their second home in La Quinta, near Palm Springs. Murray preferred to remain as anonymous as possible. He would beg Linda not to engage the neighbors, which he felt would inevitably lead to drinks, dinner, and more socializing. He did not need any more friends, he told her. He wanted peace, quiet, and maybe a little golf, just the two of them. Linda enjoyed the social scene, however, and Murray enjoyed the company of old friends, so the two spent their share of time on the party circuit. Al Davis remembered attending an event thrown by Los Angeles Clippers owner Donald Sterling at which Linda and Murray were present. It was a celebrity-filled affair, billed as a "the wedding-gown white party," and guests were asked to dress entirely in white. Murray appeared supremely uncomfortable in a white tuxedo. "Jim didn't feel right in that type of atmosphere," Davis said. Davis and Murray found a quiet corner in Sterling's mansion and began analyzing the Raiders' roster, position by position. "That scene wasn't our cup of tea. Our cup of tea was sitting around the table, talking sports," Davis said.[30]

Everybody wanted to talk sports with Murray, radio and television hosts included. His inability to say no landed him on the airwaves more than he would have liked. National programs like *The Jim Rome Show*, as well as Southern California–based shows, came calling, and Murray would, more often than not, oblige the requests, but he would tell friends privately that he found the experience uncomfortable. His friend Roy Firestone hosted the popular interview program *Up Close* on ESPN, and Firestone fought to get Murray on his show often, despite protests from ESPN network executives who wanted bigger draws. But Murray's depth of knowledge made him an ideal interview subject in Firestone's eyes. Murray had no interest, however, in adapting himself to fit the medium. "He absolutely couldn't have cared less," Firestone said. "He didn't care about embellishing, or being a winning personality. He didn't care about the performance; he didn't know where the camera was. He didn't care. He didn't want to see the tape played back; he didn't want a copy of the show. His attitude was: Just ask the questions. I'll answer them. Let's go."[31]

Media requests never failed to surprise Murray, who thought himself the least interesting of subjects. That was the same reaction he had when he was approached to write his autobiography by a literary agent. He had liked the feeling of seeing his compilations of columns in book form, however, so once he was convinced of the economic feasibility of the project, he agreed to write it. He began work on it in 1992 and found that it did not come easily. By sheer mental-muscle memory, he was now programmed to turn out his prose in eight-hundred-word chunks. "Get in and get out" was one of his writing mottoes. Earlier in his career, he had freelanced for magazines, which offered him the opportunity to write in different genres and lengths. He had intermittently produced feature stories for the *Los Angeles Times Magazine* and for national publications such as *TV Guide* and *Golf Digest*, but he had stopped accepting most freelance work when he no longer needed the paycheck. Now he was undertaking a completely new form, with the added twist of being asked to turn the microscope back on himself, an act that, to him, felt completely unnatural.

When the book was released by Macmillan Publishing in the spring of 1993, his reticence could be easily seen on the page. It was titled simply *Jim Murray: An Autobiography,* with a cover photo of a contemplative Murray lounging in the empty grandstand of an unnamed ballpark, wearing a golf shirt, gray slacks, and a sport coat. The back cover featured his Pulitzer Prize plaque, glasses, his beloved Remington typewriter, and assorted sports memorabilia. In the acknowledgments, Murray thanks three editors from his career: Frank McCulloch, Sid James, and Bill Dwyre, as well *Times* publisher Otis Chandler. He dedicated the book to Linda, but the dedication was inadvertently left out in the first printing of the book. Murray made sure that the dedication was included when the paperback edition came out, and Linda later framed and mounted the formal apology from the publisher.[32]

Inside the book, readers find a strange combination of personal memoir and sports commentary. The first forty pages read like a traditional autobiography, following Murray's life from childhood through the founding of *Sports Illustrated.* From there, however, the book changes directions and becomes what amounts to a greatest-hits collection. Profiles on great athletes and coaches are mixed with anecdotes from memorable sporting events that he covered for the *Times.* Many observations and phrases from his newspaper writing find their way into these sections. Muhammad Ali "didn't have fights, he gave recitals." Tommy Lasorda "was a baseball manager right out of central casting."[33] Chapters are loosely divided by sports, and Murray included some personal stories of his interactions with sports personalities, while concentrating mostly on the personalities themselves. Al Davis warranted seventeen pages; Pete Rose's life was afforded ten pages.

His editors prodded him to concentrate more on himself. It was, after all, supposed to be a book about Jim Murray, they told him. Murray resisted. "I kept telling them, 'Hey, we're observers. We talk about what they do.' When you go about leading a life, it doesn't seem like a big deal." Still, he acquiesced, to a degree. Further into the book, he devoted a chapter to his marriage to Gerry, a chapter to the loss of Ricky, and a chapter to his vision problems. These sections are by far the most emotionally charged of the book. He found the self-examination that went into writing about these issues severely draining. "You feel guilty, like you're opening a closet you shouldn't," he told David Leon Moore of *USA Today.* "Writing is hard work, anyway. Writing about yourself, and being honest about it, is the hardest work of all." At the book's conclusion, Murray portrays a sense of peace with his life's work: "I covered the circus. I felt privileged to have done so. Some of the happiest hours of my life were spent in a press box. Sure, I helped keep the hype going, the calliope playing. I can live with that. It's what I am."[34]

Jim Murray: An Autobiography was a financial success, thanks in part to Murray's network of friends and admirers throughout the media. The book received a nice wave of publicity. Columnists across the country devoted full columns to Murray, and sports editors assigned feature profiles on him and the book. His close friends in the business related personal stories of working with Murray, and those who had admired him from afar related the briefest of personal encounters with him. His friend Dave Anderson gave the book a glowing review in the *New York Times Book Review. Newsday,* the *Salt Lake Tribune,* the *Austin-American Statesman,* and other newspapers ran lengthy excerpts from the book, over a number of days. Murray enjoyed the praise and spent a considerable amount of time publicizing the book, both on the airwaves and at book signings.

The pressures of a major book project behind him, Murray fell back into his routine. Another experience that would break that routine was right around the corner, though. In the fall of 1994, he began mentioning to Linda that, increasingly, he was having difficulty catching his breath. "You know you're having problems when you get out of breath climbing stairs. But when you're out of breath going down stairs, it's time to call the doctor," he told her.

What he was feeling was the slow deterioration of a porcine valve that had been transplanted into his heart twelve years earlier. Just months after the death of his son, the remnants of the disease that had left him bedridden for so much of his preadolescence had returned to put him back into the hospital. The aortic valve in his heart, weakened in childhood by rheumatic fever, was failing. At the time, pig-valve replacement surgery was a relatively new procedure. In early September 1982, Dr. Jack Matloff successfully performed the procedure at Cedars-Sinai Medical Center in Los Angeles. Six weeks after the procedure, Murray was back in the pages of the *Times,* having fun with the fact that he was now "trafe." His personal physician, Dr. Gary Sugarman, provided the punch line: "This means you can never go into a Beverly Hills delicatessen as long as you live."[35]

Pig valves have a life span of twelve to fourteen years, so in 1994, Murray's valve was deteriorating right on schedule. Murray was back on the operating table, with a team of physicians at his side, including Matloff and Sugarman.[36] This time, the surgery did not go as smoothly as before. Doctors were using a mechanical valve this time, and in the process of attaching it, the original valve deteriorated, and Murray began to bleed out. He came very close to dying on the table and was placed on life support, but, after eleven hours of surgery, doctors were able to successfully attach the mechanical valve. Murray spent three days in the intensive-care unit and two more weeks in the hospital.

Recovery was a much longer process this time. A therapist was hired to come to the house on Bellagio Terrace to work one-on-one with Murray. At first, he could barely make it around the house, but, in time, Linda was taking him to Century City Mall to walk. His strength eventually returned, and by February, he was back to work, making the trip to the desert to cover the Bob Hope Chrysler Classic. In time, the new valve actually improved his quality of life beyond where it had been before the surgery.[37]

His health was very precarious at this stage of his life, however, and he was in and out of the hospital a few more times. One of those scares was the impetus that led to Murray's becoming, after thirteen years, a married man once again. In early 1997, he began experiencing regular dizzy spells. During a previous hospital stay, Linda had a difficult time gaining access to Murray because of hospital regulations that limited visitation to family. Their marital status, or lack thereof, was the problem. So when Sugarman proposed to put Murray back in the hospital for tests, Linda was upset, to put it mildly. "I told him, you make sure everything is in order, or you can take a cab," Linda recalled. Murray made a call to his attorney, and it went to voice mail. As they walked to the car to head to the hospital, he had a little surprise for her. "Well, you know. There are ways of getting around this."

"Yeah, like what?" Linda asked.

"Well, we could, you know, get married."

Linda was flabbergasted. "What did you say?"

"Well," Murray said, "then you don't have to go through all the bullshit."

"Are you asking me to marry you?"

"Well, yeah."

"Well, then ask me!"

Murray turned to her. "Will you marry me?"

"Oh, God, I don't know. This is so sudden." Then the tears came. "Of course I'll marry you," she said.

On the way to Cedar-Sinai, they discussed marriage plans.

"Maybe I should call a judge and have him come to the hospital," Linda said. "Is that soon enough?"

"I'm not going to die," Murray said.

"You better not."[38]

They sealed the deal in early March, on the Monday after the Los Angeles Open, played at Murray's beloved Riviera Country Club. It was a small ceremony at the house of some friends, and in the days following, Linda waited patiently to see if the milestone would make it into the Column. Finally, on Thursday, there it was, twenty-two paragraphs deep, tacked onto the end of a preview of the AC Delco Classic Bowling Tournament. "Team Murray underwent a roster change, a lineup revamp last Monday," he wrote. "The beauteous

Linda McCoy signed on. We got married. . . . Jerry Reinsdorf thinks he pulled the coup of the year signing Albert Belle for the White Sox? Fergetaboudit! I signed the real pennant winner. The Unreal McCoy. I wish I could have invited you all to the wedding, but home plate at Dodger Stadium was busy."[39]

"What a Grand Man You Were"

In 1974, Murray used the occasion of the death of New York Giants outfielder Fred Snodgrass to ruminate on his own obituary. Snodgrass was the infamous goat of the 1912 World Series, and Murray imagined an obit that framed his own life similarly, leading with his most embarrassing moments. He took a shot in his column at a few of the possibilities: "Datelines and obits flashed before my eyes. 'Jim Murray, 86, who stole a handful of walnuts from the fruitstand of the First National Store in West Hartford in 1932, died yesterday.' 'Jim Murray, ticketed for double-parking on a busy thoroughfare in Watchung, N.J., in 1938, died yesterday at the age of 90.' 'Jim Murray, who once told a girl in the fifth grade in 1925 that his grandfather owned a gold mine and that he himself was a direct descendent of Chief Sitting Bull, died yesterday at his home.'"[40]

Seriously discussing his legacy was not an activity that Murray would have ever considered engaging in, but, as he had written in his autobiography, he was now resigned to, and content with, his name being tied, in perpetuity, to the Column. *It's what I am.* It had ruled his existence since he had signed on. He had begun to understand its hold from the very first month on the job, when he first realized he was, as he put it, "riding the tiger": "You may not want to stay on. But you don't dare get off. Either way, it's liable to eat you alive." He had planned his sign-off in his mind and told people of those plans many times, yet he was still writing. He fantasized about retirement and did not like the idea of writing all the way up to his death. "I don't want to die in a Holiday Inn," he told his friend Bob Pastin of the *St. Louis Post-Dispatch* in 1993. "I'd like to get a gold watch at least."[41] Yet he was still writing. He could barely see, had undergone open-heart surgery twice, and was on his third aortic valve, yet he was still writing.

In that respect, he was far from alone among those in his chosen profession. Writers know better than anyone that every story needs an end. Many of the legends of his own genre had written as long as their fingers would type and died before their final words became ink on the page. Grantland Rice, the first dean of sportswriters, finished writing his final column, turned it in, then went back to his office and suffered a massive stroke. His last thoughts, about the constant rebirth of sporting greatness from generation to generation, reached his readers hours after Rice had taken his last breath.[42] Jimmy

Cannon, the alpha dog among the pack of New York sports columnists in the mid-twentieth century, would not give up his column even after suffering a debilitating stroke. Physically unable to type, he rehabilitated himself just enough to allow himself to dictate his column to a secretary. His spoken words found their way into the newspaper for another few months until another stroke sidelined him for eternity.[43] Red Smith, dying from a failing heart and kidney, was finally persuaded by editors and family members not to stop writing, but to cut down from four columns a week to three. His final column, informing readers of his decision, ran on a Monday; on Friday he was gone. His last printed words were drenched with melancholic irony. "One of the beauties of this job is that there is always tomorrow," he wrote.[44] The type of person who could truly master this particular skill, it seemed, was the same type who was most susceptible to its eternal grasp.

Unlike Smith and Cannon, Murray did not limp toward the grave, desperately hanging onto the keyboard. In the final weeks of his life, he was enjoying the benefits of his status—he had long since released himself from the pressures of deadlines and intense self-evaluation. "Our last three weekends were the happiest we had ever spent together," Linda said. The first of those weekends, at the beginning of August 1998, Murray and Linda went down to Del Mar to spend a couple of days at the track. This time, however, Murray went as a spectator and amateur horse player, not as a sportswriter. There was no column to be written, just time to spend with Linda, some old friends, and the ticket window. One evening, Linda and Murray dined with jockey Chris McCarron, a friend of Murray's and frequent column subject, at Rancho Santa Fe. McCarron spent some of the dinner asking Murray about one of Murray's favorite subjects: Ben Hogan. "I used to love to ask Murray about Hogan and players like that," McCarron said, sharing one story. "He told me Hogan very seldom, almost rarely, asked any advice of a caddie for a particular shot. And one day at Riviera, Mr. Hogan looked at the caddie and said, 'What do you think we got here?' And the caddie says, 'Mr. Hogan, I think it's 145, maybe 146 yards.' Hogan looked at him and said, 'Well, make up your mind.'"[45]

The following weekend, Murray bought something he had always longed for—a car with an open roof. After fifty years of watching them on the freeways of Southern California, he still had not had one to call his own. Since he still felt his Irish complexion could not handle a full convertible, he decided on a café latte–colored Chrysler with a sunroof. He drove the car off the lot with Linda, and the couple reminisced about their first week spent together in an open-roofed vehicle, in Indianapolis, three decades before.[46]

The Pacific Classic was set to go off on Saturday, August 15, so Murray and Linda headed back down the coast to Del Mar on Friday and checked into the Hilton San Diego, right across the street from the track. Murray was on the job this time; he was scheduled to write a column about the race, and Bill Christine was to handle the straight race story for the *Times*. The two joined the rest of the turf writers and went through the usual track rituals—interviewing jockeys and trainers in the barn area, watching the race from the press box, and conducting postrace interviews.

The Pacific Classic went off Saturday afternoon and was won by Free House, with McCarron aboard. Because the sunlight was bothering his eyes, Murray asked his old *Times* colleague Dan Smith, who now worked in public relations for Del Mar Racetrack, if he could use Smith's office to write his column. Free House had finished in the money in each of the Triple Crown races the previous year but had not won any of them. Murray found his angle in that fact— here was a horse, he told readers, who had been allowed to mature and was just starting to reach his potential.[47] Now, he had finally earned his place in the sun. "The bridesmaid finally caught the bouquet," he wrote. "The best friend finally got the girl in the Warner Bros. movie for a change. The sidekick saves the fort."[48] The column was rich in horse-racing history, a tour of the sport, starting in the early twentieth century. Many of the great American thoroughbreds warranted a mention: Man o' War, Citation, Count Fleet, Secretariat. And, in comparing the longevity of the greats in other sports to the best in horse racing, Murray even found a way to bring Babe Ruth into the conversation. Ruth had decades in the spotlight, he wrote; great thoroughbreds have but a few short years.

The next day was Sunday, and Linda and Murray decided to spend another day at the track before driving back to Bel Air. Murray took Linda to the barn area, where they chatted with McCarron and some of the other jockeys and trainers. Linda noticed that he was acting tired, dragging behind her as the two of them walked through the paddocks. Later, Murray made his way up to the press box. Dan Smith and some of the writers had seen his column about Free House in the *Times* that morning. "We were all very complimentary, you know, and Jim was always pleased, if you complimented him on his column," Smith recalled. "He always acted a little surprised, funny, and he said, 'You really liked it?' And we said, 'Yeah, Jim, we thought it was terrific.'"[49] Murray and Linda spent much of the day in the director's room at Del Mar, stayed for all ten races, and then climbed into the Chrysler for the trip home.

They arrived home earlier than expected and were enjoying a nice, leisurely evening around the house, with no column deadline in sight. A little before eleven, Murray went downstairs and changed into his pajamas and robe and then came up to watch the local news. The Bill Clinton–Monica Lewinsky affair was leading the news every night, and the following day Clinton would become the first president to testify before a grand jury and would address the country afterward. Murray was following the drama intently. "This is history in the making," he told Linda.

The news came on, and the two watched together, Murray sitting in his favorite recliner. Then the first block of commercials began airing, and Murray hit the mute button on the remote control. The commercials ended, and the news program came back on the screen. As Murray hit the mute button to bring the sound back on, he said, "Oh, Linda, something's wrong."

After a lifetime of extended physical suffering from a variety of ailments, the end came very quickly. Murray was gone in an instant, the click of a button. Murray's aortic valve, weakened from two transplant surgeries and eight decades of living, had finally disintegrated. His breathing stopped, and his face turned a deep shade of crimson. Linda called his doctor and then dialed 911. At the instruction of the paramedics, she somehow managed to get him out of the chair and onto the floor so she could attempt CPR, but it was useless. His heart was no longer functional. "I thought there was just a breath of light left there and we've got to find it," Linda said. "But he was gone."

News of his death spread quickly the next day. Christine got a call from the sports desk Monday morning. "You could have knocked me over with a feather. I had just seen him and worked with him the day before. It was so unbelievable," he said. Since he had died late Sunday evening, the *Times* was not able to publish the news of Murray's death until Tuesday morning. But the timing gave the staff a full day to prepare coverage, and in Tuesday's *Times,* Murray's death received more ink than most presidents. His obituary ran on A1, and the sports section devoted most of the front page and five full pages inside the section to Murray's life. The dominant image on the front of the sports section was a cartoon of a baseball jersey with Murray's name across the back hanging in a darkened locker, amid bats, balls, and gloves. The inside of the section was filled with remembrances from friends and luminaries. With a full day to report, the *Times* staff got to virtually everybody. "I idolized Jim Murray," wrote Bob Hope. "He should be in every sports hall of fame." Ronald Reagan, Jack Lemmon, California governor Pete Williams, Arnold Palmer, Tommy Lasorda, and dozens of others offered condolences. Twenty writers and columnists, from the *Times* and from newspapers across the country, contributed columns about Murray. Several of his most memorable columns were reprinted, along with many excerpts and quotes. Coverage continued through the week, and four days later, the day after Murray's funeral, the *Times* published a *Sports Extra,* headlined "Farewell to a Friend," with another four pages dedicated to the newspaper's most famous voice.

The Murray funeral had a similar cast of characters to the Murray memorial editions of the *Times.* St. Martin of Tours Church in Brentwood was standing-room only at 11:00 a.m. when the ceremony was set to begin. The sports community was represented by athletes and executives from every sport. "The signatures in the guest book could command a small fortune in the sports memorabilia market," wrote J. A. Adande, a young columnist covering the funeral for the *Times*. Hollywood had its share of representation, from Dabney Coleman to Peter Falk to comedian Red Buttons, whom Murray had met through his friend Will Fowler all the way back in the 1940s. The entire *Times* sports staff, as well as sportswriters and broadcasters from across the country, lined the pews. Just as the ceremony was getting started, Mike Tyson, who had flown in from Las Vegas specifically for the funeral, walked into the church and took a place in the back of the building. Throughout the church, heads turned to see the enigmatic boxer. Tyson's attendance was commented upon not only because of his outlaw image, but because the *Times*, just four days before, had reprinted Murray's column about Tyson's infamous ear-bite fight with Evander Holyfield, in which Murray referred to Tyson as "America's Wolfman." But in death, as in life, Murray's relationships transcended his printed words. "I had the greatest respect for him," Tyson said.[50]

The service had a strong Irish flavor. It began with a processional led by a bagpiper, followed by a number of traditional Irish ballads, including "Danny Boy" and "Galway Bay." Murray's children and grandchild, along with Linda, Bill, and other family members, watched from the front row. Broadcaster and essayist Jack Whitaker, another longtime friend of Murray's, was chosen to deliver the eulogy. He spoke of Murray's love of California, his lifelong passion for sports, his old-fashioned values. Mourners should allow themselves to laugh, because that, after all, was what Murray had wanted all his life, he said. "Jim Murray knew better than most that the only proper tools with which to journey through this vale of tears were the generosity of the human spirit and wit and humor," Whitaker told the congregation. "He got through it in great style. If we emulate him, they will get us through too. James Patrick Murray, my, what a grand man you were."[51]

Whitaker, like many of those who eulogized Murray in print, said that finding the right words to describe Murray was nearly impossible, because the man himself had already done it, better, thousands of times before. Adande offered the same idea in the column he wrote following the funeral. Then he symbolically turned the keyboard over to Murray himself, using Murray's column about the conclusion of the 1984 Los Angeles Olympics to supply Murray's own epitaph:

> Turn out the lights. The party's over. Pack up the costumes. Put away the paper hats. Turn off the loudspeaker. Pay the band. We'll take one more cup of kindness yet for days of Auld Lang Syne, then pick up all the glasses and put them in the sink. Never mind the dishes. We'll take care of those tomorrow. Drive carefully. We don't want to lose anybody.
>
> It's been a ball. Don't cry. Go out the way we came in, singing and dancing. A toast to absent friends, to loved ones who couldn't be here. Promise to write. Keep in touch. Thanks for the memories.

At the conclusion of the ceremony, tenor Dennis McNeil sang "When Irish Eyes Are Smiling" as the casket was carried out down the aisle.[52] Speakers had been set up outside for the overflow crowd. As the hearse and the limousine stopped traffic on Sunset Boulevard, people got out of their cars and mourners lined the street, waving and dabbing their eyes as the vehicles pulled away from the church.[53]

Bill Thomas, Bill Dwyre, and a number of the Geezers served as pallbearers and rode in the vehicles as they headed to Holy Cross Cemetery in Los Angeles. Murray was to be laid to rest alongside Gerry and Ricky. The pallbearers took hold of the casket and began moving toward the grave site, where the burial ceremony would take place. As they walked through the cemetery, one of the Geezers, perhaps channeling Murray's irreverent sense of humor, found just the right note to bid farewell to their friend. The group carried the casket down a small hill, and a voice cut through the silence: "Jim wouldn't have liked this," he observed. "It's gonna be a downhill lie."[54]

Epilogue

A month and five days later, a crowd of twenty-five hundred, made up of Jim Murray's most loyal fans, friends, and readers, walked through the turnstiles at Dodger Stadium for one last chance to gather and memorialize the man whose words had started their morning for four decades. It was a gray day, and the clouds hung low over the baseball diamond, but Vin Scully, one of the speakers assembled to pay homage to Murray, said the weather should not cast a pall over the proceedings. To the contrary, he said, it was the ideal conditions in which to speak about an Irishman like Murray. "This is not an overcast day, nor is it a gloomy day," Scully said. "The Irish would call it a soft day."[1]

Along with Scully, Al Davis, Jerry West, Chris McCarron, Al Michaels, Chick Hearn, and Ann Meyers Drysdale took the podium to share their remembrances of Murray with the assembled crowd. Bill Dwyre opened the ceremony, and then Al Michaels took to the microphone and discussed the impact Murray had upon him personally and upon sportswriting in general. He compared Murray's writing to ABC's *Wide World of Sports* in terms of innovation: "I think of [*Wide World of Sports*] in concert with what took place on February 12, 1961, when Jim Murray's first column appeared in the *Los Angeles Times*, and the signal moment that that was, not only for sports journalism in this area, but for the country, and what it did for the profession."

As Al Davis ascended to the podium, Raiders fans unveiled a banner with the words "WE LOVE OUR RAIDERS," referring to Davis's team, which he had moved back up the coast to Oakland four years before. Davis acknowledged the Raider faithful and then dug into his own treasure trove of anecdotes to remember his ever-humble friend. Davis's relationship with Murray went back to when Davis was an assistant football coach at USC and had remained strong through the decades, despite Murray's occasional shot across the bow. Davis recalled for the crowd a reception held while the Raiders were still in Los Angeles. "I certainly refrained from speaking engagements, but one group came up with a great idea: they would give Jim Murray some kind of honor, and they would ask me to present. And both of us accepted, and I said to Jim before the presentation, 'Is there anything you want me to say?' And he said, 'Well, don't be to laudatory.' And I said, 'Don't worry, Jim, I won't be. There's not that much there.'"

Both West and Hearn discussed that long-ago trip to West Virginia with the Lakers, where Murray's commentary had managed to enrage the local population. West told the crowd how Murray had written that people in West Virginia were fond of "sewing patches on their cars with needle and thread." Hearn was also along on that early-1960s Lakers road trip. "I was in that wagon," he said. "Hell, it wasn't getting in [that was difficult], it was trying to get out of town. By that time, they'd formed a posse." Then Hearn managed to sum up the reason that most of the assembled crowd were in attendance, spending a Saturday morning remembering a newspaper writer who had died more than a month earlier: "He could write about a cockfight, he could write about an automobile race, he could write about anything, and find the heart and soul of the subject and put it into words. . . . That's something that is God given, but it has to be mastered by someone with unbelievable, unequaled ability. And that's what Jim had. He could start your day with a smile."

Linda took to the podium and articulated what those closest to the man knew would have been Murray's reaction to the proceedings. "Jim, I tell you, would be embarrassed by this fanfare. He'd probably say, 'Enough already. Don't you have anything else to do?'" she said. "No, Jim, we don't."[2]

Murray, of course, laughed at the idea of "his legacy." He would say to Linda, "Hell, I won't be out of here six months and they'll be saying 'Jim who?'" That particular statement remained on her mind, percolated, and eventually led her to devote her life to proving it wrong.

A few months after the Dodger Stadium memorial, she was sitting in Murray's office, looking at the plaques and awards on the wall, and asking herself, "What am I going to do with all of this?" The statement played over and over in her mind. *They'll be saying "Jim who?"* "And I sat up, and I said, 'I don't think so. I have to do something with this.'"

That spark was the genesis of what is known today as the Jim Murray Memorial Foundation, an organization dedicated to keeping alive Murray's memory and supporting sports journalism students across the country. The foundation, born as a simple response to Murray's innate self-deprecation, has continued to grow in the years since his death. An annual sports essay contest, judged by the top professional sportswriters in the country, was chosen as the vehicle through which to award funds to the students. Murray's wide network of friends throughout the sports and media industries helped provide the intellectual weight and financial support to launch Linda's effort.

On the one-year anniversary of his death, supporters gathered at Murray's beloved Riviera Country Club for the inaugural JMMF golf tournament. The event was a tremendous success and launched the organization in a number of directions. Soon, Linda was piling up the frequent-flier miles, visiting universities from coast to coast to speak to students about Murray and what he represented. The golf tournament continued for nine years, and, as the organization grew, other events were added. An annual banquet was held in which awards were given out to athletes and journalists who represented the JMMF credo, written, of course, with Murray in mind, of "honesty, humility, and integrity." The number of universities participating in the scholarship program continues to grow, and, as of this writing, has reached thirty, from the University of Hawaii at Manoa to Murray's alma mater, Trinity University in Hartford. And as the foundation grows, Linda travels the country, spreading the gospel of Jim Murray from school to school, discovering and creating new disciples along the way. "It's a two-way street," she says. "Really, it's wonderful for them, and it's wonderful for me and for the foundation as well."

They'll be saying "Jim who?" Although since his death, sports journalism has morphed into something he would barely recognize, Murray did not really need a foundation to keep his name alive. His contemporaries who are still active and those who followed pay homage to him in print and over the airwaves regularly. His tremendous modesty was only one part of the formula that has made him a generational icon throughout the close-knit fraternity of sportswriters, editors, and broadcasters. His inimitable style and humor, his longevity, his approachability, his consistency, his integrity, and his unwavering ability to entertain had allowed him, along with Red Smith, to become a patron saint for two generations of sportswriters. He had become, by the time of his death, what Grantland Rice had been a half century before, respected and beloved by subjects and peers alike.

In the weeks following his death, writers across the country, those who knew him well and those who admired him from afar, penned tributes to Murray's greatness. In an industry that literally and figuratively moved in herds, they wrote, he was an outlier, a melodious voice that pierced the din. Everybody had a dozen favorite lines they could quote from Murray. One scribe wrote that if there was a *Bartlett's Book of Quotations* for sports, 75 percent of the lines would have come from Murray's columns.

Longtime sports columnist and author Leonard Koppett, a contemporary of Murray's, penned a thoughtful piece a month after his death that attempted to define Murray's place in the history of the genre. Murray, he wrote, along with Smith and Jimmy Cannon were the three great innovators of their generation and the generation that followed. Smith brought literate prose to the sports page, Cannon taught readers that athletes were real people, and Murray "showed us the true difference between reportage and commentary." Smith and Cannon could, and often did, write with great humor, Koppett observed. But Murray's humor was at his core as a writer. "Murray integrated his wittiness into everything he dealt with, by cleverness in language and sharp-eyed observation. The other two could be funny sometimes. He was really funny most of the time," Koppett concluded.[3]

A twenty-year journalism apprenticeship had prepared Murray to let loose his well-informed wit on the public. A decade of writing for weekly magazines had taught him to put zest into every line, every paragraph he wrote, and he brought that technique along with him to the land of daily deadlines. By the time he got to the *Times,* he was a fully formed writer and humorist with an incomparable breadth of knowledge. He had come along at the right time and stumbled into the right place. As he matured under the endless sun of Southern California, spectator sports matured with him, and with his help. And in a city that became synonymous with entertainment, he was, in his heart, an entertainer himself. *Entertain, then inform.* It was an ethos that allowed him to appreciate and respect his subjects, on the screen, and then on the field of play. And it earned him the same from them. Readers came along for the ride; Murray was their tour guide, the guy who could open their day with a quip or two or twenty and remind them to laugh a little. It was, after all, just a game.

In 2005, Linda put Murray's 1946 Remington typewriter up for auction, along with a number of other items and documents from Murray's career. The final three bidders for the typewriter were the *Los Angeles Times,* the Los Angeles Dodgers, and Southern California businessman Steve Soboroff. Soboroff was in New York for the Sotheby's auction to sell a glove worn by Sandy Koufax when the Dodger star had pitched one of his four no-hitters. The Koufax auction was first, and the glove sold for a lot more than Soboroff had expected, netting $120,000.

At the event, he became aware of the typewriter auction and, as a lifelong Murray devotee, decided that the typewriter would be going back to Los Angeles with him, if the price was right. He had a decided advantage because he was bidding for himself, and the representatives of the *Times* and the Dodgers had to clear each bid with the office back in Los Angeles. For $18,000, Soboroff became the owner of the Remington, Murray's glasses, and a framed oil painting of Murray. Fearing his wife did not want a portrait of Jim Murray on the wall of the family's living room, he allowed the *Times* to take the painting off his hands, and it now hangs in the *Times* sports department.

Having purchased it on a whim, Soboroff now, for the first time, began to think about what to do with Murray's typewriter. The typewriter had not worked in years—Murray had grudgingly acquiesced to technological advancement and moved on, first to an electric typewriter, then to word processors and computers. Soboroff discovered it was difficult and expensive to repair a sixty-year-old typewriter, but found someone who was able to get the machine in working order. Once repaired, he decided he did not want his new possession to sit in a vault. He wanted it to serve a purpose. "So now I got it, and I asked myself, what am I going to do it? What do collectors do with stuff?" he said. He got in touch with Linda, whom he had known years before, and soon the two were making plans to take the Remington on tour.

In the years since Soboroff's purchase, Jim Murray's favorite typewriter has made some of the rounds that were made by its original owner while he was still alive. The typewriter has spent time in the press box at some of Murray's favorite old haunts, such as Del Mar Racetrack and Dodger Stadium. It has tagged along with Linda as she spread the Murray gospel to student journalists at universities around the United States. Soboroff dove headfirst into typewriter collecting, and now, when it is not on the road, Murray's Remington is in high literary company, residing with typewriters formerly owned by Ernest Hemingway, Jack London, and George Bernard Shaw, among others.

When the typewriter is on tour, Soboroff allows Murray admirers young and old to try it out. Linda supplies him with Murray's embossed *Los Angeles Times* stationery, and those who are interested are invited to roll in a page and start banging away. For visitors who grew up in the age of the computer keyboard, it is often the first time they have used a manual typewriter, and it does not come easily. At one JMMF event, Soboroff and Rick Reilly were observing as students took a seat in front of the machine, one by one, and tried the keys. One young attendee struggled for a few minutes to type a legible sentence, to no avail. He stared down at the typos on his page for a beat and then looked up at Reilly. "Where's the delete key?" he asked.

Some of the happiest hours of my life were spent in press boxes. In 2006, Soboroff allowed the Remington to spend the entire baseball season in the press box at Dodger Stadium. The Dodgers were in contention that summer, and the facilities were full most of the time. The Remington, along with Murray's old glasses, were placed in a Lucite case and set up in the second row, the very seat Murray had occupied for hundreds of Dodger games over the years. Soboroff would attend games occasionally throughout the summer and visit the machine. As the summer dragged on, less attention was paid to the typewriter. Stat sheets and newspapers and hot-dog wrappers would pile up on the press-box tables around Murray's old seat. Soboroff noticed that no matter how messy it got, the reporters made sure that the table in front of the Remington remained debris free.

As the summer turned into fall and the Dodgers waged a tight battle with the San Diego Padres for the Western Division pennant, occupancy increased in the press box. Murray's seat in the second row was still left vacant. Amid the laptops and Blackberries and cell phones, the Remington was conspicuous in its obsolescence, a relic of a long-lost era when newspapers were still vibrant and information, like life, moved at a slower pace. That long-lost era was Jim Murray's time, and he was gone too, but to those who still practiced his craft, who aimed to spin stories and express ideas and entertain with words, his name still had deep meaning. As the season wound down and the press box filled up, the local reporters made a habit of improvising their own little tours of sports journalism history, taking the out-of-town writers over to the vacant seat on the second row. "It's a Remington Rand," they would say. "This is the typewriter used, many years ago, by the great Jim Murray."[4]

Notes

Introduction

1. Jim Murray, "Looking at the Losers," *Los Angeles Times,* August 25, 1961.
2. Jim Murray, "Please, No Flowers," *Los Angeles Times,* August 24, 1961.
3. Jim Murray, "Thar She Blows!," *Los Angeles Times,* January 31, 1962.
4. Jim Murray, "There Are Hardships," *Los Angeles Times,* August 26, 1961.
5. "It Began in Cincinnati," *Dayton Journal Herald,* February 13, 1974.
6. Linda McCoy-Murray, *Quotable Jim Murray: The Literary Wit, Wisdom, and Wonder of a Distinguished American Sports Columnist,* 20.
7. Ibid., 31.
8. Ibid., 50.
9. Ibid., 40.
10. Ibid., 25.
11. Jim Murray, "Living Color," *Los Angeles Times,* November 29, 1961.
12. Jim Murray, *Jim Murray: An Autobiography,* 42.
13. Jim Murray, "Ride on a Tiger," *Los Angeles Times,* March 12, 1961. Murray wrote those lines after only one month on the job.
14. Roy Firestone, interview with the author, December 15, 2009.
15. Frank Deford, interview with the author, January, 2008.

Chapter 1

1. Murray, *Jim Murray: An Autobiography,* 1.
2. Matt Allen, interview with the author, February 12, 2009. The history of the Murray family in Tobbercurry was compiled by genealogical researchers at the behest of Allen. Allen, Jim Murray's grandnephew, has traveled to the region several times and maintained a relationship with members of the Murray family still living in Ireland.
3. Jim Murray, "Only Irish Need Read," *Los Angeles Times,* March 17, 1961.
4. Carl Wittke, *The Irish in America,* 8–9.
5. Ibid., 23–25.
6. Glenn Weaver, *Hartford: An Illustrated History of Connecticut's Capital,* 80–81, 116.
7. Jim Murray, "Old School Is Fine, Thank You," *Los Angeles Times,* August 31, 1995.
8. Much of this account comes from genealogical research done at the behest Matt Allen. The *Hartford, Connecticut, City Directory* lists a Hartford address for the Murrays in 1900 and 1910. By 1930, the directory lists them as living in West Hartford.
9. Gerald Suppicich, interview with the author, November 19, 2008.

10. US Department of Commerce, Bureau of the Census, *Fourteenth Census of the United States,* Hartford, Connecticut, 1920, series T625, Roll 183, page 164.

11. Murray, *Jim Murray: An Autobiography,* 3.

12. Dr. Winkler Weinberg, interview with the author, February 2009.

13. US Department of Commerce, Bureau of the Census, *Fourteenth Census of the United States,* Hartford, Connecticut, 1920, series T625, Roll 183, page 164.

14. Suppicich interview.

15. "Arrest Druggist as Delaney's Aid: James P. Murray Stored Liquor and Sold Liquor, Police Assert," *Hartford Courant,* January 13, 1922.

16. "Druggist Murray Sentenced to Jail," *Hartford Courant,* January 29, 1922. James Murray gave notice of appeal and furnished bond of twelve hundred dollars at the time. The *Courant* did not report further on the case, so the question remains as to whether the appeal was heard and whether Murray served the sentence. James Murray would work for other pharmacists to earn a living for the rest of his life, in addition to other jobs. On his application for admission to Trinity College in 1939, Jim Murray listed his father's occupation as factory worker.

17. Carol Hamel, interview with the author, January 29, 2008.

18. Marie Hewins, interview with the author, January 24, 2008.

19. Suppicich interview.

20. Murray, *Jim Murray: An Autobiography,* 3.

21. Jim Murray, *Sporting World,* 32–33.

22. Ibid., 34.

23. Murray, *Jim Murray: An Autobiography,* 7.

24. Jim Murray, "Uncle Ed Would Be a Proud Name Dropper," *Los Angeles Times,* July 12, 1990. Murray wrote this column on the occasion of the first running of the Jim Murray Handicap at Hollywood Park in Los Angeles.

25. Hewins interview.

26. Murray, *Sporting World,* 34.

27. Eric Sandburg, interview with the author, November 14, 2008; Murray, *Jim Murray: An Autobiography,* 2.

28. Suppicich interview. Suppicich said Jim's mother traveled to visit Jim in California about four times between 1943, when Jim moved West, until 1968, when she died.

29. Sandburg interview.

30. Rose D'Ambrosia, interview with the author, February 2008.

31. Suppicich interview.

32. Linda McCoy-Murray, interview with the author, February 19, 2009.

33. Sandburg interview.

34. Jim Murray, "Tiger Not Tenzing," *Los Angeles Times,* February 11, 1964.

35. Jim Murray, "Young Twice," *Los Angeles Times,* March 7, 1965.

36. Murray, *Jim Murray: An Autobiography,* 3.

37. Weinberg interview.

38. Hamel interview. Jim's grandparents died in 1934, and his aunt Peg, whose married name was Margaret Foley, assumed the role of primary caretaker for Jim.

39. Murray, *Jim Murray: An Autobiography,* 3.

40. D'Ambrosia interview.

41. Jim Murray, unpublished, undated manuscript, 1. This manuscript appears to be the first three pages of an autobiographical piece.

42. Richard Patrissi, interview with the author, January 7, 2008. Joey Patrissi served in the US Army Air Corps in Panama during World War II. He died at age forty-two.

43. Murray, *Jim Murray: An Autobiography,* 12–13. Murray may have misremembered when he actually saw Ruth hit the home run. In his autobiography, and in his column, he sets the date for the game as Labor Day 1933. On that day, the Yankees did indeed play a

doubleheader against the A's, but Ruth did not hit a home run. He played in the first game and sat out the nightcap, in which Lou Gehrig hit a game-winning home run.

44. McCoy-Murray interview.

45. Christopher J. Lucas, *American Higher Education: A History*, 247–48.

46. Trinity College, "College History."

47. Murray, *Jim Murray: An Autobiography*, 8.

48. As a campus correspondent for the *Times*, Murray worked for city editor Max Farber. He remembered Farber telling him that newspapers were palladiums of democracy. "I was mightily impressed—as soon as I looked up 'palladium,' which I had associated in my mind more with Benny Goodman than the Hartford Times," Murray wrote.

49. In his autobiography, Murray recounts a story in Murray family lore in which his uncle Mike purchased Eugene O'Neill's house in Connecticut and found some of O'Neill's papers. Uncle Mike was not aware of O'Neill and told his real estate agent to burn the papers.

50. James Murray, "The Last Tomorrow."

51. James Murray, "Prelude to Defeat."

52. Murray, *Jim Murray: An Autobiography*, 4.

53. Murray, unpublished, undated manuscript, 1–2.

54. Hamel interview.

55. *Trinity Ivy*, 33.

56. Suppicich interview.

57. Thomas Parrish, ed., *The Simon and Schuster Encyclopedia of World War II*, 560.

58. Nebraska Studies, "Recruits: The 4-F Classification"; Suppicich interview.

59. "60 Seniors Graduated by Trinity: Masters Degree Given to Nine at Commencement Program; Local Men in Group Honored," *Hartford Courant*, May 16, 1943.

60. McCoy-Murray interview.

61. "Heat Creates Great Demand for Ice Cream: Sabbath Business Exhausts Supplies of Most Parlors at 6 P.M.," *New Haven Register*, June 22, 1943.

62. "Gun Carriers at Dice Game Fined, Jailed," *New Haven Register*, 1943.

63. Murray, unpublished, undated manuscript, 2.

64. Murray also sold a thirteen-line brief titled "Seeks Apartment of Suicide 5 Minutes after Her Death" to the *Bridgeport Sunday Herald*, a local weekly facetiously called "The Bible" because the locals would buy it on the way home from church. For this story, Murray received one dollar. The story is about a New Haven resident who called to inquire about an apartment vacancy immediately after the apartment's resident had committed suicide. The landlord had alerted the police.

65. "Army vs. Yale," *New Haven Register*, October 24, 1943.

66. Eleanor Welch, *Time*, to Jim Murray, August 18, 1943. "Thank you for your piece on candidate Odell. Since his is so far a one-man campaign, we could not use it. However, if he indulges in any more high jinks and becomes more of a public figure, let us know," Welch wrote.

67. "Two Men Held in Wooster St. Shooting Fray: Feud Boils over into Gunplay—No One Hurt," *New Haven Register*, November 14, 1943. The shooter in this case was James "Fats" Gambardella, who fired his automatic weapon at Roco Candella after a dispute over the setting up of a clothesline.

68. "Third Person Involved in Wife Beating: Curtis Gives Version of Assault as Victim Takes Turn for the Worse," *New Haven Register*, December 4, 1943; "$400,000 Loss in Broadway Fire: 13 Business Places Ruined during the Night," *New Haven Register*, December 24, 1943.

69. Jim Murray, "Football's Finest Hour," *Los Angeles Times*, August 10, 1973.

70. Will Fowler, *Reporters: Memoirs of a Young Newspaperman*, 115–16.

71. Suppicich interview.

72. McCoy-Murray interview.

73. "Clinton Woman Now Suspected in Man's Death: State Police Commissioner Reports Miss Betrand on 'Definite' List," *New Haven Register,* December 30, 1943. On March 17, 1944, when Murray was two months into his job at the *Los Angeles Examiner,* he received a letter from Connecticut State Police chief Leo F. Carroll. "Well it is lots of work, but remember this always, that if it were not for this violent and untimely death, your path and mine would not have crossed," Carroll wrote.

74. Delphine Betrand pleaded guilty to a reduced charge of manslaughter and was sentenced to ten to fifteen years in prison on April 11, 1944. She admitted to shooting James Streeto and bludgeoning him with the butt of the pistol after Streeto told her he would not marry her, as he had previously promised. "Woman Gets 10–15 Years in Slaying," *Hartford Courant,* April 12, 1944.

Chapter 2

1. Leonard Pitt and Dale Pitt, *Los Angeles A to Z: An Encyclopedia of the City and County,* 403.
2. Linda McCoy-Murray, interview with the author, February 19, 2009.
3. W. Fowler, *Reporters,* 116.
4. Jim Murray, personal journal of newspaper clippings.
5. Pitt and Pitt, *Los Angeles A to Z,* 363.
6. W. Fowler, *Reporters,* 116.
7. Murray, *Jim Murray: An Autobiography,* 1–2.
8. Rob Leicester Wagner, *Red Ink, White Lies: The Rise and Fall of Los Angeles Newspapers, 1920-1962,* 9–10.
9. "Career of Hearst Marked by Power, Increased Wealth, Crusading, and Controversy," *New York Times,* August 15, 1951.
10. Edwin Emery and Michael Emery, *The Press and America: An Interpretive History of the Mass Media,* 285–95.
11. "Hearst Built Corporate Empires in Newspapers, Magazines, Radio, and Real Estate," *New York Times,* August 15, 1951.
12. David Nasaw, *The Chief: The Life of William Randolph Hearst,* 170. Hearst's name was presented for the presidential nomination at the Democratic convention in St. Louis in July 1904, but he lost the nomination to Alton B. Parker.
13. W. Fowler, *Reporters,* 145–47.
14. Melvin Durslag, interview with the author, January 30, 2009.
15. Joe Santley, interview with the author, February 3, 2009.
16. Jim Murray to Ed Copps, *Time,* August 6, 1957, 3. Background notes for *Time* story "City Editor," August 19, 1957.
17. Durslag interview.
18. "City Editor," *Time,* August 19, 1957.
19. Murray to Copps, *Time,* August 6, 1957, 4.
20. Ibid., August 9, 1957, 3. Additional background notes for *Time* story "City Editor," August 19, 1957.
21. W. Fowler, *Reporters,* 7–8.
22. Santley interview.
23. Murray to Copps, *Time,* August 6, 1957, 12.
24. W. Fowler, *Reporters,* 23.
25. Louella O. Parsons, "Loretta Young Awaits Stork: 'So Happy,' Declares Film Star, Wife of Lieut. Col. Tom Lewis," *Los Angeles Examiner,* March 5, 1944.
26. "Father Sees Girl Injured," *Los Angeles Examiner,* February 18, 1944.
27. Jim Murray, "Goodbye to a Friend," *Los Angeles Times,* January 11, 1962.

28. McCoy-Murray interview.

29. Murray, *Jim Murray: An Autobiography*, 18.

30. "Many Favorite Stars in Week's Film Bill," *New Haven Register*, fall 1943.

31. Jim Notopoulos to Alan Scott, January 17, 1944. It is not clear whether Murray or Notopoulos had any personal connection to Scott. Scott was nominated for best original screenplay for the film *So Proudly We Hail!* that same month, his only Academy Award nomination.

32. Robert Osborne, *65 Years of the Oscar: The Official History of the Academy Awards*, 78–79. The ceremony held in 1944 was also the first in which the winners of the best supporting actress and best supporting actor awards received Oscar statuettes. Prior to that year, they received only plaques. The ceremony was also broadcast via radio to the armed forces serving overseas. The radio broadcast was hosted by Jack Benny.

33. "Academy Awards," *Los Angeles Examiner*, March 3, 1944.

34. Murray to Copps, *Time*, August 6, 1957, 2.

35. Jim Richardson, *For the Life of Me*, 49–50.

36. "Fiancé Declares Girl's Tragic Suicide Mistake," *Los Angeles Examiner*, December 14, 1944.

37. "Miss Farmer Found Guilty of Vagrancy," *Los Angeles Examiner*, July 29, 1944.

38. James Murray, "Man Sightless for 30 Years, Regains Vision," *Los Angeles Examiner*, July 3, 1944.

39. Murray, *Jim Murray: An Autobiography*, 125.

40. Frank McCulloch, interview with the author, April 3, 2008.

41. Santley interview.

42. W. Fowler, *Reporters*, 120–23.

43. McCoy-Murray interview.

44. W. Fowler, *Reporters*, 117.

45. Ibid., 11.

46. Jim Murray, "Last of the Bison," *Los Angeles Times*, July 2, 1961.

47. "Author Gene Fowler Dies at 70," Associated Press, July 3, 1960.

48. "Gene Fowler Is Dead on Coast; Author and Newspaper Man, 70," *New York Times*, July 3, 1960. A prolific writer, Gene Fowler is known for two lines in particular. He is credited with writing, "I think I'll slip out of these clothes and into a martini," though it has often been credited to Robert Benchley. And he originated this line, still found in journalism texts: "Writing is easy; all you do is sit staring at a blank sheet of paper until the drops of blood form on your forehead."

49. W. Fowler, *Reporters*, 6, 95–97. W. C. Fields died on Christmas Day 1946.

50. Durslag interview.

51. Murray, *Jim Murray: An Autobiography*, 124–25.

52. Murray's salary was soon raised to fifty dollars a week when he threatened to jump from the *Examiner* to the Associated Press.

53. Pitt and Pitt, *Los Angeles A to Z*, 383.

54. W. Fowler, *Reporters*, 119.

55. Kevin Nelson, *The Golden Game: The Story of California Baseball*, 257–62.

56. Richard E. Beverage, *The Hollywood Stars: Baseball in Movieland, 1926–1957*, 102.

57. Murray, *Jim Murray: An Autobiography*, 128.

58. "New Super Highway Connecting San Fernando Valley, L.A. Planned," *Los Angeles Examiner*, April 22, 1944. The Hollywood Freeway was completed in 1948.

59. James Murray, "Gioia Admits She Fell in Love with Arizonan," *Los Angeles Examiner*, February 25, 1947.

60. James Murray, "'Didn't Intend to Kill,' Bridget Sobs on Witness Stand," *Los Angeles Examiner*, October 30, 1946.

61. W. Fowler, *Reporters*, 146–47.

62. Richardson, *For the Life of Me*, 3–5.

63. Murray, *Jim Murray: An Autobiography*, 129.

64. James Murray, "New Waters Defense Plan: War Bride May Claim Slaying of Husband Justifiable," *Los Angeles Examiner*, October 22, 1946.

65. "Waters Judge Aided Her Once," *Los Angeles Examiner*, October 21, 1946.

66. W. Fowler, *Reporters*, 147.

67. James Murray, "3-In. Revolver Killed Waters," *Los Angeles Examiner*, October 28, 1946.

68. Gene Sherman, "Bridget Waters Jailed for One to Five Years," *Los Angeles Times*, November 7, 1946.

69. Murray, *Jim Murray: An Autobiography*, 129. Waters served time in Carson City, Nevada, and was paroled on May 3, 1948, and deported to Ireland. *Los Angeles Times*, May 4, 1948.

70. James Murray, "8-Ball Parade," 6–8.

71. Richardson, *For the Life of Me*, 296.

72. Durslag interview.

73. Wagner, *Red Ink, White Lies*, 208–9.

74. W. Fowler, *Reporters*, 75.

75. "Jack Smith, Urbane and Wry *Times* Columnist, Dies," *Los Angeles Times*, January 10, 1996. Smith was also credited by many as the writer who coined the moniker "Black Dahlia." However, in memoirs, both Richardson and Fowler wrote that the nickname came from the *Examiner*'s Long Beach correspondent Bevo Means, after hearing Elizabeth Short referred to in that way by customers at the coffee shop where she often ate lunch in the months before the murder.

76. Wagner, *Red Ink, White Lies*, 213–14.

77. W. Fowler, *Reporters*, 85.

78. Wagner, *Red Ink, White Lies*, 218.

79. W. Fowler, *Reporters*, 85.

80. Richardson, *For the Life of Me*, 282.

81. Wagner, *Red Ink, White Lies*, 220.

82. W. Fowler, *Reporters*, 128–29.

83. Wagner, *Red Ink, White Lies*, 221–22.

84. Richardson, *For the Life of Me*, 289–91.

85. Wagner, *Red Ink, White Lies*, 222.

86. W. Fowler, *Reporters*, 130.

87. Wagner, *Red Ink, White Lies*, 224.

88. Gene Sherman, "Beulah, Bud Acquitted; Crowd at Court Cheers," *Los Angeles Times*, October 6, 1947. Louise Overell married a guard from the Santa Ana jail nine months after the trial. The couple divorced a short time later. Overell died of acute alcohol poisoning in Las Vegas in 1965.

89. Santley interview; McCulloch interview.

90. W. Fowler, *Reporters*, 132.

91. Murray, *Jim Murray: An Autobiography*, 131.

Chapter 3

1. James T. Patterson, *Grand Expectations: The United States, 1945–1974*, 61–65.

2. KTLA, the first commercial television station in Southern California, broadcast for the first time on January 22, 1947.

3. George Moss, *America in the Twentieth Century,* 273–77.

4. Emery and Emery, *Press and America,* 459–60.

5. Robert T. Elson, *The World of Time, Inc.: The Intimate History of a Publishing Enterprise,* 182–83, 436–37.

6. Ibid.

7. Pat Barbee, "Seasoned Pro," 7.

8. Jim Murray, "Oz Was Wizard," *Los Angeles Times,* March 11, 1963.

9. The Ozzie Osborne referred to here is George Hamilton "Ozzie" Osborne, a thirty-four-year-old Virginia man who set the record for flagpole sitting—fifty-two days, thirteen hours, fifty-eight minutes—not the bat-eating glam rocker who emerged four decades later.

10. Los Angeles memo, Time/Life, October 1, 1948.

11. "Manners & Morals," *Time,* September 20, 1948.

12. Murray also reported that Hearst's influence was so strong that even editors at the rival *Los Angeles Times* were afraid to keep a prewritten Hearst obituary in its newsroom, for fear of retribution from the Hearst chain.

13. James Murray, research memo to *Time,* New York office, July 28, 1948.

14. Richard Maltby, *Hollywood Cinema,* 154–55.

15. Murray, *Jim Murray: An Autobiography,* 19.

16. "Big Dig," *Time,* August 22, 1949.

17. Eric Sandburg, interview with the author, November 14, 2008.

18. After diligently hunting down the details of a Sinatra-Gardner quarrel, his report read, "Here is what took place in the Gardner-Sinatra dispute pieced together from interviews with Ava's sister, Bappie, and Bappie's friend Charlie Guest, plus Ava's business agent Benton Cole. Since both Bappie and Ben Cole were present, this version is, I'm satisfied, authoritative." Murray to Terry Colman, *Time* research memo, October 24, 1952.

19. Murray to Barren Beshoar, *Time* research memo, September 25, 1953.

20. Murray, *Jim Murray: An Autobiography,* 21.

21. Rick Reilly, "King of the Sports Page," 82.

22. One report he sent to the *Time* New York office read, in total, "Marilyn Monroe was born June 1, 1926, and we have the birth certificate to prove it. Regards." Monroe's age had been a subject of debate throughout the Hollywood press.

23. Murray to Colman, *Time* research memo, July 25, 1952.

24. Nelson, *Golden Game,* 256.

25. "Storybook Romance," *Time,* January 25, 1954.

26. John Scheibe, *On the Road with Jim Murray: Baseball and the Summer of '79,* 41.

27. Murray, *Jim Murray: An Autobiography,* 19.

28. Ibid., 27.

29. Sandburg interview.

30. Sam Kashner and Jennifer Kashner, *The Bad and the Beautiful: Hollywood in the Fifties,* 278–92.

31. "A Tiger in the Reeds," *Time,* October 11, 1954.

32. Brando appears to have misremembered the name of Gerry Murray.

33. Marlon Brando to Jim Murray, October 9, 1953.

34. Frank McCulloch, interview with the author, April 3, 2008.

35. "The Wages of Virtue," *Time,* March 2, 1954.

36. Murray, *Jim Murray: An Autobiography,* 24.

37. John Wayne to Jim Murray, February 28, 1952.

38. Gerald Suppicich, interview with the author, November 19, 2008.

39. W. Fowler, *Reporters,* 133.

40. Pitt and Pitt, *Los Angeles A to Z,* 375.

41. McCulloch interview.

42. Jason Felch and Marlena Telvick, "Unsung Hero."

43. Ibid. It was a phone call from Howard Hughes to Frank McCulloch that exposed Clifford Irving's biography of Hughes as a fraud. Irving claimed to have worked with Hughes on the book and had sold the rights to *Life*, when Hughes called McCulloch to tell him that he had never met Irving.

44. "Sickle for the Harvest," *Time*, November 14, 1949.

45. Billy Graham to Jim Murray, November 28, 1949.

46. Patterson, *Great Expectations*, 256–57.

47. Murray, *Jim Murray: An Autobiography*, 36–40.

48. Patterson, *Great Expectations*, 256–57.

49. Tom Callahan, "For Crying Out Loud."

50. Richard Nixon to Jim Murray, February 20, 1953. Murray later wrote that he flew home early from a vacation in Hawaii in 1960 to cast his vote for Nixon. He said he felt he still owed him for his help in the Checkers incident.

51. An oft-repeated story concerning the practice of rewriting at *Time* came from international correspondent Theodore White, who once posted a sign on his door that read: "Any resemblance to what is written here and what is printed in Time magazine is purely coincidental."

52. McCulloch interview.

53. James Murray to Sid James, February 3, 1955.

54. Jim Murray, "That Was the LIFE," *Los Angeles Times*, December 12, 1972.

55. James Murray, "I Hate the Yankees," 26–36.

56. Letters to the editors, *Life*, April 24, 1950.

57. Murray addressed the topic of New York Yankee dominance many times once he became a full-time sports columnist, often humorously. Filing from the 1962 World Series in San Francisco, he wrote, "The New York Yankees are not a baseball team. They're a monopoly in spikes and batting helmets. First Place, Inc. If they were a normal business, they'd be trust-busted into four first-division teams." "Yankees, THE A.L.," *Los Angeles Times*, October 12, 1962.

58. Two examples are similar lines found in the October 21, 1953, and January 6, 1954, issues of the *Sporting News*.

59. Jim Murray, "The Old Breed," *Los Angeles Times*, February 23, 1966. Bennett Cerf was a founding publisher of Random House and published a number of compilations of stories, jokes, and puns.

60. Murray, *Jim Murray: An Autobiography*, 14.

61. Barbee, "Seasoned Pro," 7.

62. "Little Ice Water," *Time*, January 10, 1949.

63. Murray, *Jim Murray: An Autobiography*, 81–83. The Hogan cover story was one of a series of articles to which the *Time* sports cover jinx can be traced. Hogan was in a life-threatening auto accident shortly after the cover appeared. Three years earlier, the Illinois racing stable of Elizabeth Arden Graham burned down the day a *Time* cover on Arden reached newsstands. A year later, baseball manager Leo Durocher was suspended as manager of the Brooklyn Dodgers the day before a cover profile on him came out. The legend later morphed into the *Sports Illustrated* cover jinx.

64. "2 Minutes to Glory," *Time*, August 2, 1948; "The Strength of Ten," *Time*, July 21, 1952.

65. "All-America," *Time*, November 9, 1953; Walt Cieplik, "Jim Murray: King of Sports," 23.

66. Byron Riggan to Jim Murray, telegram, October 31, 1953. Notre Dame defeated Navy, 38–7.

Chapter 4

1. Jim Murray, "Henry Luce: The Printed Word's Dearest Friend," *Los Angeles Times*, March 2, 1967.

2. Michael MacCambridge, *The Franchise: A History of "Sports Illustrated" Magazine*, 19.

3. Murray, "Henry Luce."

4. Charles Champlin, "Memories of Henry Luce, His Life and Time," *Los Angeles Times*, March 5, 1967.

5. Frank McCulloch, interview with the author, April 3, 2008.

6. Murray, "Henry Luce."

7. Champlin, "Memories of Henry Luce."

8. Elson, *World of Time, Inc.*, xi–xiii.

9. Champlin, "Memories of Henry Luce."

10. Elson, *World of Time, Inc.*, 339–41.

11. MacCambridge, *Franchise*, 14–15.

12. After leaving Time/Life, Clay Felker achieved success as the editor of *New York Magazine*, cultivating the careers of writers such as Tom Wolfe, Gloria Steinem, and Jimmy Breslin.

13. Murray, *Jim Murray: An Autobiography*, 34–35.

14. MacCambridge, *Franchise*, 20–21.

15. Murray, *Jim Murray: An Autobiography*, 35.

16. MacCambridge, *Franchise*, 20–21.

17. Elson, *World of Time, Inc.*, 343.

18. Ernie Haverman to Jim Murray, September 30, 1953.

19. Murray, *Jim Murray: An Autobiography*, 41.

20. Elson, *World of Time, Inc.*, 344.

21. MacCambridge, *Franchise*, 32.

22. Jim Murray to Sid James, May 17, 1954.

23. For sentimental reasons, the prototype was tested in the same way that *Life* was introduced eighteen years earlier, right down to the first sentence of the mailing: "The enthusiasm now prevailing in the offices of *Time* and *Life* is one which I hope you will share in the very near future."

24. Henry Luce to Jim Murray, December 26, 1953; Murray to Luce, December 29, 1953.

25. Murray, *Jim Murray: An Autobiography*, 42.

26. MacCambridge, *Franchise*, 45–47.

27. Elson, *World of Time, Inc.*, 353–54. The magazine first turned a profit in 1964, and revenue grew steadily thereafter.

28. Jim Murray, "Magazine Illustrated Sports Importance," *Los Angeles Times*, October 19, 1997.

29. MacCambridge, *Franchise*, 68.

30. Andy Crichton, interview with the author, August 29, 2007.

31. Jim Murray, "Strub's Santa Anita."

32. Mary Simon, *Racing through the Century: The Story of Thoroughbred Racing in America*, 153–54.

33. Jim Murray, "California Gets a Gleam in the Eye," 12.

34. Simon, *Racing through the Century*, 170–71.

35. Murray, "California Gets a Gleam in the Eye," 12.

36. Simon, *Racing through the Century*, 170.

37. Jim Murray, "The Derby and Swaps," *Los Angeles Times*, May 2, 1961.

38. Simon, *Racing through the Century*, 165.

39. Jim Murray, "At Home with Swaps in California," 52–57.

40. Jim Murray, "The Derby and Swaps," *Los Angeles Times*, May 2, 1961.

41. Craig Harzmann, "The Boy of Summer: Swaps' Magical Spree Delighted Fans 50 Years Ago." In a strange footnote to *Sports Illustrated*'s coverage of the Swaps-Nashua rivalry, the magazine chose William Woodward Jr. as the magazine's sportsman of the year for 1955. James and the editors were ready to approve a photo of Woodward, his wife, Ann, jockey Eddie Arcaro, and Nashua for the cover when it was learned that Ann Woodward had shot and killed her husband. The editors substituted Brooklyn Dodgers pitcher Johnny Podres for Woodward for the honor.

42. MacCambridge, *Franchise*, 71, 73–74.

43. Jim Murray, "All Right, Louie, Drop the Jib," "The Gary Coopers' Sporting Life," and "The Wicket Men of Hollywood."

44. Elson, *World of Time, Inc.*, 359–60.

45. James Murray, "American League? Phooey!," 11–13, 74; Jim Murray, "Nationals—Phooey!," *Los Angeles Times*, July 9, 1961. In this column, Murray blamed the virulent response to his *Sports Illustrated* article on the editor: "It wasn't angry enough for my editor. So he hung a title on it that was certain to win me the rotten-egg award for 1956—'American League? Phooey!' That satisfied him enough to hang my name under it and send it out in a world he was sure would include a lot of American League fans."

46. James Murray, "The Case for the Suffering Fan," 36–43. Murray revisited this topic in his column in 1970, when the Philadelphia Phillies broke ground on a new ballpark. He discussed his *Sports Illustrated* article and reported that most of the Major League Baseball franchises had, since his article, moved into new stadia. Murray also noted in that column that his reference to being seated behind a pole had come to fruition. He had been seated behind a pole during the 1962 World Series and had watched the entire game reporting to Prescott Sullivan of the *San Francisco Examiner* what was happening on the left side of the pole, while Sullivan did the same for the right side. Jim Murray, "New Parks = More Fans," *Los Angeles Times*, August 5, 1970.

47. Robert Creamer, interview with the author, March 22, 2007.

48. W. Fowler, *Reporters*, 134.

49. Pitt and Pitt, *Los Angeles A to Z*, 313–14, 397.

50. W. Fowler, *Reporters*, 134.

51. Gerald Suppicich, interview with the author, November 19, 2008. Bob Dylan purchased the property in 1973, along with three other homes in the area, to create a small compound overlooking the Pacific. He divorced shortly thereafter, and his wife and several children remained.

52. Ibid.

53. Jim Murray, "That Was the LIFE," *Los Angeles Times*, December 12, 1972.

54. Frank McCulloch, interview with the author, December 17, 2007.

55. Murray, *Jim Murray: An Autobiography*, 131–32.

56. "Walter in Wonderland," *Time*, April 28, 1958; Melvin Durslag, interview with the author, January 30, 2009.

57. Norman Dyhrenfurth and James Murray, "Ordeal on the Approaches," 35–49; Dyhrenfurth and Murray, "The Thrust to the Summit," 47–53.

58. Jim Murray, "A Trip for Ten Tall Men," 52–59.

59. David Halberstam, *The Powers That Be*, 286.

60. McCulloch interview.

61. MacCambridge, *Franchise*, 86–88.

62. Both Murray's friend Will Fowler, in his book *Reporters*, and John Scheibe, in his book *On the Road with Jim Murray*, write that Murray was offered the position of managing editor (or in Fowler's case editor in chief) of *Sports Illustrated*. It seems unlikely, however, since André Laguerre had been promoted to that position just months before. It is more

likely that Luce saw Murray as a good candidate to take a high-level editor position at the magazine and assist Laguerre, with whom Murray was well acquainted.

63. W. Fowler, *Reporters*, 134.

64. Durslag interview.

65. Sidney James to Jim Murray, January 18, 1961; Murray, *Jim Murray: An Autobiography*, 133.

Chapter 5

1. John Caughey and Laree Caughey, *Los Angeles: Biography of a City*, 399–401.

2. Bill Shirley, ed., *Sports Pages of the "Los Angeles Times,"* 8.

3. Wagner, *Red Ink, White Lies*, 287.

4. *Editor & Publisher, Editor & Publisher International Yearbook*, 34–36.

5. Halberstam, *The Powers That Be*, 107–8.

6. Dennis McDougal, *Privileged Son: Otis Chandler and the Rise and Fall of the "L.A. Times" Dynasty*, 219.

7. "*Times* Again Sets New National Records in '60: Leads All Papers in News Published (Ninth Year), Advertising (Sixth Year)," *Los Angeles Times*, February 12, 1961. The *Times* held this title consecutively until 1975.

8. McDougal, *Privileged Son*, 215–19.

9. Bill Thomas, interview with the author, December 12, 2008.

10. John Hall, interview with the author, January 23, 2009.

11. Nick Williams, "Members of the All-Star Team," *Los Angeles Times*, February 12, 1961.

12. Frank Haven and Frank McCulloch, *Los Angeles Times* memo titled "Sports Columnist," 1961.

13. Dan Smith, interview with the author, January 15, 2010. The Grba column was Murray's second.

14. Frank McCulloch, interview with the author, April 3, 2008; Melvin Durslag, interview with the author, January 30, 2009.

15. "Jim Murray to Write Feature Sports Column in *Times*," *Los Angeles Times*, February 5, 1961, M1.

16. William Randolph Hearst Sr. died in 1951, and his son took over as chief of operations for Hearst, Inc.

17. "Durslag's Column Now National Feature: Hearst Service Gaines *Examiner* Writer; Continues Top Local Sports Coverage," *Los Angeles Examiner*, February 12, 1961.

18. Jim Murray, "Let's Dot Some I's," *Los Angeles Times*, February 12, 1961.

19. Jim Murray, "Boos and Bravos," *Los Angeles Times*, April 28, 1961.

20. Scheibe, *On the Road*, 39.

21. Jim Murray, "Ride on a Tiger," *Los Angeles Times*, March 12, 1961.

22. Durslag interview.

23. Jim Murray, "Chess and Cobwebs," *Los Angeles Times*, August 16, 1961. The championships featured an eighteen-year-old Bobby Fisher, who refused to show up for the final match, which ended in forfeit.

24. "Ruth's Mark Safe after 154 Games," *Los Angeles Times*, July 18, 1961.

25. Jim Murray, "Ford Frick's Gopher Ball," *Los Angeles Times*, July 25, 1961.

26. Jim Murray, "Week of Schneider," *Los Angeles Times*, August 1, 1961.

27. "Cronin Disagrees with Frick, Says 162 Games OK," *Los Angeles Times*, September 15, 1961.

28. Jim Murray, "M&M, Chi, and Rain," *Los Angeles Times*, September 14, 1961.

29. David Halberstam, *October 1964*, 168–70.

30. Jim Murray, "Mantle's Life Was Hit and Myth," *Los Angeles Times,* August 20, 1995.

31. Ibid., 169.

32. "Jim Murray, "Failure at 58?," *Los Angeles Times,* September 20, 1961.

33. Frank Finch, "Maris Comes Out Swinging, Hits 61," *Los Angeles Times,* October 2, 1961.

34. Halberstam, *October 1964,* 169.

35. Jim Murray, "I Love Maris," *Los Angeles Times,* October 3, 1961.

36. "A Bear at 'Bama," *Time,* November 17, 1961.

37. Moss, *America in the Twentieth Century,* 330.

38. Jim Murray, "Bedsheets and 'Bama," *Los Angeles Times,* November 20, 1961. Alabama won the game, beating Georgia Tech, 10–0.

39. John W. Bloomer to Mrs. W. C. Farrar, December 1, 1961.

40. Jim Murray, "Living Color," *Los Angeles Times,* November 29, 1961.

41. John Herbers, "Wallace Denies Yielding to U.S.: Backers Are Said to Stress Fear of School Rioting," *New York Times,* September 5, 1963.

42. Jim Murray, "End of a Charade," *Los Angeles Times,* September 11, 1970.

43. Jim Murray, "Series Fun in Cincy," *Los Angeles Times,* October 9, 1961.

44. Douglass Looney, "Public Snitch Lets Quips Fall Where They May," *National Observer,* August 19, 1972.

45. McCulloch interview.

46. Jim Murray, "Malibu to Zero Plus," *Los Angeles Times,* February 1, 1962; Murray, "Candy for the Lakers," *Los Angeles Times,* February 5, 1962; Murray, "A Side of Beef," *Los Angeles Times,* February 6, 1962.

47. Jim Murray, "Fire When Ready, Suh," *Los Angeles Times,* March 6, 1962.

48. Durslag interview.

49. Jim Murray, "Man at Mach 1," *Los Angeles Times,* March 6, 1962.

50. Jim Murray, "A Root for Home," *Los Angeles Times,* March 7, 1962.

51. Bill Christine, interview with the author, December 19, 2008. Don Rickles, in fact, was a friend of Murray's, and Murray occasionally went to Rickles for material for his column. He would often credit Rickles for particular lines in a column.

52. Advertisement, *Los Angeles Times* Syndicate, 1962.

53. Jim Murray, "Slag Heap of the East," *Los Angeles Times,* August 17, 1962.

54. Jim Murray, "A Taste of Rubble," *Los Angeles Times,* August 20, 1962.

55. H. K. Baum, letter to the editor, *Los Angeles Times,* August 30, 1962; Jim Murray, "Now for Philly," *Los Angeles Times,* August 22, 1962.

56. Looney, "Public Snitch."

57. Jim Murray, "Kook's Tour," *Los Angeles Times,* February 26, 1962.

58. Looney, "Public Snitch."

59. "Good Sports," *Time,* September 1, 1961. The article went on to list some other top sportswriters, including Durslag and Furman Bisher of the *Atlanta Journal.* Red Smith was still the "best, most polished, literate and readable of them all," *Time* determined.

60. "Jim Murray Nominated for Award," *Los Angeles Times,* January 7, 1963; "Jim Murray Cited by City Council," *Los Angeles Times,* November 29, 1962; Jim Murray, "A Year Later," *Los Angeles Times,* February 13, 1962.

Chapter 6

1. Bill Thomas, interview with the author, December 12, 2008.

2. Bill Christine, interview with the author, December 19, 2008.

3. Emery and Emery, *Press and America,* 657–59.

4. Thomas interview.

5. McDougal, *Privileged Son,* 315–16.

6. Jim Murray, "Beauty and the Beast," *Los Angeles Times*, March 3, 1961. In fact, Rickles supplied jokes for Murray's column on more than one occasion. Murray covered the Sugar Ray Robinson–Gene Fulmer middleweight championship bout in Las Vegas, where Rickles was performing, for this particular column. The column set up the premise that Robinson was the flashy, stylish one, while Fulmer was the country throwback. Then Rickles offered some one-liners for the column: "When he was a kid, for kicks, Ray would ask a girl to dance. Gene would go up to his brother and say 'Let's rassle!' When Ray was stompin' at the Savoy, Gene was stompin' on crickets."

7. Jim Murray, *The Best of Jim Murray*, 152.

8. Gerald Suppicich, interview with the author, November 19, 2008.

9. Dave Kindred, "He Kept the Calliope Playing," *Sporting News*, August 31, 1998.

10. Jim Murray, "It's a Bird! a Car! a Bullet! . . . It's Super Jerry," *Los Angeles Times*, April 27, 1969.

11. Jim Murray, "The New Breed," *Los Angeles Times*, December 8, 1965.

12. Jim Murray, "Places Everyone! Sandy's on Camera," *Los Angeles Times*, March 27, 1966.

13. "Jim Murray, "Can't Make the War, Sarge. It's My Knee," *Los Angeles Times*, May 11, 1966.

14. Jim Murray, "When in Doubt, Pun," *Los Angeles Times*, August 8, 1965.

15. Melvin Durslag, interview with the author, January 30, 2009.

16. Emery and Emery, *Press and America*, 657.

17. Jim Murray, "Derby Day at Churchill Downs Is Perfume and Mink," *Los Angeles Times*, May 5, 1968.

18. Murray Sperber, *Onward to Victory: The Crises That Shaped College Sports*, 30–31. Sperber owes a debt for this spectrum to others. See Stanley Walker, *City Editor*, 126–27.

19. Murray, *Sporting World*, 14.

20. Luther Nichols to Jim Murray, July 9, 1962.

21. In the foreword to *The Sporting Life of Jim Murray*, Murray discussed the difficulty in naming sequels and offered several alternate titles: "Love Finds Jim Murray," "The Son of the Best of Jim Murray," and, for his enemies, "The Slow Lingering Death of Jim Murray."

22. Martin Kane, "Booktalk: Jim Murray Moves Gracefully from Newspaper Column into Hardcover"; Jim Murray, "Author and Critic," *Los Angeles Times*, January 7, 1965.

23. Roland Lazenby, *The Show: The Inside Story of the Spectacular Los Angeles Lakers in the Words of Those Who Lived It*, 13–54.

24. Jim Murray, "A Coming of Age?," *Los Angeles Times*, February 12, 1962.

25. Murray, *Jim Murray: An Autobiography*, 105.

26. In the team's first year in Los Angeles, management could not find any radio or television station to broadcast Laker games. The team made the playoffs, and in the final game of the Western Conference Finals against St. Louis, Short arranged for Chick Hearn, then working at KNX in St. Louis, to broadcast the game. Hearn joined the Lakers the following year.

27. Jack Disney, interview with the author, January 8, 2009.

28. Jerry West, interview with the author, November 6, 2009.

29. Disney interview.

30. Ibid.

31. Jim Murray, "Basketball Road Trip: One of Life's Vacuums," *Los Angeles Times*, February 19, 1969. Air travel was a regular theme of Murray's Laker coverage. The year before the team arrived in Los Angeles, it was involved in an actual plane crash. On January 18, 1960, the team plane landed in a cornfield in the town of Carroll, Iowa, during a flight from St. Louis to Minneapolis. Nobody was injured, but the incident became part of team lore and was a regular point of reference on road trips.

32. Jim Murray, "Elgin Has Elegance," *Los Angeles Times*, February 3, 1963.

33. Jim Murray, "Where'd They Go?," *Los Angeles Times*, January 13, 1965.

34. Morton Sharnik, "Death of a Champion."

35. Nat Fleischer and Sam Andre, *An Illustrated History of Boxing*, 354–55.

36. Jim Murray, "Stop the Fight!," *Los Angeles Times*, March 24, 1963.

37. "Moore Dies: Rope Snap Caused Injury, Study of Pictures Indicates," *Los Angeles Times*, March 25, 1963.

38. John Hall, "Moore's Death Saddens Ring World: Olympic Calls Off Mitt Card," *Los Angeles Times*, March 26, 1963.

39. "Ban on Boxing Urged: Brown, Legislators Demand Action as Davey Moore Sinks," *Los Angeles Times*, March 23, 1963.

40. "Pope Raps Boxing, Calls It Barbaric," Associated Press, March 25, 1963.

41. Murray, untitled, undated manuscript. The document is three pages of a biographical manuscript found in Murray's personal files. Christopher Battalino, a Hartford native, was featherweight champion of the world from 1929 to 1931. Kid Kaplan was a native of Ukraine who reigned as featherweight champion from 1925 to 1927.

42. Jim Murray, "A Big Shaver," *Los Angeles Times*, March 16, 1965.

43. Jim Murray, "Big Train on Time," *Los Angeles Times*, September 23, 1965.

44. Jim Murray, "Boxing's Requiem," *Los Angeles Times*, March 27, 1962; Murray, "No Rose for Benny," *Los Angeles Times*, April 5, 1962.

45. Jim Murray, "The Last Time I Saw Lavo," *Los Angeles Times*, July 10, 1962.

46. Jim Murray, "The Prize Is Death," *Los Angeles Times*, September 30, 1962; John Hall, "Unbeaten Clay Stops Lavorante in 5th," *Los Angeles Times*, July 21, 1962.

47. John Hall, "Lavorante Wages Battle for His Life: Argentine Heavy's Condition Remains Critical after 4-Hour Surgery," *Los Angeles Times*, September 23, 1962.

48. Murray, "The Prize Is Death."

49. Jim Murray, "Christmas in 254," *Los Angeles Times*, December 17, 1962.

50. "Boxing Furor: California, Federal Suspension Urged," *Los Angeles Times*, March 26, 1963.

51. Paul Zimmerman, "Amateur Feud Goes On and On," *Los Angeles Times*, April 27, 1966.

52. Don Page, "Boxing on Ropes? Not So, Say TV Ratings," *Los Angeles Times*, April 27, 1963.

53. Jim Murray, "Fight Fans: Blood Brothers Just Waiting for the Kill," *Los Angeles Times*, June 25, 1969.

54. Scheibe, *On the Road*, 79.

55. Murray, "Boxing's Requiem."

56. David Farber and Beth Bailey, *The Columbia Guide to America in the 1960s*, 55–58.

57. Todd Gitlin, *The Sixties: Years of Hope, Days of Rage*, 5.

58. Bruce Jenkins, interview with the author, August 16, 2009.

59. Murray, *Jim Murray: An Autobiography*, 223–24.

60. Jim Murray, "Vacation on Wheels," *Los Angeles Times*, July 28, 1965.

61. Jenkins interview.

62. Eric Sandburg, interview with the author, June 13, 2008.

63. Jenkins interview.

64. As noted, Murray eventually sold the house at Point Dume to Bob Dylan. When Murray gave the news to his sister, he referred to Dylan as "some guitar player." And in his autobiography, he wrote that the sight of a guitar "evokes the same emotional reaction in me that the sight of a swastika would in a rabbi."

65. Murray, *Jim Murray: An Autobiography*, 219–22.

66. Jim Murray, "The Violent States of America: A Nation in Surgery," *Los Angeles Times*, June 6, 1968. Murray also wrote a column eulogizing Robert Kennedy that was published

after Kennedy's funeral. Rose Kennedy signed a copy of the column, and Murray had it bronzed and hung it in his office.

67. "Murray's Column on Kennedy Murder Draws Praise, Criticism," *Los Angeles Times*, June 9, 1968.

68. Jim Murray, "The Russians and Humanism," *Los Angeles Times*, July 21, 1966.

69. Jim Murray, "Tennis to Menace," *Los Angeles Times*, November 6, 1962.

70. Lyle Kenyon Engel, *The Indianapolis "500": The World's Most Exciting Auto Race.*

71. "Indianapolis Fans Tune Up on Beer, Jazz, and Chevalier," *New York Times*, May 30, 1964.

72. Murray, *Jim Murray: An Autobiography,* 134–35.

73. Russell Jaslow, interview with the author, September 5, 2010.

74. Dan Gurney, interview with the author, September 21, 2010.

75. Jim Murray, "A Wave Goodbye," *Los Angeles Times*, March 27, 1974.

76. Mario Andretti, interview with the author, October 7, 2009.

77. Jim Murray, "It Was Eddie," *Los Angeles Times,* June 2, 1964.

78. Frank M. Blunk, "Second-Lap Crash Fatal to Sachs and MacDonald," *New York Times,* May 31, 1964.

79. William N. Wallace, "'500' Crash Vivid for TV Viewers: Start of Race and Pit Stops Are Shown in Detail," *New York Times*, May 29, 1964.

80. Murray, "It Was Eddie."

81. Jim Murray, "The 500: 'Gentlemen, Start Your Coffins!,'" *Los Angeles Times,* May 29, 1966.

82. Robert F. James, "Indy's Somber Trial by Fire and Rain."

83. Jim Murray, "Now They're Starting to Burn," *Los Angeles Times*, May 29, 1973.

84. James, "Indy's Somber Trial by Fire and Rain."

85. John Radosta, "Auto Safety Measures Create Other Problems," *New York Times,* June 20, 1973.

86. Andretti interview.

87. Jim Murray, "Marring the Races," *Los Angeles Times*, August 1, 1973.

88. Jim Murray, "Indianapolis 500: Death Is on the Pole against 33 Lives," *Los Angeles Times*, May 25, 1971.

89. Jim Murray, "Faultless Phillie," *Los Angeles Times*, August 31, 1965.

90. James Murray, "Fame Is for Winners."

91. Jim Murray, "Flags for Fame?," *Los Angeles Times,* June 23, 1966; Baseball Almanac, "Baseball Hall of Fame BBWAA Voting Percentages"; Ted Williams to Jim Murray, July 13, 1995.

92. Liston was convicted of robbery after holding up a café in St. Louis and stealing thirty-seven dollars when he was twenty years old. He was arrested for a few other minor crimes around the same time.

93. David Remnick, *King of the World: Muhammad Ali and the Rise of an American Hero*, 21.

94. Jim Murray, "Stop, Look, 'n Liston," *Los Angeles Times*, September 23, 1962.

95. Ferdie Pacheco, interview with the author, June 24, 2009. Pacheco and Murray had a friendly relationship, and Murray on occasion would stay at Pacheco's home on visits to Miami.

96. Jim Murray, "The Brave Bulls," *Los Angeles Times*, April 25, 1962.

97. Jim Murray, "Come Out Talking!," *Los Angeles Times*, November 7, 1963.

98. Remnick, *King of the World,* 150.

99. Jim Murray, "Upset—or Setup?," *Los Angeles Times*, February 26, 1964.

100. Jim Murray, "God in My Corner," *Los Angeles Times*, February 27, 1964. The meeting between Murray, Young, Pye, and Ali is also discussed in Murray's autobiography.

101. Remnick, *King of the World,* 244–45.

102. Jim Murray, "A Way Down East," *Los Angeles Times,* May 21, 1965. An editorial published in the *Bangor Daily News* on May 29, 1965, called out Murray: "The worst slander upon the state was committed by Jim Murray of the Los Angeles Times. Though he has connections in Maine, he devoted an entire column to calling the state 'by cracky' country and 'Wal, I swan' territory. His syndicated column appears in papers from California to Florida. What a lovely image of Maine he spread about."

103. Jerry Izenberg, interview with the author, July 30, 2009.

104. John Hall, interview with the author, January 23, 2009.

105. Jim Murray, "A Fight of Shame," *Los Angeles Times,* May 23, 1965.

106. The photo of Ali standing over Liston that night, fist raised, challenging him to rise, is probably the most iconic image of Ali's boxing career. It was taken by *Sports Illustrated* photographer Neil Liefer.

107. John Hall, "It Only Takes a Minute to Kill Boxing: Clay KO's Liston in 1st Round . . . We Think," *Los Angeles Times,* May 26, 1965.

108. Jim Murray, "The Drubbing."

109. Jim Murray, "Now Hear This," *Los Angeles Times,* June 10, 1965.

110. Thomas Hauser, *Muhammad Ali: His Life and Times,* 133.

111. Pacheco interview.

112. Jim Murray, "Come On, Ali, I Want to Talk to Cassius Clay," *Los Angeles Times,* November 4, 1966.

113. Jim Murray, "Louisville Loudmouth Secedes from the Union," *Los Angeles Times,* April 27, 1967.

Chapter 7

1. Jim Murray, "Ravages of Time," *Los Angeles Times,* December 30, 1969.

2. National Sportscasters and Sportswriters Association, "National Winners." Murray was honored with the award for national sportswriter of the year in 1964, from 1966 through 1977, and again in 1979. Red Smith, then of the *New York Herald-Tribune,* won in 1965, and Will Grimsley of the Associated Press won in 1978.

3. Douglas Looney, "For Jim Murray, Everything Is Fair Game," *National Observer,* August 19, 1972.

4. Jim Murray, "Shucks, It's All in Fun," *Los Angeles Times,* November 15, 1972.

5. "PGA Board Votes to Drop 'Clause'—L.A. Open Restored," Associated Press, May 18, 1961.

6. Jim Murray, "PGA Does Turnabout," *Los Angeles Times,* May 18, 1961.

7. Charlie Sifford, with James Gullo, *Just Let Me Play: The Story of Charlie Sifford, the First Black PGA Golfer,* 12–14, 120–23, 150–51.

8. Ron Rapoport, *The Immortal Bobby: Bobby Jones and the Golden Age of Golf,* 272–73.

9. Sifford, *Just Let Me Play,* 172–79.

10. Jim Murray, "Sifford Made His Way with Par, Not Politics," *Los Angeles Times,* January 9, 1969.

11. Robert T. Jones to Jim Murray, February 28, 1969; Jones to Charles Sifford, July 18, 1968.

12. Jones to Murray, February 28, 1969.

13. Jim Murray, "Sifford's Due a Bid," *Los Angeles Times,* February 5, 1969.

14. Jim Murray, "As White as the KKK," *Los Angeles Times,* April 6, 1969.

15. Bill Shirley, "Elder Gets in the Front Door," *Los Angeles Times,* April 10, 1975.

16. Jim Murray, "A Master Caddy's Great Day at the Masters," *Los Angeles Times,* April 11, 1975.

17. Jim Murray, "Fame or Shame," *Los Angeles Times*, June 21, 1964.

18. Jim Murray, "Baseball's Injustice," *Los Angeles Times*, February 14, 1971.

19. "Paige Becomes Regular Member of Hall of Fame," United Press International, July 8, 1971.

20. Jim Murray, "Move Over, Satch," *Los Angeles Times*, August 12, 1971. By 2006 there were thirty-five former Negro League players in the Baseball Hall of Fame.

21. Skip Bayless, "The Ram Family: A House Somewhat Divided," *Los Angeles Times*, January 28, 1977.

22. Erwin Baker, "Harris Furor Spreads to the L.A. City Council," *Los Angeles Times*, February 15, 1977.

23. Jim Murray, "Rams Forced to Punt . . . but Watch for QB Sneak," *Los Angeles Times*, February 2, 1977.

24. A. S. "Doc" Young to Jim Murray, February 9, 1977; Doc Young, "Sickness in the Land," *Los Angeles Sentinel*.

25. Jim Murray, "QB Issue at City Hall," *Los Angeles Times*, February 24, 1977.

26. Jim Murray, "Apartheid, U.S. Style," *Los Angeles Times*, December 20, 1967.

27. Jackie Robinson to Jim Murray, December 20, 1967.

28. Jim Murray, "The Final Rundown," *Los Angeles Times*, October 26, 1971.

29. Simon Reeve, *One Day in September: The Full Story of the 1972 Munich Olympics Massacre and the Israeli Revenge Operation "Wrath of God,"* x–xi.

30. Jim Murray, "A Yank in Der Vaterland," *Los Angeles Times*, August 27, 1972; Jim Murray, "Swan Song for Avery," *Los Angeles Times*, August 29, 1972.

31. Scheibe, *On the Road*, 111.

32. Howard Cosell, *Cosell*, 4–5.

33. Scheibe, *On the Road*, 111.

34. Dave Kindred, *Sound and Fury: Two Powerful Lives, One Fateful Friendship*, 182.

35. Jim Murray, "Olympics New and Tragic Event—Murder," *Los Angeles Times*, September 6, 1972.

36. Jim Murray, "Blood on Olympus," *Los Angeles Times*, September 7, 1972.

37. Jim McKay, *My Wide World*, 230–34.

38. Jim Murray, "Olympic Awards," *Los Angeles Times*, September 12, 1972.

39. Gerald Suppicich, interview with the author, November 19, 2008.

40. Mike Downey, e-mail interview with the author, June 23, 2009.

41. Jim Murray, "Missing: Ocean of Joy," *Los Angeles Times*, December 25, 1973. Murray adhered to the sales contract by withholding Dylan's name. He wrote: "To the person who bought my house, I leave more than the bricks, the land, the mountain backdrop to the north and east." The column also generated a strong response from readers, many of whom chastised Murray for never using his position at the *Times* to fight for conservationist causes in Malibu. Murray expressed little sympathy. "Well, as they say, you might get away from the environment. But you'll never get away from the environmentalists," he wrote.

42. "It Began in Cincinnati," *Dayton Journal Herald*, February 13, 1974.

43. Kenyon was also a screenwriter who wrote several movies in the 1940s and dozens of television episodes in the 1950s, '60s, and '70s.

44. James Murray, "A Number on His Back," untitled, undated screenplay.

45. James Murray, untitled, undated screenplay.

46. Jim Murray, untitled, undated manuscript.

47. Jim Murray, "An Idea for a Television Series," untitled, undated television treatment. *Gangbusters* was a popular radio police drama that was broadcast from the 1930s into the 1950s.

48. Jim Murray, "Debut of an Artist," *Los Angeles Times*, December 28, 1962.

49. Margaret Harford, "*Wall of Noise*: Racetrack Story Melodramatic," *Los Angeles Times*, September 7, 1963.

50. Frank Deford, interview with the author, January 21, 2007.

51. Jim Murray, "Blasting a Golf Trail," *Los Angeles Times*, August 25, 1974.

52. Reilly, "King of the Sports Page."

53. Bill Thomas, interview with the author, December 12, 2008.

54. Murray estimated that for 75 percent of the rounds of golf he played in his lifetime, Vic Hunter was in the foursome. Hunter died in 1980 on the second hole at Riviera.

55. Jim Murray, "The Game of the Name," *Los Angeles Times*, December 4, 1974.

56. Bill Dwyre, interview with the author, August 20, 2010.

57. The simulated fight was the brainstorm of radio and television producer Murray Warner. The computer simulation was turned into a script for the fight, which was filmed with fifteen different endings. Who won depended on where the fight was being viewed. In New York and Chicago, Ali won; in Philadelphia, it was a draw. Marciano won by knockout in Italy.

58. Ferdie Pacheco, *Blood in My Coffee: The Life of the Fight Doctor*, 62–63.

59. Jim Murray, "Is This Being a Martyr?," *Los Angeles Times*, December 6, 1970.

60. Jim Murray, "Amateur Night," *Los Angeles Times*, March 12, 1971.

61. Jim Murray, "Feet of Clay," *Los Angeles Times*, March 9, 1971.

62. Murray, *Jim Murray: An Autobiography*, 199.

63. Muhammad Ali to Jim Murray, 1973.

64. Foreman had won the heavyweight title from Frazier in a second-round knockout in Kingston, Jamaica, in 1973.

65. Jerry Izenberg, interview with the author, July 30, 2009.

66. Jim Murray, "On the Road to Zaire," *Los Angeles Times*, October 24, 1974.

67. Jim Murray, "Nightmare in Zaire," *Los Angeles Times*, November 1, 1974.

68. Jim Murray, "Muhammad's Back on Top of the Mountain," *Los Angeles Times*, October 30, 1974.

69. Murray, "Nightmare in Zaire."

70. Jim Murray, "It's 'the Greatest' Lie of All," *Los Angeles Times*, July 21, 1992.

71. Reilly, "King of the Sports Page," 82.

72. Jim Murray, "The Ballad of Muhammad Ali: A Sad Song at the End," *Los Angeles Times*, October 3, 1980.

73. Murray, "It's 'the Greatest' Lie of All"; Murray, *Jim Murray: An Autobiography*, 200.

74. Jim Murray, "Shoulda Stood in Bed," *Los Angeles Times*, October 19, 1978.

75. Jim Murray, "The Joy of Seeing," *Los Angeles Times*, February 13, 1979.

76. Bill Shirley, "The Return of Murray: He's Not Talking about Elvin Hayes When He Says HE Can Barely Make Out the Big E," *Los Angeles Times*, June 28, 1979.

77. Jim Murray, "If You're Expecting One-Liners, Wait a Column," *Los Angeles Times*, July 1, 1979.

78. Scheibe, *On the Road*, 59.

79. Murray, *Jim Murray: An Autobiography*, 204.

80. Scheibe, *On the Road*, 33–34.

81. Ibid., 70 (quote), 159.

82. John Hall, "The Love Game," *Los Angeles Times*, September 28, 1979.

83. Scheibe, *On the Road*, 59.

84. Ibid., 85, 129.

85. Ibid., 165–67.

86. Murray, *Jim Murray: An Autobiography*, 206.

87. Pete Thomas, "Hey Jim, This One's for You," *Los Angeles Times*, August 18, 1998.

88. Scheibe, *On the Road*, 168.

89. Murray, *Jim Murray: An Autobiography,* 207.

90. Blackie Sherrod, interview with the author, December 8, 2008.

Chapter 8

1. Benjamin G. Rader, *In Its Own Image: How Television Transformed Sports,* 206–7.

2. Daniel Machalaba, "*Sports Illustrated* Runs Hard to Keep Ahead of the Field," *Wall Street Journal,* January 23, 1981.

3. Dennis Ahlburg and James Dworkin, "Player Compensation in the National Football League," in *The Business of Professional Sports,* edited by Paul Staudohar and James Mangan, 62.

4. Ron Powers, *Supertube: The Rise of Television Sports,* 15–16.

5. Bill Shirley, "The Columnists: These Days, They Jump Teams, Earn Big Money, and for Better or Worse, Write Their Own Ticket," *Los Angeles Times,* February 13, 1985.

6. Mike Littwin, interview with the author, May 26, 2010.

7. *Sports Illustrated* was a losing proposition while Murray was there, but it finally began to turn a profit in 1964, and by 1981 it was the fifth-largest magazine in the United States in terms of revenue, behind *Time, TV Guide, Reader's Digest,* and *Newsweek.* That year, circulation climbed above 2.25 million, and revenue was estimated to be $188 million.

8. John Scheibe, interview with the author, October 7, 2010.

9. Scheibe, *On the Road,* 73.

10. Littwin interview.

11. Scott Ostler, interview with the author, May 19, 2010.

12. Littwin interview.

13. Ibid.

14. John Hall, interview with the author, January 23, 2009.

15. Littwin interview.

16. Mike Goodman and Al Delugach, "Big Profits in Super Bowl Ticket Deals," *Los Angeles Times,* January 14, 1981.

17. Hall interview.

18. Littwin interview.

19. Howard Cosell, with Peter Bonventre, *I Never Played the Game,* 22.

20. Gerald Suppicich, interview with the author, November 19, 2008.

21. Mike Downey, interview with the author, June 23, 2009.

22. Reilly, "King of the Sports Page."

23. Jay Berwanger was a University of Chicago halfback in the mid-1930s and the first recipient of the Heisman Trophy.

24. Jim Murray, "A Day with the Ambassador to Cincinnati," *Los Angeles Times,* July 15, 1976.

25. Gerald Ford to Jim Murray, August 30, 1977.

26. Jim Murray, "The Hall of What?," *Los Angeles Times,* April 4, 1978.

27. Downey interview.

28. Jim Murray, interview with Murray Olderman, March 29, 1991.

29. Cieplik, "Jim Murray."

30. Bill Milsaps, interview with the author, June 16, 2009.

31. Blackie Sherrod, "Columnist's Aura Creates Wonder, Envy," *Dallas Morning News,* July 7, 1993.

32. Al Davis, interview with the author, June 12, 2010.

33. Rick Reilly, interview with David Bulla, March 20, 2007.

34. Jim Murray, "Jordan Hits Out of Bounds," *Los Angeles Times,* June 8, 1993.

35. Scheibe, *On the Road,* 68–69.

36. Milsaps interview.

37. Ostler interview.

38. Linda McCoy-Murray, interview with the author, February 19, 2009.

39. Michael Eigner to Jim Murray, March 7, 1988; David Lunz to Murray, March 3, 1988.

40. Scheibe, *On the Road*, 98.

41. Littwin interview.

42. Edwin Pope, interview with the author, June 9, 2009.

43. McCoy-Murray interview.

44. Douglas Looney, "For Jim Murray, Everything Is Fair Game," *National Observer*, August 19, 1972.

45. Bob Steiner, interview with the author, January 23, 2009; Murray interview with Olderman.

46. Murray interview with Olderman.

47. Jim Murray, "Wanna Be a Writer?," *Los Angeles Times*, April 27, 1972.

48. Cieplik, "Jim Murray."

49. Jon Sandberg, interview with the author, February 25, 2008.

50. James Sogg, "Hemingway in a Press Box," *L.A. Village View*, October 15, 1993.

51. Shirley, "The Columnists."

52. Sogg, "Hemingway."

53. Ibid.

54. Murray interview with Olderman.

55. Ibid.

56. Murray, *Jim Murray: An Autobiography*, 222–27.

57. Bruce Jenkins, interview with the author, August 18, 2009.

58. Ibid.

59. Murray, *Jim Murray: An Autobiography*, 229–32.

60. Scheibe interview.

61. Bill Dwyre, "A Christmas Gift: These Words Will Endure," *Los Angeles Times*, December 25, 1998.

62. Jim Murray, "She Took the Magic and Happy Summer with Her," *Los Angeles Times*, April 3, 1984.

63. "Jim Murray's Grief Is Shared by Many Readers," *Los Angeles Times*, April 7, 1984.

64. W. Fowler, *Reporters*, 140.

65. Reilly, "King of the Sports Page."

66. Ibid.

67. Rick Reilly, interview with the author, December 18, 2010.

68. Linda McCoy-Murray, podcast interview with Al Beaton and Greg Eno, September 20, 2010.

69. Roy Firestone, interview with the author, December 15, 2009; Bill Thomas, interview with the author, December 12, 2008.

70. Mike Penner, "The First Priority at Candlestick Was to Get Out of the Park Safely," *Los Angeles Times*, October 18, 1989.

71. Jim Murray, "Nature Took Terrible Swing," *Los Angeles Times*, October 18, 1989.

72. Ken Peters, interview with the author, August 30, 2010.

73. Murray, "Nature Took Terrible Swing."

74. Pope interview.

Chapter 9

1. Bill Dwyre, interview with the author, August 20, 2010.

2. Jim Murray, acceptance speech for J. G. Taylor Spink Award, Baseball Hall of Fame, Cooperstown, New York, August 1, 1988.

3. J. Douglas Bates, *The Pulitzer Prize: The Inside Story of America's Most Prestigious Award*, 11–13.

4. Ibid., 155, 158, 188–90.

5. These three and Murray are the only journalists to win the award for general sports-writing. In 1935, Bill Taylor of the *New York Herald-Tribune* was awarded a Pulitzer for news coverage of the America's Cup yacht race, and in 1953, Max Kase of the *New York Journal-American* won a special citation for coverage of a college basketball scandal.

6. Ira Berkow, *Red: A Biography of Red Smith*, 142–44.

7. Ira Berkow, "Red Smith, Sports Columnist Who Won Pulitzer, Dies at 76," *New York Times*, January 16, 1982.

8. Tom Callahan, "Murray: Reflecting Truth and Our Age," *Washington Post*, April 15, 1990.

9. Dave Anderson, interview with the author, May 14, 2010.

10. Jurors select finalists for each category, and a winner is then chosen by the Pulitzer Board. The board has the option of accepting one of the finalists, choosing another entry, or declining to choose a winner.

11. Bill Dwyre, nomination for Pulitzer Prize, General Commentary category, 1989.

12. Callahan, "Murray: Reflecting Truth and Our Age." Murray's little joke proved prescient. Eight years later, the first sentence of Murray's obituary, filed by the Associated Press, read, "Jim Murray, the Los Angeles Times columnist who won a Pulitzer Prize and put heart, humor and humanity on America's sports pages for nearly four decades, is dead at 78."

13. "Jim Murray Wins Pulitzer Prize: Veteran *Times* Sports Columnist Honored for Commentary," *Among Ourselves*, April 1990.

14. Jerry Izenberg, interview with the author, July 30, 2009.

15. Blackie Sherrod, "Columnist's Aura Creates Wonder, Envy," *Dallas Morning News*, July 7, 1993.

16. Dwyre interview.

17. Alex Jones, "The *National Sports Daily* Closes with Today's Issue," *New York Times*, June 13, 1991.

18. Frank Deford, interview with the author, January 21, 2007. Bill Dwyre remembers the offer to be one million dollars a year, but published reports around the time of the launch of the *National* had the top salary figures in the neighborhood of $250,000, the figure Deford mentioned.

19. Dwyre interview.

20. Bill Milsaps, interview with the author, June 16, 2009.

21. "Greenville News' Sports Editor, Columnist Dies," Associated Press, May 26, 2009.

22. Dwyre interview.

23. Jim Murray, "It's the 'Jim Murray,' Racing's Newest Classic," *Los Angeles Times*, December 7, 1967.

24. John Hall, interview with the author, January 23, 2009.

25. The inaugural Jim Murray Handicap was won by Shotiche, a ten-to-one shot trained by Bobby Frankel. It paid $23.80.

26. Jim Murray, "Uncle Ed Would Be a Proud Name Dropper," *Los Angeles Times*, July 12, 1990.

27. Bill Christine, interview with the author, December 19, 2008; Jim Murray, "Racing Lady Is No Champ," *Los Angeles Times*, August 31, 1992.

28. "Everything but Flappers from the Roaring '20s," *Los Angeles Times*, June 6, 1998.

29. Scott Ostler, interview with the author, May 19, 2010.

30. Al Davis, interview with the author, June 12, 2010.

31. Firestone interview.

32. Bill Plaschke, "She Was Right Woman at Right Time for Murray," *Los Angeles Times*, August 21, 1998.

33. Murray, *Jim Murray: An Autobiography*, 61, 187.

34. David Leon Moore, "Murray Touch as a Wordsmith Sight to Behold," *USA Today*, June 22, 1993; Murray, *Jim Murray: An Autobiography*, 262.

35. Jim Murray, "There's Been No Change of Heart," *Los Angeles Times*, October 24, 1982.

36. Jim Murray, "As I Was Saying before I Was So Rudely Interrupted . . . ," *Los Angeles Times*, February 16, 1995.

37. Linda McCoy-Murray, interview with the author, October 15, 2010.

38. Ibid.

39. Jim Murray, "Up Lanes and Down Aisles," *Los Angeles Times*, March 6, 1997.

40. Jim Murray, "Downing's Epitaph," *Los Angeles Times*, April 10, 1974.

41. Jim Murray, "Ride on a Tiger," *Los Angeles Times*, March 12, 1961; Bob Pastin, "The Columnist Jim Murray's Law Reflected in Book: Nothing's Sacred," *St. Louis Post-Dispatch*, July 7, 1993.

42. William A. Harper, *How You Played the Game: The Life of Grantland Rice*, 508, 53.

43. Red Smith, "When Jimmy Wrote to End Writing," *New York Times*, December 7, 1973.

44. Berkow, *Red*, 282–84.

45. Chris McCarron, speech at Jim Murray memorial tribute, September 26, 1998.

46. Plaschke, "She Was Right Woman."

47. Murray had written a column the previous week about Free House, comparing him to other great horses and athletes that had been forgotten because they missed out on victory by a nose. Jim Murray, "Chasing Greatest Is Own Reward," *Los Angeles Times*, August 6, 1998.

48. Jim Murray, "You Can Teach an Old Horse New Tricks," *Los Angeles Times*, August 16, 1998.

49. Dan Smith, interview with the author, January 15, 2010.

50. J. A. Adande, "Others' Words Can't Do Justice," *Los Angeles Times*, August 22, 1998.

51. Jack Whitaker, "Jim Murray: 1919–1998; Jack Whitaker's Tribute: 'My, What a Grand Man You Were,'" *Los Angeles Times*, August 22, 1998.

52. Eric Malnic, "Funeral: Jim Murray Is Remembered as a Great Writer and Person at Brentwood Mass," *Los Angeles Times*, August 22, 1998.

53. McCoy-Murray interview.

54. Furman Bisher, interview with the author, December 1, 2008.

Epilogue

1. Mike Penner, "A Tribute to Jim Murray: To This Team of L.A. All-Stars, a Writer Was Most Valuable," *Los Angeles Times*, September 27, 1998.

2. Murray, *The Last of the Best*, 309–20.

3. Leonard Koppett, "What Made Murray Great? It's a Funny Thing," *Los Angeles Times*, September 23, 1998.

4. Steve Soboroff, interview with the author, December 2, 2010.

Bibliography

Apfelbaum, Jim, ed. *The Gigantic Book of Golf Quotations: Thousands of Notable Quotables from Tommy Armour to Fuzzy Zoeller*. New York: Skyhorse, 2007.

Ball, Don, Jr., and Rogers E. M. Whitaker. *Decade of the Trains: The 1940s*. Boston: New York Graphic Society, 1977.

Barbee, Pat. "Seasoned Pro." *Beverly Hills 1-2-3*, June 3, 1992.

Baseball Almanac. "Baseball Hall of Fame BBWAA Voting Percentages." http://www.baseball-almanac.com/hof/hofmem4.shtml (accessed August 29, 2010).

Bates, J. Douglas. *The Pulitzer Prize: The Inside Story of America's Most Prestigious Award*. New York: Birch Lane Press, 1991.

Baughman, James L. *Henry R. Luce and the Rise of the American News Media*. Boston: Twayne, 1987.

Berkow, Ira. *Red: A Biography of Red Smith*. Lincoln: University of Nebraska Press, 2007.

Betts, John Rickard. *America's Sporting Heritage, 1850–1950*. Reading, MA: Addison-Wesley, 1974.

Beverage, Richard E. *The Hollywood Stars: Baseball in Movieland, 1926–1957*. Placentia, CA: Deacon Press, 1984.

Boyle, Robert H. *Sport: Mirror of American Life*. Boston: Little, Brown, 1963.

Callahan, Tom. "For Crying Out Loud." *Golf Digest*, November 1998.

Caughey, John, and Laree Caughey. *Los Angeles: Biography of a City*. Berkeley and Los Angeles: University of California Press, 1976.

Champlin, Charles. *A Life in Writing: The Story of an American Journalist*. Syracuse, NY: Syracuse University Press, 2006.

Cieplik, Walt. "Jim Murray: King of Sports." *Writer's Digest*, August 1977.

Coblentz, Edmond D., ed. *William Randolph Hearst: A Portrait in His Own Words*. New York: Simon and Schuster, 1952.

255

Cosell, Howard. *Cosell.* New York: Pocket Books, 1974.

Cosell, Howard, with Peter Bonventre. *I Never Played the Game.* New York: Avon Books, 1985.

Deford, Frank. "*Sportswriter* Is One Word." Lecture, University of Notre Dame, Notre Dame, Indiana, August 2010.

Dyhrenfurth, Norman, and James Murray. "Ordeal on the Approaches." *Sports Illustrated,* August 29, 1960.

———. "The Thrust to the Summit." *Sports Illustrated,* September 3, 1960.

Editor & Publisher. Editor & Publisher International Yearbook. New York: Editor & Publisher, 1961.

Elson, Robert T. *The World of Time, Inc.: The Intimate History of a Publishing Enterprise.* Vol. 2, *1941–1960.* New York: Atheneum, 1973.

Emery, Edwin, and Michael Emery. *The Press and America: An Interpretive History of the Mass Media.* 5th ed. Englewood Cliffs, NJ: Prentice-Hall, 1984.

Engel, Lyle Kenyon. *The Indianapolis "500": The World's Most Exciting Auto Race.* New York: Four Winds Press, 1970.

Evensen, Bruce J. *When Dempsey Fought Tunney: Heroes, Hokum, and Storytelling in the Jazz Age.* Knoxville: University of Tennessee Press, 1996.

Farber, David, and Beth Bailey. *The Columbia Guide to America in the 1960s.* New York: Columbia University Press, 2001.

Felch, Jason, and Marlena Telvick. "Unsung Hero." *American Journalism Review* (June–July 2004).

Fleischer, Nat, and Sam Andre. *An Illustrated History of Boxing.* 5th ed. Secaucus, NJ: Citadel Press, 1997.

Fountain, Charles. *Sportswriter: The Life and Times of Grantland Rice.* New York: Oxford University Press, 1993.

Fowler, Gene. *Skyline: A Reporter's Reminiscence of the '20s.* New York: Viking Press, 1961.

Fowler, Will. *Reporters: Memoirs of a Young Newspaperman.* Malibu, CA: Roundtable, 1991.

———. *The Young Man from Denver: A Candid and Affectionate Biography of Gene Fowler.* Garden City, NY: Doubleday, 1962.

Garrison, Bruce. *Sports Reporting.* Ames: Iowa State University Press, 1985.

Gitlin, Todd. *The Sixties: Years of Hope, Days of Rage.* New York: Bantam Books, 1993.

Gottlieb, Robert, and Irene Wolt. *Thinking Big: The Story of the "Los Angeles Times," Its Publishers, and Their Influence on Southern California.* New York: G. P. Putnam's Sons, 1977.

Halberstam, David. *October 1964.* New York: Fawcett Columbine, 1994.

———. *The Powers That Be.* New York: Alfred A. Knopf, 1979.

Harper, William A. *How You Played the Game: The Life of Grantland Rice.* Columbia: University of Missouri Press, 1999.

Hart, Jack R. *The Information Empire: The Rise of the "Los Angeles Times" and the Times Mirror Corporation*. Washington, DC: University Press of America, 1981.

Harzmann, Craig. "The Boy of Summer: Swaps' Magical Spree Delighted Fans 50 Years Ago." *Blood Horse*, June 2006.

Hauser, Thomas. *Muhammad Ali: His Life and Times*. New York: Simon and Schuster, 1991.

Hearn, Chick, and Steve Springer. *Chick: His Unpublished Memoirs and the Memories of Those Who Knew Him*. Chicago: Triumph Books, 2004.

Hollander, Zander, ed. *The NBA's Official Encyclopedia of Pro Basketball*. New York: Times Mirror, 1981.

Holtzman, Jerome. *No Cheering in the Press Box*. New York: Henry Holt, 1995.

Jack, Zachary Michael, ed. *Inside the Ropes: Sportswriters Get Their Game On*. Lincoln: University of Nebraska Press, 2008.

James, Robert F. "Indy's Somber Trial by Fire and Rain." *Sports Illustrated*, June 11, 1973.

Jessup, John, ed. *The Ideas of Henry Luce*. New York: Atheneum, 1969.

Kane, Martin. "Booktalk: Jim Murray Moves Gracefully from Newspaper Column into Hardcover." *Sports Illustrated*, April 12, 1965.

Kashner, Sam, and Jennifer MacNair. *The Bad and the Beautiful: Hollywood in the Fifties*. New York: W. W. Norton, 2002.

Kindred, Dave. *Sound and Fury: Two Powerful Lives, One Fateful Friendship*. New York: Free Press, 2006.

Koppett, Leonard. *The Rise and Fall of the Press Box*. Toronto: Sport Classic Books, 2003.

Lazenby, Roland. *The Show: The Inside Story of the Spectacular Los Angeles Lakers in the Words of Those Who Lived It*. New York: McGraw-Hill, 2006.

Lucas, Christopher J. *American Higher Education: A History*. 2nd ed. New York: Palgrave Macmillan, 2006.

MacCambridge, Michael. *The Franchise: A History of "Sports Illustrated" Magazine*. New York: Hyperion, 1997.

Maltby, Richard. *Hollywood Cinema*. 2nd ed. Malden, MA: Blackwell, 2003.

Martin, J. A., and Thomas F. Saal. *American Auto Racing: The Milestones and Personalities of a Century of Speed*. Jefferson, NC: McFarland, 2004.

McCoy-Murray, Linda. *Quotable Jim Murray: The Literary Wit, Wisdom, and Wonder of a Distinguished American Sports Columnist*. Nashville, TN: TowelHouse, 2003.

McDougal, Dennis. *Privileged Son: Otis Chandler and the Rise and Fall of the "L.A. Times" Dynasty*. Cambridge, MA: Perseus, 2001.

McKay, Jim. *My Wide World*. New York: Dutton/Penguin, 1998.

Moss, George. *America in the Twentieth Century*. Englewood Cliffs, NJ: Prentice-Hall, 1989.

Mott, Frank Luther. *American Journalism: A History, 1690–1960.* 3rd ed. New York: Macmillan, 1962.

Murray, Jim. "All Right, Louie, Drop the Jib." *Sports Illustrated,* April 30, 1956.

———. "American League? Phooey!" *Sports Illustrated,* June 11, 1956.

———. "At Home with Swaps in California." *Sports Illustrated,* July 18, 1955.

———. *The Best of Jim Murray.* Garden City, NY: Doubleday, 1965.

———. "California Gets a Gleam in the Eye." *Sports Illustrated,* February 28, 1955.

———. "The Case for the Suffering Fan." *Sports Illustrated,* August 20, 1956.

———. "The Drubbing." *Sports Illustrated,* June 7, 1965.

———. "8-Ball Parade." In *8 Ball Final.* 4th annual ed. Los Angeles: Los Angeles Press Club, 1950.

———. "Fame Is for Winners." *Sports Illustrated,* April 15, 1957.

———. "The Gary Coopers' Sporting Life." *Sports Illustrated,* June 1, 1959.

———. "I Hate the Yankees." *Life,* April 17, 1950.

———. *Jim Murray: An Autobiography.* New York: Macmillan, 1993.

———. *The Jim Murray Collection.* Dallas: Taylor, 1988.

———. "The Last Tomorrow." *Trinity Review* (January 1941).

———. "Once Upon a Time It Was Dreamsville." *Los Angeles Magazine,* July 1970.

———. "Prelude to Defeat." *Trinity Review* (May 1940).

———. *The Sporting World of Jim Murray.* Garden City, NY: Doubleday, 1968.

———. "Strub's Santa Anita." *Sports Illustrated,* January 10, 1955.

———. "A Trip for Ten Tall Men." *Sports Illustrated,* January 30, 1961.

———. "The Wicket Men of Hollywood." *Sports Illustrated,* January 30, 1956.

Nasaw, David. *The Chief: The Life of William Randolph Hearst.* Boston: Houghton Mifflin, 2000.

National Sportscasters and Sportswriters Association. "National Winners." http://www.nssafame.com/General/15266 (accessed September 9, 2010).

Nebraska Studies. "Recruits: The 4-F Classification." http://www.nebraskastudies.org/0800/frameset_reset.html?http://www.nebraskastudies.org/0800/stories/0801_0106.html (accessed March 19, 2009).

Nelson, Kevin. *The Golden Game: The Story of California Baseball.* San Francisco: California Historical Society Press, 2004.

Osborne, Robert. *Academy Awards Illustrated: A Complete History of Hollywood's Academy Awards in Words and Pictures.* La Habra, CA: Ernest E. Schworck, 1969.

———. *65 Years of the Oscar: The Official History of the Academy Awards.* New York: Abbeville Press, 1994.

Pacheco, Ferdie. *Blood in My Coffee: The Life of the Fight Doctor.* Champaign, IL: Sports Publishing, 2005.

Parrish, Thomas, ed. *The Simon and Schuster Encyclopedia of World War II.* New York: Simon and Schuster, 1978.

Patterson, James T. *Grand Expectations: The United States, 1945–1974.* New York: Oxford University Press, 1996.

Pitt, Leonard, and Dale Pitt. *Los Angeles A to Z: An Encyclopedia of the City and County.* Berkeley and Los Angeles: University of California Press, 1997.

Powers, Ron. *Supertube: The Rise of Television Sports.* New York: Coward-Mc-Cann, 1984.

Rader, Benjamin G. *In Its Own Image: How Television Transformed Sports.* New York: Free Press, 1984.

Radosta, John. *The "New York Times" Complete Guide to Auto Racing.* Chicago: Quadrangle Books, 1971.

Rapoport, Ron. *The Immortal Bobby: Bobby Jones and the Golden Age of Golf.* Hoboken, NJ: John Wiley and Sons, 2005.

Reeve, Simon. *One Day in September: The Full Story of the 1972 Munich Olympics Massacre and the Israeli Revenge Operation "Wrath of God."* New York: Arcade, 2006.

Reilly, Rick. "King of the Sports Page." *Sports Illustrated,* April 21, 1986.

Remnick, David. *King of the World: Muhammad Ali and the Rise of an American Hero.* New York: Random House, 1998.

Richardson, Jim. *For the Life of Me.* New York: G. P. Putnam's Sons, 1954.

Scheibe, John. *On the Road with Jim Murray: Baseball and the Summer of '79.* Encino, CA: Encino Media, 2007.

Sharnik, Morton. "Death of a Champion." *Sports Illustrated,* April 1, 1963.

Shirley, Bill, ed. *Sports Pages of the "Los Angeles Times."* New York: Harry N. Abrams, 1983.

Sifford, Charlie, with James Gullo. *Just Let Me Play: The Story of Charlie Sifford, the First Black PGA Golfer.* New York: British American Publishing, 1992.

Simon, Mary. *Racing through the Century: The Story of Thoroughbred Racing in America.* Irvine, CA: Bowtie Press, 2002.

Smith, Curt. *Pull Up a Chair: The Vin Scully Story.* Dulles, VA: Potomac Books, 2009.

Smith, Red. *The Red Smith Reader.* New York: Random House, 1982.

Sperber, Murray. *Onward to Victory: The Crises That Shaped College Sports.* New York: Henry Holt, 1998.

Startt, James D., and Wm. David Sloan. *Historical Methods in Mass Communication.* Hillsdale, NJ: Lawrence Erlbaum Associates, 1989.

Staudohar, Paul, and James Mangan, eds. *The Business of Professional Sports.* Urbana: University of Illinois Press, 1991.

Taft, William H. *Newspapers as Tools for Historians.* Columbia, MO: Lucas Brothers, 1970.

Trinity College. "College History." http://www.trincoll.edu/AboutTrinity/CollegeHistory.htm (accessed March 19, 2009).

Trinity Ivy. Hartford, CT: Trinity College, 1943.

Underwood, Agness. *Newspaperwoman.* New York: Harper and Brothers, 1949.

Wagner, Rob Leicester. *Red Ink, White Lies: The Rise and Fall of Los Angeles Newspapers, 1920–1962.* Upland, CA: Dragonflyer Press, 2000.

Walker, Stanley. *City Editor.* Baltimore: Johns Hopkins University Press, 1999.

Wanta, Wayne. "The Coverage of Sports in Print Media." In *Handbook of Sports Media,* edited by Arthur A. Raney and Jennings Bryant. Mahwah, NJ: Lawrence Erlbaum Associates, 2006.

Weaver, Glen. *Hartford: An Illustrated History of Connecticut's Capital.* Woodland Hills, CA: Windsor Publications, 1982.

Winkler, John K. *William Randolph Hearst: A New Appraisal.* New York: Hastings House, 1955.

Wittke, Carl. *The Irish in America.* Baton Rouge: Louisiana State University Press, 1956.

Wojciechowski, Gene. *Pond Scum and Vultures: America's Sportswriters Talk about Their Glamorous Profession.* New York: Macmillan, 1990.

Zingg, Paul J., and Mark D. Medeiros. *Runs, Hits, and an Era: The Pacific Coast League, 1903–1958.* Urbana: University of Illinois Press, 1994.

Index